Study Guide

for use with

Principles of Economics

Third Edition

Robert H. Frank
Cornell University

Ben S. Bernanke
Princeton University (formerly)
Chairman of the President's Council of Economic Advisers

Prepared by
Jack Mogab
Texas State University – San Marcos

Louis Johnston
The College of Saint Benedict/Saint John's University

 McGraw-Hill
Irwin

Boston   Burr Ridge, IL   Dubuque, IA   Madison, WI   New York   San Francisco   St. Louis
Bangkok   Bogotá   Caracas   Kuala Lumpur   Lisbon   London   Madrid   Mexico City
Milan   Montreal   New Delhi   Santiago   Seoul   Singapore   Sydney   Taipei   Toronto

McGraw-Hill
Irwin

Study Guide for use with
PRINCIPLES OF ECONOMICS
Robert H. Frank, Ben S. Bernanke

Published by McGraw-Hill/Irwin, an imprint of The McGraw-Hill Companies, Inc., 1221 Avenue of the Americas, New York, NY 10020. Copyright © 2007 by The McGraw-Hill Companies, Inc. All rights reserved.

1 2 3 4 5 6 7 8 9 0 QPD/QPD 0 9 8 7 6 5

ISBN-13: 978-0-07-321006-3
ISBN-10: 0-07-321006-4

www.mhhe.com

The McGraw-Hill Companies

To the Student

Welcome to the study of economics. We believe you will find the subject thoroughly intriguing. As you become an "economic naturalist" you will gain a clearer understanding of many important issues that currently may be perplexing to you. For example, what determines the cost of a car, or the salary you will earn when you graduate? Why does the economy experience booms and busts? How does the banking system create money? Why are federal deficits and surpluses so controversial?

These and many other topics are addressed in *Principles of Economics, Principles of Microeconomics,* and *Principles of Macroeconomics,* 3rd Editions by Robert H. Frank and Ben S. Bernanke, for which these Study Guides have been written. The Study Guide chapters parallel the chapters in the corresponding textbook, and each contains the following eight sections designed to assist your learning and to enhance your understanding of economics:

1. **Pretest.** This will test what you really know about the basic concepts and principles in the chapter and what you need to review before continuing on with more in-depth testing.
2. **Key Point Review.** The Learning Objectives for the chapter are listed to identify important concepts to master. The chapter's main ideas are summarized, and new terms are defined. **Hints** and **Notes** are provided to alert you to "tricks, clues and short-cuts".
3. **Self-Test: Key Terms**. All new terms are listed. Check your knowledge of key definitions by matching the term in the right-hand column with the appropriate definitions in the left-hand column.
4. **Self-Test: Multiple-Choice Questions.** Strengthen your grasp of the chapter material by choosing the correct answer from the alternatives for each question. Your ability to answer multiple-choice questions should serve as a good indicator of success on exams. You may wish to study for exams by reviewing these questions.
5. **Self-Test: Short Answer/Problems.** Here you will discover how the tools of economics can be applied to explore and clarify important issues. Problems are developed step by step. You are asked to analyze graphs and tables, to perform basic computations, and to select the best answers to a variety of fill-in statements.
6. **Economic Naturalist Applications.** Become an economic naturalist by applying the tools of economics to discuss these real-world issues with your classmates.
7. **Solutions**. Solutions, with explanations for the more complex and difficult items in the self-tests, are provided for the key-term, and multiple-choice questions, as well as for the short answer/problems.

The following suggestions will help make your study of economics successful:

Class Preparation or Must I Turn Off the TV?
It is essential that you prepare assignments BEFORE attending class so that you can understand the lecture and ask questions. Your instructor typically will not present all the materials in the text, but rather will concentrate on explaining the more complex ideas and applications. In preparing for class, first read the "Key Point Review" to identify the

learning objectives for the chapter. Next, go to the chapter in the text. Read the "Summary," "Core Principles," and the "Key Terms" at the **end** of the chapter. Then, read the introductory section that will provide an overview of the topics to be covered in the chapter. The number of topics will range from 4 to 7. Read and study one topic at a time, i.e., begin at the bold, upper-case red color heading and read until you get to the "Recap" box. Look for the paragraphs in the chapter that define and explain the concepts, principles, and laws related to that topic. These concepts, principles, and laws are listed at the end of each chapter as "Key Terms." As you read, mark these "terms" (as many as 3 to 5 per topic). You will notice that each topic can be presented in three modes--verbal, numerical (tables), and visual (graphs). This variety of presentation is important since economics is communicated through all three modes, and the test questions will reflect all three. After you have completed reading a topic, take a few minutes to read the Recap box. Verify that (1) you know (i.e. remember) the topic and important terms; (2) you understand (i.e. comprehend) that material; (3) you can relate the terms to one another when appropriate; and (4) you can relate the topic to the other topics in the chapter. Complete all the assigned topics in the above manner and write down any questions you have for the instructor.

Class Attendance or Why Not Go To the Rec Center?
Frankly, economics is such a demanding course that you will need all the help you can get. A great deal of that help comes from your instructor's lectures. The instructor's style and presentation will show you not only what the instructor considers to be important, but also how s/he approaches this subject. Getting notes from a friend will not give you this information. If you have followed the above suggestions in preparing for class, you will have some knowledge and understanding of the assigned topics. In class, the trick is to carefully combine four classroom skills - listening, taking notes, answering questions, and responding to questions. Listen with your mind. Be selective in what you write down. If you try to write everything that the instructor says, you will not have time to learn anything. For example, do not write a definition that has been given in the text. Listen for examples that differ from those in the text, special emphasis on a relationship between topics, and frequently repeated principles. Asking questions is the responsibility of the student. If you don't know enough to ask questions, you haven't done your job. If you have difficulty formulating questions during class, you should spend some time before class developing a list of questions you need to have answered. On the other side of the coin, you should also respond to the instructor's questions. You should not be shy about answering questions in class. An incorrect answer given in class is a free shot, while the same wrong answer on the test is very costly. The most effective way to use class time is to develop your ability to comprehend and apply economics concepts.

After Class or Do I Have To Do This Again?
Even if you have meticulously prepared for class and performed those four classroom behaviors, you still have a couple of things to do before you will be at the mastery level of the material. First, your class notes should be sketchy. You need to rewrite these notes in a more complete way before they get cold. Next, return to the Study Guide. Complete the three Self-Tests without referring to the text, and check your answers with the Solutions at the end of the Study Guide chapter. If your answers are correct, go onto the

Economic Naturalist section. If your answers to some of the questions are incorrect, go back and review the text and your class notes for those topics. Then return to the Study Guide Self-Tests to complete the questions you answered incorrectly (to further test your mastery of the material, go to the Electronic Learning Session in the Student Center at the Frank/Bernanke web site: http://www.mhhe.com/economics/frankbernanke3). If you still do not understand the answers to the questions, either ask questions in the next class or go see your instructor for help.

If You Want To Learn It, Teach It.
To further test your comprehension of a topic, try explaining it in your own words to a classmate. Illustrate the idea with an example. If you can explain it clearly and give a good example, you have mastered the concept and its time to move on to the next chapter.

A Final Word
If the strategy outlined above seems like a lot of work, it is. You cannot achieve success in economics without hard work. It is estimated that the average student should spend 2-3 hours of quality study time for every hour spent in class.

Acknowledgments
It is a pleasure to acknowledge the assistance and support of Irwin McGraw-Hill in the preparation of this Study Guide. Particular thanks go to our capable and patient editors Tom Thompson and Paul Shensa.

Contents

Chapter 1
Thinking Like An Economist

I. Pretest: What Do You Really Know?
Circle the letter that corresponds to the best answer. (Answers appear immediately after the final question).

1. When economists say there is no such thing as a free lunch, they mean that
   A. we must pay money for everything we get.
   B. it is against the law to accept goods or services without paying for them.
   C. the more lunch a person eats the more weight the person will gain.
   D. each day we decide to eat lunch is another day we must pay out money.
   E. every choice we make involves a tradeoff.

2. The concept of scarcity applies equally to Bill Gates and a homeless person because
   A. both have the same legal rights protected by the U.S. constitution.
   B. they have the same access to the markets for goods and services.
   C. there are only 24 hours in the day for both of them.
   D. the cost and benefit of picking up a $100 bill from the sidewalk would be the same to each of them.
   E. both must breathe air in order to live.

3. People who have well-defined goals and try to fulfill those goals as best they can are known as
   A. rational.
   B. macroeconomists.
   C. microeconomists.
   D. maximizers.
   E. opportunists.

4. When someone makes a choice, the value of the next best alternative not selected defines
   A. marginal costs.
   B. opportunity costs.
   C. opportunity benefits.
   D. average costs.
   E. economic surplus.

5. Which of the following is true of economic models and how they are used to study behavior?
   A. Economists believe people literally behave according to the model.
   B. Economic models capture every detail of a given situation not matter how small.
   C. Economists rely exclusively on verbal descriptions of their models.
   D. Economic models explain everyone's behavior.
   E. Economic models are simplifications of a given situation with the important details included.

6. Sunk costs are _____ when deciding between alternatives.
   A. irrelevant
   B. highly important
   C. important
   D. slightly important
   E. the only factor to consider

7. Which of the following is not a synonym for "marginal" in economics?
   A. Extra.
   B. Additional.
   C. One more.
   D. Change.
   E. Average.

8. Economics is conventionally divided into two subjects called
   A. marginal benefit and marginal cost.
   B. reservation price and opportunity cost.
   C. microeconomics and macroeconomics.
   D. rational economics and irrational economics.
   E. economic surplus and economic deficit.

9. In deciding the number of students to allow to enroll in the economics classes, the Chairperson of the Economics Department is making a(n) _____ decision.
   A. microeconomic
   B. macroeconomic
   C. economic surplus
   D. marginal choice
   E. imperfect

10. Which of the following topics is most likely to be studied in microeconomics?
    A. Tax policies.
    B. The rate of inflation.
    C. National output.
    D. The auto market.
    E. The unemployment rate.

Solutions and Feedback to Pretest
For each question you incorrectly answered, we strongly recommend taking the time to review the appropriate material before continuing. In the table below are listed for each question the pertinent Learning Objective from the following Key Point Review.

Correct Answer	Learning Objective
1. E	1
2. C	1
3. A	2
4. B	2
5. E	3
6. A	4
7. E	4
8. C	5
9. A	5
10. D	5

II. Key Point Review
The Forest

Chapter one presents the essence of economics as a field of study and as a way of thinking about the world around you. The central questions you need to be able to answer are:

- How does the Scarcity Principle affect the choices that people make?
- How do rational people resolve trade-offs?
- What is the role of models in economics?
- What are four decision pitfalls to avoid in making decisions?
- How can you become an economic naturalist?

The Trees

Learning Objective 1: Define the field of study known as economics. Explain the logical relationship between the Scarcity Principle and the Cost-Benefit Principle. Understand the universality of the two principles.
Economics is the study of how people make choices under conditions of scarcity and how the results of those choices affect society. The **Scarcity Principle** (aka the **No-Free-Lunch Principle**) indicates that all the resources available to the individual are finite, but the needs and wants of the individual are infinite. Satisfying all, or even most, of people's requirements and desires is impossible. Thus, people are forced to make choices because more of one item means less of some other item. The **Cost-Benefit Principle** of economics suggests people will choose to take an action, if and only if, the extra benefits from the action are greater than or equal to the extra cost of the action. Importantly, these two fundamental principles apply to all people, societies, countries, and to the entire history of mankind as well as the modern age.

Learning Objective 2: Discuss the meaning of a rational person in an economic context. How do the concepts of economic surplus and opportunity cost relate to rational behavior?
A **rational person** is one who has well-defined goals and endeavors to fulfill them as best they can. The Cost-Benefit Principle is one tool that assists individuals in making rational choices. The difference between the benefits of taking an action and the costs of the action defines **economic surplus**. Rational behavior, therefore, means taking the actions for which the economic surplus is positive and refusing those with negative economic surplus. The **opportunity cost** of a choice or decision yet to be made is the value of the next-best alternative that must be sacrificed. To practice rational behavior, the opportunity cost of the alternatives being considered must be recognized and counted, even if they do not involve explicit monetary payments.

Learning Objective 3: Explain economist's use of models to explain behavior.
Economists use abstract models to describe and predict behavior. The Cost-Benefit Principle is an example of a behavioral model: it indicates how an idealized rational person can maximize his economic surplus when choosing among alternatives. All fields of study that describe or predict behavior, from Physics to Sociology, use models. A model is a simplified version of reality. Superior models capture the most important elements of reality and ignore minor relationships and inconsequential details. A model that included every facet of a particular behavior wouldn't be a model; it would be reality. If reality could be understood, then a model would not have been needed initially. A frequent but misguided criticism directed at the field of economics indicts the use of models to describe and predict behavior. The critics point out that people do not explicitly calculate the net benefits of going to a movie or a basketball game when deciding how to spend a Friday night. Of course this is correct, but it misses the point. People behave *as if* they do the calculations using their experiences and trial and error to approximate the value of benefits and costs. Of course mistakes are made and people fail to choose rationally. But believing people are constantly using their calculators to assess whether to have Chinese take-out or pizza delivered is **not** necessary to use the Cost-Benefits Principle as a description of how people make choices.

Hint: In order to understand economics and perform well on exams, you must think in terms of the ideas presented in the textbook and lectures. Do not give in to the temptation to create your own model. In a physics class it is unlikely you would question the existence or behavior of gravity. Even though you have made many economic decisions already, it does not mean you fully understand all the underlying concepts anymore than being held down to the planet means you fully understand the physicist's model of gravity.

Learning Objective 4: List and differentiate among the four decision-making pitfalls and relate the pitfalls to the Incentive Principle.
The usefulness of the Cost-Benefit Principle, at either an intuitive level or for an explicit calculation, depends on the proper assessment of the costs and benefits of the choices. While everyone may have a natural tendency to weigh costs and benefits, a natural tendency to accurately measure costs and benefits may not exist and certainly can be improved.

Measuring costs and benefits as proportions rather than absolute values defines the first decision-making pitfall. As the examples in the textbook emphasize, if it is worthwhile to take an action that saves you $10, then it is worthwhile when the list price of the item is $1,000 (a 1% savings) or $20 (a 50% savings). Net benefits (economic surplus) are measured in dollars, not percentages. The extent of the relative savings has no bearing on the decision to take the action, only the extent of the absolute savings should be considered.

Another common oversight is ignoring opportunity costs. Choosing a particular alternative means an infinite number of alternatives will not be chosen. To accurately gauge the net benefits of a decision, one must recognize the alternatives and value them honestly. If spending a beautiful, sunny Wednesday afternoon at the lake means you take an unpaid day off from work, then the forgone earnings must be included in the assessment of costs. The reason class attendance is nearly 100% on the day of an exam but noticeably less on lecture days stems from the difference in opportunity costs of not attending class.

> **Note:** Frequently, to introduce the concept and importance of opportunity costs, economists use time and the resulting forgone earnings as example. Do not be misled by our tendencies. All choices have an opportunity cost. Buying a car means not buying a lot of other consumer goods, the most valuable of which measures the opportunity cost.

The third pitfall in evaluating the costs and benefits stems from including costs that are irrelevant. Costs that cannot be recovered define the concept of **sunk costs**. For example, suppose you purchased a nonrefundable, nontransferable front row ticket to see your favorite pop star. Suppose further your economics professor announces at the last minute a test on the day after the concert. Whether you go to the concert depends on your valuation of the costs and benefits. However, it is entirely incorrect to include the cost of your ticket in the decision. The ticket has been paid for and cannot be sold, given away, or refunded; it is a sunk cost. The temptation to count the ticket price is strong but it will lead to an inaccurate (overstated) estimate of the costs.

The fourth common pitfall in quantifying the consequence of choosing a particular alternative stems from a failure to distinguish between average and marginal measures. The change in the total costs of an activity resulting from a one unit change in the level of the activity defines **marginal costs**. The resulting change in total benefits of an activity when a one unit change in the level of activity occurs identifies the **marginal benefits**. The Cost-Benefit Principle indicates that as long as the marginal benefits are greater than the marginal costs, the level of the activity should be increased. The other type of measurement variables are the average measures. **Average benefits** are the total benefits of n units of the activity divided by n. The total costs of n units of the activity divided by n defines the **average costs**. Measuring average costs and benefits is much easier than measuring marginal costs and benefits, which contributes to the frequent reliance on averages to guide decision-making. The convenience of average measures, unfortunately, does not change the inappropriateness of using average measures to make marginal decisions. If the average benefits of a given level of activity exceed the average costs of the same level of activity, increasing the activity is not necessarily the maximizing choice. A comparison of the average benefit to the average cost offers no guidance on whether to lessen or expand the level of the activity to reach maximization.

> **Note:** The mathematically inclined reader may realize that comparing the marginal benefits to the marginal costs is an application of the first derivative test from calculus. Seeking to maximize the net benefits (total benefits minus total costs) of an activity results in choosing the level of activity where the marginal benefits equal the marginal costs

The four pitfalls listed above suggest that sometimes people make irrational choices. Most of the time, however, people make rational choices. Thus, economists focus on rational choices to offer useful advice, and to provide a basis for predicting and explaining human behavior. Rational choices can be summed up in the Incentive Principle. The Incentive Principle states that a person (or firm, or society) is more likely to take an action if its benefit rises, and less likely to take it if its cost rises.

Learning Objective 5: Distinguish between Normative and Positive Economics, and between Macroeconomics and Microeconomics.

Economic models are based upon the principles of rational choice. The models, therefore, do not always describe how people actually behave, but rather predict how people will behave. Thus, economists differentiate between normative economics and positive economics. A normative economic principle is a principle that says how people *should* behave, while a positive economic principle is a principle that *predicts* how people will behave.

Economics divides into two major sub-fields. **Microeconomics** concentrates on the choices individuals make under scarcity and the implications for prices and quantities in individual markets. The impact of a future war with Iraq on the price of gasoline would form a microeconomic topic. **Macroeconomics** studies the performance of economies at the national level and the effect of governmental policies on the national economy's output. The resulting change in gross domestic product from President Bush's tax reform proposal is a proper macroeconomic question.

Learning Objective 6: Recognize the abundance of opportunities to apply economic reasoning — to practice "Economic Naturalism."

Economic naturalism refers the to the application of the basic tenets of economics to understand and explain everyday behaviors. The textbook gives several examples of common phenomenon which can be easily understood by applying the Cost-Benefit Principle. Setting the specific examples aside, the main point is to encourage you to use what you are learning to understand behavior that has seemed perplexing or inconsistent. You may find actions or choices that once confused or baffled you can now be easily comprehended. Of particular importance, the behavior of the political process is more clearly grasped within the simple framework of the Cost-Benefit Principle.

Learning Objective 7 (Appendix): Understand how to translate a verbal statement into an equation. Clearly define the following: equation, variable, dependent variable, independent variable, constant (parameter).

Economic models are frequently expressed in mathematical terms. A mathematical model allows for a greater degree of precision than a model expressed in verbal terms. But, model development always begins with verbal statements before proceeding to a mathematical version of the statements. An **equation** is a mathematical expression of the relationship between two or more variables. **Variables** are items thought to be related and that can take on different numerical values. By convention, the variable (or variables) which is thought to determine the magnitude of some other variable is placed on the right-hand side of the equation; the variable being determined is placed on the left hand side. The right-hand side variables are called **independent variables** and the left-hand side variable is called the **dependent variable**. Often a **constant** (or **parameter**) is included on the right-hand side of the equation with a value that is fixed. The statement "I think my GPA will improve this semester because I got a laptop for Christmas" can be translated into an equation like GPA = f(new laptop). GPA is the dependent variable and the laptop is the independent variable. The laptop presumably improves your productivity in some fashion and, in turn, improves your test scores and your GPA. Obviously, GPA does not "cause" a laptop but a laptop may "cause" a higher GPA. Use the term cause with reservation; to say X "causes" Y is a difficult proposition to prove. More accurately, say X "strongly influences" or X has a "significant effect" on Y.

Learning Objective 8 (Appendix): Starting with an equation, illustrate the equation with a graph. Define the following: vertical intercept, slope, rise, run.

For an equation of the form $Y = a + b*X$, Y is the dependent variable and X is the independent variable. The **vertical intercept** is the value of Y when X is zero; it is the value of "a" in the equation above. The **slope** of the equation, signified by "b" in the equation above, is the ratio of the change in Y when some change in X occurs. The change in Y is termed **rise** and the change in X is called **run**. These terms come from the orientation of the graph: X is on the horizontal axis (hence run) while Y is placed on the vertical axis (hence rise). Slope is often defined as rise over run. To plot an equation, first determine the vertical intercept's value and put a point on the vertical axis at this value (remember X=0). Then calculate a value of Y when X is not equal to 0 (pick easy X values like 1 or 10). To accomplish this, take the value of X you picked, multiple it by "b" and then add "a" to arrive at the value of Y. For linear relationships (straight lines), two pairs of coordinates are enough to completely describe the equation. Thus, after marking the vertical intercept and calculated value of Y, you can run a line through the two points. You have now illustrated the equation in the form of a graph.

Learning Objective 9 (Appendix): Starting with a graph, determine the underlying equation.

If this were a repair manual for a car, it would say installation is the reverse of disassembly. Look at the graph and note where the curve crosses or intersects the vertical axis. This is the vertical intercept "a." Now calculate the slope. Depending on the scale (the units X and Y are measured in) of the graph, pick two X values and note the resulting Y values in the graph. Say the values of X are 10 and 15 and the corresponding values for Y are 30 and 20. Slope is calculated as $(20-30)/(15-10) = (-10)/(5) = -2$. The rise of the graph is -10 when the run is 5. A negative relationship exists between X and Y, i.e., as X gets larger, Y gets smaller. Now simply take your results for "a" and "b" and write it out in equation form (as in the preceding learning objective).

Learning Objective 10 (Appendix): Demonstrate how a change in 1) the vertical intercept and 2) the slope affect the graph of the equation.
Continuing with the Y = a +b*X example, a change in the vertical intercept means a change in how large Y is when X = 0. When "a" changes, the position of the line in the graph changes. The change in position can be called a "shift" in the curve. It shifts up if the value of "a" gets larger and it shifts down if the value of "a" decreases. Note that the slope of the equation is the same as before and therefore the new line *must* be parallel to the original line. When the slope changes, the shape of the line in the graph changes. The line pivots through the unchanging vertical intercept. The new line will be steeper if the absolute value of the slope is greater than it was before; the line will be flatter if the absolute value of the slope is smaller than it was before. Recall that the flattest line is a horizontal line with a slope of zero and the steepest line is a vertical line with a slope of infinity.

Learning Objective 11 (Appendix): Beginning with a table of data, know how to construct a graph and how to determine the underlying equation.
When working with tabular data, first figure out which variable is the dependent variable and which is the independent variable. Next, write the name of the dependent variable on the vertical axis of your graph and the independent variable on the horizontal axis. Plot some of the data points by locating the value of the dependent variable and the associated value of the independent variable. Now use the techniques outlined above to either graph the function or determine the underlying equation.

III. Self-Test

<u>Key Terms</u>
Match the term in the right-hand column with the appropriate definition in the left-hand column by placing the letter of the term in the blank in front of its definition. (Answers are given at the end of the chapter.)

1. _____ The study of how individuals make choices under conditions of scarcity and the resulting effects.   a. average benefit

2. _____ A person with well-defined goals and tries to achieve them.   b. average cost

3. _____ The subfield of economics that concentrates on the performance of the national economy and the effects of governmental policies.   c. economics

4. _____ The value of the next best alternative not selected.   d. economic surplus

5. _____ The difference between the benefits of taking an action and the costs of taking the action.   e. macroeconomics

6. _____ The extra benefit experienced as a result of a one unit increase in the amount of activity chosen.   f. marginal benefit

7. _____ The total cost of *n* units of activity divided by *n*.   g. marginal cost

8. _____ The subfield of economics that concentrates on the behavior of individual markets.   h. microeconomics

9. ____ The extra costs experienced as a result of a one unit increase in the amount of activity chosen.

i. normative economic principle

10. ___ Costs that cannot be recovered regardless of the alternative chosen.

j. opportunity cost

11. ___ The total benefits of *n* units of activity divided by *n*.

k. positive economic principle

12. ___ A principle that predicts how people will behave.

l. rational person

13. ___ A principle that says how people should behave.

m. sunk cost

Appendix

Appendix

14. ___ A value in an equation that is fixed.

n. Constant (or parameter)

15. ___ The variable or variables that cause or determine the relationship in an equation.

o. dependent variable

16. ___ In a straight line, the ratio of the vertical distance to the corresponding horizontal distance between any two points.

p. equation

17. ___ The variable that is caused by or is being determined in an equation.

q. independent variable

18. ___ A mathematical statement of the relationship between two or more variables.

r. rise

19. ___ Items thought to be related which can take on different numerical values.

s. run

20. ___ When calculating slope, the vertical distance a straight line travels between any two points.

t. slope

21. ___ The value of the dependent variable when the value of the independent variable is zero.

u. variables

22. ___ When calculating slope, the horizontal distance a straight line travels between any two points .

v. vertical intercept

Multiple-Choice Questions

Circle the letter that corresponds to the best answer. (Answers are given at the end of the chapter.)

1. The scarcity principle indicates that
   A. no matter how much one has, it is never enough.
   B. compared to 100 years ago, individuals have less time today.
   C. with limited resources, having more of "this" means having less of "that."
   D. because tradeoffs must be made, resources are therefore scarce.
   E. the wealthier a person is, the fewer the number of tradeoffs he must make.

2. Benny has one hour before bedtime and he can either watch TV or listen to his new Korn CD. He chooses to listen to the CD. The scarcity principle's influence on Benny is seen in
   A. the decision to listen to music.
   B. the decision not to watch TV.
   C. the fixed amount of time before bed.
   D. the decision to choose between TV and music.
   E. Benny's taste in music.

3. Choosing to study for an exam until the extra benefit (improved score) equals the extra cost (mental fatigue) is
   A. not rational.
   B. an application of the cost-benefit principle.
   C. an application of the scarcity principle.
   D. the relevant opportunity cost.
   E. less desirable than studying for the entire evening.

4. The scarcity principle indicates that _____ and the cost-benefit principle indicates

   _____.
   A. choices must be made; how to make the choices
   B. how to make the choices; choices must be made
   C. choices must be made; just one of many possible ways to make the choices
   D. choices must be made; the choices will be poor
   E. choices must be made; the costs can never outweigh the benefits of the choices

5. Amy is thinking about going to the movies tonight to see Star Wars III: Revenge of the Siths. A ticket costs $7 and she will have to cancel her dog-sitting job that pays $30. The cost of seeing the movie is
   A. $7.
   B. $30.
   C. $37.
   D. $37 minus the benefit of seeing the movie.
   E. indeterminate.

6. The use of economic models, such as the cost-benefit principle, means economists believe that
   A. this is how people explicitly chose between alternatives.
   B. this is a reasonable abstraction of how people chose between alternatives.
   C. those who explicitly make decisions this way are smarter.
   D. with enough education, all people will start to explicitly make decisions this way.
   E. this is the way the world ought to explicitly make decisions.

7. Tony notes that an electronics store is offering a flat $20 off of all prices in the store. Tony reasons that if he wants to buy something with a price of $50 that it is a good offer but if he wants to buy something with a price of $500 it is not a good offer. This is an example of
   A. inconsistent reasoning; saving $20 is saving $20.
   B. the proper application of the cost-benefit principle.
   C. rational choice because in the first case he saves $40% and in the second case he saves 4%.
   D. marginal cost equals marginal benefit thinking.
   E. opportunity costs.

8. That individuals make inconsistent choices and the inconsistencies have a strong pattern is, in the view of the textbook,
   A. evidence of the severe limitations of economic models.

B. an indication of widespread irrationality.
C. support for the study of economics to improve decision making.
D. of limited importance.
E. a well-kept secret that should remain that way.

9. Sunk cost are different from other concepts of cost in that they
   A. can be either variable or fixed.
   B. cannot be lessened by choosing any particular course of action.
   C. influence the decision of which activity to do or not do.
   D. rise as the level of the activity rises.
   E. must be included for an accurate cost-benefit analysis.

10. Which of the following questions would not be part of microeconomics?
    A. What college major to select.
    B. How to make the largest profit.
    C. Whether to study or watch TV tonight.
    D. How will an early freeze in California affect the price of fruit.
    E. Should the federal budget always be balanced.

11. When making a decision, the important costs to identify and consider are the _____
    costs and the _____ costs.
    A. opportunity; marginal
    B. opportunity; fixed
    C. sunk; marginal
    D. marginal; average
    E. marginal; fixed

12. Janie can either mow the lawn or wash clothes, earning her a benefit of $30 or $45,
    respectively. Janie will therefore choose to _____ because the economic surplus is
    _____.
    A. mow; greater
    B. wash; greater
    C. mow; smaller
    D. wash; smaller
    E. mow; the same as for washing

13. Anytime one purchases a ticket in advance of an event, if the ticket is non-refundable and
    non-transferable then on the day of the event, then the ticket is
    A. part of the cost of going.
    B. a variable cost.
    C. part of the cost of going if it was expensive.
    D. a sunk cost and should play no role in the decision to go or not.
    E. a fixed cost but not a sunk cost.

14. The average cost of 20 units of an activity is the
    A. total cost of 20 units of the activity divided by 20.
    B. 20 divided by the total cost of 20 units of the activity.
    C. extra cost of 20 units of the activity divided by 20.
    D. reciprocal of the total cost of 20 units of the activity.
    E. change in total cost of the activity.

15. Class attendance on exam days is nearly 100% but on lecture days it is less. The likely
    explanation for this would be
    A. the opportunity cost of not attending on exam day is much higher than usual.
    B. random chance.
    C. the episode of Jerry Springer was a rerun.
    D. students thought today's class was a review.
    E. the opportunity cost of attending on exam day is much higher than usual.

16. To avoid the mistake of ignoring opportunity costs, the textbook recommends framing
    questions in the form of
    A. should I do A?
    B. should I do B?
    C. why should I do A?
    D. should I do A or B?
    E. should I do A or B or C or… Z?

17. On the first day of the semester, David finds he has one hour of time in the evening to
    allocate. He can do one of two things. He can watch TV for one hour or he can open his
    economics textbook and read for an hour. The benefit of watching TV is 30; the benefit or
    reading about economics is 20. The cost of watching TV is _____ and the cost of
    reading his economics textbook is _____.
    A. 20; 30
    B. 0; 0
    C. 30; 20
    D. 20; 0
    E. indeterminate; indeterminate

18. Continuing with the information in question 17, if David applies the cost-benefit principle
    accurately, he will
    A. read his economics textbook.
    B. watch TV.
    C. watch TV but fret that he should be reading.
    D. read his economics textbook but resent missing TV.
    E. flip a coin because the net benefits are the same.

19. Continuing with the information in question 17, suppose that instead of the first day of the
    semester, it is the night before David's first exam in economics. One could reasonably predict
    that
    A. the benefit of watching TV will rise.

B. the benefit of reading about economics will fall.

C. the cost of watching TV will rise.

D. the cost of reading economics will rise.

E. he will continue to make the same choice.

20. In general, to make optimal decisions, one needs information on the
   A. average benefits and marginal costs.
   B. marginal benefits and marginal costs.
   C. marginal benefits and average costs.
   D. average benefits and average costs.
   E. benefits and costs, which can be either average or marginal.

Short Answer Problems
(Answers and solutions are given at the end of the chapter.)

1. Enid has 2 exams tomorrow: one in economics and one in marketing. She has a total of 4 hours available for studying. The table below shows the test scores she will make with different amounts of studying time. For example, if she spends one hour studying economics, she makes a 77 on the economics test and makes a 79 on the marketing test, having spent 3 hours (4-1) studying for it.

	Hours Spent Studying Economics				
	0	1	2	3	4
Economics Score	65	77	86	89	91
Marketing Score	80	79	77	70	50

   A. The scarce resource Enid is allocating is (time/intelligence) _____. The opportunity cost of an extra hour studying economics is the (improvement in economics score/reduction in marketing score) _____.

   B. Calculate the marginal benefit of spending 1, 2, 3, and 4 hours studying economics: the 1st hour ____; the 2nd _____; the 3rd ____; and the 4th ____.

   C. Calculate the marginal cost of spending 1, 2, 3, and 4 hours studying economics: the 1st hour ____; the 2nd _____; the 3rd ____; and the 4th ____.

   D. If Enid is rational, she should spend _____ hours studying economics and _____ hours studying marketing.

   E. Calculate the total points from both tests when 0 to 4 hours are spent studying economics: 0 hours ____; 1 hour ____; 2 hours _____; 3 hours _____; and 4 hours _____. Does the answer to "D" agree with the answer here (yes/no) _____.

2. Ontel engineers proposed developing a 5 Gigahertz microprocessor in early 2003 at a cost of $50 million for a working prototype. By mid 2004, the $50 million had been spent with no prototype. The engineers request an additional $10 million to finish the project. For

convenience, assume 1) the marginal cost of producing the chip once it is developed is zero and 2) with the additional funding, the probability of a prototype is 1.

A. In January, 2003 the sunk costs of this project was _____ and in July 2004, the sunk costs of the project are _____.

B. Assume Ontel estimates it will earn revenues of $40 million on a 5 Gigahertz chip. If the extra funding is not approved, then Ontel will lose ($50 million/$10 million) _____. If the extra $10 million is granted, Ontel will lose ($60 million/$20 million) _____. Therefore, the extra $10 million (should/should not) _____ be granted.

3. The following table contains information about the costs and benefits of engaging in different amounts of an activity. Assume that cost data reflects both monetary and opportunity costs.

Units of Activity	Costs	Benefits	Average Costs	Average Benefits	Marginal Costs	Marginal Benefits
0	$0	$0	$0	$0	n/a	n/a
1	30	100				
2	35	150				
3	50	180				
4	70	200				
5	120	205				

A. Calculate the average costs and benefits for the different levels of activity. Likewise, calculate the marginal costs and benefits.

B. The level of activity consistent with the Cost-Benefit Principle occurs at (4/5) _____ units. The (4/5) _____ units would represent excess activity because the (marginal costs/average costs) _____ are greater than the (marginal benefits/average benefits) _____.

C. The difference between the benefits and the costs is the same for units (3 and 4/2 and 3) _____. Why then is there only one maximum point? Explain. _____
_____.

IV. Economic Naturalist Application

A frequent complaint of the wealthy is that, while they can purchase virtually any item they want, the one item they can't purchase more of is time. How are the wealthy identical to the lower classes with respect to time? Is their a difference in their opportunity cost of time compared with the lower classes? Suppose some wealthy person decides to retire. Will he still lament his lack of time? Why?

V. Self-Test Solutions

Key Terms

1. c
2. l
3. e
4. j
5. d
6. f
7. b
8. h
9. g
10. m
11. a
12. k
13. i
Appendix
14. n
15. q
16. t
17. o
18. p
19. u
20. r
21. v
22. s

Multiple-Choice Questions

1. C
2. C
3. B
4. A
5. C
6. B
7. A
8. C
9. B
10. E
11. A
12. B
13. D
14. A
15. A
16. D

17. A
18. B
19. C
20. B

Short Answer Problems

1.
A. time; reduction in marketing score
B. 12; 9; 3; 2.
C. 1; 2; 7; 20.
D. 2; 2.
E. 145; 156; 163; 159; 141. yes.

2.
A. 0; $50 million.
B. $50 million. $20 million. should.

3.

Units of Activity	Costs	Benefits	Average Costs	Average Benefits	Marginal Costs	Marginal Benefits
0	$0	$0	$0	$0	n/a	n/a
1	30	100	30.0	100	$30	$100
2	35	150	17.5	75	5	50
3	50	180	16.7	60	15	30
4	70	200	17.5	50	20	20
5	120	205	24.0	41	50	5

A. See table.

B. 4. 5; marginal costs; marginal benefits.

C. 3 and 4. The difference is *maximized* at 4 units; if one stops at 3 units, the maximum net benefits will not be realized.

Chapter 2
Comparative Advantage:
The Basis for Exchange

I. Pretest: What Do You Really Know?

Circle the letter that corresponds to the best answer. (Answers appear immediately after the final question).

1. Bill can write one computer program in an hour while Larry can write two computer programs in one hour. In this case,
   A. Larry has a comparative advantage in writing simple computer programs.
   B. Bill has a comparative advantage in writing simple computer programs.
   C. Larry has an absolute advantage in writing simple computer programs.
   D. Bill has an absolute advantage in writing simple computer programs.
   E. neither person has an absolute advantage.

2. The Principle of Comparative Advantage implies that
   A. each person should specialize in those tasks in which he or she does not have a comparative advantage.
   B. each person should specialize in those tasks in which he or she has a comparative advantage.
   C. each person should be self-sufficient.
   D. each person will be poorer if they trade with others.
   E. each person should specialize in those tasks in which they have an absolute advantage.

3. The production possibilities curve shows
   A. the minimum combinations of two goods that can be produced by a country.
   B. the only combinations of two goods that can be produced by a country.
   C. the maximum combinations of two goods that can be produced by a country.
   D. the minimum combinations of two resources that a country needs to produce a good.
   E. the maximum combinations of two resources that a country needs to produce a good.

4. A production possibilities curve slopes downward because
   A. in order to produce more of one good you must produce less of another good.
   B. in order to produce more of one good you must produce more of another good.

    C. in order to produce less of one good you must produce less of another good.
    D. it just has to, that's all.
    E. resources are unlimited.

5. All points on the production possibilities curve are
    A. unattainable points.
    B. efficient points.
    C. inefficient points.
    D. attainable points.
    E. both efficient and attainable points.

6. The Principle of Increasing Opportunity Cost states that
    A. wherever you go, there you are.
    B. to increase the production of a good, a country must produce less of another good.
    C. to increase the production of a good, a country should first employ those resources with the highest opportunity cost and then turn to resources with lower opportunity costs.
    D. to increase the production of a good, a country should first employ those resources with the lowest opportunity cost and then turn to resources with higher opportunity costs.
    E. to increase the production of a good, a country must improve its technology.

7. A production possibilities curve that reflects The Principle of Increasing Opportunity Cost will
    A. slope downward.
    B. be bowed outward.
    C. be bowed inward.
    D. be a straight line.
    E. slope upward.

8. Which of the following will *not* cause a production possibilities curve to shift outward?
    A. An increase in a country's productivity.
    B. An increase in a country's resources.
    C. An improvement in a country's technology.
    D. Specialization in the production of one good.
    E. All of the above will cause a production possibilities curve to shift outward.

9. Bill can write one computer program or one speech in an hour. Larry can write one computer program or two speeches in an hour. In this case,
    A. Larry should write computer programs and Bill should write speeches because these are the tasks in which each has a comparative advantage.
    B. Larry should write speeches and Bill should write computer programs because these are the tasks in which each has a comparative advantage.
    C. They should each write computer programs and speeches and not specialize.
    D. Bill has an absolute advantage in speeches and should therefore write speeches.
    E. Larry has an absolute advantage in speeches and should therefore write speeches.

10. Which of the following is a benefit of specialization and trade on the basis of comparative advantage?
   A. Two countries can produce more of two goods with no change in their resources or productivities.
   B. Both countries' production possibilities curves will shift outward.
   C. The opportunity costs of both goods will increase for both countries.
   D. The opportunity cost of one good will rise in both countries.
   E. Both countries production possibilities curves will shift inward.

Solutions and Feedback to Pretest
The answers to the pretest are provided below along with the relevant Learning Objective from the Key Point Review. We strongly recommend that you take the time to review the appropriate material for each question you answered incorrectly.

Correct Answer	Learning Objective
1. C	1
2. B	2
3. C	3
4. A	3
5. E	4
6. D	5
7. B	5
8. D	6
9. B	7
10. A	8

II. Key Point Review
The Forest

This chapter focuses on the concepts of specialization and trade. You will apply these ideas throughout your work in economics. In particular, the study of international trade is built with these tools. It is therefore very important to master these concepts now.

The central questions you need to be able to answer are as follows:
- What is absolute advantage?
- What is comparative advantage?
- How is opportunity cost related to comparative advantage?
- How does comparative advantage determine specialization?
- What is the production possibilities curve?
- How is the production possibilities curve used to determine comparative advantage, specialization and trade patterns?

The Trees

Learning Objective 1: define and contrast these terms: absolute advantage, comparative advantage.

A person has an **absolute advantage** over another person if she can complete a task using fewer resources than the other person. A person has a **comparative advantage** over another person if she has a lower opportunity cost of completing a task than the other person.

For example: many professors have teaching assistants (TAs) to help them grade student work. Suppose that in a ten minute period, a professor can either grade one exam or enter 30 scores into a spreadsheet. In the same amount of time, a TA can either grade one-half of an exam or enter 20 scores.

- The professor has an absolute advantage in both tasks: she can grade an exam in ten minutes while it will take the TA twenty minutes, and she can enter 30 scores in 10 minutes while the TA can only enter 20.
- The professor has a comparative advantage in grading exams: her opportunity cost of grading an exam is 30 scores while the TA's opportunity cost is 40. The TA, however, has a comparative advantage in entering scores since his opportunity cost is 1/40 of an exam per score versus 1/30 of an exam for the professor.

Learning Objective 2: Define and explain the importance of The Principle of Comparative Advantage. Briefly identify some of the sources of comparative advantage for individuals and countries.

The Principle of Comparative Advantage states that everyone does best when each person or country concentrates on the activities for which his or her opportunity cost is lowest.

For example, since the TA has a comparative advantage in entering scores and the professor has a comparative advantage in grading exams, the best thing to do is to have the professor grade the exams and then have the TA enter the scores in a spreadsheet.

Note: This might not fit your intuition; you might think that since the professor has absolute advantage she should do both tasks. This is an important example of why it is important to learn how to think like an economist: economic concepts often lead to conclusions that are correct but are not intuitively obvious.

The sources of comparative advantage for individuals include education and training, life experience, and innate abilities. Climate, natural resources, and historical circumstances are three among many sources of comparative advantage for nations and regions.

Learning Objective 3: Define the production possibilities curve and explain how the slope of the production possibilities curve is related to The Scarcity Principle.

You must learn how to apply production possibilities curves in two ways: to individuals and to countries. The definition of the production possibilities curve is the same for both: it shows the maximum amount of two goods that can be produced given the person or country's productivity and resources.

The Scarcity Principle states that having more of one good thing usually means having less of another. The production possibilities curve obeys this principle: the negative slope of the production possibilities curve is caused by the fact that in order to produce more of one good, a person or country must produce less of another good.

Note: The absolute value of the slope of the production possibilities curve is equal to the opportunity cost of the good plotted on the horizontal axis.

Hint: The slope of a line is discussed in both the textbook (appendix to Chapter 1) and this study guide (Chapter 1).

Learning Objective 4: For a given production possibilities curve, explain the differences among attainable points, unattainable points, efficient points, and inefficient points.

Attainable points are points that are inside or on the production possibilities curve. **Unattainable points** lie outside the production possibilities curve. Points on the production possibilities curve are **efficient points** while those that are inside the production possibilities curve are **inefficient points.** Thus, all efficient points are attainable but all attainable points are not efficient. This is important since much of economics consists of distinguishing efficient economic outcomes from attainable, but inefficient, ones.

Learning Objective 5: Define and explain The Principle of Increasing Opportunity Cost (also called the "Low-Hanging-Fruit Principle").
The Principle of Increasing Opportunity Cost states that to expand the production of any good, a person or country should first employ those resources with the lowest opportunity cost, and only afterward turn to resources with higher opportunity costs.

For example: suppose that a professor is grading exams and has only two red pens, one that works well and one that does not. The Principle of Increasing Costs implies that the professor should use the pen that works well first and use the other pen only after the better one runs out of ink.

Learning Objective 6: Identify and discuss the reasons why a production possibilities curve might shift.

There are two reasons why a production possibilities curve might shift. The first is that a person or country acquires more resources such as human capital, physical capital or natural capital. The second is that the person or country increases its productivity holding its resources fixed. This can happen through improvements in technology and advancements in knowledge.

Note: A shift in the production possibilities curve can turn a point that was previously considered to be unattainable into an attainable point. Indeed, this is the central story of the past 200 years of world economic history!

Learning Objective 7: Identify and explain the relationships among these concepts: comparative advantage, specialization, and trade.

Comparative advantage determines **specialization**: each person or country should specialize in the task in which they have a comparative advantage. (This is the Principle of Comparative Advantage.) The people or countries should then **trade** with one another for those tasks in which they do not have a comparative advantage.

For example: we discussed the professor and the TA in Learning Objectives 1 and 2 and found that the professor has a comparative advantage in grading and the TA in entering scores. This implies that the professor should specialize in grading, the TA in entering scores and then they should trade (i.e. work together) to complete the grading and the entering of scores for the class.

Learning Objective 8: Discuss the benefits and costs of specialization and trade. Do this for both individuals and countries.

There are two important benefits of specialization and trade. The first is that it allows two people or two countries to produce and consume more goods and services than they could produce or consume if they worked independently. This provides both with higher living standards. Second, specialization allows people or countries to get better at what they do, what economists call "learning-by-doing." Of course, excessive specialization can impose costs as well as benefits. For example, a country may have a comparative advantage in producing oil. This means that it will not be able to take advantage of learning-by-doing in other areas and may be stuck producing oil rather than manufacturing other goods. Further, specialization can lead to mind-numbing, repetitive work if it is carried too far.

III. Self-Test

Key Terms
Match the term in the right-hand column with the appropriate definition in the left-hand column by placing the letter of the term in the blank in front of its definition. (Answers are given at the end of the chapter.)

1. _____ A combination of goods that cannot be produced using a person's current resources and productivity.

    a. absolute advantage

2. _____ A person can perform a task with fewer resources (for example, in less time) than another person.

    b. attainable point

3. _____ A combination of goods that can be produced using a person's current resources and productivity.

    c. comparative advantage

4. _____ A graph that shows the maximum combinations of goods that can be produced by a person given their current resources and productivity.

    d. efficient point

5. _____ A person can perform a task at a lower opportunity cost than another person.

    e. inefficient point

6. _____ A combination of goods in which the production of one good can be increased without reducing the production of another good.

    f. production possibilities curve

7. _____ A combination of goods in which the production of one good cannot be increased without reducing the production of another good.

    g. unattainable point

Multiple-Choice Questions
Circle the letter that corresponds to the best answer. (Answers are given at the end of the chapter.)

1. If Kirby can perform a task using fewer resources than Frank, we say that Kirby
    A. has a comparative advantage in this task.
    B. has an absolute advantage in this task.
    C. has increasing opportunity costs in this task
    D. has a comparative disadvantage relative in this task.
    E. has an absolute disadvantage in this task.

2. If Kirby can perform a task at a lower opportunity cost than Frank, we say that Kirby
    A. has a comparative advantage in this task.
    B. has an absolute advantage in this task.
    C. has increasing opportunity costs in this task
    D. has a comparative disadvantage relative in this task.
    E. has an absolute disadvantage in this task.

Use the following information for problems 3 and 4: Bob can do 7 loads of laundry or make 3 complete meals per day. Carol can do 10 loads of laundry or make 2 complete meals per day.

3. Given the information above, Carol has
   A. no absolute advantage in either task but a comparative advantage making meals.
   B. an absolute advantage doing laundry and a comparative advantage doing laundry.
   C. an absolute advantage making meals and a comparative advantage making meals.
   D. an absolute advantage in doing laundry but no comparative advantage in either task.

4. According to the Principle of Comparative Advantage and given the information above,
   A. Bob should do the laundry and Carol should make the meals.
   B. Carol should do the laundry and Bob should make the meals.
   C. they should alternate tasks depending on the day of the week since neither of them has an absolute or comparative advantage in either task.
   D. Bob should make 2 meals and do 3 loads of laundry and Carol should make 1 meal and 7 loads of laundry.
   E. we cannot tell which person should do which task since not enough information is provided.

5. Production possibilities curves
   A. always slope downward.
   B. slope downward only if the Principle of Increasing Cost applies.
   C. bow inward if the Principle of Increasing Cost applies.
   D. always slope upward.
   E. slope downward only if the Principle of Comparative Advantage applies.

6. Which of the following will cause a production possibilities curve to bow outward?
   A. Scarcity.
   B. The Principle of Comparative Advantage.
   C. The Principle of Increasing Cost.
   D. Absolute advantage.
   E. None of the above will cause the production possibilities curve to bow outward.

Use the following information for problems 7, 8, and 9: Jan can crochet two headbands or 4 purses in one day. Marcia can crochet 5 headbands or one purse in one day.

7. If we plot each woman's production possibilities curve with headbands on the vertical axis and purses on the horizontal axis,
   A. the absolute value of the slope of Jan's production possibilities curve will be ½ and Marcia's will be 1/5.
   B. the absolute value of the slope of Jan's production possibilities curve will be ½ and Marcia's will be 2/5.
   C. the absolute value of the slope of Jan's production possibilities curve will be 2 and Marcia's will be 1/5.
   D. the absolute value of the slope of Jan's production possibilities curve will be ½ and Marcia's will be 5.
   E. the absolute value of the slope of Jan's production possibilities curve will be 2 and Marcia's will be 5.

8. Given the information above, Marcia has
    A. an absolute advantage crocheting headbands and a comparative advantage crocheting purses.
    B. no absolute advantage in either task but a comparative advantage crocheting purses.
    C. an absolute advantage crocheting headbands and a comparative advantage crocheting headbands.
    D. an absolute advantage crocheting purses and a comparative advantage crocheting purses.
    E. an absolute advantage in crocheting purses but no comparative advantage in either task.

9. According to the Principle of Comparative Advantage and given the information above, Jan should
    A. yell, "Marcia, Marcia, Marcia!"
    B. only crochet purses and trade them for any headbands she wants.
    C. only crochet headbands and trade them for any purses she wants.
    D. crochet both headbands and purses and not engage in trade.
    E. produce nothing since she does not have an absolute advantage in either headbands or purses.

10. Billie can compose two songs in one day or sing and record 4 songs in one day. Given this information, a combination of composing one song and singing and recording 4 songs all in one day is an
    A. efficient and attainable point.
    B. efficient point but is also an unattainable point.
    C. inefficient point but is also an attainable point.
    D. inefficient and unattainable point.
    E. unattainable point.

11. A point on a production possibilities curve is
    A. an efficient point.
    B. an inefficient point.
    C. an efficient but unattainable point.
    D. an inefficient but attainable point.
    E. an unattainable point.

12. An increase in a country's resources will
    A. cause that country's production possibilities curve to bow outward.
    B. cause that country's production possibilities curve to bow inward.
    C. shift that country's production possibilities curve outward.
    D. have no effect on that country's production possibilities curve.
    E. shift that country's production possibilities curve inward.

13. A worker learns a new skill that is applicable in his or her job. This will cause the worker's production possibilities curve to
    A. bow inward.
    B. bow outward.

  C. shift inward.
  D. shift outward.
  E. remain unchanged.

Use the following information for problems 14, 15, and 16: Mr. Jones can photocopy 10 pages from a book or type 2 pages of handwritten text in 10 minutes. Mr. Smith can photocopy 40 pages from a book or type 3 pages of handwritten text in 10 minutes.

14. Given the information above, Mr. Jones has
  A. an absolute advantage in photocopying and a comparative advantage in photocopying.
  B. an absolute advantage in typing and a comparative advantage in typing.
  C. no absolute advantage in either task but a comparative advantage in photocopying.
  D. no absolute advantage in either task but a comparative advantage in typing.
  E. absolute advantage in neither task nor a comparative advantage in either task.

15. Given the information above, if Mr. Smith and Mr. Jones follow the Principle of Comparative Advantage
  A. Mr. Smith will do all of the typing and Mr. Jones will do all of the photocopying.
  B. Mr. Smith will do all of the photocopying and Mr. Jones will do all of the typing.
  C. Mr. Jones will photocopy 5 pages and type one page, and Mr. Smith will photocopy 20 pages and type 2 pages.
  D. Mr. Smith will photocopy 5 pages and type one page, and Mr. Jones will photocopy 20 pages and type 2 pages.
  E. they will not know what to do since not enough information is provided.

16. Given the information above, if Mr. Jones takes a course and learns how to type 3 pages in 10 minutes and can still photocopy 10 pages in 10 minutes, then
  A. Mr. Smith will do all of the typing and Mr. Jones will do all of the photocopying.
  B. Mr. Smith will do all of the photocopying and Mr. Jones will do all of the typing.
  C. Mr. Jones will photocopy 5 pages and type one page, and Mr. Smith will photocopy 20 pages and type 2 pages.
  D. Mr. Smith will photocopy 5 pages and type one page, and Mr. Jones will photocopy 20 pages and type 2 pages.
  E. they will not know what to do since not enough information is provided.

17. Which of the following statements reflects the correct relationship among absolute advantage, comparative advantage, specialization and trade?
  A. People should specialize in those tasks in which they have an absolute advantage and have someone else perform those tasks in which they do not have an absolute advantage.
  B. People should specialize in those tasks in which they have a comparative advantage and have someone else perform those tasks in which they do not have a comparative advantage.
  C. People should specialize in those tasks in which they have comparative advantage but only have others perform those tasks in which they do not have an absolute advantage.
  D. People should specialize in those tasks in which they have an absolute advantage but only have others perform those tasks in which they do not have a comparative advantage.

E. People should only specialize in those tasks in which they have both comparative and absolute advantage and have others perform those tasks in which they have neither comparative nor absolute advantage.

18. A benefit of specialization and trade between two people is that
   A. each can consume more than before they traded with no increase in resources or productivity.
   B. each can consume the same amount as before they traded with fewer resources and no change in productivity.
   C. each can consume the same amount as before they traded with the same resources and lower levels of productivity.
   D. None of the above are correct.
   E. Answers A, B and C are all correct.

19. If a production possibilities curve obeys The Principle of Increasing Opportunity Cost, then the absolute value of the slope this production possibilities curve will
   A. be constant.
   B. rise.
   C. fall.
   D. rise then fall.
   E. not be affected.

20. Paula has absolute advantage in two tasks compared to Olivia. Paula has a comparative advantage in one task while Olivia has a comparative advantage in the other. This implies that
   A. Olivia will gain from trading with Paula but Paula will not gain from trading with Olivia
   B. Paula will gain from trading with Olivia but Olivia will not gain from trading with Paula.
   C. both Olivia and Paula will gain from trading with each other.
   D. neither Olivia nor Paula will gain from trading with each other.
   E. there is not enough information to know whether or not either or both will gain from trade.

Short Answer Problems
(Answers and solutions are given at the end of the chapter.)

1. A production possibilities curve for an economy
   The table below presents data on the country of Johnnyland, an economy that produces two goods: potato chips and computer chips:

Potato chips (millions of bags)	0	2	4	6	8
Computer chips (millions of chips)	30	27	21	12	0

A. Draw the production possibilities curve on the graph below.

A. If Johnnyland is producing 21 million computer chips and 2 million bags of potato chips this is a(n) _____ point.
B. Suppose Johnnyland is producing 30 million computer chips and no potato chips. If this country decides to start producing potato chips, the opportunity cost of the first 2 million bags of potato chips will be _____ computer chips.
C. Suppose Johnnyland is producing 27 million computer chips and 2 million bags of potato chips. If this country decides to produce 2 million more bags of potato chips, the opportunity cost will be _____ computer chips.
D. Suppose Johnnyland is producing 21 million computer chips and 4 million bags of potato chips. If this country decides to produce 2 million more bags of potato chips, the opportunity cost will be _____ computer chips.
E. Given your answers to parts (C), (D) and (E), does this production possibilities curve obey The Principle of Increasing Opportunity Cost? _____ . Why? _____
_____
F. Does the shape of the production possibilities curve you drew in part (A) support your answer to part (F)? _____ Explain why or why not: _____
_____

2. **Production Possibilities and Comparative Advantages for Two People**

Let's return to Susan and Tom, the people discussed in Chapter 2 of the text who gather nuts and pick coffee. Susan can gather 2 pounds of nuts or pick 4 pounds of coffee per hour while Tom can gather 4 pounds of nuts or pick 2 pounds of coffee per hour. Suppose that they each work 6 hours per day.

A. Draw the production possibilities curve for both Tom and Susan on the graph below.

B. Susan has a comparative advantage in _____ and Tom has a comparative advantage
    in _____. We can see this on the graph because the slope of Susan's production
    possibilities frontier is (steeper/flatter) _____ than Tom's.
C. Suppose that Susan and Tom decide to work together so that they can maximize their
    production of nuts and coffee. If both Susan and Tom only gather nuts, they will gather
    _____ pounds of nuts in 6 hours. If both Susan and Tom only pick coffee, they will
    pick _____ pounds of coffee in 6 hours. If Susan and Tom specialize according to
    their comparative advantages they will pick _____ pounds of coffee and
    _____ pounds of nuts in 6 hours.
D. Use the information from part (C) to draw the production possibilities curve for Susan and
    Tom working together.

E. Compare the graphs you drew in parts (A) and (D) and explain how they are related to one
    another:

    _____

    _____

3. **Production Possibilities and the Gains from Trade**

    Suppose that each worker in the United Kingdom (UK) is identical and can produce 72
    computers or 180 tons of grain per year. There are 30 million workers in the UK. Suppose that
    each worker in Finland is identical and can produce 48 computers or 48 tons of grain per year.
    There are 3 million workers in Finland.

    A. (The UK/Finland) _____ has an absolute advantage in computer production and
        (the UK/Finland) _____ has an absolute advantage in grain production.
    B. The UK has an opportunity cost of _____ per computer and an opportunity cost of
        _____ per ton of grain. Finland has an opportunity cost of _____ per
        computer and an opportunity cost of _____ per ton of grain.
    C. The information in part (B) tells us that _____ has a comparative advantage in
        grain production and _____ has a comparative advantage in computer production.
        This is because _____.
    D. Suppose that Finland offered to specialize in the production of computers and trade
        computers to the UK for grain at the rate of 1 computer for 2 tons of grain. The UK should
        (accept/reject) _____ this offer because the UK produces computers at a
        (lower/higher) opportunity cost than 1 computer for 2 tons of grain.
    E. Suppose that Finland offered to specialize in the production of computers and trade
        computers to the UK at the rate of 1 computer for 3 tons of grain. The UK should
        (accept/reject) _____ this offer because the UK can produce grain at a
        (lower/higher) opportunity cost than 1 computer for ½ ton of grain.
    F. Suppose that the ability of UK workers to produce computers improved so that their
        productivity in computer making doubled. This means that the UK now has an opportunity
        cost of _____ per computer and an opportunity cost of _____ per ton of
        grain.
    G. Given the information in part (F), the comparative advantages of the UK and Finland
        (have/have not) _____ been changed from your answer in part (C). This is
        because _____.
    H. Given the information in part (F) and your answer to part (G), suppose that Finland
        offered to specialize in the production of computers and trade computers to the UK for
        grain at the rate of 1 computer for 2 tons of grain. The UK should (accept/reject)
        _____ this offer because the UK can produce grain at a (lower/higher) opportunity
        cost than 1 computer for 2 tons of grain.

IV. Becoming an Economic Naturalist: Case Study

Farmers in Minnesota and South Dakota grow sunflower seeds and soybeans. The table below provides data on yields per acre for both crops in 2004:

State	Soybeans (bushels per acre)	Sunflower seeds (pounds per acre)
Minnesota	33	1068
South Dakota	34	1462

The table below contains data on the number of acres planted in all crops, in soybeans and in sunflower seeds for each state (in 1000s of acres):

State	All crops	Soybeans	Sunflower seeds
Minnesota	19,481	7,050	415
South Dakota	17,146	4,120	530

Source: U.S. Department of Agriculture website (www.usda.gov)

Using these data, identify which state has a comparative advantage in each crop. Do you think that The Principle of Comparative Advantage explains the planting behavior of farmers in Minnesota and South Dakota? Why or why not?
Answer:

V. Self-Test Solutions
Key Terms
1. g
2. a
3. b
4. f
5. c
6. e
7. d

Multiple-Choice Questions
1. B
2. A
3. B; Carol can do more laundry in a day than Bob (absolute advantage). Her opportunity cost of a load of laundry is 2/10 of a meal, which is lower than Bob's opportunity cost of a load of laundry (3/7 of a meal).
4. B
5. A; this is because of The Scarcity Principle.

6. C
7. D
8. C; Marcia's opportunity cost of headbands is 1/5 of a purse while Jan's is 2 purses.
9. B
10. E
11. A
12. C; the opportunity costs are not affected but the country can now produce more of both goods.
13. D
14. C
15. A
16. A; Mr. Jones still has a lower opportunity cost of typing. Neither Mr. Jones nor Mr. Smith now has an absolute advantage in typing.
17. B
18. E
19. B
20. C

Short Answer Problems

1. A. See graph at right.

    B. inefficient point. They could produce 4 million bags of potato chips but do not.
    C. 3 million.
    D. 4 million.
    E. 9 million
    F. Yes. The opportunity cost of producing 2 million bags of potato chips rises from 3 million computer chips to 4 million computer chips to 9 million computer chips.
    G. Yes. The production possibilities curve is bowed out, implying that the absolute value of the slope is increasing. The absolute value of the slope is equal to the opportunity cost of potato chips, and thus the graph shows that opportunity cost of potato chips is indeed increasing.

2. A. See graph below:

B. Coffee; nuts; flatter.

C. 36; 36; 24; 24.

D. See graph below

E. The upper segment of the graph is Susan's production possibilities curve shifted up by 36 units, 24 of which consist of Tom only gathering nuts and Susan gradually shifting from gathering nuts to picking coffee. When Susan is picking 24 pounds of coffee, she is using all of her resources and in order for the two of them to produce more coffee Tom must move from gathering nuts to picking coffee. This segment of the graph is thus Tom's production possibilities curve shifted to the right by 24 units. Notice: Susan shifts out of nuts first! She has the comparative advantage in coffee and so they will gain more coffee if Susan gathers it instead of Tom. This is an illustration of the The Principle of Increasing Opportunity Cost.

3. A. UK, UK

  B. 2.5 tons of grain, 0.4 computers; 1 ton of grain, 1 computer.

  C. the UK; Finland. This is because the UK has a lower opportunity cost of grain in terms of computers than does Finland, and Finland has a lower opportunity cost of computers in terms of grain than does the UK.

  D. accept; higher. Note: 2.5 tons of grain per computer is higher than 2 tons of grain per computer.

E. reject; lower. Note: 2.5 tons of grain per computer is lower than 3 tons of grain per computer.
F. 1.25 tons of grain; 0.8 computers.
G. have not. This is because the UK still has a lower opportunity cost of grain in terms of computers than does Finland, and Finland still has a lower opportunity cost of computers in terms of grain than does the UK. The differences in opportunity costs have narrowed but still yield the same comparative advantages.
H. reject; 1.25 tons of grain per computer is lower than 2 tons of grain per computer.

Chapter 3
Supply and Demand:
An Introduction

I. Pretest: What Do You Really Know?

Circle the letter that corresponds to the best answer. (Answers appear immediately after the final question).

1. Which of the following is not one of the basic economic questions that every society must answer?
   A. What goods will be produced?
   B. Where will goods be produced?
   C. How will goods be produced?
   D. How will goods be distributed to members of society?
   E. None of the above is a basic economic question.

2. The demand for milk slopes downward because
   A. a lower price of milk allows a buyer to purchase more milk.
   B. a lower price of milk allows a buyer to substitute milk for other beverages.
   C. a lower price of milk causes sellers to produce less milk.
   D. both (A) and (B) are correct.
   E. of gravity.

3. An increase in the price of beef will probably cause
   A. the demand for chicken to decrease.
   B. the demand for beef to increase.
   C. the demand for chicken to increase.
   D. the quantity demanded of beef to increase.
   E. the demand for beef to decrease.

4. As the price of milk increases, suppliers will
   A. increase the supply of milk.
   B. increase the quantity supplied of milk.
   C. decrease the supply of milk.
   D. decrease the quantity supplied of milk.
   E. be unaffected and not change their behavior at all.

5. An increase in the price of chicken feed will
   A. cause the supply of chicken to fall.
   B. cause the demand for chicken to fall.
   C. cause the demand for chicken to rise.
   D. cause the supply of chicken to rise.
   E. cause the quantity supplied of chicken to rise.

6. If a market is in equilibrium, then
   A. the quantity demanded equals the quantity supplied.
   B. the buyer's reservation price equals the seller's reservation price.
   C. there is no excess demand or excess supply.
   D. (A), (B) and (C) are all true.
   E. none of the above answers are true.

7. The price of milk is currently above the equilibrium price in the milk market. This means that
   A. there will be excess supply at this price.
   B. there will be excess demand at this price.
   C. there will be a decrease in demand.
   D. there will be a decrease in supply.
   E. the equilibrium price of milk will rise.

8. If the price of tea falls, then the price of coffee will
   A. rise because the demand for coffee will rise.
   B. fall because the demand for coffee will fall.
   C. rise because the supply of coffee will rise.
   D. fall because the supply of coffee will fall.
   E. be unaffected because the price of tea only affects the market for tea.

9. If the price of gasoline is $2.50 per gallon and the buyer's reservation price is $3.00 per gallon, then
   A. the buyer's surplus is $0.50 per gallon.
   B. the seller's surplus is $0.50 per gallon.
   C. the market is in equilibrium.
   D. the demand for gasoline will fall.
   E. the demand for gasoline will rise.

10. Economic efficiency means that
    A. all machines in the economy are running at their full capacity.
    B. there is "cash on the table."
    C. the socially optimal amount of the good is being bought and sold.
    D. the buyer's reservation price is greater than the seller's reservation price.
    E. the seller's reservation price is greater than the buyer's reservation price

cancer; they will want to buy more of the good regardless of even if the prices of other goods stay the same and their incomes remain constant. This will cause the demand curve to shift to the right.

5. A change in buyers' expectations. This can also cause the demand curve to shift either to the right or the left. For example, if people believe that a good will not be available next week, they will increase their demand for the good this week.

The **buyers' reservation price** is the highest price that buyers are willing to pay for a given quantity of a good. This gives us a second way to define a demand curve: a **demand curve** shows the buyers' reservation price for every possible quantity of the good.

Learning Objective 3: Understand the supply curve. Specifically,
- **define a supply curve;**
- **explain the difference between a change in quantity supplied and a change in demand;**
- **list the variables that cause a supply curve to shift and explain why they do this.**
- **explain the concept of the sellers' reservation price and how the supply curve can be interpreted in two ways.**

A **supply curve** shows the quantity of a good that sellers are able to sell and wish to sell (the quantity supplied) at each possible price holding everything other than price constant. A **change in quantity supplied** is movement along a supply curve; this is *only* caused by a change in the price of a good. A **change in supply** is a shift of the entire supply curve and can be caused by the following:

1. A change in the number of sellers. An increase in the number of sellers will shift the supply curve to the right while a decrease in the number of sellers will shift the supply curve to the left.

2. A change in the price of resources used to produce the good. An increase in resource prices will cause the supply curve to shift to the left while a decline in resource prices will shift the supply curve to the right.

3. A change in the technology used to produce the good. An improvement in technology will shift the supply curve to the right; a technological decline will shift the supply curve to the left.

4. A change in sellers' expectations. This can also cause the supply curve to shift either to the right or the left. For example, if sellers believe that buyers will need the good next week, they may decrease their supply of the good this week.

The **sellers' reservation price** is the lowest price that sellers are willing to receive for a given quantity of a good. This gives us a second way to define a supply curve: a **supply curve** shows the sellers' reservation price for every possible quantity of the good.

Hint: Much of the language we used to describe the supply curve is parallel to the words we employed to describe the demand curve. This is something to look for whenever you are working with supply and demand: if a concept is important for one curve there is probably a parallel concept that is important for the other curve.

Learning Objective 4: Define the following terms: equilibrium, equilibrium price, equilibrium quantity and market equilibrium.
Equilibrium is a condition where nothing will change unless an outside force acts on the situation. Think of throwing a ball: if the ball lands on the ground it will not move unless something else happens (e.g. someone picks it up and throws it.) The ball is thus in equilibrium.

We apply the same idea to markets; we just need to be careful about what we mean by a situation where nothing will change. This means we must focus on the two key variables of the supply and demand model: prices and quantities. An **equilibrium price** is a price at which the quantity demanded equals the quantity supplied. An **equilibrium quantity** is the quantity that buyers and sellers agree to at the equilibrium price. **Market equilibrium** is a situation where an equilibrium price has established an equilibrium quantity.

Learning Objective 5: Define excess supply and excess demand and explain how they differ from market equilibrium.
Excess supply exists when the quantity supplied of a good exceeds the quantity demanded of a good at a given price. **Excess demand** exists when the quantity demanded of a good exceeds the quantity supplied of a good at a given price. Both of these are situations where a market is not in equilibrium.

> Note: You cannot talk about excess supply or excess demand without reference to a price. For example, the phrase "there is excess demand for gasoline" does not make sense since a high enough price for gasoline will eliminate the excess demand. The phrase "there is excess demand for gasoline at $1.50 per gallon" is a correct way to describe the situation.

Learning Objective 6: Use shifts in supply and/or demand to analyze and explain changes in market equilibria.
This is the culmination of ALL THE PREVIOUS LEARNING OBJECTIVES. You have learned about how all of the individual parts of the supply and demand model work and now you have to apply them. There is a simple, 3-step rubric for applying the model:

1. Draw a pair of supply and demand curves at an initial equilibrium of P_0 and Q_0:

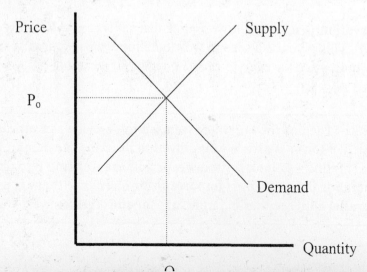

2. Use Learning Objectives 2 and 3 to identify whether the supply curve shifts and in what direction, the demand curve shifts and in what direction or both curves shift and what directions. For example: suppose that the number of buyers in a particular market increases. This will cause the demand curve to the right and will have no effect on the supply curve. Draw this out:

3. Find the new market equilibrium and compare it to the initial market equilibrium. For example: since the demand curve shifted to the right, the graph shows that the new market equilibrium, P_1 and Q_1 will be at both a higher equilibrium price and a higher equilibrium quantity.

> **Hint: Figures 3.17, 3.18, and 3.19 in the text illustrate all of the possible outcomes of shifts in supply and demand. IT DOES NOT PAY TO MEMORIZE THIS INFORMATION! Rather, use the rubric above and let the graph do the work.**

Learning Objective 7: Define the following terms: buyer's surplus, seller's surplus and total surplus. Explain how these terms are related to the concept of "cash on the table."
Buyer's surplus is the difference between the buyers' reservation price and the market price for a given quantity of a good. Similarly, the **seller's surplus** is the difference between the market price and the sellers' reservation price for a given quantity of a good. The **total surplus** is the difference between the buyers' reservation price and the sellers' reservation price for a given quantity of a good.

When total surplus for a given quantity of a good is positive, that means that the buyer and the seller can both gain by agreeing to a price that is between their reservation prices. The buyer will gain because he pays less than his reservation price and the seller will gain since she receives a price that is higher than her reservation price. **Cash on the table** is the name economists give to a situation when the buyer and seller cannot take advantage of this difference in their reservation prices, either because they cannot come to an agreement or something else prevents them from doing so (e.g. a law or regulation).

Learning Objective 8: Explain the relationship between the socially optimal quantity of a good and economic efficiency. Use this relationship to explain the relationship between the Efficiency Principle and the Equilibrium Principle.

The **socially optimal quantity of a good** is that quantity where there is no cash on the table. **Economic efficiency** results when all goods and services are produced at their socially optimal quantities. The **Efficiency Principle** states that economic efficiency is an important goal for society to achieve since economic efficiency means that there are no unexploited gains from exchange, i.e. there is no cash on the table.

Now, consider a market that is in equilibrium. At the equilibrium quantity, the buyer's reservation price is equal to the seller's reservation price. This means there is no cash on the table and thus the market is producing the socially optimal quantity of the good. Thus, we have economic efficiency when a market is in equilibrium, and this leads to the **Equilibrium Principle**: a market in equilibrium leaves no unexploited opportunities for individuals, but there may be gains achievable through collective action.

Note: Collective action can mean either private or public action. For example, a group of people getting together on their own to do something is private, while the same group of people acting through their city government would constitute a public action. The equilibrium principle says nothing about which type of collective action will allow a group to reap the unexploited gains, only that some type of collective action will do this.

Learning Objective 9 (Appendix): Solve for the equilibrium price and equilibrium quantity for a market using equations for the supply and demand curves.

Supply and demand curves can be expressed as linear equations and then solved to find the equilibrium price and equilibrium quantity. This is an application of the "two equations, two unknowns" types of problems you did in high school algebra. In this case, the two equations are the supply curve and the demand curve and the two unknowns are the equilibrium price and the equilibrium quantity.

III. Self-Test
<u>Key Terms</u>
Match the term in the right-hand column with the appropriate definition in the left-hand column by placing the letter of the term in the blank in front of its definition. (Answers are given at the end of the chapter.)

1. ____ A graph that shows the quantity of a good that buyers wish   a. buyer's reservation price
to buy and are able to buy at each possible price holding
everything other than price constant.

2. ____ A type of good where the amount buyers are willing and   b. buyer's surplus
able to purchase at every price rises when buyers' income rises.

3. _____ Movement along a supply curve.

4. _____ A price at which the quantity of a good that buyers wish to buy and are able to buy equals the quantity of a good that sellers wish to sell and are able to sell.

5. _____ A situation where the quantity demanded exceeds the quantity supplied at a given price.

6. _____ The difference between the market price and the sellers' reservation price.

7. _____ The result of there being a difference between the buyers' reservation price and the sellers' reservation price.

8. _____ A pair of goods in which an increase in the price of one good will cause an increase in the demand for the other good.

9. _____ The highest price that a buyer is willing to pay for a given quantity of a good.

10. _____ the difference between the buyers' reservation price and the market price.

12. _____ A state of affairs where nothing will change unless it is disturbed by an outside force.

13. _____ A maximum price at which buyers and sellers can make exchanges legally.

14. _____ A situation where the quantity supplied exceeds the quantity demanded at a given price.

15. _____ The lowest price that a seller is willing to receive for a given quantity of a good.

16. _____ The condition of a market when the quantity of a good buyers wish to buy and are able to buy equals the quantity of a good that sellers wish to sell and are able to sell.

17. _____ A pair of goods in which an increase in the price of one good will cause a decrease in the demand for the other good.

18. _____ A decrease in the price of a good allows buyers to purchase a larger quantity of that good with the same income.

19. _____ The name of the quantity at which the quantity of a good that buyers wish to buy and are able to buy equals the quantity of a good that sellers wish to sell and are able to sell.

20. _____ A change in the amount sellers are willing and able to offer for sale at every price.

21. _____ A group of buyers and sellers of a single good who interact through prices.

22. _____ The response of buyers to a change in the price of a good.

23. _____ The concept of all markets producing the socially optimal quantity of a good.

24. _____ the difference between the buyers' reservation price and the sellers' reservation price.

25. _____ A type of good where the amount buyers are willing and able to purchase at every price falls when buyers' income rises.

26. _____ A decrease in the price of a good causes people to increase

c. cash on the table

d. change in demand

e. change in quantity demanded

f. change in quantity supplied

g. change in supply

h. complements

i. demand curve

j. economic efficiency

k. equilibrium

l. equilibrium price

m. equilibrium quantity

n. excess demand

o. excess supply

p. income effect

q. inferior good

r. market

s. market equilibrium

t. normal good

u. price ceiling

v. seller's reservation price

w. seller's surplus

x. socially optimal quantity

y. substitutes

their purchases of the good and buy less of another good.

27. ____A change in the amount buyers are willing and able to   z. substitution effect
purchase at every price.

28. ___ A quantity at which there is no difference between buyers'   aa. supply curve
reservation price and sellers' reservation price.

29. ___A graph that shows the quantity of a good that sellers wish   bb. total surplus
to sell and are able to sell at each possible price holding everything
other than price constant.

Multiple-Choice Questions
Circle the letter that corresponds to the best answer. (Answers are given at the end of the chapter.)

1. A market
    A. allows buyers and sellers of a good to communicate through prices.
    B. is a way society answers the three basic economic questions.
    C. consists of supply and demand when drawn in a graph.
    D. (A), (B) and (C) all are true of a market
    E. None of the above is true of a market.

2. The last time that you went to the store milk was $2.50 per gallon. You go to the store with
    $5 and intend to buy two gallons of milk but find that the price has risen to $3.00 per gallon.
    Since you can only buy one gallon of milk, you have experienced
    A. the substitution effect.
    B. the income effect.
    C. a price ceiling.
    D. excess supply.
    E. excess demand

3. You usually buy a particular brand of bottled water. If you purchase a different beverage
    when the price of bottled water rises, you have experienced
    A. the substitution effect.
    B. the income effect.
    C. a price ceiling.
    D. excess supply.
    E. excess demand

4. If buyers' reservation price falls,
    A. There will be an increase in the quantity demanded of a good.
    B. There will be an increase in the demanded for a good.
    C. There will be no effect on the quantity supplied or the quantity demanded.
    D. There will be an increase in the quantity supplied of a good.
    E. There will be an increase in the supply of a good.

5. If sellers' reservation price rises,
    A. There will be an increase in the quantity demanded of a good.

B. There will be an increase in the demanded for a good.

C. There will be no effect on the quantity supplied or the quantity demanded.

D. There will be an increase in the quantity supplied of a good.

E. There will be an increase in the supply of a good.

6. Suppose that bread and butter are complements. If the price of bread rises, then
   A. the supply of butter will increase.
   B. the demand for butter will increase.
   C. the demand for butter will decrease.
   D. the demand for bread will increase.
   E. the quantity demanded of butter will increase.

7. If orange juice and pineapple juice are substitutes,
   A. an increase in the price of orange juice will cause the demand for pineapple juice to fall.
   B. an increase in the price of orange juice will cause the demand for pineapple juice to rise.
   C. an increase in the demand for orange juice will cause a decrease in the demand for pineapple juice.
   D. an increase in the demand for orange juice will cause an increase in the demand for pineapple juice.
   E. a decrease in the price of orange juice will cause the demand for pineapple juice to rise.

8. Which of the following would *not* cause an increase in the US supply of gasoline?
   A. A decrease in the price of crude oil.
   B. A technological improvement in gasoline refining.
   C. An increase in the fuel efficiency of cars.
   D. An increase in the number of refineries in the US.
   E. None of the above would cause an increase in the US supply of gasoline.

9. Suppose that shoe producers think that flip-flops will go out of fashion next year. This will
   A. cause the supply of flip-flops to decrease next year.
   B. cause the supply of flip-flops to increase next year.
   C. cause an increase in the quantity of flip-flops supplied next year.
   D. cause a decrease in the quantity of flip-flops supplied next year.
   E. cause the demand for flip-slops to increase next year.

10. If a market is *not* in equilibrium at a given price, then
    A. there is excess demand.
    B. there is excess supply.
    C. the equilibrium price is not equal to the current price.
    D. (A), (B) and (C) all are possible for market that is not in equilibrium.
    E. None of the above is true of a market that is not in equilibrium.

11. A new medical study is published showing that eating oatmeal reduces the risk of colon cancer. We should observe that
    A. the price of oatmeal falls.
    B. the price of oatmeal rises.

C. the equilibrium quantity of oatmeal falls.
D. the supply of oatmeal falls.
E. the demand for oatmeal falls.

12. An increase in the price of gasoline will most likely cause
    A. the supply of low gas mileage cars to increase and the price of low gas mileage cars to rise.
    B. the supply of low gas mileage cars to decrease and the price of low gas mileage cars to fall.
    C. excess supply in the market for low gas mileage cars.
    D. the demand for low gas mileage cars to increase and the price of low gas mileage cars to rise.
    E. the demand for low gas mileage cars to decrease and the price of low gas mileage cars to fall.

Use the graph below for problems 13, 14 and 15; it represents the market for songs downloaded from the internet:

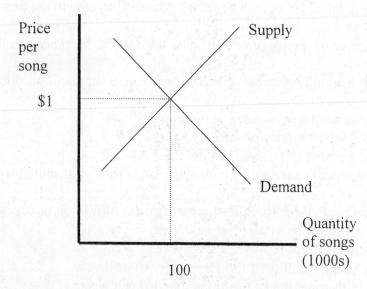

13. An increase in the demand for music downloads would
    A. not affect the equilibrium price or equilibrium quantity.
    B. cause an increase in the equilibrium price and a decrease in the equilibrium quantity.
    C. cause a decrease in the equilibrium price and an increase in the equilibrium quantity.
    D. cause an increase in the equilibrium price and an increase in the equilibrium quantity.
    E. cause a decrease in the equilibrium price and a decrease in the equilibrium quantity.

14. An improvement in the technology used to place downloads on the internet would
    A. not affect the equilibrium price or equilibrium quantity.
    B. cause an increase in the equilibrium price and a decrease in the equilibrium quantity.
    C. cause a decrease in the equilibrium price and an increase in the equilibrium quantity.
    D. cause an increase in the equilibrium price and an increase in the equilibrium quantity.
    E. cause a decrease in the equilibrium price and a decrease in the equilibrium quantity.

15. If a price ceiling of $0.50 per song was placed on music downloads,
    A. not affect the equilibrium price or equilibrium quantity.
    B. this would create excess demand.
    C. this would create excess supply.
    D. this would cause a decrease in demand and an increase in supply.
    E. this would cause an increase in demand and a decrease in supply.

16. An increase in consumer income will
    A. cause the equilibrium price of a normal good to fall if supply remains constant.
    B. cause the equilibrium price of a normal good to rise if supply remains constant.
    C. not affect the equilibrium price of a good.
    D. cause the equilibrium price of an inferior good to rise if supply remains constant.
    E. cause the supply of a good to fall.

Use the graph below for problems 17 and 18:

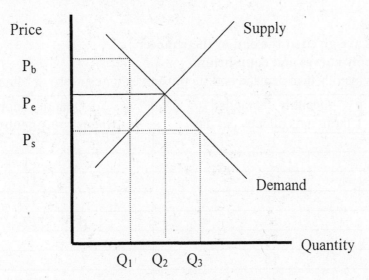

17. If P_e is the equilibrium price, a price ceiling at P_s will
    A. create a situation where there is "cash on the table."
    B. generate excess demand.
    C. create a greater amount of buyers' surplus at Q_1 than when the market is in equilibrium.
    D. cause (A), (B) and (C) to all happen.
    E. have none of the effects given in (A), (B) or (C).

18. If P_e is the equilibrium price, a price ceiling at P_b will
    A. create a situation where there is "cash on the table."
    B. generate excess demand.
    C. create a greater amount of buyers' surplus at Q_1 than when the market is in equilibrium.
    D. cause (A), (B) and (C) to all happen.
    E. have none of the effects given in (A), (B) or (C).

19. The socially optimal quantity of a good
     A. cannot be produced in a market.
     B. is that quantity where there are no unexploited opportunities for gain.
     C. is that quantity where there are unexploited opportunities for gain.
     D. is a situation where quantity supplied exceeds quantity demand.
     E. is a situation where quantity demanded exceeds quantity supplied.

20. According to the Equilibrium Principle,
     A. there is no "cash on the table" for individuals but there may be "cash on the table" for society as a whole.
     B. there is no "cash on the table" for society as a whole but there may be "cash on the table" for individuals.
     C. every market is always in equilibrium.
     D. no market is ever in equilibrium.
     E. None of the above is true according to the Equilibrium Principle.

Short Answer Problems
(Answers and solutions are given at the end of the chapter.)
1. Demand curves, supply curves and equilibrium
The table below provides hypothetical demand and supply curves for espresso in Minneapolis:

Price per cup	Quantity demanded (thousands of cups per day)	Quantity supplied (thousands of cups per day)
$4.00	0	24
$3.50	3	21
$3.00	6	18
$2.50	9	15
$2.00	12	12
$1.50	15	9
$1.00	18	6
$0.50	21	3

     A. Graph the supply and demand curves on the axes below.

B. Label the equilibrium price and the equilibrium quantity on the graph.
C. Suppose that a price ceiling is imposed at $1.50 per cup. What is the quantity demanded?
    _____ What is the quantity supplied? _____ This information implies that at
    $1.50 per cup there is (excess demand / excess supply / equilibrium in the market)
    _____.

D. Suppose that a price ceiling is imposed at $3.50 per cup. What is the quantity demanded?
    _____ What is the quantity supplied? _____ This information implies that at
    $3.50 per cup there is (excess demand / excess supply / equilibrium in the market)
    _____.

2. Working with supply and demand shifts

Suppose that the market for ice cream cones in St. Cloud, Minnesota, is represented by the demand
and supply curves below:

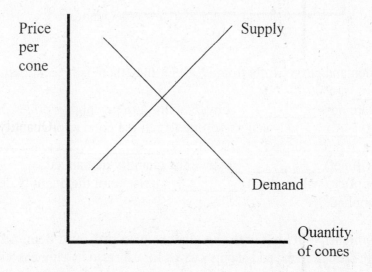

A. Label the equilibrium price and equilibrium quantity on the graph above.
B. A heat wave will (increase/decrease) _____ the demand for ice cream cones.
    Draw this on the graph above.
C. As a result of part (B), the equilibrium price will (rise/fall) _____ and the
    equilibrium quantity will (rise/fall) _____. Label the new equilibrium price and
    new equilibrium quantity on your graph.
D. Suppose that the heat wave also encourages new sellers to offer ice cream cones. This
    will (increase/decrease) _____ the (demand/supply) _____. Draw this on
    the graph above.
E. Compared to the original equilibrium, the action you analyzed in part (D) will cause the
    equilibrium price to (rise/fall/either rise or fall depending on the size of the change)
    _____ and the equilibrium quantity to (rise/fall/either rise or fall depending on the
    size of the change) _____.

3. **Understanding why equilibrium prices and quantities change.** Consider the graph below:

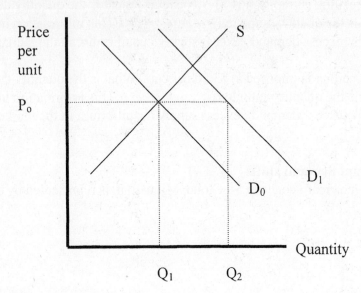

A. When the demand curve shifts from D_0 to D_1 then there is (excess demand/excess supply) _____ at P_0.
B. There (are/are not) _____ buyers willing to pay higher prices than P_0. There (are/are not) _____ sellers willing to sell the good at prices higher than P_0.
C. An increase in price above P_0 (will/will not) _____ increase the quantity supplied and (will/will not) _____ reduce the quantity demanded.
D. The market price (will/will not) _____ rise until the quantity demanded equals the quantity supplied.

4. **(Appendix problem) Working with the algebra of supply and demand**
Suppose that hypothetical demand and supply curves for espresso in Minneapolis/St. Paul are given by the following equations:

$$\text{Demand:} \quad P = 4 - \frac{1}{6}Q \quad ; \quad \text{Supply:} \quad P = \frac{1}{6}Q$$

A. Solve for the equilibrium price and equilibrium quantity in this market:

B. Compare your answers in part (A) to your answers in question 1, part (B) above. Are they the same? _____. Explain why or why not _____
_____
_____

IV. Becoming an Economic Naturalist: Case Study

A story in the March 15, 2005 issue of the *Minneapolis Star-Tribune* reported that

- the price of coffee beans more than tripled between 2001 and 2005. The quantity of coffee purchased over this period
- "Americans are drinking more coffee than they have in a decade;"

Explain how these two facts can both be true using supply and demand analysis. In particular, consider whether the either the demand for coffee changed or the supply of coffee changed or both; and take into account the size of the changes in supply and/or demand in your analysis.

Answer:

V. Self-Test Solutions

Key Terms

1. i	6. w	11. k	16. h	21. e	26. d
2. t	7. c	12. u	17. p	22. j	27. x
3. f	8. y	13. o	18. m	23. bb	28. aa
4. l	9. a.	14. v	19. g	24. q	
5. n	10. b	15. s	20. r	25. z	

Multiple-Choice Questions

1. D	6. C	11. B	16. B
2. D	7. B	12. E	17. D
3. A	8. C	13. D	18. E
4. A	9. A	14. C	19. B
5. D	10. D	15. B	20. A

Short Answer Problems

1. A and B:

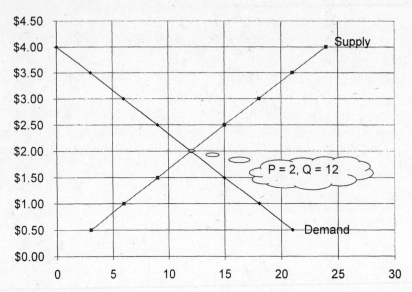

C. quantity demanded = 15, quantity supplied = 9; there is excess demand.
D. quantity demanded and quantity supplied both are 12. There is equilibrium in this market because the price ceiling is placed above the equilibrium price.

2. Graph for all sections:

B. increase. See graph above for demand shift.
C. Rise, rise. In the graph, equilibrium price rises from P_0 to P_1 and equilibrium quantity rises from Q_0 to Q_1.
D. Increase, supply. The supply curve will shift to the right (not drawn on graph above.)

E. Either rise or fall depending on the size of the change, rise. Since both supply and demand are shifting to the right the equilibrium quantity will definitely rise. However, depending on the size of the shifts in demand and supply the equilibrium price could rise, fall or stay the same relative to the original market equilibrium.

3. A. excess demand

B. are, are.

C. will, will

D. will. This problem illustrates the way that markets respond to shifts in demand and supply: excess demand or excess supply is created and prices either rise or fall to establish a new equilibrium.

4. A. In equilibrium the price to the buyer and to the seller must be the same. Thus,

$$4 - (1/6)\, Q = (1/6)Q$$

This implies

$$4 = (1/3)\, Q$$

And hence

$$Q = 12$$

The equilibrium price is found by substituting $Q = 12$ into either the demand or supply curve:

Demand: $P = 4 - (1/6)(12) = 4 - 2 = 2$
Supply: $P = (1/6)(12) = 2$

B. The answers are the same. This is because the equations used in this problem generate the same supply and demand curves as does the table in question 1.

Chapter 4
Elasticity

I. Pretest: What Do You Really Know?

Circle the letter that corresponds to the best answer. (Answers appear immediately after the final question).

1. The price elasticity of demand measures
    A. the amount by which a demand curve shifts when buyers' income rises.
    B. the amount by which the demand for a good changes when the price of the good changes.
    C. the amount by which the quantity demanded for a good changes when the price of the good changes.
    D. the amount by which the demand for a good changes when the price of another good changes.
    E. the amount by which the quantity demanded for a good changes when the price of the good changes.

2. To say that a demand curve is elastic is the same thing as saying
    A. the quantity demanded of a good is insensitive to changes in the price of the good.
    B. the quantity demanded of a good is sensitive to changes in the price of the good.
    C. the quantity demanded of a good is sensitive to changes in the price of another good.
    D. the quantity demanded of a good is insensitive to changes in the price of the good.
    E. the demand for a good is sensitive to changes in the price of the good.

3. A good for which there are many substitutes will have
    A. a price elasticity of demand equal to zero.
    B. an indeterminate price elasticity of demand.
    C. a relatively low price elasticity of demand.
    D. a relatively high price elasticity of demand.

4. The price elasticity of demand for a good will be relatively low when
    A. there are few substitutes for the good.
    B. people spend a small fraction of their income on the good.
    C. there is a short time horizon during which people can substitute for the good.
    D. none of the above is true.
    E. (A), (B) and (C) are all true.

5. If a 10% increase in the price of light bulbs causes a 5% decrease in the quantity demanded of light bulbs, then
    A. the price elasticity of demand for light bulbs is equal to 0.5.
    B. the price elasticity of demand for light bulbs is equal to 2.
    C. the price elasticity of demand for light bulbs is equal to 50.
    D. the price elasticity of demand for light bulbs is equal to 15.
    E. the price elasticity of demand for light bulbs cannot be determined from this information.

6. If you know that the price elasticity of demand for a good is equal to 2, then
    A. a 10% decrease in price will lead to a 5% increase in the quantity demanded.
    B. a 10% increase in price will lead to a 5% decrease in the quantity demanded.
    C. a 5% decrease in price will lead to a 10% increase in the quantity demanded.
    D. a 5% decrease in price will to a 10% decrease in the quantity demanded.
    E. a 2% decrease in price will lead to a 2% increase in the quantity demanded.

7. The price elasticity of demand for cigarettes is 0.5. This means that
    A. an increase in the price of cigarettes will lead to a decrease in total expenditure.
    B. an increase in the price of cigarettes will lead to an increase in total expenditure.
    C. an increase in the price of cigarettes will have no effect on total expenditure.
    D. a decrease in the price of cigarettes will lead to an increase in total revenue.
    E. a decrease in the price of cigarettes will have no effect on total revenue.

8. A measure of the responsiveness of the quantity demanded of one good to the price of another good is
    A. the price elasticity of demand.
    B. the income elasticity of demand.
    C. the price elasticity of supply.
    D. the cross-price elasticity of demand.
    E. not possible to calculate.

9. The phrase "elastic supply" means that
    A. the quantity supplied of a good is relatively sensitive to changes in the price of a good.
    B. the quantity supplied of a good is relatively insensitive to changes in the price of a good.
    C. the quantity supplied of one good is relatively sensitive to changes in the price of another good.
    D. the price of one good is relatively sensitive to changes in the quantity demanded of another good.
    E. the supply curve is vertical.

10. Which of the following is not a determinant of the price elasticity of supply:
    A. flexibility of inputs.
    B. mobility of inputs.
    C. the tastes of buyers.
    D. ease of producing substitute inputs
    E. time.

Solutions and Feedback to Pretest
The answers to the pretest are provided below along with the relevant Learning Objective from the Key Point Review. We strongly recommend that you take the time to review the appropriate material for each question you answered incorrectly.

Correct Answer	Learning Objective
1. C	1
2. B	1
3. D	2
4. E	2
5. A	3
6. C	3
7. B	4
8. D	5
9. A	6
10. C	7

II. Key Point Review
The Forest

This chapter focuses on a single concept, elasticity, and its applications to both supply and demand.

The central questions you need to be able to answer are:
- What is the price elasticity of demand?
- What is the difference between elastic demand and inelastic demand?
- How is the price elasticity of demand computed?
- How does a price change affect total expenditure depending on the price elasticity of demand?
- What is the price elasticity of supply?

The Trees

Learning Objective 1: Define the price elasticity of demand. Differentiate among the following types of demand: perfectly elastic demand, elastic demand, unit elastic demand, inelastic demand, perfectly inelastic demand.

The **price elasticity of demand**, denoted by the Greek letter epsilon (ε) is defined as the percentage change in the quantity demanded of a good caused by a one percent change in the price of a good holding everything other than price constant. It measures the responsiveness of the quantity demanded of a good to a change in its price holding everything other than price constant. For example, the price elasticity of the demand for gasoline measures how sensitive is the quantity demanded of gasoline to changes in the price of gasoline.

The price elasticity of demand is calculated by comparing a given percentage change in price with the resulting change in the quantity demanded of a good. For example, if the price of gasoline rises by 10% and we find that the quantity demanded of gasoline falls by 1%, then the price elasticity of demand for gasoline is

$$\varepsilon = \frac{percentage\ change\ in\ quantity\ demanded}{percentage\ change\ in\ price} = \frac{-1\%}{10\%} = -0.1$$

The demand curve always slopes down and so this number will always be negative, so for convenience we drop the negative sign and express the price elasticity of demand as a positive number (0.1, not -0.1 in the example above.)

A good with a price elasticity of demand greater than 1 has **elastic demand.** A good with a price elasticity of demand equal to one has **unit elastic demand.** A good with a price elasticity of demand less than 1 has **inelastic demand.** A good with a price elasticity of demand equal to zero has **perfectly inelastic demand.** A good with an infinite price elasticity of demand has **perfectly elastic demand.**

Hint: Another way to remember these relationships is using to use simple mathematics:

Elastic demand: $\varepsilon > 1$
Unit elastic demand: $\varepsilon = 0$
Inelastic demand: $\varepsilon < 1$
Perfectly inelastic demand: $\varepsilon = 0$
Perfectly elastic demand: $\varepsilon = \infty$ (infinity)

Learning Objective 2: Explain the determinants of the price elasticity of demand. Provide examples using actual goods and services.

There are three **determinants of the price elasticity of demand** for a good: substitution possibilities for the good, the share of the good in buyers' budgets, and the time horizon under consideration.

Goods with few possible substitutes will have lower price elasticities than goods with more possible substitutes. For example: if you own a car, there are few substitutes for gasoline as your fuel. This means that the price elasticity of gasoline will be relatively low relative to other goods.

The smaller the share of a good in buyers' budgets the lower will be the price elasticity. For example, if the price of lip balm doubles the quantity demanded will probably not change much since the share of most peoples' budgets that is spent on lip balm is quite low. Lip balm will therefore have a relatively low price elasticity of demand compared to goods that constitute a larger share of buyers' budgets.

A longer time horizon allows for more substitution possibilities. For example, if the price of gasoline rises, people will still have to put gasoline in their cars immediately after the price rises. However, if the price of gasoline remains high people will trade in their cars over time for more fuel efficient autos or cars that run on alternative fuels such as diesel or ethanol.

Learning Objective 3: Calculate the price elasticity of demand using information from a demand curve.

You will be asked to calculate the price elasticity of demand in one of two ways: using 2 given points on a demand curve or from a single point on a demand curve along with the equation for that demand curve.

- From given points: suppose you are told that the price of a good originally was P_0 and the quantity demanded at this price was Q_0. The price then changed (i.e. rose or fell) to P_1 and the quantity demanded at this price was Q_1. The price elasticity of demand is then:

$$\varepsilon = \frac{percentage\ change\ in\ quantity\ demanded}{percentage\ change\ in\ price} = \frac{\dfrac{Q_1 - Q_0}{Q_0}}{\dfrac{P_1 - P_0}{P_0}}$$

Hint: Unless you are very comfortable with math, it is not a good idea to use this formula directly. Rather, calculate the percentage change in price, then calculate the percentage change in quantity demanded, then plug the two numbers results into the formula.

Note: Remember to ignore the negative sign in when you are finished with the calculation!

- From a single point and an equation: suppose you are told that the current price of a good is P_0 and that the quantity demanded at P_0 is Q_0. You are also given the equation for demand curve:

$$P = b - m \cdot Q$$

Where 'b' is the vertical intercept of this line and 'm' is the slope of this line. The price elasticity of demand is then

$$\varepsilon = \frac{P_0}{Q_0} \cdot \frac{1}{m}$$

Learning Objective 4: Define total revenue and total expenditure. Understand how changes in the price of a good affect total revenue and total expenditure depending on the price elasticity of demand for the good.

Suppose that the current price of a good is P_0 and that the quantity demanded at P_0 is Q_0. The **total revenue** earned by sellers and the **total expenditure** of buyers are equal to $P_0 \cdot Q_0$. A change in price will cause the quantity demanded to change; the amount by which quantity demanded changes will depend on the price elasticity of demand.

- If a good has elastic demand ($\varepsilon > 1$), then an increase in the price of the good will lead to a decrease in total revenue and total expenditure. A decrease in the price of the good will lead to an increase in total revenue and total expenditure.
- If a good has inelastic demand ($\varepsilon < 1$), then an increase in the price of the good will lead to an increase in total revenue and total expenditure. A decrease in the price of the good will lead to a decrease in total revenue and total expenditure.
- If a good has unit elastic demand ($\varepsilon = 1$), then total revenue and total expenditure will be unaffected by either an increase or decrease in the price of the good.

For example:

- Electricity has a price elasticity of demand equal to 1.20. This means that an increase in the price of electricity will lead to a decrease in total revenue for electric utilities and a decrease in total expenditures by electric utility customers.
- Coffee has a price elasticity of demand equal to 0.25. This means that an increase in the price of coffee will lead to an increase in total revenue for coffee sellers and an increase in total expenditures by coffee buyers.

> **Note: Do not confuse revenue with profit! Sellers may earn more revenue but we do not know what happens to their costs when they sell different amounts.**

Learning Objective 5: Define the cross-price elasticity of demand and the income elasticity of demand.

The **cross-price elasticity of demand** measures the responsiveness of the quantity demanded of one good to a change in the price of another good. This is a useful measure because it tells us whether or not two goods are substitutes or complements. Two goods are substitutes if their cross-price elasticity of demand is positive while two goods are complements if their cross-price elasticity of demand is negative.

The cross-price elasticity of demand is calculated as follows:

$$\varepsilon_c = \frac{percentage\ change\ in\ quantity\ demanded\ of\ one\ good}{percentage\ change\ in\ price\ of\ another\ good}$$

The **income elasticity of demand** measures the responsiveness of the quantity demanded of a good to a change in buyers' income. This is handy since it tells us whether a good is a normal good or an inferior good. A good is a normal good if its income elasticity is positive; a good is an inferior good if its income elasticity is negative.

$$\varepsilon_1 = \frac{percentage\ change\ in\ quantity\ demanded}{percentage\ change\ in\ buyers'\ income}$$

Learning Objective 6: Define the price elasticity of supply. Differentiate among the following types of supply: perfectly elastic supply, elastic supply, unit elastic supply, inelastic supply, perfectly inelastic supply.

The **price elasticity of supply** is defined as the percentage change in the quantity supplied of a good caused by a one percent change in the price of a good holding everything other than price constant. It measures the responsiveness of the quantity supplied of a good to a change in its price holding everything other than price constant. For example, the price elasticity of the supply of gasoline measures how sensitive is the quantity supplied of gasoline to changes in the price of gasoline.

The price elasticity of supply is calculated by comparing a given percentage change in price with the resulting change in the quantity supplied of a good. For example, if the price of gasoline rises by 10% and we find that the quantity supplied of gasoline rises by 1%, then the price elasticity of supply for gasoline is

$$price\ elasticity\ of\ supply = \frac{percentage\ change\ in\ quantity\ supply}{percentage\ change\ in\ price} = \frac{1\%}{10\%} = 0.1$$

The supply curve always slopes up and so this number will always be positive.

A good with a price elasticity of supply greater than 1 has **elastic supply.** A good with a price elasticity of supply equal to one has **unit elastic supply.** A good with a price elasticity of supply less than 1 has **inelastic supply.** A good with a price elasticity of supply equal to zero has **perfectly inelastic supply.** A good with an infinite price elasticity of demand has **perfectly elastic supply**.

> Note: Price elasticity of supply is calculated using the same formulas provided in Learning Objective 3.

Learning Objective 7: Explain the determinants of the price elasticity of supply. Provide examples using actual goods and services.

There are three **determinants of the price elasticity of supply** for a good: flexibility of inputs, mobility of inputs, ease of producing substitute inputs and time.

Some goods use inputs that can be employed in many other products. These types of goods will have a higher price elasticity of supply than goods that do not have flexible inputs since an increase in price can attract resources more easily (and thus increase output by a larger amount) than goods that lack input flexibility. For example: the production of paper boxes requires relatively unskilled labor and an increase in the price of paper boxes can induce a large increase in production since new workers can be hired fairly easily. The supply of paper boxes will thus have a higher price elasticity of supply than other goods.

Mobility of inputs works in a similar way. If inputs can be moved quickly and brought into production rapidly, then an increase in price can cause a large increase in output. So, for example, if the price of software produced by companies in San Francisco rises, computer professionals from other regions can quickly move to the Bay Area and increase production of software.

The ease of producing substitute inputs is directly related to the price elasticity of supply. For example, if airfares rise then airlines can offer more flights but only up to a point after which they need more planes. Planes are produced relatively slowly so a large increase in airfares does not produce a big increase in quantity supplied. But, if planes could be produced more rapidly the response of airlines in terms of flights offered would be much greater.

A longer time horizon allows for any or all of the above factors to come into play and thus increases the price elasticity of supply.

Learning Objective 8 (Appendix): Calculate the price elasticity of demand using the midpoint formula.

The **midpoint formula** is a way of calculating an elasticity using an average of two points rather than the points themselves. Specifically, suppose that you are told that the price of a good originally was P_0 and the quantity demanded at this price was Q_0. The price then changed (i.e. rose or fell) to P_1 and the quantity demanded at this price was Q_1. Rather than using P_0 and Q_0 as the initial points and quantity, we use an average of P_0 and P_1 to calculate the percentage change in price and an average of Q_0 and Q_1 to calculate the percentage change in quantity. This leads to the formula:

$$\varepsilon = \frac{percentage\ change\ in\ quantity\ demanded}{percentage\ change\ in\ price} = \frac{(\frac{Q_1 - Q_0}{\frac{Q_1 + Q_0}{2}})}{\frac{P_1 - P_0}{(\frac{P_1 + P_0}{2})}} = \frac{\frac{Q_1 - Q_0}{Q_1 + Q_0}}{\frac{P_1 - P_0}{P_1 + P_0}}$$

III. Self-Test

Key Terms
Match the term in the right-hand column with the appropriate definition in the left-hand column by placing the letter of the term in the blank in front of its definition. (Answers are given at the end of the chapter.)

1. ____ A horizontal demand curve.

2. ____ A supply curve with a price elasticity of supply equal to zero.

3. ____ A price elasticity of demand or supply less than 1.

4. ____ A vertical demand curve.

5. ____ The quantity of a good a buyer purchases multiplied by the price per unit.

6. ____ Measures the responsiveness of the quantity supplied of a good to a change in the price that good.

7. ____ A price elasticity of demand or supply equal to 1.

8. ____ Measures the responsiveness of the quantity demanded of a good to a change in buyers' income.

9. ____ the quantity of a good a seller sells multiplied by the price per unit.

10. ____ A horizontal supply curve.

11. ____ A price elasticity of demand or supply greater than 1.

12. ____ Measures the responsiveness of the quantity demanded of one good to a change in the price of another good.

13. ____ Measures the responsiveness of the quantity demanded of a good to a change in the price that good.

a. cross-price elasticity of demand

b. elastic

c. income elasticity of demand

d. inelastic

e. perfectly elastic demand

f. perfectly elastic supply

g. perfectly inelastic demand

h. perfectly inelastic supply

i. price elasticity of demand

j. price elasticity of supply

k. total expenditure

l. total revenue

m. unit elastic

Multiple-Choice Questions
Circle the letter that corresponds to the best answer. (Answers are given at the end of the chapter.)

1.   The price elasticity of demand for a good measures the sensitivity of
   A.   demand to a one percent change in price of that good.
   B.   demand to a one percent change in price of another good.
   C.   quantity demanded to a one percent change in price of that good.
   D.   quantity demanded to a one percent change in price of another good.
   E.   demand to a one percent change in buyers' income.

2.   If the price of canned soup falls by one percent and the quantity demanded rises by three percent, then the price elasticity of demand for canned soup is
   A.   0.03
   B.   0.30

      C.   0.333
      D.   3
      E.   30

3.   Suppose that the price elasticity of demand for apples is 0.25. A 5% increase in the price of apples will lead to a
      A.   1.25% decrease in the quantity demanded of apples.
      B.   1.25% increase in the quantity demanded of apples.
      C.   20% decrease in the quantity demanded of apples.
      D.   0.05% decrease in the quantity demanded of apples.
      E.   5% decrease in the quantity demanded of apples.

4.   Shoes of all types have fewer close substitutes than specific brands of shoes such as Nike, Adidas and others. This implies that the demand for shoes of all types would be _____ than the demand for a specific brand of shoe.
      A.   more elastic
      B.   perfectly inelastic
      C.   less elastic
      D.   unitary elastic
      E.   none of the above

5.   Items of furniture such as sofas have _____ price elasticities of demand compared to low budget items such as hand soap.
      A.   higher
      B.   lower
      C.   similar
      D.   infinite
      E.   unit

6.   Suppose that an online music service allows downloads at $1.50 per song and averages 50,000 downloads per month. The service then decides to lower the price per download to $1 and finds that they now average 60,000 downloads per month. These data imply that the price elasticity of music downloads is
      A.   1.67
      B.   0.00005
      C.   0.05
      D.   0.6
      E.   6

Use the following information for problems 7, 8, and 9: A college is trying to decide what price to charge for student parking permits during the school year. The college currently charges $450 per car for the school year. They sell 2,000 parking permits per year. They conduct a survey and find that if they raise the price to $500 per year they will sell 1,950 permits.

7.   The price elasticity of demand for parking permits at the current price of $450 is
     A.   22.5   D.   4.44
     B.   2.25   E.   0.44
     C.   0.225

8.   The total revenue from parking permits at $450 per permit is
     A. $900,000
     B. $877,500
     C. $1,000,000
     D. $975,000
     E.   impossible to calculate because not enough information is provided.

9.   If the college wants to increase the revenue it earns from parking permits,
     A.   it should decrease the price of parking permits.
     B.   it should increase the price of parking permits.
     C.   it should not change the price of parking permits because a price change will not
          affect the revenue it earns.
     D.   it should allow free student parking in campus lots and eliminate parking permits,
     E.   it should eliminate permits and ban student parking in campus lots.

10. A company finds that when it decreases the price of its product the total revenue it earns
     from sales of the product rises. The company president says, "this doesn't make sense!"
     You explain to him that it does if
     A.   the price elasticity of demand for the company's product is equal to zero.
     B.   the price elasticity of demand for the company's product is inelastic.
     C.   the price elasticity of demand for the company's product is equal to one.
     D.   the price elasticity of demand for the company's product is elastic.
     E.   the price elasticity of supply for the company's product is elastic.

11. A firms that produces a good for which there are very few substitutes will find that
     A.   lowering the price of the good increases total revenue.
     B.   lowering the price of the good decreases total revenue.
     C.   raising the price of the good increases total revenue.
     D.   raising the price of the good decreases total revenue.
     E.   total revenue remains the same regardless of whether they raise or lower the price
          of the good.

12. The demand curve for a good is given by the equation $P = 100 - Q$. If the price of the
     good is 30, then the price elasticity of demand at that price is
     A.   1
     B.   7/3
     C.   3/7
     D.   100
     E.   21

13.   Consider these two demand curves:

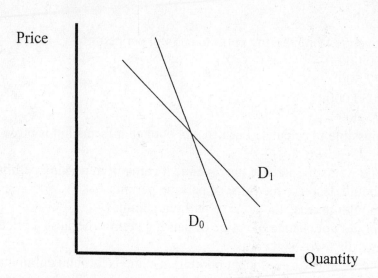

From the point where the two demand curves intersect, we can infer that
A. D_1 is more elastic than D_0.
B. D_0 is more elastic than D_1.
C.   both demand curves are equally elastic.
D. D_1 is elastic and D_0 is inelastic.
E. D_0 is elastic and D_1 is inelastic.

14.   A company that makes computer games learns that manufacturers of game consoles are going to lower their prices. A statistic that will provide information on how this action will affect the quantity demanded of computer games is
A.   The price elasticity of demand for computer games.
B.   The income elasticity of demand for computer games.
C.   The price elasticity of supply for computer games.
D.   The cross-price elasticity of computer games with respect to game consoles.
E.   The price elasticity of supply for game consoles.

15.   A market researcher finds that the income elasticity of a product is negative. This means that:
A.   the good has a low price elasticity of demand.
B.   the good has a high price elasticity of demand.
C.   the good is an inferior good.
D.   the good is a normal good.
E.   the good has perfectly inelastic demand.

16.   You observe that a large increase (in percentage terms) in the price of gasoline leads to only a small increase (in percentage terms) in the quantity of gasoline supplied. You conclude that
A.   the demand for gasoline is inelastic.   D.   the demand for gasoline is elastic.
B.   the supply of gasoline is inelastic.   E.   gasoline is an inferior good.
C.   the supply of gasoline is elastic.

17.   Consider these two supply curves:

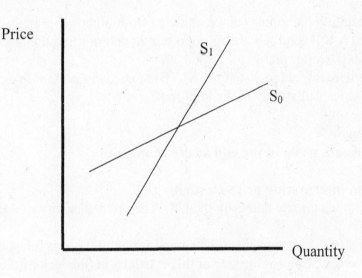

From the point where the two supply curves intersect, we can infer that
A. S_1 is more elastic than S_0.
B. S_0 is more elastic than S_1.
C.   both supply curves are equally elastic.
D. S_1 is elastic and S_0 is inelastic.
E. S_0 is elastic and S_1 is inelastic.

18.   Suppose that the price of milk rises from $3 per gallon to $4 per gallon, leading to an increase in quantity supplied from 1,000,000 gallons to 1,200,000 gallons. These data imply that the price elasticity of supply for milk is:
A.   6
B.   1.65
C.   0.6
D.   0.165
E.   0.06

19.   A restaurant makes cheeseburgers and double cheeseburgers. The price elasticity of double cheeseburgers is
A.   high because the inputs used to make cheeseburgers and double cheeseburgers are the same.
B.   low because the inputs used to make cheeseburgers and double cheeseburgers are the same.

C.   low because cheeseburgers are a small part of buyers' budgets.
D.   high because cheeseburgers are a small part of buyers' budgets.
E.   zero because cheeseburgers and double cheeseburgers are so similar.

20.   The price elasticity of supply for a good is usually higher in the long run than in the short run
A.   because inputs can be drawn from other uses to produce the good.
B.   because substitutes for critical inputs can more easily be found in a long period of time.
C.   because additional inputs can be attracted from other geographic areas.
D.   because (A), (B) and (C) are all important in determining the price elasticity of supply in the long run.
E.   because none of factors listed in (A), (B) or (C) is important in determining the price elasticity of supply in the long run.

Short Answer Problems
(Answers and solutions are given at the end of the chapter.)

1. **Understanding and interpreting price elasticity**
    Natural gas is used to heat many homes in the US. The price elasticity of demand for natural gas is 0.15.
    A. A price elasticity of 0.15 means that the demand for natural gas is (elastic/inelastic) _____. One reason for the size of this elasticity is (the lack of/the wide availability of) _____ substitutes for natural gas during a (short/long) _____ period of time.
    B. A hurricane that causes a 50% increase in the price of natural gas will cause a _____% decrease in the quantity demanded of natural gas.
    C. A hurricane that causes a 50% increase in the price of natural gas will cause (an increase/a decrease) _____ in total expenditure on natural gas.
    D. A 50% increase in the price of natural gas that is not reversed over time will probably cause the price elasticity of natural gas to (increase/decrease) _____. Explain your reasoning:_____
    _____

2. **Price elasticity of demand and setting prices**
    Assume that the current price for a basketball ticket at a local college is $8 and that the demand for tickets is given by this demand curve:
    $$P = 20 - 0.01*Q$$
    A. Calculate the quantity demanded and total revenue: Q = _____, total revenue = _____.
    B. Calculate the price elasticity of demand: ε = _____. Is the demand for basketball tickets elastic or inelastic? _____.
    C. The athletic department wants to raise more revenue from ticket sales. One group says, "raise ticket prices by 10%." Another group says, "no, lower ticket prices by 10%." Calculate total revenue under each of these scenarios:
        •   total revenue with 10% price increase = _____.

- total revenue with 10% price decrease =_____.

D. Compare your answers to part (C) with the price elasticity of demand you calculated in part (B). Do you results confirm the assertions regarding price elasticity and total revenue you have studied in the text? Why or why not? _____

_____

3. Understanding the price elasticity of supply

The price elasticity of supply for onions is 0.35 in the short run and 1.00 in the long run.

A. If the price of onions rises by 10% in the short run, sellers will increase their quantity supplied by _____ %.

B. If the price of onions rises by 10% in the long run, sellers will increase their quantity supplied by _____ %.

C. Why would the price elasticity of supply be higher in the long run than in the short run? Explain: _____

_____

4. (Appendix problem) Using the midpoint formula

You are given the following information on the demand for coffee:

Price (dollars per pound)	Quantity demanded (pounds)
3	10,000
5	5,000

A. Calculate the price elasticity of demand using equation (4.2), assuming that the price increases from $3 per pound to $5 per pound: $\varepsilon =$ _____.

B. Calculate the price elasticity of demand using equation (4.2), assuming that the price decreases from $5 per pound to $3 per pound: $\varepsilon =$ _____.

C. Compare your answers to parts (A) and (B). If they are different, explain why. If they are the same, explain why: _____

_____

D. Calculate the price elasticity of demand using the midpoint formula: $\varepsilon =$ _____.
Compare and contrast your answer to your calculations in parts (A) and (B).

IV.   Becoming an Economic Naturalist: Case Study

Price elasticity of demand is one of the most common economic concepts you will see used in everyday life. You never know where it will appear; for example, consider the following passage from John Hassler's novel *Grand Opening* (Ballantine Books;, 1988). The owner of the town's funeral home is speaking to the town's new grocer:

Haven't I told you about the economics of groceries as compared to the economics of death? ...I average twenty-four funerals a year in this town and there's no way short of murder I can change that number. If I offered a hot price on caskets, how many people would die to save a few bucks? Now you, on the other hand, you can mount a sale as often as you feel like it, and people will flock to your groceries like cows to a salt lick. You're in complete control of your business, Hank. My business is run by the angel of death (p. 114).

What does this passage say about the price elasticity of funerals? What does the quote tell us about the price elasticity of groceries? How will the total revenue of the funeral director respond to an increase in the price of funerals? How will the total revenue of the grocer respond to a decrease in the price of groceries?

Answer:

V. Self-Test Solutions

Key Terms

1. e	5. k	8. c	11. b
2. h	6. j	9. l	12. a
3. d	7. m	10. f	13. i
4. g			

Multiple-Choice Questions

1. C	5. A	9. B	13. A	17. B
2. D	6. D	10. D	14. D	18. C
3. A	7. C	11. C	15. C	19. A
4. C	8. A	12. C	16. B	20. D

Short Answer Problems

1.   A.   inelastic, the lack of, short
     B.   7.5% (a 50% increase multiplied by the elasticity of 0.15)
     C.   an increase since the demand is inelastic.
     D.   increase. Over time people can buy heating systems that use fuels other than natural gas and thus substitute away from natural gas.

2.   A. $Q = 1,200$ and total revenue = 9600

B.   2/3, meaning that demand is inelastic.

C.   10% increase: total revenue = 9856 (since P = 8.8 and Q = 1120)
10% decrease: total revenue = 9216 (since P = 7.2 and Q = 1280)

D.   Yes, since the text argued that if demand is inelastic a price increase causes total revenue to increase.

3.   A.   3.5%

B.   10%

C.   Price elasticity is higher in the long run since resources and technology can move into the industry (in this case, onion production) where prices have risen.

4.   A.   0.75 (since % change in Q = 50%, % change in P = 67%)

B.   2.5 (since % change in Q = 100% and change in P = 40%)

C.   They diverge because the different starting points on the demand curve lead to different percentage changes of Q and P.

D.   1.33. Notice that this is between the two estimates in (A) and (B).

Chapter 5
Demand: The Benefit Side of the Market

I. Pretest: What Do You Really Know?
Circle the letter that corresponds to the best answer. (Answers appear immediately after the final question).

1. According to the Law of Demand, a person will
   A. buy more of one good if the price of another good rises.
   B. buy more of a good if the price of that good rises.
   C. buy more of a good if the price of that good falls.
   D. buy more of a good if the person's income rises.
   E. buy more of a good if the price of another good falls.

2. The Law of Demand and the Rational Spending Rule apply to
   A. goods and services that people purchase for bare subsistence.
   B. goods and services that people purchase above bare subsistence.
   C. goods and services that people consider luxuries.
   D. (A), (B) and (C).
   E. (B) and (C).

3. When the term "utility" is used by economists it refers to
   A. the usefulness of a good or service
   B. the satisfaction a consumer gains from purchasing goods and services.
   C. the electrical needs of a good or service.
   D. the degree of need a consumer has for the good or service.
   E. the price of a good or service.

4. The marginal utility of a good or service is
   A. the additional utility gained by purchasing an additional unit of the good or service.
   B. the additional cost of purchasing an additional unit of the good or service.
   C. the additional usefulness gained by purchasing an additional unit of the good or service.
   D. the additional energy needed to produce an additional unit of the good or service.
   E. the additional space that will be needed to store an additional unit of the good or service.

5. Suppose that you eat two ice cream cones, one right after the other. If you enjoyed the
   second cone, but not as much as the first, then your behavior obeys
   A. the Principle of Increasing Opportunity Cost.
   B. the Cost-Benefit Principle.
   C. the Scarcity Principle.
   D. the law of diminishing marginal utility.
   E. the Equilibrium Principle.

6. The Rational Spending Rule states that a person should purchase two goods, A and B, until

   A. the marginal utility per dollar of both goods are equal, i.e. $\dfrac{MU_A}{P_A} = \dfrac{MU_B}{P_B}$

   B. the price of good A equals the price of good B, i.e. $P_A = P_B$.
   C. the marginal utility of good A equals the marginal utility of good B, i.e. $MU_A = MU_B$.
   D. the marginal utility of good A equals the price of good B and the marginal utility of good
      B equals the price of good A, i.e. $MU_A = P_B$ and $MU_B = P_A$.
   E. the marginal utility of each good is zero, i.e. $MU_A = 0$ and $MU_B = 0$.

7. Suppose that a person is buying two goods, X and Y. After making his choices, the person
   finds that the marginal utility per dollar for good X is greater than the marginal utility per
   dollar for good Y. If this person follows the Rational Spending Rule he should
   A. buy less X and more Y.   D. buy more X and less Y.
   B. buy less of both goods.   E. make no change in his selections.
   C. buy more of both goods.

8. Ernie is buying nectarines and plums at the grocery store. A worker comes along and puts
   out a new sign that increases the price of nectarines. Ernie decides to buy fewer nectarines
   and more plums. This is an example of
   A. the substitution effect only.
   B. the income effect only.
   C. the substitution and income effects working together.
   D. the law of diminishing marginal utility.
   E. the Equilibrium Principle.

9. The relationship between individual demand curves for a good and the market demand curve
   for a good is
   A. the market demand curve is the vertical summation of the individual demand curves.
   B. the market demand curve is the horizontal summation of the individual demand curves.
   C. the individual demand curves are downward sloping but the market demand curve is
      upward sloping.
   D. the individual demand curves are upward sloping but the market demand curve is
      downward sloping.
   E. irrelevant since they are not related.

10. For a given demand curve, consumer surplus is
    A. equal to the area below the demand curve and above the current price of the good.
    B. equal to the price of the good times the quantity of the good.

C. equal to the area between the current price of the good and the supply curve for the good.
D. equal to the area above the demand curve.
E. equal to the current price of the good.

Solutions and Feedback to Pretest
The answers to the pretest are provided below along with the relevant Learning Objective from the Key Point Review. We strongly recommend that you take the time to review the appropriate material for each question you answered incorrectly.

Correct Answer	Learning Objective
1. C	1
2. D	1 and 3
3. B	2
4. A	2
5. D	2
6. A	3
7. D	3
8. C	4
9. B	5
10. A	6

II. Key Point Review
The Forest

This chapter focuses on the demand side of markets. The central questions you need to be able to answer are:
- What is the Law of Demand?
- How are individual wants translated into demand?
- What is the rational spending rule and how is it applied?
- How is the rational spending rule related to substitution and income effects?
- What is the relationship between individual demand curves and a market demand curve?
- What is the relationship between demand and consumer surplus?

The Trees

Learning Objective 1: Define the Law of Demand and distinguish between needs and wants.
The **Law of Demand** states that people will do less of what they want to do as the cost of doing it rises. The costs include *all* of the relevant costs, monetary and nonmonetary, that people weigh when making decisions.

Economists focus on wants and not needs. For example, humans *need* minimum levels of caloric intake and water in order to survive. However, humans do not need specific foods in order to meet these needs; rather, people can choose many combinations of fruits, vegetables, meats and beverages that will provide the needed calories and hydration. Thus economists focus on what people *want*, i.e. we assume that they meet there basic needs and now have choices about how to meet these needs.

Learning Objective 2: Define utility and marginal utility. Use these terms to define and explain the law of diminishing marginal utility.

Utility is the term economists use to denote the amount of satisfaction a person receives when they consume a good or service. Economists know that a person's utility cannot be measured like their body temperature but it is a useful fiction that allows us to model individual decision making.

> **Hint: The text uses the term "utils" as the unit of measure for utility. This may seem confusing or strange so think of a measurement that is more relevant and memorable for you. For example, instead of utils think of satisfaction as being measured in terms of smiles or little hearts.**

When someone consumes more of a good, we say that their utility increases. **Marginal utility** is the amount of additional utility a person gains by consuming an additional unit of a good. For example, suppose that you get 100 utils from consuming one cookie and your utility rises to 150 utils when you eat a second cookie. The marginal utility of the first cookies is therefore 100 utils (the jump from zero to 100 utils) and that of the second cookie is 50 utils (the jump from 100 to 150.)

The **law of diminishing marginal utility** states that after a certain level of consumption, the additional utility from consuming a good will start to fall. The cookie example illustrates this principle as well: the first cookie gave 100 utils of marginal utility but the second only gave 50 utils of marginal utility.

> **Note: Keep in mind that diminishing means "getting smaller," not "becoming negative." We assume that goods always provide some satisfaction and thus the marginal utility of a good is always positive.**

Learning Objective 3: State the Rational Spending Rule and explain the reasoning behind it.

The **Rational Spending Rule** states that a person's spending should be allocated so that the marginal utility per dollar is the same for every good purchased. This can also be expressed in symbols: let MU_X stand for the marginal utility of good X and P_x stand for the price of good X. The rational spending rule for two goods A and B is thus

$$\frac{MU_A}{P_A} = \frac{MU_B}{P_B}$$

The rational spending rule is actually an extension of the **Cost-Benefit Principle**. The Cost-Benefit Principle states that a consumer should purchase goods in such a way that the marginal benefit of purchasing another unit of a good is at least as great as the marginal cost of the good. The rational spending rule says that this principle must apply to *all of the goods a person buys.*

Here is a way to see this: suppose a person purchases apples until the marginal utility of the last apple they purchase is exactly equal to its marginal cost. Since the price of an apple is its marginal cost, we can write

$$MU_{apple} = P_{apple}$$

We can divide both sides of this equation by the price of an apple; we then have

$$\frac{MU_{apple}}{P_{apple}} = 1$$

Now, suppose that this same person behaves the same way when they buy bananas:

$$MU_{banana} = P_{banana}$$

This then implies that

$$\frac{MU_{banana}}{P_{banana}} = 1$$

Thus, it must be the case that

$$\frac{MU_{apple}}{P_{apple}} = \frac{MU_{banana}}{P_{banana}}$$

Learning Objective 4: Explain how the Rational Spending Rule is the basis for the substitution effect and the income effect.

Note: The authors explained the substitution effect and the income effect intuitively in Chapter 3. You should review this material before proceeding.

The easiest way to explain this relationship is to use an example, so let's continue using apples and bananas. Suppose that the price of a banana rises; this will make $\frac{MU_{banana}}{P_{banana}}$ fall; now the

marginal utility per dollar for an apple will be greater than the marginal utility per dollar for a banana and the Rational Spending Rule is no longer satisfied. How can a person restore the balance? The key is the law of diminishing marginal utility: she can purchase fewer bananas and increase the marginal utility per dollar of bananas or she can purchase more apples and decrease the marginal utility per dollar of apples. This is the substitution effect. Since the price of bananas has risen, she cannot purchase the same amount as before unless she purchases fewer apples (which wouldn't make sense) or gets more income (which we assume is fixed). Thus she must decrease her banana purchases and spend the remaining income on apples. This is the income effect.

> **Note: The substitution effect and the income effect work together to cause the quantity demanded of bananas to fall when the price of bananas rises. That is, we have just proved why demand curves slope down using the Rational Spending Rule!**

Learning Objective 5: Explain the relationship between the individual demand curves for a good and a market demand curve for a good.

The **market demand curve** shows for each price the quantity demanded by all buyers in a market. We can construct the market demand curve in two steps:

1. At each price, find the quantity demand by each individual at that price, and then add together all of the individual quantities demanded. We then have a price and the quantity demanded by all of the buyers in that market at that price.
2. Repeat step one for all known prices. The result will be a list of prices and the associated quantity demanded by all of the buyers in that market at each price. This list is the market demand curve.

This two step process is called "horizontal addition."

Learning Objective 6: Define and explain the significance of the term consumer surplus. Show how it is calculated on a graph with a linear demand curve.

Consumer surplus measures the dollar value of the benefit buyers receive from buying a good at the market price. It is important because changes in consumer surplus allow us to see how consumer welfare changes as the market price changes. It is found by calculating the area underneath the demand curve and above the market price as shown in the graph below:

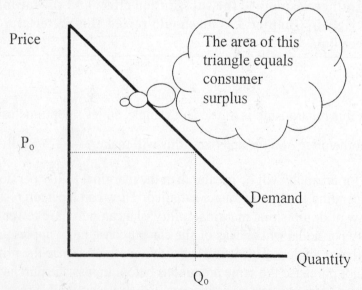

As shown in the graph above, consumer surplus is the area of a triangle, since the area of a right triangle is always ½*(base)*(height) this is also the way consumer surplus is calculated for a linear demand curve.

> **Note: Consumer surplus is the economic surplus received by buyers. The concept of economic surplus was introduced in Chapter 1 and you should review this material to be sure that you understand consumer surplus.**

Learning Objective 7 (Appendix): Understand budget constraints. Specifically,
- **define a budget constraint and explain how the slope is related to the prices of two goods the two;**
- **explain how changes in income shift the budget constraint;**
- **explain how changes in prices change the slope of the budget constraint.**

The **budget constraint** for two goods, A and B, and income M is

$$P_A*A + P_B*B = M$$

Re-writing this equation so that B is measure on the vertical axis of a graph, we have

$$B = \frac{M}{P_B} - \frac{P_A}{P_B}A$$

This equation shows how prices and income shift the budget constraint. A change in income, M, shifts the entire budget constraint since it changes the vertical intercept, $\frac{M}{P_B}$. A change in either price will affect the slope of the line, $\frac{P_A}{P_B}$

Learning Objective 8 (Appendix): Understand indifference curves. Specifically, define what an indifference curve is and explain how the slope is related to marginal rate of substitution between two goods.

An **indifference curve** is a line that connects all combinations of two goods, A and B, that a consumer prefers equally. In other words, a consumer gets equal utility from any combination of goods along an indifference curve. The marginal rate of substitution (MRS) is the slope of an indifference curve and is the amount of one good a person must give up when they consume an additional unit of another good *in order to remain at the same level of utility*. It turns out that this is equal to $\frac{MU_A}{MU_B}$.

Learning Objective 9 (Appendix): Define the best affordable bundle and how this point is related to the Rational Spending Rule.

The **best affordable bundle** is the combination of goods where the consumer maximizes his/her utility. This is found where $MRS = \dfrac{P_A}{P_B}$. Since $MRS = \dfrac{MU_A}{MU_B}$, the best affordable bundle is found where $\dfrac{MU_A}{MU_B} = \dfrac{P_A}{P_B}$. Re-writing this equation we have the Rational Spending Rule:

$$\frac{MU_A}{P_A} = \frac{MU_B}{P_B}$$

III. Self-Test

Key Terms
Match the term in the right-hand column with the appropriate definition in the left-hand column by placing the letter of the term in the blank in front of its definition. (Answers are given at the end of the chapter.)

1. _____ The amount of additional satisfaction a person gains by consuming an additional unit of a good.

a. consumer surplus

2. _____ The combination of goods in which the marginal utility per dollar for each good is equal.

b. law of demand

3. _____ People will do less of what they want to do as the cost of doing it rises.

c. law of diminishing marginal utility

4. _____ The dollar price of a good relative to general level of all prices.

d. marginal utility

5. _____ The absolute price of a good in dollar terms.

e. nominal price

6. _____ The dollar value of the benefit buyers receive from buying a good at the market price.

f. optimal combination of goods

7. _____ Choose a combination of goods such that the marginal utilities per dollar all goods are equal.

g. rational spending rule

8. _____ After a certain level of consumption, the additional utility from consuming a good will start to fall.

h. real price

Multiple-Choice Questions
Circle the letter that corresponds to the best answer. (Answers are given at the end of the chapter.)

1. According to the law of demand, as the cost of an activity
   A. falls, less of the activity will occur.
   B. falls, the level of the activity will increase at all possible costs.
   C. rises, more of the activity will occur.
   D. rises, the level of the activity will decrease at all possible costs.
   E. falls, more of the activity will occur.

2.   Which of the following statements is not an example of the law of demand?
      A.   "I am going to wait until 6 pm to leave work so as to miss the heaviest traffic."
      B.   "I read that DVDs are on sale at a local store. I wasn't going to buy any but since they are on sale I am going to buy a couple of them."
      C.   "The World Wide Web has made it much easier to get information on used cars, so I do a lot more research before I buy than I did before the World Wide Web was available."
      D.   "I've heard that economics tutors are paid $10 per hour at the tutoring center. I think that I'll go down there and offer my services."
      E.   "The price of coffee at the local coffee shop has risen so I'm going to buy only one cup per day instead of my usual two cups."

3.   Economists use the terms "needs" and "wants" to mean that after certain subsistence levels of food, shelter, and clothing are provided for,
      A.   all other goods and services are "needs."
      B.   many goods and services are "needs."
      C.   all other goods and services are "wants."
      D.   a few goods and services are "needs."
      E.   all other goods and services are "luxuries."

Use the following information for problems 4, 5, and 6: you like hot dogs and so you decide to participate in a hot dog eating contest during the 4th of July celebration in your town. You really enjoyed the first two hot dogs, the third one was fine, but when you ate the 4th one you decided that you like hot dogs but did not want to get sick so you quit the contest.

4.   Your total utility _____ with each hot dog you ate up through the 4th one.
      A.   increased   D.   first increased than decreased
      B.   decreased   E. · first decreased than increased
      C.   stayed the same

5.   The additional satisfaction you received from eating each hot dog is called the _____ of eating the hot dog.
      A.   marginal cost   D.   total cost
      B.   marginal utility   E.   usefulness
      C.   total utility

6.   The 4th hot dog was the last one you ate because you thought that the additional satisfaction of eating a 5th hot dog would be _____ the additional cost you would incur from eating it.
      A.   more than
      B.   more than but not very much more
      C.   less than
      D.   much more than
      E.   infinite compared to

Use the table below for problems 7, 8, and 9: suppose we know the following information on Woodruff's consumption of soda pop:

Number of cans of soda pop per day	Total utility (in utils)
1	20
2	35
3	38
4	39

7.   Woodruff's total utility from drinking 4 cans of soda pop is
   A.   39 utils
   B.   19 utils
   C.   4 utils
   D.   1 util
   E.   0 utils

8.   Woodruff's marginal utility from the 4th can of soda pop is
   A.   39 utils
   B.   19 utils
   C.   4 utils
   D.   1 util
   E.   0 utils

9.   Woodruff's total utility _____ as he drinks additional cans of soda pop and his marginal utility always_____ with each additional can of soda pop he drinks.
   A.   at first decreases then increases, decreases
   B.   at first increases then decreases, decreases
   C.   always decreases, increases
   D.   always increases, increases
   E.   always increases, decreases

Use the table below for problems 10, 11 and 12: we have the following information on D.W., an avid movie watcher:

Number of movies per month	Total utility from watching movies on DVD (in utils)	Total utility from watching movies at the local theater (in utils)
1	30	42
2	58	72
3	72	96
4	80	108

10. If the price of a DVD rental is $1 and the price of watching a movie at the local theater is $3, then if D.W. obeys the Rational Spending Rule she will watch _____ movies on DVD and _____ movies at the theater in a month.
A. 4, 3   B. 3, 4   C. 4, 4   D. 3, 3   E. 1, 2

11. If the price of a DVD rental is $2 and the price of watching a movie at the local theater is $3, then if D.W. obeys the Rational Spending Rule she will watch _____ movies on DVD and _____ movies at the theater in a month.
A. 1, 2   B. 3, 4   C. 4, 4   D. 3, 3   E. 4, 3

12. If the price of a DVD rental rises to $2 and the price of watching a movie at a theater rises to $6, then if D.W. obeys the Rational Spending Rule she will watch _____ movies on DVD and _____ movies at the theater in a month.
A. 1, 1   B. 2, 1   C. 4, 2   D. 3, 2   E. 4, 3

13. Suppose that Bessie is buying bread and milk. After making her initial selections, she finds that her marginal utility per dollar for bread is greater than her marginal utility per dollar for milk. If Bessie follows the Rational Spending Rule she should
A.   buy more milk and less bread.
B.   buy fewer of both goods.
C.   buy more of both goods.
D.   buy more bread and less milk.
E.   make no change in her selections since she is maximizing her utility.

Use the table below for problems 14, 15 and 16: Mr. D likes to buy donuts and scones for breakfast. Donuts cost $0.50 each and scones cost $1 each. We have the following information on Mr. D's utility from eating donuts and scones:

Number purchased:	Marginal utility from donuts (in utils)	Marginal utility from scones (in utils)
1	20	45
2	15	30
3	10	25

14. If Mr. D. buys and eats 3 scones, his marginal utility per dollar is _____.
A. 6.25   B. 7.5   C. 11.25   D. 15   E. 25

15. If Mr. D buys and eats 3 donuts, his marginal utility per dollar is _____.
A. 20   B. 10   C. 5   D. 2.5   E. 1.25

16. What is Mr. D's optimal combination of donuts and scones if he follows the Rational Spending Rule?
A.   1 donut and 3 scones.   D.   1 donut and 1 scone.
B.   3 donuts and 1 scone.   E.   3 donuts and 3 scones.
C.   2 donuts and 2 scones

17.   You have information on the individual demand curves for gasoline for all buyers in a
        city. If you sum the quantities demanded by all consumers at each price, the result will
        be
        A.   the market supply curve for gasoline in this city.
        B.   the market demand curve for gasoline in this city.
        C.   the total expenditures on gasoline in this city.
        D.   nonsense; you should sum the prices, not the quantities demanded.
        E.   the total utility of all buyers in the city.

18.   Suppose that ½ of the buyers in a region think that hamburger is an inferior good and the
        other ½ of the buyers think that hamburger is a normal good. An increase in the income
        of all buyers will result in _____ the market demand curve for hamburger in
        this region.
        A.   a shift to the right of
        B.   a shift to the left of
        C.   no effect on
        D.   an indeterminate effect on
        E.   a shift first to the right, then to the left of

19.   You walk into a coffee shop and are willing to pay $5 for a latte and find that the price is
        $3 for a latte. When you buy the latte, your consumer surplus is
        A. $0   B. $1.67   C. $2   D. $3   E. $5

20.

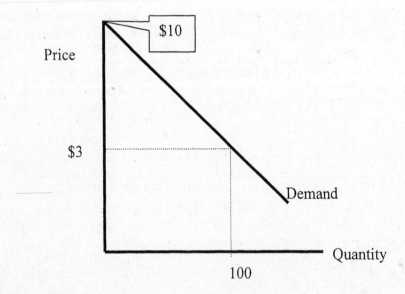

        For the demand curve shown above, consumer surplus is _____.
        A. $7   B. $10   C. $100   D. $150   E. $300

Short Answer Problems
(Answers and solutions are given at the end of the chapter.)

1. Understanding and calculating total and marginal utilities
You are given the following information about a consumer:

Units of good purchased	Total utility	Marginal utility
0	0	*Ignore this cell*
1	50	
2	80	
3		20
4	115	
5		3

A.   Explain why the total utility is zero when zero units of the good are purchased:
_____
_____
_____

B.   Fill in the missing values in the table for total utility and marginal utility.

C.   Do these numbers obey the law of diminishing marginal utility? Explain your reasoning. _____
_____
_____
_____

2. Applying the Rational Spending Rule
You are given the following information about a consumer who likes to listen to music. She can listen to music either by downloading songs from the internet and listening to them on her MP3 player or by purchasing a vinyl record and playing it on her record player.

Number of songs per day	Total utility from listening to songs downloaded from the internet (in utils)	Marginal utility from listening to songs downloaded from the internet (in utils)	Marginal utility per dollar from listening to songs downloaded from the internet (in utils)	Total utility from listening to songs on vinyl records (in utils)	Marginal utility from listening to songs on vinyl records (in utils)	Marginal utility per dollar from listening to songs on vinyl records (in utils)
1	20			32		
2	48			52		
3	62			86		
4	70			90		

A. Calculate her marginal utility for each number of songs for each type of music and fill in the appropriate blanks in the table.

B. Suppose that the price of a song is $1 when she downloads it from the internet and $3 when she purchases a record. Calculate her marginal utility per dollar for each number of songs for each type of music and fill in the appropriate blanks in the table.

C. Assume that she follows the Rational Spending Rule. What combination of downloaded songs and songs from vinyl records will she choose? _____ downloads and _____ songs from vinyl records.

D. Suppose that the price of downloads increases to $2 per song. How, if at all, will this affect the combination of downloaded songs and songs from vinyl records will she choose? Explain your reasoning. _____

_____

_____

_____

3. Constructing the market demand curve from individual demand curves

The table below provides information on three individual demand curves:

Price per haircut ($)	Haircuts demanded per year		
	Larry	Moe	Curly
$5	12	6	3
$7	8	5	2
$9	5	4	1
$11	3	3	0

A. At a price of $5, the market quantity demanded is _____.

B. At a price of $7, the market quantity demanded is _____.

C. At a price of $9, the market quantity demanded is _____.

D. At a price of $11, the market quantity demanded is _____.

E. Draw the market demand curve on the axes below.

4. Calculating and interpreting consumer surplus

Suppose that the market demand curve for a good is given by the equation $P = 500 - 0.2*Q$.

    A.   The quantity demanded will equal zero at a price of _____.

    B.   The quantity demanded when the market price is $250 is _____.

    C.   The consumer surplus when the market price is $250 is _____.

    D.   Suppose that the market price falls from $250 to $200. This will cause the consumer surplus to (rise/fall) _____.

    E.   The consumer surplus when the market price is $200 is _____.

5. (Appendix problem) Finding the best affordable bundle using indifference curves and budget constraints.

Use the graph below to answer the following questions:

A. Draw a budget constraint for a consumer who is buying bulk cereal and bulk milk. (This means that he can purchase any fraction of cereal and milk he pleases.) The price of cereal is $2.50 per pound and milk is $2 per gallon. The consumer has $10 to spend.

B. Suppose that the consumer chooses to buy 2 pounds of cereal and 2.5 gallons of milk. On the graph above, draw an indifference curve that obeys this decision given the budget constraint you drew in part (A).

C. What is the marginal rate of substitution when the consumer chooses to buy 2 pounds of cereal and 2.5 gallons of milk? Explain your reasoning. _____

_____

_____

IV. Becoming an Economic Naturalist: Case Study

This chapter focuses on *how* consumers make choices. The Rational Decision Rule states that a consumer equalizes the marginal utility per dollar for each good that they purchase. The substitution effect and the income effect follow from the Rational Decision Rule and thus provide the reasons why the Law of Demand holds.

Barry Schwartz, a professor of psychology at Swarthmore College, points out that many people today have difficulty making decisions because they have *too many* choices. How do they deal with this problem? In his book *The Paradox of Choice* (New York: Ecco, 2004) Schwartz hypothesizes that people "satisfise," i.e. they rank their choices and then try to choose so that they meet a satisfactory level of utility

Does the Rational Decision Rule only apply to a small number of goods or does it apply to any number of goods? Can a person have "too many choices" according to this rule? If Schwartz's hypothesis is true, does this disprove the Law of Demand?

Answer:

V. Self-Test Solutions
Key Terms

1. d	3. b	5. e	7. g
2. f	4. h	6. a	8. c

Multiple-Choice Questions

1. E	5. B	9. E	13. D	17. B
2. D	6. C	10. A	14. E	18. D
3. C	7. A	11. C	15. A	19. C
4. A	8. D	12. E	16. C	20. D

Short Answer Problems

1. A. We assume that people derive satisfaction, i.e. utility from purchasing and consuming goods. Since the consumer bought nothing they cannot gain any utility from the good.
    B. Total utility: 100, 118; marginal utility: 50, 30, 15
    C. Yes; marginal utility falls from 50 to 30 to 20 to 15 to 3.

2.   A and B: this table

Number of songs per day	Total utility from listening to songs downloaded from the internet (in utils)	Marginal utility from listening to songs downloaded from the internet (in utils)	Marginal utility per dollar from listening to songs downloaded from the internet (in utils)	Total utility from listening to songs on vinyl records (in utils)	Marginal utility from listening to songs on vinyl records (in utils)	Marginal utility per dollar from listening to songs on vinyl records (in utils)
1	20	20	20	33	33	11
2	48	28	28	63	30	10
3	62	14	14	87	24	8
4	70	8	8	99	12	4

C.   Choose 4 downloads and 3 songs from records since this equalizes the marginal utility per dollar spent.

D.   She will buy another song on vinyl. The increase in the price of downloads causes the marginal utility of downloads to fall; to restore balance according to the Rational Spending Rule, she must increase her purchase of songs on vinyl in order to decrease the marginal utility per dollar of songs on vinyl.

3.   A. 21 (= 12 + 6 + 3)
          B. 15 (= 8 + 5 + 2)
          C. 10 (= 5 + 4 + 1)
          D. 6 (=3 + 3 + 0)

4.   A.   500
          B.   1250
          C. $156,250; this is equal to the area ½ *base*height = ½*(1250)*(500-250)
          D.   rise; the fall in price will increase the area of the triangle under the demand curve and above the market price.
          E. $225,000, computed from ½*(1500)*(500-200)

5.   A.   Cereal intercept: 4 pounds ($10 divided by $2.50 per pound); milk intercept: 5 gallons ($10 divided by $2 per gallon).
          B.   You should draw an indifference curve that is tangent to the budget constraint at the point 2 pounds of cereal and 2.5 gallons of milk.
          C.   The marginal rate of substitution is equal to the slope of the budget line. This will be equal to 1.25 gallons of milk per pound of cereal or 0.8 pounds of cereal per gallon of milk, depending on which good you put on which axis.

Chapter 6
Perfectly Competitive Supply:
The Cost Side of the Market

I. Pretest: What Do You Really Know?

Circle the letter that corresponds to the best answer. (Answers appear immediately after the final question).

1. The basic goal of most private firms is to
   A. minimize their costs.
   B. maximize their market share.
   C. maximize their profit.
   D. maximize their output.
   E. stay in business regardless of whether or not they make a profit or loss.

2. Which of the following is not a characteristic of a perfectly competitive market:
   A. Firms sell the same standardized product.
   B. Firms are price takers.
   C. There are many buyers and sellers.
   D. Productive resources are immobile.
   E. Buyers and sellers are well informed.

3. The key difference between the short run and the long run is
   A. the presence of fixed factors of production in the short run.
   B. the presence of fixed factors of production in the long run.
   C. the short run is measured in months while the long run is measured in years.
   D. factors of production are used in the short run but not in the long run.
   E. the presence of variable factors of production in the short run.

4. An example of a fixed factor of production for a school is:
   A. The number of substitute teachers hired each day.
   B. The number of regular teachers working each day.
   C. The amount of electricity used each day.
   D. The amount of paper used each day.
   E. The amount of water used each day.

5. A perfectly competitive firm will maximize its profit in the short run when
    A. average total cost equals price.
    B. average variable cost equals price.
    C. fixed costs are zero.
    D. average total cost equals marginal cost.
    E. marginal cost equals price.

6. The Cost-Benefit Principle implies that in the short run a firm should
    A. increase its production if price is greater than marginal cost.
    B. increase its production if price is less than marginal cost.
    C. increase its production if price is greater than average total cost.
    D. increase its production if price is greater than average variable cost.
    E. only produce if it can earn a positive profit.

7. A firm that is experiencing a loss in the short run should
    A. immediately cease production.
    B. utilize more variable inputs in order to increase output.
    C. utilize more fixed inputs in order to increase output.
    D. cease production if the loss they are experiencing is greater than their fixed costs.
    E. cease production if the loss they are experiencing is less than their fixed costs.

8. A firm that experiences an increase in its fixed costs will
    A. decrease their output in the short run.
    B. increase their output in the short run.
    C. make no change in their output in the short run.
    D. experience an increase in profit.
    E. cease production immediately.

9. The firm's supply curve is the same as its
    A. average total cost curve.
    B. average variable cost curve.
    C. fixed cost.
    D. marginal cost curve.
    E. profit.

10. Producer surplus is the difference between
    A. the price a firm actually receives and the firm's reservation price.
    B. the firm's reservation price and its variable cost.
    C. the firm's variable cost and its fixed cost.
    D. the price a firm actually receives and its fixed cost.
    E. a buyer's reservation price and the firm's reservation price.

Solutions and Feedback to Pretest
The answers to the pretest are provided below along with the relevant Learning Objective from the Key Point Review. We strongly recommend that you take the time to review the appropriate material for each question you answered incorrectly.

1. C	1
2. D	2
3. A	3
4. B	4
5. E	5
6. A	5
7. D	6
8. C	7
9. D	8
10. A	9

II. Key Point Review
The Forest

This chapter focuses on how individual sellers operate in an environment that economists call perfect competition. These sellers are known as perfectly competitive firms. This chapter focuses on perfect competition in the short run; Chapter 8 extends the discussion to the long run. The central questions you need to be able to answer regarding these firms are:

- How much output will a perfectly competitive firm produce in the short run?
- How much profit will perfectly competitive firm earn in the short run?
- At what price will a perfectly competitive firm shut down?
- How is a firm's marginal cost related to its supply curve?
- What is producer surplus and what is it measured?

The Trees

Learning Objective 1: Define and explain the significance of the following terms: profit, profit maximing firm.

Profit is the difference between a firm's total revenue and its total cost. **Profit maximizing firms** choose an output level that makes this difference as large as possible. Not all firms are profit maximizing but, as stressed in the chapter, most private firms that produce goods and services have this as their goal. It is thus a good starting point for analyzing the behavior of individual sellers.

> **Hint:** Chapter 8 has a more detailed discussion of profit that you may find helpful before you proceed

Learning Objective 2: Define and explain what a perfectly competitive firm is and explain the four conditions that are characteristic of perfectly competitive markets.

A **perfectly competitive firm** is a seller that operates in a perfectly competitive market. A perfectly competitive market has **four characteristics**:

1. **All firms sell a standardized product.** This means that the output of one seller cannot be distinguished from the output of another seller and thus a buyer will purchase from whoever sells the product at the lowest price.
2. **The market has many buyers and sellers**, each of which buys or sells only a small fraction of the market quantity. This implies that buyers and sellers are **price takers**: they have no influence over the price at which they exchange goods and services.
3. **Factors of production are mobile.** Mobility of inputs allows firms to enter or leave the market at any time. The inputs they employ are not specific to a particular industry.
4. **Buyers and sellers are well informed.** Buyers and sellers have all the information that they need to operate in the market and no one agent has more information than any other agent.

Markets for agricultural products are good examples of perfectly competitive markets. Consider the market for soybeans in 2002[1]. There were 317,611 farms that produced 2,707,719,216 bushels of soybeans. Clearly there are many soybean farms and once soybeans have been harvested it is impossible to tell what farm produced them. Minute-by-minute information on soybean prices is available via radio, television and the world-wide web; buyers and sellers are thus quite well-informed and no one farm can influence this price. Finally, inputs to soybean production such as farm machinery and land are quite mobile and can used in the production of other crops.

Learning Objective 3: Define and explain what is meant by the terms short run and long run. Relate these concepts to the following terms: factors of production, fixed factors of production, variable factors of production and the law of diminishing returns.

The resources that firms use to produce goods and services are called **factors of production**. These factors can be categorized as fixed or variable. **Fixed factors of production** cannot be varied for a given period of time while variable factors can be. For example, a farmer can choose any amount of fertilizer to be applied to a 200 acre soybean farm; by contrast, once 200 acres have been planted the amount of land become a fixed factor since it cannot be varied until the crop is harvested.

This leads to two conceptions of time. The **short run** is a period of time during which at least one factor of production is fixed. Thus, the short run for a soybean farm would be one cycle of planting and harvesting. The **long run** is a time period during which all factors of production are variable.

The **law of diminishing returns** states that as a firm employs more units of a variable factor

---

[1] All data are from Census of Agriculture, 2002, Table 1: Historical Highlights: 2002 and Earlier Census Years.

while keeping at least one factor fixed, the additional output gained will get progressively smaller. For example, if a soybean farmer applies fertilizer to 200 acres of land then soybean production will rise. A second application will cause output to increase further and a third application will increase output even more. However, the law of diminishing returns implies that the additional output gained from the second application will be smaller than that gained from the first use, and the additional bushels produced from a third application will be smaller still.

Learning Objective 4: Relate the terms given in Learning Objective 3 to the following terms: fixed cost, variable cost, total cost and marginal cost.

Fixed cost is the sum of all costs associated with fixed factors of production. **Variable cost** is the sum of all costs associated with variable factors of production. **Total cost** equals fixed cost plus variable cost.

Marginal cost is the additional total cost incurred when output increases by one unit. For example, if a farmer must spend $200 to produce another 100 bushels of soybeans, then the marginal cost is $2 per bushel. The law of diminishing returns implies that marginal cost is increasing, i.e. that each additional unit costs more and more to produce.

> **Note:** There is another way to look at marginal cost: when the firm increases production, the additional total cost incurred must be equal to the additional <u>variable</u> cost incurred. Fixed cost does not change when we increase output! Thus, an equivalent definition of marginal cost is that it is the additional <u>variable</u> cost incurred when output increases by one unit. This is useful in understanding Learning Objective 7 below.

Learning Objective 5: Explain how a perfectly competitive firm chooses an output level that maximizes its profit. Do this both in words and using a graph. Connect this condition to the concept of marginal cost using the Cost-Benefit Principle. Show how profit can be calculated using the concepts of price, quantity and average total cost.

A perfectly competitive firm will produce at an output level where the price at which it sells the good is equal to the marginal cost of producing the good.

This is the single most important concept to understand in this chapter and is a direct application of the Cost-Benefit Principle. Suppose that a perfectly competitive firm produces one unit of a good. It will earn additional revenue equal to the price per unit; this is the marginal benefit it gains from producing the good. It will incur additional cost equal to the marginal cost. The Cost-Benefit Principles implies that the firm should produce additional units of the good as long as the price per unit (the marginal benefit) is at least as great as the marginal cost.

When will this process end? We can find out by applying what we know about perfectly competitive firms. The price faced by a perfectly competitive firm is constant. However, the law of diminishing returns implies that marginal cost is increasing. Hence, at some point marginal cost and price will be equal to one another. The firm should produce at this output level and not any higher.

Graphically, we can find the profit-maximizing output level using the marginal cost curve (MC) and the price:

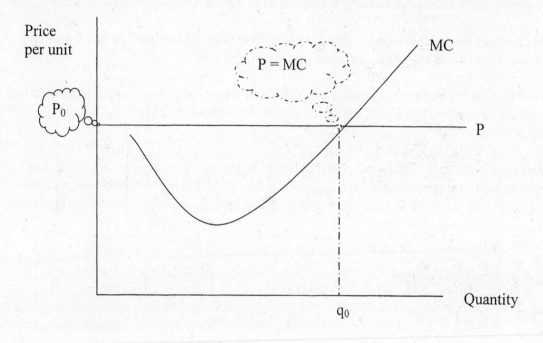

We can find the profit earned by the firm by adding the average total cost curve (ATC) to the graph:

The difference between the P_0 and ATC_0 tells us the profit per unit sold; since the number of units sold is q_o, profit is equal to $(P_o - ATC_0)*q_o$. This is the same as the area of the shaded rectangle in the graph. THIS IS USEFUL because the size of the box varies as the price varies; thus, we can easily see what happens to a firm's profit as the price changes by watching the size of the rectangle!

Learning Objective 6: Explain the condition under which a perfectly competitive firm will continue to operate despite making a loss. Do this both in words and using a graph. Connect this condition to the concept of average variable cost.

A firm should continue to operate *even if it is making a loss* when the loss from operating is less than the loss from shutting down. The loss from operating is

$$\text{total cost} - \text{total revenue}$$

The loss from shutting down is equal to the firm's fixed cost. Thus, we can write our condition for operating as

$$\text{fixed cost} > \text{total cost} - \text{total revenue}$$

Since total cost equals variable cost plus fixed cost, we have

$$\text{fixed cost} > \text{variable cost} + \text{fixed cost} - \text{total revenue}$$

and hence

$$0 > \text{variable cost} - \text{total revenue}$$

If we look at this in per unit terms (i.e. divide by q), we have

$$0 > AVC - P$$

Thus another way to state our condition for operating is that

$$P \geq AVC$$

i.e. the price at which they sell their product should cover their average variable cost. This is handy because we can show it on the graph:

This allows you to always know the lowest price at which a firm will produce: it's at the minimum point of AVC.

Learning Objective 7: Compare and contrast the effect of a change in variable cost on the profit maximizing output level with the effect of a change in fixed cost.

A change in fixed cost will not affect marginal cost; since a firm chooses a profit maximizing output level where price equals marginal cost, a change in fixed cost will not affect the profit maximizing output level. Similarly, a change in variable cost *does* affect marginal cost and thus does affect the profit maximizing output level.

> **Note: Graphically, a change in fixed cost shifts the average variable cost curve but not the marginal cost curve. Thus, a change in fixed cost will affect the firm's profit but not the quantity they produce. A change in variable cost shifts both the average variable cost curve and the marginal cost curve and thus affects both the quantity produced and profit.**

Learning Objective 8: Explain how Learning Objectives 6 and 7 lead to the conclusion that the firm's marginal cost curve is that firm's supply curve as well.

A firm's supply curve shows the quantity of a good that the firm is able to sell and wishes to sell (the quantity supplied) at each possible price holding everything other than price constant. Learning Objective 6 shows that for each price the firm will produce an output level where price is equal to marginal cost as long as price is greater than average variable cost. Thus, the portion of the marginal cost curve that is above average variable cost must be the firm's supply curve!

Learning Objective 7 shows that changes in variable cost shift the marginal cost curve. Changes in input prices and changes in technology both shift variable cost and thus the firm's supply curve as well.

Learning Objective 9: Define and explain the significance of the term producer surplus. Show how it is calculated on a graph with a linear supply curve.

Producer surplus measures the dollar value of the benefit sellers receive from selling a good at the market price. It is important because changes in producer surplus allow us to see how producer welfare changes as the market price changes. It is found by calculating the area below the market price and above the supply curve as shown in the graph below.

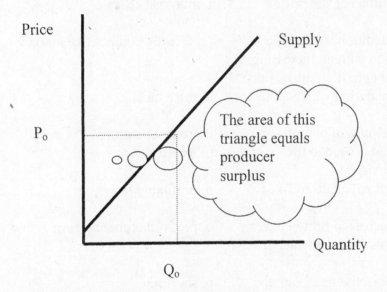

As shown in the graph above, producer surplus is the area of a triangle. Since the area of a right triangle is always ½*(base)*(height) this is also the way producer surplus is calculated for a linear supply curve.

Note: Producer surplus is the economic surplus received by sellers. The concept of economic surplus was introduced in Chapter 1 and you should review this material to be sure that you understand producer surplus.

III. Self-Test

Key Terms
Match the term in the right-hand column with the appropriate definition in the left-hand column by placing the letter of the term in the blank in front of its' definition. (Answers are given at the end of the chapter.)

1. _____ The additional cost incurred when a firm increases its output by one unit.

a. average total cost (ATC)

2. _____ A firm earning total revenue that is greater than total cost.

b. average variable cost (AVC)

3. _____ A factor of production whose amount cannot be changed for a given period of time.

c. factor of production

4. _____ Fixed cost plus variable cost.

d. fixed cost

5._____ A period of time during which at least one of a firm's factors of production is fixed.

e. fixed factor of production

6. _____ Total cost per unit of output.

f. imperfectly competitive firm

7. _____ A firm that cannot influence the price at which it sells its product.

g. law of diminishing returns

8. _____ The difference between the price at which a firm sells its product and its reservation price.

h. long run

9. _____ A firm that can influence the price at which it sells its product.

i. marginal cost

10. _____ As a firm uses additional units of a variable factor of production without increasing its fixed inputs, the additional output produced falls.

j. perfectly competitive market

11. _____ A period of time during which all factors of production are variable.

k. price taker

12. _____ Variable cost per unit of output.

l. producer surplus

13. _____ Any resource that is used in the production of a good or service.

m. profit

14. _____ The sum of all of payments to fixed factors of production.

n. profitable firm

15. _____ A market in which each firm believes that it has no control over the price at which it sells its product.

o. profit-maximizing firm

16. _____ A firm whose objective is to earn the highest possible profit.

p. short run

17. _____ An input whose amount changes depending on the amount of output being produced.

q. total cost

18. _____ The difference between a firm's total revenue and its total cost.

r. variable cost

19. _____The cost of all variable factors of production.

s. variable factor of production

Multiple-Choice Questions
Circle the letter that corresponds to the best answer. (Answers are given at the end of the chapter.)

1.   Total revenue minus total cost is equal to
  A.   gross earnings.
  B.   net worth.
  C.   profit.
  D.   retained earnings.
  E.   rate of return.

2.   A firm whose goal is to maximize its profit will produce at an output level where
        A.   total cost is the lowest.
        B.   the difference between total revenue and total cost is highest.
        C.   variable cost is the lowest.
        D.   marginal cost is lowest.
        E.   fixed cost is lowest.

3.   Which of the following is a characteristic of a perfectly competitive firm?
        A.   Its goal is to minimize its total cost.
        B.   It faces the downward-sloping, market demand curve for its product.
        C.   It always earns a positive profit.
        D.   It can sell any amount of output that it chooses at the market price.
        E.   It sells a product that is distinct and different from its competitors.

4.   A good example of a perfectly competitive market is
        A.   The market for corn.
        B.   The market for corn flakes cereal.
        C.   The market for athletic shoes.
        D.   The market for computer operating system software.
        E.   The market for automobiles.

Use the following information for problems 5 and 6: the local photocopy shop has the following information on the number of copies it can produce:

Labor (in worker hours)	Output (number of copies)
0	0
1	700
2	1100
3	1400
4	1600
5	1700

5.   The average product of labor for 4 hours of labor is _____.
        A. 200   B. 400   C. 700   D. 750   E. 1600

6.   The marginal product of the 3rd hour of work is _____.
        A. 1600   B. 1400   C. 466.67   D. 300   E. 233.33

7.   The law of diminishing returns states that as a firm adds more units of a variable factor of production,
        A.   profits increase but at a decreasing rate
        B.   price increases but at a decreasing rate.
        C.   total cost increases but a decreasing rate.
        D.   the average product of the variable factor increases at a decreasing rate.

E.   output increases but at a decreasing rate.

8.   The short run is a period
      A.   in which at least one factor of production is variable.
      B.   in which at least one factor of production is fixed.
      C.   of no more than 90 days.
      D.   in which all factors of production are fixed.
      E.   in which all factors of production are variable.

9.   Marginal cost is the additional total cost incurred
      A.   by adding one more unit of a variable input.
      B.   by adding one more unit of any input, variable or fixed.
      C.   when the market price increases by $1.
      D.   when one more unit of output is produced.
      E.   by an insignificant input.

Use the following information for problems 10, 11 and 12: the local dry-cleaning shop has the following costs: it pays $1000 per month to rent space, a flat fee of $500 per month for all of its equipment and supplies, and $10 per hour to its employees.

10.   The dry-cleaning shop's fixed cost is
      A. $1000   D. $10 times the number of hours its employees work.
      B. $500   E.   impossible to tell from the given information.
      C. $1500

11.   Suppose that one worker works one hour at the shop and cleans one hundred pounds of clothes. The average cost per pound of clothes is
      A. $1 per pound.   D. $15 per pound.
      B. $5 per pound.   E. $15.10 per pound.
      C. $10 per pound.

12.   Suppose that a second worker comes to the shop, works one hour, and cleans an additional 50 pounds of clothes. The marginal cost of this output is
      A. $1500 per pound.   D. $10 per pound.
      B. $1000 per pound.   E. $0.20 per pound.
      C. $500 per pound.

13.   The "price equals marginal cost" rule for profit maximization is a specific example of which of the following core principles?
      A.   The Scarcity Principle.   D.   The Efficiency Principle.
      B.   The Equilibrium Principle.   E.   The Principle of Comparative Advantage.
      C.   The Cost-Benefit Principle.

14.   Suppose that a perfectly competitive firm can sell its output at $10 per unit. The firm is trying to decide on its production level for the day and finds that if it produces 500 units, the marginal cost will be equal to $11. The firm should
       A.   lower its price.   D.   produce exactly 500 units.
       B.   raise its price.   E.   produce fewer than 500 units.
       C.   produce more than 500 units.

15.   A perfectly competitive firm is currently producing 100 units of a good and the marginal cost of the good is equal to $5 at this level of output. This implies that if the firm is maximizing its profit,
       A.   total revenue exceeds total cost.
       B.   the price at which it can sell the good is equal to $5.
       C.   the price at which it can sell the good is less than $5.
       D.   total revenue must be greater than $500.
       E.   total cost must exceed total revenue.

16.   A perfectly competitive firm is currently producing 1000 units of output. Variable cost is equal to $3000 at this output level and its fixed cost is equal to $500. The firm is able to sell its output at $5 per unit. If the price of the product drops to $3.50 per unit, should this firm continue operation during the short run?
       A.   No, because P < ATC   D.   No, because P > ATC
       B.   Yes, because P > AVC   E.   No, because P < AVC
       C.   Yes, because P > ATC

17.   A perfectly competitive firm is currently producing 750 units of a good and the marginal cost of the good is equal to $5 at this level of output. The firm learns that its fixed cost is rising from $1000 to $2000. In the short run, this firm should
       A.   continue to produce at its current output level.
       B.   decrease its output.
       C.   increase its output.
       D.   raise its price.
       E.   lower its price.

18.   For a perfectly competitive firm, an increase in variable cost will
       A.   increase marginal cost and therefore shift the firm's supply curve to the left.
       B.   increase marginal cost and therefore shift the firm's supply curve to the right.
       C.   decrease marginal cost and therefore shift the firm's supply curve to the left.
       D.   decrease marginal cost and therefore shift the firm's supply curve to the right.
       E.   have no affect on either marginal cost or the firm's supply curve.

19.   Consider the following cost curves for a perfectly competitive firm:

The supply curve for this firm consists of
A.   The entire marginal cost (MC) curve.
B.   The portion of the marginal cost (MC) curve that is above the average total cost
       (ATC) curve.
C.   The portion of the marginal cost curve that is below the average total cost (ATC)
       curve.
D.   The entire average variable cost (AVC) curve.
E.   The portion of the marginal cost (MC) curve that is above the average variable
       cost (AVC) curve.

20.   Suppose that a coffee shop always sells 100 cups of coffee per hour. It currently sells
       coffee at $1.50 per cup and has a reservation price of $1 per cup. If coffee becomes more
       popular so that the price at which it can sell its coffee rises to $2 per cup, then
A.   consumer surplus will rise from $50 to $100 per hour.
B.   consumer surplus will fall from $100 to $50 per hour.
C.   producer surplus will rise from $50 to $100 per hour.
D.   producer surplus will fall from $100 to $50 per hour.
E.   neither producer surplus nor consumer surplus will be affected.

Short Answer Problems
(Answers and solutions are given at the end of the chapter.)

1. Inputs, output and productivity
You are given the following information on the hourly operations of a sandwich shop:

Labor (Number of workers)	Capital (Size of sandwich shop in square feet)	Output (Number of sandwiches produced)	Average product of labor	Marginal product of labor
0	1000	0	N/A	N/A
5	1000	25		
10	1000	65		
15	1000	95		
20	1000	115		
25	1000	125		
30	1000	130		

A.   (labor/capital) _____ is the fixed factor of production because it (changes/does not change) _____ as the amount of output increases. This means that the sandwich shop is operating in the (short run / long run) _____.

B.   Fill in the column for the average product of labor. What units is this expressed in? _____ Explain why:

_____

C.   Fill in the column for the marginal product of labor. What units is this expressed in? _____ Explain why:

_____

D.   Does this sandwich shop obey the law of diminishing returns? _____ Explain your reasoning: _____

_____

_____

2. All those costs: understanding fixed, variable, total and marginal cost

Let's return to the Paducah Slugger Company, maker of fine baseball bats. (See problems 3 and 4 at the end of Chapter 6 in the text.) Acme Sporting Goods supplies Paducah with lumber and then pays $10 for each finished bat. Paducah's only factors of production are lathe operators and a small building with a lathe. The number of bats per day it produces depends on the number of employee-hours per day as given in the table below:

Number of bats per day	Number of employee-hours per day	Fixed Cost ($/day)	Variable Cost ($/day)	Total Cost ($/day)	Average Variable Cost ($/day)	Average Total Cost ($/day)	Marginal Cost ($/day)
0	0						
5	1						
10	2						
15	4						
20	7						
25	11						
30	16						
35	22						

A. This firm is operating in the (short run / long run) _____ because there is at least one (fixed / variable) _____ factor of production.
B. Suppose that workers are paid $10 per hour and that the fixed cost for the lathe and building is $60.
 i) Fill in the columns for fixed cost, variable cost and total cost.
 ii) Fill in the columns for average variable cost, average total cost and marginal cost.
C. Plot your data for average variable cost, average total cost and marginal cost on the graph below.

3. The profit maximizing level of output under various scenarios

Let's use the information you developed in question 3 above.

 a. On the graph you drew in question 3 above, draw a line at $10 to indicate the price at which Paducah can sell finished bats. At what quantity does it intersect the marginal cost curve?_____ Is this the quantity where price equals marginal cost in the table of data in question 3? _____ Why or why not?

 _____

 b. On the graph you drew in part (A), show the firm's profit.
 c. Suppose the price of finished bats fell to $8 per bat. Show the new profit maximizing level of output on the graph above.
 d. Suppose the price of finished bats fell to $4 per bat. At what output level should the firm produce?_____Will the firm make a profit or a loss?_____?
 Should the firm produce at this output level or would it be better off (i.e. make a greater profit or incur a smaller loss) if it shut down?

 _____

4. Calculating and interpreting producer surplus

Suppose that the market demand curve for a good is given by the equation $P = 100 + 0.2*Q$.
 A. The quantity supplied will equal zero at a price of _____.
 B. The quantity supplied when the market price is $250 is _____.

C.   The producer surplus when the market price is $250 is _____.

D.   Suppose that the market price rises from $250 to $300. This will cause the producer surplus to (rise/fall) _____.

E.   The producer surplus when the market price is $300 is _____.

IV. Becoming an Economic Naturalist: Case Study

Movie theaters have many of the characteristics of perfectly competitive firms. They produce a standard product; they act as price takers; the inputs to the process are quite mobile; and information on movie prices and other factors is available to all. The *Christian Science Monitor* ("Cinema Owners Worry About Ticket Prices Too," March 25, 2005) reported the following as the most important costs of running a movie theater:

- Employee salaries
- Utilities
- Lease or mortgage payments

- Concession equipment
- Projection equipment

- Maintenance
- Film rental fees

Which of these are fixed costs? Which of these are variable costs? If a movie theater is losing money, which costs will be relevant to its shut down decision? Do you think that these costs would result in the types of cost curves presented in Chapter 6? Why or why not?

Answer:

V. Self-Test Solutions

Key Terms

1. i	6. a	11. h	16. o
2. n	7. k	12. b	17. s
3. e	8. l	13. c	18. m
4. q	9. f	14. d	19. r
5. p	10. g	15. j	

Multiple-Choice Questions

1. C	5. B	9. D	13. C	17. A
2. B	6. D	10. C	14. E	18. A
3. D	7. E	11. E	15. B	19. E
4. A	8. B	12. E	16. B	20. C

Short Answer Problems

1.   A. Capital; does not change; short run
        B and C calculations:

Labor (Number of workers)	Capital (Size of sandwich shop in square feet)	Output (Number of sandwiches produced)	Average product of labor	Marginal product of labor
0	1000	0	N/A	N/A
5	1000	25	5.00	5
10	1000	65	6.50	8
15	1000	95	6.33	6
20	1000	115	5.75	4
25	1000	125	5.00	2
30	1000	130	4.33	1

   B. Units: sandwiches per worker since you are dividing sandwiches produced by the number of workers.

   C. Units: sandwiches per worker since you are dividing the additional output produced by an additional worker.

   D. Yes; after 10 workers the marginal product of labor falls from 8 to 6, then 4, 2, and 1.

2.   A. short run, fixed.
        B.

Number of bats per day	Number of employee-hours per day	Fixed Cost ($/day)	Variable Cost ($/day)	Total cost ($/day)	Average variable cost ($/day)	Average total cost ($/day)	Marginal cost ($/day)
0	0	60	0	60			
5	1	60	10	70	2.00	14.00	2
10	2	60	20	80	2.00	8.00	2
15	4	60	40	100	2.67	6.67	4
20	7	60	70	130	3.50	6.50	6
25	11	60	110	170	4.40	6.80	8
30	16	60	160	220	5.33	7.33	10
35	22	60	220	280	6.29	8.00	12

2 (C) and 3:

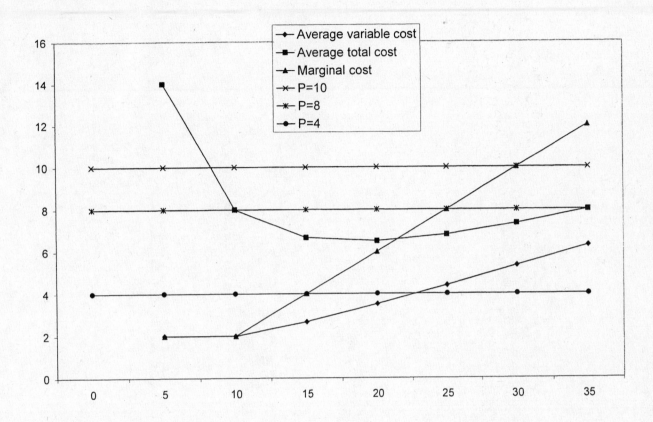

4.   A.   100
      B.   750
      C. $56,250; this is equal to the area ½ *base*height ==½*(750)*(250-100)
      D.   rise; ; the rise in price will increase the area of the triangle under the market price
            and above the supply curve.
      E. $100,000; this is equal to the area ½ *base*height ==½*(1000)*(300-100)

Chapter 7
Efficiency and Exchange

I. Pretest: What Do You Really Know?

Circle the letter that corresponds to the best answer. (Answers appear immediately after the final question).

1. A market that is in equilibrium
    A. causes prices to be lower for buyers than for sellers.
    B. causes prices to be higher for buyers than for sellers.
    C. is efficient.
    D. is inefficient.
    E. causes quantity demanded to exceed quantity supplied.

2. A market equilibrium will *not* be efficient if
    A. the quantity supplied equals the quantity demanded.
    B. consumer surplus is smaller than producer surplus.
    C. producer surplus is smaller than consumer surplus.
    D. individual supply curves fail to include all relevant costs of production.
    E. individual demand curves include all relevant benefits from buying a good.

3. A price ceiling will cause
    A. total economic surplus to rise.
    B. demand to decrease.
    C. quantity supplied to increase.
    D. quantity demanded to decrease.
    E. producer surplus to fall.

4. First-come, first-served policies cause
    A. total economic surplus to fall.
    B. demand to decrease.
    C. quantity supplied to increase.
    D. quantity demanded to decrease.
    E. consumer surplus to rise.

5. If market efficiency is an important goal, then the answer to the question, "how should governments price their services?" is
   A. charge a price equal to the average cost of producing the service.
   B. charge a price equal to the marginal cost of producing the service.
   C. charge a price equal to the total cost of producing the service.
   D. charge a price equal to the variable cost of producing the service.
   E. charge a price of zero since people already pay taxes.

6. A $2 per pack tax on cigarettes that is imposed on sellers will cause
   A. the demand curve for cigarettes to shift down by $2.
   B. the demand curve for cigarettes to shift up by $2.
   C. the supply curve for cigarettes to shift up by $2.
   D. the supply curve for cigarettes to shift down by $2.
   E. no change in either the demand or supply of cigarettes.

7. A per unit tax imposed on sellers
   A. affects only the sellers.
   B. affects only the buyers.
   C. affects only the government that imposes the tax.
   D. has no effect on a market
   E. affects both buyers and sellers.

8. The deadweight loss created by a per unit tax is equal to
   A. the amount of revenue collected by the government via the tax.
   B. the loss of producer surplus caused by the tax.
   C. the loss of consumer surplus caused by the tax.
   D. the loss of total economic surplus caused by the tax.
   E. the change in the equilibrium price caused by the tax.

9. The more elastic is the demand for a good, the _____ will be the burden of the tax borne by the _____.
   A. smaller; consumers
   B. larger; consumers
   C. larger; producers and consumers
   D. smaller; producers
   E. smaller; producers and consumers

10. The deadweight loss caused by a tax will be
    A. larger the more inelastic is the demand for a good.
    B. smaller the more inelastic is the demand for a good.
    C. smaller the more inelastic is the supply of a good.
    D. smaller the more inelastic is the demand for a good or the supply of a good.
    E. unaffected by the elasticity of either demand or supply.

Solutions and Feedback to Pretest
The answers to the pretest are provided below along with the relevant Learning Objective from the Key Point Review. We strongly recommend that you take the time to review the appropriate material for each question you answered incorrectly.

Correct Answer	Learning Objective
1. C	1
2. D	1
3. E	2
4. A	2
5. B	3
6. C	4
7. E	4
8. D	5
9. A	5
10. D	5

II. Key Point Review
The Forest

This chapter focuses on the relationship between market equilibrium and market efficiency. This is a relationship that you will examine and apply throughout the coming chapters so now is the time to master it!

The central questions you need to be able to answer are:
- What is efficiency?
- How do various policies, both public and private, affect efficiency?
- How does the concept of efficiency help determine the "right" price for public services?
- How does the imposition of taxes affect efficiency?

The Trees

Learning Objective 1: Define efficiency and explain how it is represented in a supply and demand diagram. Understand why efficiency is *an* important social goal but not the *only* social goal.

Efficiency (or **Pareto efficiency**) is a situation where no one in a group can be made better off without making at least one person in the group worse off. This is represented in a supply and demand diagram by the market equilibrium, i.e. when the quantity demanded equals the quantity supplied. It is an important goal because efficiency creates the largest possible amount of economic surplus; this surplus can then be used to address other social goals such as reducing income inequality.

> **Hint: This is a restatement of the Efficiency Principle from Chapter 3. You should review this Principle now since the concepts in this chapter are applications and extensions of it.**

Learning Objective 2: Investigate how public and private policies affect efficiency. Specifically, analyze how price ceilings, price subsidies and first-come, first-served policies affect efficiency.

Public and private policies affect efficiency by changing the prices at which buyers and sellers make transactions. Policies that prevent markets from reaching their equilibrium price prevent markets from being efficient. Each of the policies discussed in the text do this in slightly different ways:

- A **price ceiling** is the maximum price at which buyers and sellers can make exchanges legally. Thus, if a price ceiling is imposed below the equilibrium price then neither the buyers' reservation price nor the sellers' reservation price will be equal to the equilibrium price.

> **Hint: You studied the effects of price ceilings in Chapter 3. If you do not remember these concepts or are still unsure about them, you should review them now.**

- A price **subsidy** is a policy in which buyers pay a lower price than the equilibrium price, with the difference between the price buyers pay and the equilibrium price covered by the government. Again, the market is no longer operating where the price paid by buyers equals the price paid by sellers and the market is no longer efficient.
- A **first-come, first-served policy** is just that: rather than using changes in prices to determine buyers' willingness to pay for a good, the seller simply sets a price for a good or service and then sells to whomever arrives first. Unless it just happens to turn out that buyers want exactly the quantity that the seller has available, this will result in excess demand for the good. Excess demand occurs when the price of a good or service is lower than the equilibrium price so, yet again, this is a market that is not in equilibrium and is therefore not efficient.

Learning Objective 3: Use the concept of efficiency to study how much governments should charge for public services.

A market is efficient when the reservation price for buyers and sellers is equal, i.e. when the market price is the equilibrium price. Government services pose a particular challenge because they are *not* sold in markets; rather, a government provides a service such as fresh water or sewage disposal without any competition. They are thus free to charge any price for the service that they wish to choose.

We can use the insight of market efficiency to price government services by remembering that in equilibrium the price received by a seller is equal to the marginal cost of producing the service. Therefore a government should charge customers a price equal to the marginal cost of providing fresh water, sewage disposal, or whatever service they are providing.

Note: This is another way to look at why price subsidies create inefficiency. Subsidizing publicly-provided drinking water, for example, will drive the price below the marginal cost of producing the water and reduce total economic surplus. This does *not* mean that the provision of clean drinking water is not an important social goal; rather, it *does* mean that by pricing the water correctly we can create the maximum possible economic surplus and from that surplus we can craft policies to help those who may not have access to adequate water supplies.

Learning Objective 4: Examine the effects of a per unit tax imposed on sellers. Specifically, discuss who collects the tax for the government versus who actually pays the tax.

A **per unit tax imposed on sellers** shifts the supply curve up by the amount of the per unit tax. The tax acts like an increase in marginal cost; every additional unit sold now costs its original marginal cost plus the per unit tax.

Notice what happens when the supply curve shifts up:

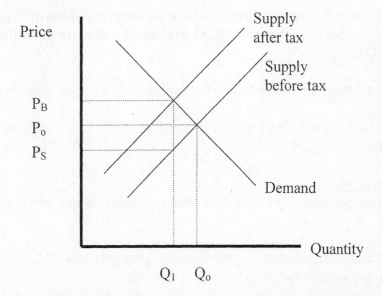

At Q_1, the price buyers pay, P_B, is higher than the price received by sellers, P_S. The difference between the two prices is the per unit tax. Further, the price that buyers pay has risen *despite the fact that the tax was imposed on the sellers*. Thus, a tax that is imposed on sellers (and hence is collected for the government by the sellers) is actually paid both by sellers (through a lower price received for their good) and by buyers (through a higher price paid for the good.)

Learning Objective 5: Show how a per unit tax imposed on sellers affects consumer surplus, producer surplus and total economic surplus.

The graph in Learning Objective 4 is useful here. The price buyers pay rises; this implies that consumer surplus falls. Similarly, the price sellers receive falls and hence producer surplus falls. Total economic surplus is the sum of consumer surplus and producer surplus and therefore total economic surplus falls as well.

The difference between the total economic surplus before the tax is imposed and the total economic surplus after the tax is imposed is the **deadweight loss** created by the tax. It consists of both lost consumer surplus and lost producer surplus.

The size of the deadweight loss and the relative amounts lost by buyers and sellers depends on the elasticity of the demand and supply curves.

- For a given supply curve, the more elastic is the demand curve the larger is the resulting deadweight loss. Further, the more elastic is the demand curve the more the deadweight loss will consist of lost producer surplus.
- For a given demand curve, the more elastic is the supply curve the larger is the resulting deadweight loss. Further, the more elastic is the supply curve the more the deadweight loss will consist of lost consumer surplus.

III. Self-Test

Key Terms
Match the term in the right-hand column with the appropriate definition in the left-hand column by placing the letter of the term in the blank in front of its definition. (Answers are given at the end of the chapter.)

1. ____ A situation where it is not possible to help some people without harming others.

2. ____ A reduction in total economic surplus caused by the adoption of a policy.

a. deadweight loss

b. efficiency (or Pareto efficiency)

Multiple-Choice Questions
Circle the letter that corresponds to the best answer. (Answers are given at the end of the chapter.)

1.   A market that is in equilibrium is considered efficient because
    A.   quantity supplied equals quantity demanded.
    B.   the price paid by buyers equals the price received by sellers.
    C.   there is no other price at which total economic surplus is larger.
    D.   there is no excess supply.
    E.   there is no excess demand.

2.   The concept of efficiency is NOT based on which of the following predetermined attributes of buyers and sellers?
      A.   Buyers' income.
      B.   Technology.
      C.   Individual worker abilities.
      D.   Policies that will most quickly increase incomes for those in poverty.
      E.   Buyers' tastes.

3.   Suppose that the market demand curve fails to capture all of the benefits of buying a good. This implies that
      A.   the equilibrium price is efficient but the quantity will be too large.
      B.   the equilibrium price and quantity are still efficient.
      C.   the government must craft policies to decrease demand for the good.
      D.   the equilibrium price is inefficiently high.
      E.   the equilibrium price is inefficiently low.

4.   When a price ceiling is imposed on a market at a price below the equilibrium price, then
      A.   the quantity demanded exceeds the quantity supplied and total economic surplus falls relative to its equilibrium level.
      B.   the quantity supplied exceeds the quantity demanded and total economic surplus falls relative to its equilibrium level.
      C.   producer surplus and total economic surplus both increase relative to their equilibrium levels.
      D.   consumer surplus and total economic surplus both increase relative to their equilibrium levels.
      E.   there is no effect on consumer surplus, producer surplus or total economic surplus.

5.   Suppose that a price ceiling on chocolate bars is imposed at a price below the equilibrium price of chocolate bars. In this situation,
      A.   the buyers' reservation price will be higher than the sellers' reservation price.
      B.   the quantity demanded exceeds the quantity supplied.
      C.   the sellers' reservation price will be higher than the buyers' reservation price.
      D.   (B) and (C) are true.
      E.   neither (A), nor (B), nor (C) is true.

6.   Suppose that the monks of St. John's Abbey produce bread at a constant marginal cost of $2 per loaf. The local government decides that residents near the abbey cannot afford this price and provide a $1 per loaf subsidy to anyone who buys St. John's bread. In this situation,
      A.   total economic surplus will increase.
      B.   total economic surplus will decrease.
      C.   total economic surplus will be unaffected.
      D.   the amount of St. John's bread that residents buy will be unaffected.
      E.   there will be an excess supply of St. John's bread.

7.   Most shopping malls promote the fact that they provide free parking, meaning that there
        is no monetary charge to park at the mall. This is an example of
        A.   A price ceiling.
        B.   A price subsidy.
        C.   A first-come, first served policy.
        D.   An efficient market.
        E.   A per unit tax.

8.   Your local government is installing a new sewage treatment system and they are trying to
        decide how to charge for this service. Their engineers report that to treat the first million
        gallons of water will cost $0.25 per gallon; the next million gallons will cost $0.30 per
        gallon, and every gallon after that will cost $0.35 per gallon. If the town expects to treat
        3 million gallons over the next month, then they should
        A.   charge $0.90 per gallon for this service.
        B.   charge $0.25 per gallon for this service.
        C.   charge $0.30 per gallon for this service.
        D.   charge $0.35 per gallon for this service.
        E.   charge $0.55 per gallon for this service.

9.   If a government provides a service at a price that is less than the marginal cost of
        producing the service,
        A.   Total economic surplus will be smaller than if they charge a price equal to
                marginal cost.
        B.   Total economic surplus will be larger than if they charge a price equal to marginal
                cost.
        C.   Total economic surplus will be unaffected by this policy.
        D.   Excess supply of the service will result.
        E.   Consumer surplus will be smaller than if they charge a price equal to marginal
                cost.

10.   You go to the local coffee shop and to buy a large cup of coffee. You pay $2.50 for it but
        you would have been willing to pay as much as $4 for it. This means that
        A.   your producer surplus is $1.50.
        B.   your consumer surplus is -$1.50.
        C.   your consumer surplus is $1.50.
        D.   your producer surplus is -$1.50.
        E.   your consumer surplus is $2.50.

11.   You run the local coffee shop and a customer comes to the counter to buy a large cup of
        coffee. You sell it to her for $2.50 but you would have been willing to sell it for as low
        as $1. This means that
        A.   your producer surplus is $1.50.
        B.   your consumer surplus is -$1.50.
        C.   your consumer surplus is $1.50.
        D.   your producer surplus is -$1.50.
        E.   your consumer surplus is $2.50.

Use the graph below for problems 12, 13 and 14: Suppose that a state increases the gasoline tax imposed on sellers by $1 per gallon and that this is represented by the demand and supply curves below:

12.   The vertical distance between the two supply curves is
        A.   less than $1.
        B.   more than $1.
        C.   equal to $0.50.
        D.   equal to $1.
        E.   unknown since not enough information is provided in the question.

13.   The equilibrium price of gasoline after the tax increase is
        A. P_2
        B. P_0
        C. P_1
        D.   between P_0 and P_1
        E.   unknown since not enough information is provided in the question.

14.   The burden of the tax increase is
        A.   zero.
        B.   borne only by the government.
        C.   borne only by the sellers.
        D.   borne only by the buyers.
        E.   borne by both the buyers and sellers.

Use the following information for problems 15, 16 and 17: suppose that a new $0.75 per pack tax on cigarettes is imposed in Minnesota. You are told that the demand for cigarettes is downward sloping.

15.   The tax will
      A.   have no effect on the price paid by buyers and decrease the price received by
            sellers.
      B.   have no effect on the price received by sellers and increase the price received by
            sellers.
      C.   decrease the price received by sellers and increase the price paid by buyers.
      D.   increase the price received by sellers and decrease the price paid by buyers.
      E.   increase the price received by sellers and increase the price paid by buyers.

16.   The tax will result in
      A.   An increase in consumer surplus, a decrease in producer surplus and no change in
            total economic surplus.
      B.   A decrease in consumer surplus, a decrease in producer surplus and a decrease in
            total economic surplus.
      C.   A decrease in consumer surplus, an increase in producer surplus and no change in
            total economic surplus.
      D.   An increase in consumer surplus, a decrease in producer surplus and an increase
            in total economic surplus.
      E.   A decrease in consumer surplus, an increase in producer surplus and an increase
            in total economic surplus.

17.   You find that the quantity of cigarettes bought and sold in Minnesota falls by 10,000
      packs. The deadweight loss of the tax is
      A. $3750
      B.   10,000 packs of cigarettes.
      C.   unknown due to insufficient information.
      D. $7500.
      E. $15,000.

18.   When a per unit tax is imposed, which of the following is NOT affected by the elasticity
      of demand?
      A.   the increase in the price paid by buyers.
      B.   the decrease in price received by the sellers.
      C.   the deadweight loss.
      D.   the size of the shift upward in the supply curve.
      E.   the amount of tax revenue earned by the government.

19.   Suppose that a per unit tax is levied on a good that has inelastic supply. The result will
      be that
      A.   the good will disappear from store shelves.
      B.   the equilibrium price will be unaffected by the per unit tax.
      C.   the deadweight loss created by the tax will be relatively large.
      D.   no deadweight loss is created by the tax.
      E.   the deadweight loss created by the tax will be relatively small.

20.   A price subsidy and a tax have the same effect on a market in that
        A.   neither of them affect the equilibrium quantity.
        B.   neither of them affect the equilibrium price.
        C.   both of them reduce total economic surplus.
        D.   neither of them reduce economic surplus.
        E.   both of them cause excess demand.

Short Answer Problems
(Answers and solutions are given at the end of the chapter.)
1. Calculating consumer surplus, producer surplus and total surplus
The table below contains data on demand and supply for a hypothetical market.

Price	Quantity demanded	Quantity supplied
0	300	0
50	250	100
100	200	200
150	150	300
200	100	400
250	50	500
300	0	600

A.   The equilibrium price in this market is _____. Calculate consumer surplus (CS),
        producer surplus (PS) and total economic surplus (TES) at the equilibrium price:
        CS: _____   PS: _____   TES: _____
B.   Suppose that a price ceiling is imposed at a price of 50. The quantity demanded is
        _____ and the quantity supplied is _____ at this price. Calculate consumer
        surplus (CS), producer surplus (PS) and total economic surplus (TES) at price =
        50:
        CS: _____   PS: _____   TES: _____

C.   The deadweight loss of the price ceiling is equal to _____.

D.   Graph the supply and demand curves on the axes below and identify the CS, PS,
        TES from parts (A) and (B) and the deadweight loss from (C).

2. Taxes and economic surplus
Now that you understand how to calculate and graph consumer surplus, producer surplus, total economic surplus and deadweight loss let's examine the effects of a tax on the same market.

A.   Suppose that the government imposes a 150 per unit tax on this good. Construct the new supply curve (i.e. the supply curve that includes the tax) by filling in the two empty columns in the table below.

Quantity supplied	Price without tax	Tax per unit	Price with tax
0	0		
100	50		
200	100		
300	150		
400	200		
500	250		
600	300		

B.   Using the supply curve in part (A) and the demand curve from the previous problem, find the new equilibrium price _____ and equilibrium quantity _____ . The price paid by buyers is _____ and the price received by sellers is _____ .

C.   At the new equilibrium price, calculate consumer surplus (CS), producer surplus (PS), the tax revenue collected by the government (TR) and total economic surplus (TES):
CS: _____   PS: _____
TR _____   TES: _____

D.   The deadweight loss caused by the tax is equal to _____ .

3. Price elasticity of demand and deadweight loss
The relationship between price elasticity of supply and deadweight loss is discussed in the text and shown in Figure 7.17 of the text. Let's examine the relationship between price elasticity of demand and deadweight loss. The diagrams below show identical supply curves with relatively elastic and inelastic demand curves, respectively :

A.   Suppose that a per unit tax is imposed on both markets. Show how this affects the equilibrium price and equilibrium quantity in each market. Note: be sure to impose the same amount of tax (e.g. $1) in both markets.

B.   Using your answers to part (A), identify the deadweight loss in each market. Which one is larger? Explain your reasoning:_____

_____

_____

IV. Becoming an Economic Naturalist: Case Study

On October 28, 1999, *The New York Times* reported that "the Coca-Cola Co. has quietly begun testing a vending machine that can automatically raise prices for its drinks in hot weather." Analyze the effects of introducing this type of vending machine in a warm climate (e.g. the article mentions the possibility of introducing this type of machine in Brazil.) Specifically, discuss the effect on consumer surplus, producer surplus and total economic surplus. Who will benefit from this development? Who will be worse off?

Answer:

V. Self Test Solutions

Key Terms
1. b
2. a

Multiple-Choice Questions

1. C	6. B	11. A	16. B
2. D	7. C	12. D	17. A
3. E	8. D	13. C	18. D
4. B	9. A	14. E	19. E
5. A	10.C	15. C	20. C

Short Answer Problems
1.   A.   100; 20,000; 10,000; 30,000. Both CS and PS are calculated with the formula ½*(base)*(height) and TES = CS + PS.

B.   250; 100. CS = 20,000 (calculated as ½*(300-200)*100 + 100*(200-50)); PS = 2500; TES = 22,500.

C.   Deadweight loss = original TES – new TES = 30,000 - 22,500 = 7,500.

D.

Before price ceiling:
CS = A + B + C
PS = D + E + F

After price ceiling:

CS = A + B + D
PS = F
Deadweight loss
= C + E

2.   A.

Quantity supplied	Price without tax	Tax per unit	Price with tax
0	0	150	150
100	50	150	200
200	100	150	250
300	150	150	300
400	200	150	350
500	250	150	400
600	300	150	450

Note: The first and last columns now give you the new supply curve.

B.   200; 100; 200; 50.

C.   CS = 5,000, PS = 2500, TR = 15,000, TES = 22,500.

D.   Deadweight loss = original TES – new TES = 30,000 - 22,500 = 7,500.
Notice that this is the same result as the price ceiling in problem 1.

3.   Deadweight loss is larger in market with more elastic demand.

Chapter 8
The Quest for Profit and the Invisible Hand

I. Pretest: What Do You Really Know?

Circle the letter that corresponds to the best answer. (Answers appear immediately after the final question).

1. Explicit costs
   A. are equal to the opportunity costs of a firm's owners.
   B. are the same thing as fixed costs.
   C. are equal to the payments made to the firm's factors of production.
   D. are always variable in the short run.
   E. are included in economic profit but not in accounting profit.

2. Implicit costs
   A. are equal to the opportunity costs of a firm's owners.
   B. are the same thing as fixed costs.
   C. are equal of the payments made to the firm's factors of production.
   D. are always variable in the short run.
   E. are included in accounting profit but not in economic profit.

3. Which of the following would *not* be included when calculating accounting profit?
   A. wages paid to workers.
   B. the salary that an owner could have earned working somewhere else.
   C. rent paid for the office space occupied by a firm.
   D. medical insurance premiums paid for workers by the owners of the firm.
   E. a firm's monthly phone bill.

4. The correct definition of economic profit is
   A. accounting profit plus implicit costs.
   B. total revenue minus implicit costs.
   C. total revenue minus the sum of fixed and variable costs.
   D. total revenue minus the sum of explicit and implicit costs.
   E. total revenue minus accounting profit.

5. Firms will enter an industry when _____ are positive and exit an industry when _____ are negative.
   A. accounting profits, accounting profits
   B. accounting profits, economic profits
   C. explicit costs, implicit costs
   D. economic profits, accounting profits
   E. economic profits, economic profits

6. Which of the following would be an example of the allocative function of price?
   A. A buyer's reservation price is higher than the market price.
   B. Finding a $5 bill on a campus sidewalk.
   C. Switching from a theater major to a finance major because salaries for college graduates with finance majors are higher than those of theater majors.
   D. A friend gives you his ticket to a baseball game.
   E. Losing a $5 bill on a campus sidewalk.

7. _____ work together to guide resources to their highest value.
   A. The rationing and allocative functions of price
   B. Fixed and variable costs of firms
   C. Explicit and implicit costs of firms
   D. Barriers to entry and exit
   E. Price floors and price ceilings

8. You apply for a job that pays $7 per hour. You are hired and told that, after looking over your qualifications, your pay will be $8 per hour. This is an example of
   A. accounting profit.   D.   an implicit cost.
   B. economic profit.   E.   economic rent.
   C. a factor of production.

9. Suppose that a company in a perfectly competitive industry develops a new production technique that reduces its costs. The result of this will be that
   A. this firm will go out of business.
   B. other firms in the industry will adopt the technique resulting in lower prices for consumers.
   C. the supply curve for this firm will shift up.
   D. the market demand curve for this good will shift to the left.
   E. nothing changes since this is the nature of perfectly competitive industries.

10. Which of the following statements is correct?
    A. When a market is in equilibrium all relevant costs and benefits are included in demand and supply.
    B. When a market is in equilibrium the reservation price of buyers exceeds the reservation price of sellers.
    C. When a market is in equilibrium it is also at a social optimum.
    D. When a market is in equilibrium it may be at a social optimum.
    E. When a market is in equilibrium all firms in that industry earn positive economic profits.

Solutions and Feedback to Pretest

The answers to the pretest are provided below along with the relevant Learning Objective from the Key Point Review. We strongly recommend that you take the time to review the appropriate material for each question you answered incorrectly.

Correct Answer	Learning Objective
1. C	1
2. A	1
3. B	1
4. D	1
5. E	2
6. C	2
7. A	2
8. E	3
9. B	4
10. D	5

II. Key Point Review
The Forest

This chapter focuses on the connections between profits and resource allocation. Resources will flow towards activities where their owners can earn profits and will leave when profits turn into losses. Adam Smith argued that this would lead to an efficient allocation of resources and referred to this process as "the Invisible Hand."

The central questions you need to be able to answer are:
- What is the difference between accounting profit and economic profit?
- How does economic profit affect the allocation of resources?
- How does the invisible hand manifest itself in everyday life?
- What is the relationship between market equilibrium and a social optimum?

The Trees

Learning Objective 1: Understand the role played by economic profit in decision-making by firms.
There are two steps to understanding the role played by economic **profit** in making economic decisions. First, you must know what economists mean by the word profit; this involves keeping in mind some basic definitions. Second, you must understand what information is conveyed by a given level of profit.

Basic **definitions:**
- **Profit** is the difference between total revenue and total cost.
  - **Total revenue** is the number or units of a good sold times the price per unit.
  - **Explicit costs** are payments made by a firm to its factors of production.
  - **Implicit costs** are the opportunity cost of all resources supplied by the owners of the firm.

> **Note: An (unstated) assumption in this chapter is that all costs, whether they are explicit or implicit, are variable.**

- **Accounting profit** is equal to total revenue minus explicit costs
- **Economic** profit is equal to total revenue minus the sum of explicit and implicit costs
- **Normal profit** is a situation where economic profit is equal to zero. This implies that the firm is earning an accounting profit that is exactly equal to its implicit costs.

> **Hint: From now on, when you see "profit" you should think "economic profit" unless you are specifically told otherwise.**

We can now formulate a **simple rule for firms**: if economic profit is positive in an industry, a firm in that industry should stay in and firms that are making less than the profit in this industry should enter it. If economic profit is negative in an industry, then a firm in that industry should exit and firms that are outside of the industry should stay out of it.

> **Note: Here is yet another application of the Cost-Benefit Principle. The benefit in this case is total revenue and the cost is the sum of explicit and implicit cost.**

> **Hint: This is the same condition for shutting down that we developed in Chapter 6. The difference is that in this chapter all costs are variable and so we need not make any distinction between variable and total costs.**

Learning Objective 2: Analyze how changes in demand and supply affect an individual firm's profits. Use this analysis to explain the allocative function of price.

Changes in demand and supply affect the equilibrium price of a good, and changes in the price of a good affect the quantity produced by a perfectly competitive firm. A firm's profit depends on the amount of output it produces. Thus, changes in demand and supply affect a firm's profit and determine whether a firm should stay in a particular line of business or get out.

Suppose that a firm is earning a positive economic profit (e.g. see Figure 8.2 in the textbook.) The simple rule we formulated above implies that the firm should stay in this industry and that other firms should enter; this means that the supply curve for this product will shift to the right (e.g. see Figure 8.3.) This process will continue until the typical firm is making a normal profit (e.g. see Figure 8.4). This is the **long run equilibrium for an industry**. The reasoning is the same for a firm earning a negative economic profit; see Figures 8.5 and 8.6 in the textbook for the relevant graphs.

The key to this entire process is the ability of firms to enter and exit an industry. A **barrier to entry** is any force that prevents this from happening; examples range from formal, legal restrictions that prevent firms from entering markets to informal conditions such as the inability for new firms to raise the capital needed to enter a particular market.

The **allocative function of price** is to direct resources away from overcrowded markets and towards markets which are underserved. The analysis above shows how this happens. For example, suppose that the price of a good rises; an individual firm will react to this by increasing its output and thus increasing its profits. The increase in profits will attract other firms, and the resources they employ, to enter the industry with the rising profits and to exit an industry with lower profits.

Adam Smith called this process "**the Invisible Hand**" because there is no central authority guiding the allocation of resources towards their most productive uses. Rather, each individual is "led by an invisible hand to promote an end which was no part of his intention."[1]

Learning Objective 3: Explain the difference between economic rent and positive economic profit.

Economic rent is the proportion of the payment made to a factor of production that exceeds the factor's reservation price. For example, in the movie *Field of Dreams* a famous ballplayer named Shoeless Joe Jackson declares, "Shoot, I'd have played this game for nothin'." Since he was paid a salary to play baseball, his economic rent was his entire salary! Positive economic profit is similar to economic rent since it is the amount of profit a firm earns above a normal profit; however, economic profits are driven to zero by the invisible hand process discussed in Learning Objective 2 whereas economic rents are not.

Learning Objective 4: Apply the invisible hand to everyday phenomena, taking into account the time value of money.
The text presents five examples of the invisible hand in action. Two examples to which you should pay particular attention are cost-saving innovations and the stock market.
- Cost-saving innovations. A cost-saving innovation will reduce a firm's average total cost and their marginal cost and therefore allow that firm to earn a positive economic profit at a given market price. However, this innovation will be adopted by the firms competitors already in the market and the positive profit will attract new entrants; both of these factors will cause the supply curve for the good to shift down, driving down the price of the good and eliminating the above-normal profit.
- The stock market. The **efficient markets hypothesis (EMH)** states that the current price of a stock incorporates all available information relevant to a company's earnings. The invisible hand provides the logic behind the EMH: the current price of a stock will change depending on the profit level of the company issuing the stock. If a company's profit rises, people will buy the stock and drive its price up and eliminating the opportunity earn above-normal returns from owning the stock.

---

[1] Adam Smith, *An Inquiry Into the Nature and Causes of the Wealth of Nations*. New York: Modern Library, 1937 (1776). The quote is on page 423.

Both of these examples take place over time and thus it is important to keep in mind the **time value of money**: the fact that the value of one dollar today is greater than the value of one dollar in the future because the dollar today can be saved and earn interest. This can be done by computing the **present value** of any payments made in the future. In particular, suppose that you will receive a payment of M dollars T years from now and that you expect the interest rate to be some amount r (in decimal form) over those T years. The present value of M dollars is then $\frac{M}{(1+r)^T}$. Further, a perpetual payment of M dollars annually has a present value of $\frac{M}{r}$.

Learning Objective 5: Understand and explain the difference between market equilibrium and a social optimum.

The invisible hand is a theory of how markets allocate resources through a process of market equilibrium. A market that is in equilibrium obeys the Equilibrium Principle, i.e. the "no-cash-on-the-table" principle. This means that there are no further opportunities for gain available to the buyers and sellers in this market.

Keep in mind, however, what this does *not* mean! First, it does not indicate that there are never any profit opportunities to be exploited; rather it simply says that if the market is in equilibrium there are no profit opportunities. A market that is not in equilibrium may very well have profit opportunities. Indeed this is how some people become very wealthy!

Second, the fact that there are no further opportunities for individual gain does not mean that there are no further opportunities for societal gain. Only when the latter is true is a market at a social optimum.

> **Note: This is the third time that this idea has appeared! You also worked with this concept in Chapter 3 and Chapter 7.**

III. Self-Test

Key Terms
Match the term in the right-hand column with the appropriate definition in the left-hand column by placing the letter of the term in the blank in front of its definition. (Answers are given at the end of the chapter.)

1. ____ The opportunity cost of all resources supplied by the owners of a firm.

    a. accounting profit

2. ____ The amount of money that must be deposited today at a given interest rate so that annual earnings of a given amount will be generated.

    b. allocative function of price

3. ____ Any force that prevents firms from entering a market in which they do not currently operate.

    c. barrier to entry

4. ____ Payments made by a firm to its factors of production.

5. ____ A situation where total revenue minus explicit costs equals implicit costs.

6. ____ The function of price that serves to direct resources away from overcrowded markets and towards markets which are underserved.

7. ____ Total revenue minus the sum of explicit and implicit costs.

8. ____ The proportion of the payment made to a factor of production that exceeds the factor's reservation price.

9. ____ The idea that the value of one dollar today is greater than the value of one dollar in the future because the dollar today can be saved and earn interest.

10. ____ The value of a firm's current stock price reflects all of the relevant information regarding its current and future earnings prospects.

11. ____ Adam Smith's proposition that the actions of independent, self-interested buyers and sellers will often result in the most efficient allocation of resources.

12. ____ Total revenue minus explicit costs.

13. ____ A situation where economic profit is negative.

14. ____ The function of price that serves to distribute goods to those buyers who value them the highest.

d. economic loss
e. economic profit
f. economic rent
g. efficient markets hypothesis
h. explicit costs
i. implicit costs
j. invisible hand theory
k. normal profit
l. present value of a perpetual annual payment
m. rationing function of price
n. time value of money

Multiple-Choice Questions
Circle the letter that corresponds to the best answer. (Answers are given at the end of the chapter.)

1. Which of the following is not an example of explicit costs?
   A. Wages paid to workers.
   B. The interest the owner could have earned on the savings she invested in the firm.
   C. Salaries paid to management.
   D. Fees paid for maintenance of the firm's website.
   E. Rent paid for office space.

2. Which of the following is not an example of implicit costs?
   A. The return stockholders could have earned by investing in a different firm.
   B. The revenue the firm could have earned from leasing out some of the office space that it owns.
   C. The revenue the firm could collect from selling off some of its office furniture.
   D. The interest the owners could have earned on the savings they invested in the firm.
   E. The salary of the firm's president.

3.   The correct definition of accounting profit is
       A.   total revenue minus explicit costs.
       B.   total revenue minus implicit costs.
       C.   total revenue minus the sum of fixed and variable costs.
       D.   total revenue minus the sum of explicit and implicit costs.
       E.   economic profit plus explicit costs.

4.   Which of the following are included when calculating economic profit?
       A.   Wages paid to workers.
       B.   The salary that an owner could have earned working somewhere else.
       C.   Rent paid for the office space occupied by a firm.
       D.   Medical insurance premiums paid for workers by the owners of the firm.
       E.   All of the above would be included when calculating economic profit.

Use the following information for problems 5, 6 and 7: Lianne used to work as a lawyer with a large law firm; she earned a yearly salary of $150,000. She got tired of working for a big firm and decided to start her own law practice. She pays her legal secretary $30,000 per year and spends $24,000 per year for rent, utilities and other miscellaneous expenses. She earns $ 200,000 in total revenue per year in her own practice.

5.   Lianne's opportunity cost of having her own law practice, also known as her
       _____, is equal to _____.
       A.   explicit cost, $54,000
       B.   explicit cost, $150,000
       C.   implicit cost, $150,000
       D.   implicit cost, $54,000
       E.   implicit cost, $200,000

6.   Lianne's accounting profit is equal to _____.
       A. $24,000
       B. $30,000
       C. $200,000
       D. $146,000
       E. $150,000

7.   Lianne is
       A.   earning negative economic profits.
       B.   earning zero economic profits.
       C.   earning positive economic profits.
       D.   earning negative accounting profits.
       E.   earning a normal profit.

8.   You observe that all of the firms in an industry are earning positive economic profits. In the near future, you would predict
    A.   many of these firms will see their economic profits rise.
    B.   many of these firms will see their economic profits fall.
    C.   new firms will enter this industry.
    D.   (B) and (C) will both occur.
    E.   none of the above would occur.

9.   A situation where there is no tendency for firms to enter or exit an industry is called
    A.   a barrier to entry.
    B.   a short run equilibrium.
    C.   a long run equilibrium.
    D.   a fixed cost.
    E.   the rationing function of price.

Use the graphs below for problems 10, 11, 12 and 13: suppose the graphs below represent the market for apples (on the left) and an individual apple orchard (on the right).

10.   Suppose that S is the current market supply curve for apples. How many pounds of apples per year should the individual apple orchard produce in order to maximize its profit?
    A.   2500
    B.   2000
    C.   1500
    D.   1000
    E.   500

11.   If S is the current market supply curve for apples, then the individual apple orchard is
    A.   earning zero profits.

B.   earning a profit of $3000
C.   earning a profit of $2000
D.   earning a profit of $1500
E.   earning a profit of $500

12.   Suppose that S is the current market supply curve for apples and all orchards are
      producing at the profit-maximizing quantity. What will happen to the supply curve in the
      long run?
      A.   Quantity supplied will increase but stay on S curve.
      B.   Supply will shift to S^1
      C.   Quantity supplied will increased and will on S1 curve
      D.   Supply will shift to S^2
      E.   Quantity supplied will decrease.

13.   In the long run, as the supply curve shifts to the right
      A.   more orchards will be planted and the individual orchard will earn a normal profit.
      B.   more orchards will be planted and the individual orchard will earn a profit of
              $3000.
      C.   more orchards will be planted and the individual orchard will earn a profit of
              $2000.
      D.   there will be no more orchards than there were to begin with and the individual
              orchard will earn a normal profit.
      E.   there will be no more orchards than there were to begin with and the individual
              orchard will earn a profit of $2000.

14.   "The allocative function of price" means that prices
      A.   guide all resources to a single market.
      B.   allocate high-priced goods among poor people.
      C.   guide resources to their highest value uses.
      D.   ensure that those who value a good highly are able to buy it.
      E.   allocate low quality goods away from buyers.

15.   Economic rents, unlike economic profits,
      A.   can be less than zero.
      B.   cannot be driven to zero through competition.
      C.   do not involve the idea of opportunity costs.
      D.   only apply to land.
      E.   can only be positive when accounting profits are zero.

16.   An apparel company develops a lower-cost method for printing logos on t-shirts. The
      invisible hand predicts that
      A.   this firm will go out of business.
      B.   other apparel companies will adopt this new method resulting in lower prices for
              consumers.
      C.   the market supply curve for t-shifts will shift to the left.
      D.   the market demand curve for t-shirts will shift to the left.

E.   nothing will change.

17.   The company for which you work awards you a bonus. You can receive $2500 now and
        $2500 one year from now, or you can receive a lump sum payment now. The annual
        interest rate is 5%. In order for the two offers to be of the same present value, the lump
        sum payment now must be equal to
        A. $50,000
        B. $5000
        C. $4881
        D. $4762
        E. $4750

18.   The efficient markets hypothesis
        A.   implies that competitive markets produce efficient outcomes.
        B.   predicts that production by competitive firms is always done efficiently.
        C.   asserts that buyers are following the rational spending rule.
        D.   states that all of the relevant information about a company's current and future
               stock price is incorporated into its current accounting profit.
        E.   states that all relevant information about a company's current and future earnings
               prospects is incorporated into its current stock price.

19.   The Efficiency Principle states that unexploited opportunities for gain
        A.   never exist.
        B.   always exist when a market is in equilibrium.
        C.   never exist when a market is in equilibrium.
        D.   can exist when a market is in equilibrium but rarely do.
        E.   always exist.

20.   When either the costs of production to individual firms or the benefits of consumption to
        individual buyers differ from those of society,
        A.   the market equilibrium will not be efficient.
        B.   the market equilibrium will be efficient.
        C.   the allocation of resources will be optimal.
        D.   the invisible hand will guarantee efficiency.
        E.   the equilibrium level of output will be the socially optimal level of output.

Short Answer Problems
(Answers and solutions are given at the end of the chapter.)

1. The firm, the market and economic profit.
You are given the following information about a firm:

Quantity sold	Total revenue	Explicit cost	Implicit cost	Accounting profit	Economic profit
10	50	36	5		
15	75	63	6		
20	100	93	7		

| 25 | 125 | 125 | 8 | | |
| 30 | 150 | 161 | 9 | | |

A.   Fill in the columns for accounting profit and economic profit. Do you see a consistent relationship between accounting profit and economic profit? What is it? _____

B.   What is the price per unit at which the firm sells its product?_____   Explain your reasoning: _____

C.   Suppose that the demand for this product rises. What will happen to the market price? _____ How will this affect this firm's economic profit? _____

D.   Ignore part (C) and suppose that the demand for this product falls. What will happen to the market price? _____ How will this affect this firm's economic profit? _____

E.   Ignore part (D) and suppose that firms leave this market. What happens to the market supply curve? _____ What will happen to the market price? _____ How will this affect this firm's economic profit?

_____

F.   Can you draw any general conclusions from this problem regarding the relationship between changes in the market price and changes in this firm's economic profit? Explain: _____

_____

2. Cost-saving innovations and the invisible hand

Let's return yet again to the Paducah Slugger Company, maker of fine baseball bats. (See problems 3 and 4 at the end of Chapter 6 in the text and problems 1 and 2 in Chapter 6 of this study guide.) Acme Sporting Goods supplies Paducah with lumber and then pays $10 for each finished bat. Paducah's only factors of production are lathe operators and a small building with a lathe. Information on the number of bats produced per day and their associated average total costs and marginal costs are given in the table below:

Number of bats per day	Average total cost ($/day)	Marginal cost ($/day)
0		
5	14.00	2
10	8.00	2
15	6.67	4
20	6.50	6
25	6.80	8
30	7.33	10
35	8.00	12

A.   Graph the Paducah Slugger Company's average total cost curve and marginal cost curve on the graph below

B.   Show the profit maximizing level of output for the Paducah Slugger Company.

C.   Suppose that Paducah develops a new method for producing bats that reduces its average and marginal costs. How will this affect Paducah's profit if it can still sell finished bats to Acme Sporting Goods at $10 per bat? _____

_____

D.   Suppose that Acme Sporting Goods learns about the new method for producing bats that Paducah has developed. How do you think they will react? Specifically, will they continue to pay $10 per finished bat? Explain your reasoning: _____

_____

_____

IV. Becoming an Economic Naturalist: Case Study

Few American households owned videocassette recorders (VCRs) in 1975, yet by 1995 over 80 percent of them did. (See Federal Reserve Bank of Dallas, *Time Well Spent*, p. 22; this is available at http://www.dallasfed.org/fed/annual/1999p/ar97.pdf). However, rather than using VCRs to record television programs most households used them to watch prerecorded movies. The explosion in VCR ownership thus created a demand for both rentals and sales of movies and television programs on videocassettes. How profitable would you suspect that a typical video rental store was in the late 1970s? What would you predict regarding the number of video rental stores in the late 1970s versus the late 1980s? What do you think happened to the profitability of owning a video rental store between the late 1970s and the late 1980s? How might stores have responded to this phenomenon during the 1980s?

Answer:

V. Self-Test Solutions

Key Terms

1. i	6. b	11. j
2. l	7. e	12. a
3. c	8. f	13. d
4. h	9. n	14. m
5. k	10. g	

Multiple-Choice Questions

1. B	6. D	11. C	16. B
2. E	7. A	12. D	17. C
3. A	8. D	13. A	18. E
4. E	9. C	14. C	19. C
5. C	10. B	15. B	20. A

Short Answer Problems

1.   A.

Quantity sold	Total revenue	Explicit cost	Implicit cost	Accounting profit	Economic profit
10	50	36	5	14	9
15	75	63	6	12	6
20	100	93	7	7	0
25	125	125	8	0	-8
30	150	161	9	-11	-20

B.   5; since total revenue equals price times quantity, price must equal total revenue divided by quantity and this is equal to 5 for every level of quantity sold.

C.   rise; profit will increase. (Hint: try increasing the price to 6 and recalculate economic profit.)

D.   fall; profit will fall. (Hint: try decreasing the price to 4 and recalculate economic profit.)

E.   shifts to the left; rise; profit will increase. (Hint: try increasing the price to 6 and recalculate economic profit.)

F.   Yes: the firm's profit is positively related to the market price.

2. A.

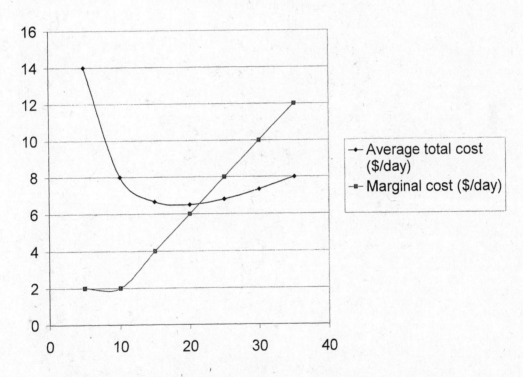

B.   the profit maximizing quantity will be at 30 bats; this is where P = MC

C.   The profit maximizing level of output will increase and the since the average cost curve shifts down Paducah's profit will rise.

D.   Acme will want to take advantage of this profit making opportunity. They will probably reduce the price they pay for finished bats and either keep the price at which they sell bats constant (in which case they will increase their profit) or reduce the price at which they sell bats to consumers (in which case they are passing along the cost-saving innovation's savings to consumers.) Note that this is just what the invisible hand predicts.

Chapter 9
International Trade

I. Pretest: What Do You Really Know?

Circle the letter that corresponds to the best answer. (Answers appear immediately after the final question).

1. The Principle of Comparative Advantage implies that each country
   A. should specialize in those tasks in which they do not have a comparative advantage.
   B. should specialize in those tasks in which they have a comparative advantage.
   C. should be self-sufficient.
   D. will be poorer if they trade with other countries.
   E. should specialize in those tasks in which they have an absolute advantage.

2. Autarky is a situation in which an economy
   A. has no diplomatic relations with other countries.
   B. has no direct access to water transportation.
   C. is economically self-sufficient.
   D. is not economically self-sufficient.
   E. does not use markets to allocate resources.

3. In a closed economy,
   A. consumption possibilities are identical to production possibilities.
   B. consumption possibilities are generally higher than production possibilities.
   C. consumption possibilities are generally lower than production possibilities.
   D. consumption possibilities are determined by the government.
   E. production possibilities are determined by the government.

4. If we compare a country before and after opening itself to trade, we generally find that
   A. total economic surplus is lower after opening to trade than before.
   B. total economic surplus is the same after opening to trade than before.
   C. total economic surplus is higher after opening to trade than before.
   D. producer surplus and consumer surplus are both higher after opening to trade than before.
   E. (C) and (D) are both true.

5. A closed economy is producing wheat at an equilibrium price that is lower than the world price. If it were to open itself to trade,
   A. the domestic price of wheat would rise and the country would import wheat.
   B. the domestic price of wheat would fall and the country would import wheat.
   C. the domestic price of wheat would be unaffected and the country would not import or export wheat.
   D. the domestic price of wheat would fall and the country would export wheat.
   E. the domestic price of wheat would rise and the country would export wheat.

6. An economy that opens itself to trade when the world price of a good is lower than the domestic price will
   A. gain consumer surplus, lose producer surplus and gain total economic surplus.
   B. lose consumer surplus, gain producer surplus and gain total economic surplus.
   C. lose consumer surplus, gain producer surplus and lose total economic surplus.
   D. gain consumer surplus, lose producer surplus and lose total economic surplus.
   E. experience no changes in consumer surplus, producer surplus or total economic surplus.

7. Protectionism is the idea that
   A. free trade must be protected against any restrictions.
   B. workers must be protected from safety hazards.
   C. free trade is injurious and should be restricted.
   D. consumption possibilities are greater than production possibilities and thus consumption possibilities protect production possibilities.
   E. child labor must be made illegal.

8. A tariff on imported sugar will
   A. raise the price received by domestic sellers.
   B. raise the price paid by domestic buyers.
   C. lower the amount of sugar that is imported
   D. cause (A), (B) and (C) all to occur.
   E. not have any effect on the price or the amount of sugar that is imported.

9. American textile producers may ask for quotas on imported textiles because
   A. consumer surplus has increased due to trade.
   B. producer surplus has decreased due to trade
   C. total economic surplus has increased due to trade.
   D. the price of textiles has risen.
   E. the amount of textiles that American producers can sell has increased.

10. Outsourcing refers to
    A. importing goods in which a country does not have a comparative advantage.
    B. exporting goods in which a country has a comparative advantage.
    C. encouraging high wage workers to emigrate.
    D. encouraging low wage workers from other countries to immigrate.
    E. moving jobs from high wage countries to low wage countries.

Solutions and Feedback to Pretest

The answers to the pretest are provided below along with the relevant Learning Objective from the Key Point Review. We strongly recommend that you take the time to review the appropriate material for each question you answered incorrectly.

Correct Answer	Learning Objective
1. B	1
2. C	2
3. A	2
4. C	3
5. E	3
6. A	3
7. C	4
8. D	4
9. B	4
10. E	5

II. Key Point Review
The Forest

This chapter focuses on international trade and discusses the reasons why countries trade and the effects of trade on a country and its citizens.

The central questions you need to be able to answer are:
- What is the primary basis for international trade?
- How does trade affect a country's consumption possibilities?
- What are the effects of international trade on consumer surplus, producer surplus and total economic surplus?
- How do trade restrictions such as tariffs and quotas affect consumer surplus, producer surplus and total economic surplus?
- What is outsourcing and what are its effects?

The Trees
Learning Objective 1: Explain why comparative advantage is the basis for trade.

The Principle of Comparative Advantage states that everyone does best when each person concentrates on the activities for which his or her opportunity cost is lowest. People should then trade with one another for those tasks in which they do not have a comparative advantage.

Hint: You should review Chapter 2 if you do not remember this concept.

Learning Objective 2: Explain the difference between production possibilities and consumption possibilities. Define a closed economy and an open economy, and then show how an open economy has consumption possibilities that are greater than its production possibilities.

A country's **production possibilities** show the maximum combinations of goods that can be produced given the country's resources and productivity. A country's **consumption possibilities** show the maximum combinations of goods that can be consumed given the country's resources and productivity. When an economy is economically self-sufficient, a situation called **autarky**, its production possibilities and consumption possibilities are identical. The same is true for an economy that does not participate in international trade; this type of economy is known as a **closed economy**.

An **open economy** is an economy that participates in international trade. When an economy opens itself to trade, its citizens can specialize according to their comparative advantages and trade for those goods in which they do not have a comparative advantage. This means that they will be able to purchase goods at lower opportunity costs than before and thus their consumption possibilities will be larger than what they could produce on their own.

Learning Objective 3: Show how consumer surplus, producer surplus and total economic surplus are affected when a country opens itself to international trade. Identify the winners and losers when an economy opens itself to international trade.

The fact that trade expands a country's consumption possibilities suggests that total economic surplus expands when a country opens itself to trade. However, this analysis says nothing about whether it is consumers, producers or both who are receiving this increased surplus. A supply and demand analysis allows us to determine who collects the gains and who might bear the losses from trade.

There is a simple, 4-step rubric for determining the gains and losses from trade:

1. Draw a pair of supply and demand curves, find the equilibrium price and quantity, and then identify consumer surplus and producer surplus in the graph. (For example, see Figure 9.6(a) and Figure 9.7(a) in the text.) This is the **closed economy equilibrium**.
2. Locate the world price on this graph. The **world price** is the price at which a good is traded on international markets, and it will be either above or below the current equilibrium price. (For example, see, in the text, Figure 9.6(b) for a price that is below the closed economy equilibrium and Figure 9.7(b) for a price that is above the closed economy equilibrium.) This is the **open economy equilibrium**.
3. Identify consumer surplus and producer surplus for the open economy equilibrium. (For example, see, in the text, Figure 9.6(b) for a price that is below the closed economy equilibrium and Figure 9.7(b) for a price that is above the closed economy equilibrium.)
4. Compare consumer surplus in the closed and open economy equilibria to see whether it has increased or decreased. Do the same for producer surplus in the closed and

open economy equilibria. You now can say whether consumers or producers gain from trade.

In general, when an economy opens itself to trade, total economic surplus will increase. Further,

- domestic consumers win and domestic producers lose when the world price is below the closed economy equilibrium price.
- domestic producers win and domestic consumers lose when the world price is above the closed economy equilibrium price.

> Hint: You should review Chapter 7 if you do not remember the concepts of consumer surplus, producer surplus and total economic surplus.

Learning Objective 4: Explain how the presence of winners and losers from trade creates pressure for protectionist policies such as tariffs and quotas. Identify how protectionism reduces economic efficiency.

No one wants to be made worse off, yet international trade can reduce either producer or consumer surplus while increasing total economic surplus. This leads to demands from the injured parties for **protectionist policies**, i.e. policies that restrict trade in order to reduce the loss in consumer or producer surplus caused by trade.

Two protectionist policies are tariffs and quotas. A **tariff** is a tax imposed on an imported good. This is typically used when the world price is below the closed economy equilibrium price; the tariff increases the price that domestic consumers pay for the good above the world price and reduces the amount of the good that is imported. This increases producer surplus relative the no-tariff situation, but it reduces consumer surplus and total economic surplus as well. There is thus a deadweight loss associated with a tariff. See, for example, Figure 9.8 in the text. A **quota** is a legal limit on the number or value of foreign goods that can be imported. This has the same effects on consumer surplus, producer surplus and total economic surplus as a tariff. See, for example, Figure 9.9 in the text.

Learning Objective 5: Define outsourcing and explain how it is related to comparative advantage and international trade.

Outsourcing is the act of replacing relatively expensive domestic workers with cheaper workers in overseas locations.

On the face of it, this idea seems very different from the rest of the chapter; outsourcing is about lowering the cost of factors of production while we have so far analyzed trade in goods and services, not factors of production. However, it turns out that outsourcing has exactly the same effect on consumer surplus and total economic surplus as opening an economy to trade when the world price is lower than the closed economy equilibrium price. Outsourcing lowers the cost of inputs and thus lowers the price buyers pay for the good and encourages them to purchase more of it; both of these factors increase consumer surplus and total economic surplus for this market.

A larger quantity of the good will be supplied and this may increase, decrease or leave unaffected producer surplus. For example, if jobs are outsourced by domestic companies, but the domestic companies continue to sell the good produced by overseas workers, they will reap the profits and thus increase their producer surplus.

Learning Objective 6 (Appendix): Analyze the effects of the world price, tariffs and quotas on domestic prices and quantities using equations for the supply and demand curves.

The Appendix to Chapter 3 showed how supply and demand curves can be expressed as linear equations and then solved to find the equilibrium price and equilibrium quantity. This is an extension of that skill; here, you need to be able to find the equilibrium price and equilibrium quantity and then show how these change when a lower or higher world price is available for the good and how this is affected by tariffs or quotas.

> **Hint: You should review the Appendix to Chapter 3 if you do not remember these concepts.**

III. Self-Test

Key Terms
Match the term in the right-hand column with the appropriate definition in the left-hand column by placing the letter of the term in the blank in front of its definition. (Answers are given at the end of the chapter.)

1. ____ A legal limit on the number or value of foreign goods that can be imported.   a. autarky

2. ____ An economy that trades with other countries.   b. closed economy

3. ____ An economy that does not trade with the rest of the world.   c. consumption possibilities

4. ____ The view that free trade is injurious and should be restricted.   d. open economy

5. ____ A tax imposed on an imported good.   e. outsourcing

6. ____ A situation in which a country is self-sufficient.   f. protectionism

7. ____ The combination of goods that a country's citizens might feasibly consume.   g. quota

8. ____ The price at which a good is traded on international markets.   h. tariff

9. ____ The act of replacing relatively expensive domestic workers with cheaper workers in overseas locations.   i. world price

Multiple-Choice Questions
Circle the letter that corresponds to the best answer. (Answers are given at the end of the chapter.)

1.   In general, a nation will enjoy a higher material standard of living by
      A.   becoming self-sufficient.
      B.   specializing according to absolute advantage and trading.
      C.   imposing tariffs and quotas.
      D.   specializing according to comparative advantage and trading.
      E.   producing only one good and trading for everything else.

2.   Suppose that the country of Benedictia is a closed economy. This means that Benedictia
      A.   is landlocked.
      B.   restricts immigration and emigration.
      C.   does not engage in international trade.
      D.   engages in international trade but only in some goods and services.
      E.   engages in international trade.

Use the following information for problems 3, 4, 5 and 6: Suppose that each worker in the United Kingdom (UK) is identical and can produce 72 computers or 180 tons of grain per year. There are 30 million workers in the UK.

3.   The production possibilities curve for the UK will be
      A.   a straight line with intercepts at 72 computers and 180 tons of grain.
      B.   a straight line with intercepts at 2160 computers and 5400 tons of grain.
      C.   a curve that is bowed out with intercepts at 72 computers and 180 tons of grain.
      D.   a curve that is bowed out with intercepts at 2160 computers and 5400 tons of grain.
      E.   a curve that is bowed in with intercepts at 2160 computers and 5400 tons of grain.

4.   The opportunity cost of computers in terms of grain is
      A.   2.5   C.   7.2   E.   180
      B.   0.4   D.   72

5.   Suppose that the world price per computer is twice as high the world price per ton of grain. The UK should
      A.   specialize in computers and trade computers for grain.
      B.   produce a some of both goods and trade for both goods.
      C.   specialize in grain and trade grain for computers.
      D.   not engage in international trade.
      E.   do something but I don't know what since there is not enough information provided.

6.   Suppose that the world price per computer is one-half of the world price per ton of grain.
        A.   specialize in computers and trade computers for grain.
        B.   produce a some of both goods and trade for both goods.
        C.   specialize in grain and trade grain for computers.
        D.   not engage in international trade.
        E.   do something but I don't know what since there is not enough information
                provided.

Use the graph below for problems 7, 8 and 9: the graph below represents a country's market for
DVD players without international trade.

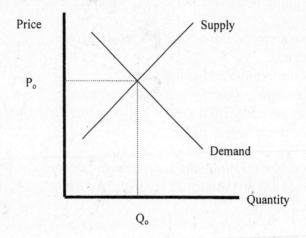

7.   Suppose that this country opens itself to international trade and that the world price of
        DVD players is lower than P_0. The price paid by domestic buyers will _____ and the price
        received by domestic producers will _____.
        A.   rise, rise
        B.   fall, fall
        C.   rise, fall
        D.   fall, rise
        E.   unaffected, unaffected

8.   Suppose that this country opens itself to international trade and that the world price of
        DVD players is lower than P_0. Buyers in this country will
        A.   purchase more DVD players and all DVD players will be imported.
        B.   purchase more DVD players, some of which will be imported.
        C.   purchase more DVD players, none of which will be imported.
        D.   purchase fewer DVD players and DVD players will be exported from this
                country.
        E.   purchase no more or fewer DVD players than they did before trade began.

9.   Suppose that this country opens itself to international trade and that the world price of
        DVD players is lower than P_0. This will cause a
        A.   gain in consumer surplus, a loss in producer surplus and a gain in total economic
                surplus.

B.   a loss in consumer surplus, a gain in producer surplus and a gain in total economic surplus.

C.   a loss in consumer surplus, a gain in producer surplus and a loss in total economic surplus.

D.   a gain in consumer surplus, a loss in producer surplus and a loss in total economic surplus.

E.   no change in consumer surplus, producer surplus or total economic surplus.

Use the graph below for problems 10, 11 and 12: the graph below represents a country's market for women's blouses without international trade.

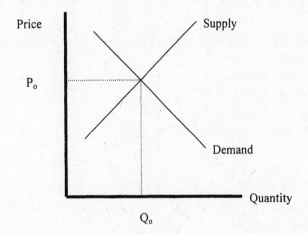

10.   Suppose that this country opens itself to international trade and that the world price of blouses is higher than P_0. The price paid by domestic buyers will ____ and the price received by domestic producers will ____.

     A.   rise, rise
     B.   fall, fall
     C.   rise, fall
     D.   fall, rise
     E.   unaffected, unaffected

11.   Suppose that this country opens itself to international trade and that the world price of blouses is higher than P_0. Buyers in this country will

     A.   purchase more blouses and all blouses will be imported.
     B.   purchase more blouses, some of which will be imported.
     C.   purchase more blouses, none of which will be imported.
     D.   purchase fewer blouses and blouses will be exported from this country.
     E.   purchase no more or fewer blouses than they did before trade began.

12.   Suppose that this country opens itself to international trade and that the world price of blouses is higher than P_0. This will cause a

     A.   gain in consumer surplus, a loss in producer surplus and a gain in total economic surplus.
     B.   a loss in consumer surplus, a gain in producer surplus and a gain in total economic

surplus.

C.   a loss in consumer surplus, a gain in producer surplus and a loss in total economic surplus.

D.   a gain in consumer surplus, a loss in producer surplus and a loss in total economic surplus.

E.   no change in consumer surplus, producer surplus or total economic surplus.

13.   If the US is a net importer of children's toys, free trade will only hurt
A.   domestic toy producers.   D.   domestic toy buyers.
B.   rich citizens of the US.   E.   foreign toy suppliers.
C.   poor citizens of the US.

14.   A country that engages in protectionist policies would enact measures to
A.   restrict imports
B.   raise the price of imports.
C.   do both (A) and (B)
D.   do neither (A) nor (B)
E.   open its borders to trade.

15.   A tariff is a
A.   legal limit on the number or value of foreign goods that can be imported.
B.   tax imposed on imports.
C.   tax imposed on exports.
D.   tax imposed on domestic producers of a good.
E.   tax imposed on illegal immigrants.

16.   Suppose that a country is currently importing a good. Imposing a tariff on this good will
A.   raise the price received by domestic sellers, lower the price paid by domestic buyers and increase total economic surplus.
B.   lower the price received by domestic sellers, raise the price paid by domestic buyers and increase total economic surplus.
C.   lower the price received by domestic sellers, raise the price paid by domestic buyers and decrease total economic surplus.
D.   raise the price received by domestic sellers, lower the price paid by domestic buyers and decrease total economic surplus.
E.   raise the price received by domestic sellers, raise the price paid by domestic buyers and decrease total economic surplus.

17.   A quota is a
A.   legal limit on the number or value of foreign goods that can be imported.
B.   tax imposed on imports
C.   tax imposed on exports.
D.   tax imposed on domestic producers of a good.
E.   tax imposed on illegal immigrants.

18.   Quotas and tariffs are similar in that both policies
        A.   generate revenue for the government.
        B.   increase the domestic price of the good on which the tariff or quota is imposed.
        C.   decrease the domestic price of the good on which the tariff or quota is imposed.
        D.   hurt domestic producers of the good and help domestic buyers of the good.
        E.   help domestic producers and domestic consumers of the good.

19.   Outsourcing is attractive to American companies because
        A.   High wage foreign workers can be replaced with low wage US workers.
        B.   High wage US workers can be replaced with low wage workers located abroad.
        C.   High wage US workers can be replaced with low wage immigrants.
        D.   Low price foreign goods can be kept out of the US.
        E.   consumer surplus is reduced.

20.   Jobs that are most likely to be outsourced are
        A.   those that can be managed with simple rules.
        B.   those that involve face-to-face contact.
        C.   those that cannot be carried out abroad.
        D.   covered by (A), (B) and (C)
        E.   not any jobs that are described by (A), (B) or (C).

Short Answer Problems
(Answers and solutions are given at the end of the chapter.)

1. Production possibilities and consumption possibilities
An economy has two workers, Paula and Ryan. For every day that they work, Paula can produce
4 computers or 16 shirts and Ryan can produce 6 computers or 12 shirts.
A.   Does the same person who has absolute advantage in the production of shirts also have
        comparative advantage in the production of shirts? Explain your reasoning.

        _____
        _____
        _____
        _____

B.   How much of each good is produced in a single day if each worker fully specializes
        according to his or her comparative advantage? Shirts:_____
        Computers:_____
C.   Suppose that this economy can trade with another economy. Specifically, suppose that
        Paula and Ryan can buy or sell any amount of shirts at $33 per shirt and they can buy or
        sell any amount of computers at $100 per computer. Would this economy's consumption
        possibilities exceed its production possibilities if it engages in trade? Explain your
        reasoning.

        _____
        _____
        _____
        _____

2. Gains and losses from trade

Suppose that the graph below represents the market for iron ore in China. The closed economy equilibrium is at P_0 and Q_0.

A.   Chinese iron mines are on the (demand/supply) _____ side of this market and Chinese steel producers are on the (demand/supply) _____ side of this market.
B.   Identify consumer surplus and producer surplus on the graph above.
C.   Suppose that the world price of iron ore is below the closed economy equilibrium price in China. Draw this on the graph above. The price paid by domestic buyers (rises/falls) _____ and the price received by domestic sellers (rises/falls) _____ .
C.   Suppose that the Chinese market for iron ore is opened to international trade. Identify the new levels of consumer surplus and producer surplus on the graph above. What happens to the level of total economic surplus? Explain: _____
_____
_____
_____

3. (Appendix problem) Working with the algebra of supply and demand in an open economy.

Suppose that domestic demand and supply curves for wheat in a small country are given by the following equations:

Demand: $Q = 5 - 0.2*P$ Supply: $Q = 1 + 0.8*P$

Quantities are measured in millions of bushels and prices are measured in dollars per bushel.

A.   Solve for the closed economy equilibrium price _____ and equilibrium quantity _____ .
B.   Suppose that this country opens itself to international trade and that the world price of wheat is equal to 5. At this price, domestic buyers will purchase _____ bushels of wheat, domestic producers will sell _____ bushels of wheat and _____ bushels of wheat will be (exported/imported) _____ .

IV. Becoming an Economic Naturalist: Case Study

The Central American Free Trade Agreement (CAFTA) was hotly debated in
Congress during 2005. Two groups spent much time and effort lobbying for and
against this treaty because it would reduce US quotas on imported raw sugar. (See,
for example, "Sugar Still a Barrier to Securing Trade Pact," *New York Times,* June 29,
2005.) One group consisted of American sugar beet farmers and American sugar cane
growers; the other group consisted of American sugar refiners who utilized primarily
imported sugar cane. Which group do you think was in favor of CAFTA and which
group opposed the treaty? Why? The article also states, "White House officials
repeatedly tried to soften the opposition of sugar producers with side deals that would
temporarily reduce the sting of the trade agreement." What types of "side deals"
could "reduce the sting?"

Answer:

Self-Test Solutions

Key Terms

1. g	6. a		
2. d	7. c		
3. b	8. i		
4. f	9. e		
5. h			

Multiple-Choice Questions

1. D	6. A	11. D	16. E
2. C	7. B	12. B	17. A
3. B	8. B	13. A	18. B
4. A	9. A	14. C	19. B
5. C	10. A	15. B	20. A

Short Answer Problems

1. A. Yes, Ryan has comparative advantage and absolute advantage in computers and
        Paula has comparative and absolute advantage in shirts.
    B. 16; 6
    C. Yes. The world price is 3 computers per shirt; if Paula and Ryan produce 16
        shirts and 6 computers they can trade away computers or shirts for larger
        quantities of either good than they could produce on their own.
2. A. supply; demand

      B.   Figure 9.6 in the text shows these effects for the case of Costa Rican computers; the graphs are identical for the case of Chinese steel imports analyzed in this problem.

3.   A.   P = $4 per bushel, Q = 4.2 million bushels

      B.   Quantity supplied = 5 million bushels, quantity demanded = 4 million bushels; since quantity supplied exceeds quantity demand, exports = 1 million bushels.

Chapter 10
Monopoly and Other Forms of Imperfect Competition

I. Pretest: What Do You Really Know?
Circle the letter that corresponds to the best answer. (Answers appear immediately after the final question).

1. Which of the following lists market structures from most to least competitive?
    A. pure monopoly, oligopoly, perfect competition, monopolistic competition.
    B. oligopoly, pure monopoly, perfect competition, imperfect competition.
    C. perfect competition, monopolistic competition, oligopoly, pure monopoly.
    D. perfect competition, economies of scale, oligopoly.
    E. monopolistic competition, oligopoly, economies of scale.

2. An imperfectly competitive firm must _____ in order to sell an additional unit of its product.
    A. raise the price that it charges
    B. decrease the number of employees it hires
    C. lower the price that it charges
    D. lower barriers to entry
    E. advertise

3. Constant returns to scale is a situation where doubling all inputs leads to
    A. a doubling in the price of inputs.
    B. more than doubling in the amount of output produced.
    C. a doubling in the price of outputs.
    D. doubling the amount of output produced.
    E. less than doubling the amount of output produced.

4. Industries with large start-up costs and low marginal costs will have
    A. constant average total costs.
    B. declining average total costs.
    C. increasing average total costs.
    D. constant marginal costs.
    E. declining marginal costs.

5. An imperfectly competitive firm differs from a perfectly competitive firm in that
   A. the latter must raise its price to sell more output while the former does not.
   B. the former must lower its price to sell more output while the latter does not.
   C. the former must lower its price to sell more output while the latter does not.
   D. the former can produce at any level of output that it chooses while the latter cannot.
   E. the latter can produce at any level of output that it chooses while the former cannot.

6. The profit maximizing level of output for a monopolist occurs at a
   A. price that is lower than marginal cost.
   B. price where marginal cost is equal to zero.
   C. quantity where marginal revenue equals marginal cost.
   D. quantity where price equals marginal cost.
   E. quantity where marginal cost is minimized.

7. When a monopoly is compared to a perfectly competitive market, we find that
   A. consumer surplus rises, producer surplus falls and total economic surplus falls.
   B. consumer surplus falls, producer surplus rises and total economic surplus rises.
   C. consumer surplus rises, producer surplus falls and total economic surplus falls.
   D. consumer surplus falls, producer surplus rises and total economic surplus falls.
   E. there is no change in consumer surplus, producer surplus or total economic surplus.

8. When compared with pure monopoly, price discrimination is
   A. uniformly bad for society.
   B. always beneficial to sellers and to society as a whole but never beneficial to buyers.
   C. always beneficial to buyers and to society as a whole but never beneficial to sellers.
   D. always beneficial to buyers, sellers and society as a whole.
   E. always beneficial to buyers and society as a whole and sometimes beneficial to sellers.

9. A perfect hurdle is a
   A. method of price discrimination.
   B. barrier to entry.
   C. fixed cost.
   D. scale economy
   E. variable input.

10. Public policy does not seek to eliminate natural monopolies because
    A. society benefits from goods produced at low average total costs.
    B. society benefits from companies that are large and stable.
    C. society cannot eliminate them anymore than they can change the weather.
    D. natural monopolies have too many barriers to entry.
    E. society benefits from goods produced at high fixed costs.

Solutions and Feedback to Pretest
The answers to the pretest are provided below along with the relevant Learning Objective from the Key Point Review. We strongly recommend that you take the time to review the appropriate material for each question you answered incorrectly.

Correct Answer	Learning Objective
1. C	1
2. C	2
3. D	2
4. B	3
5. C	1
6. C	4
7. D	5
8. D	6
9. A	6
10. A	7

II. Key Point Review
The Forest

This chapter focuses on monopoly and the general characteristics of imperfect competition. This is the first of two chapters on imperfect competition; Chapter 11 continues the discussion and focuses on monopolistic competition and oligopoly.

The central questions you need to be able to answer are:
- What is imperfect competition and how does it differ from perfect competition?
- What is market power and how does this affect the demand curve facing the firm?
- How do start-up costs affect economies of scale and market power?
- How does a monopolist choose an output level that maximizes its profit?
- How does monopoly affect consumer surplus, producer surplus and total economic surplus?
- What is price discrimination and what are its effects?
- What are some of the public policies applied to natural monopolies?

The Trees

Learning Objective 1: Define imperfect competition and explain how it differs from perfect competition. Discuss the three types of imperfect competition.

Imperfect competition is a situation in which firms have some ability to set their own prices. This differs from perfect competition in that perfectly competitive firms have no power to affect the price at which they sell their product.

Another way to describe the difference between imperfect and perfect competition is to say that perfectly competitive firms are **price takers** (i.e. they cannot influence the price at which they sell their product) while imperfectly competitive firms are **price setters** (i.e. they have at least some influence over the price at which they sell their product.)

The three types of imperfect competition are monopoly, oligopoly and monopolistic competition. A **monopoly** is an industry in which there is a single supplier of a unique product with no close substitutes. An **oligopoly** is an industry in which a small number of large firms produce products that are either close or perfect substitutes. **Monopolistic competition** is an industry in which a large number of firms produce slightly differentiated products that are reasonably close substitutes for one another.

Hint: You should review the characteristics of perfectly competitive firms (in Chapter 6) so that you can compare and contrast them with those of monopoly, oligopoly and monopolistic competition.

Learning Objective 2: Explain the term market power and relate this to the demand curve facing a firm. Discuss five important sources of market power.

Market power refers to a firm's ability to raise the price of a good without losing all of its sales. This implies that as the firm raises its price it will sell fewer units but will still have customers who want to buy their product, i.e. the demand curve for the firm is downward sloping.

There are generally five sources of market power. **Exclusive control over important inputs, possession of patents and copyrights**, and **control of licenses or franchises** are similar in that they are barriers to entry, i.e. they are methods of preventing other firms from entering a market.

Hint: Barriers to entry and their effects were discussed in Chapter 8. You should review this concept if you do not remember it.

Economies of scale refers to a situation in which a proportional increase in all factors of production leads to a greater than proportional increase in output. This means that an existing firm can actually reduce its average total costs as it increases its production. This confers an advantage on a firm that is already producing a product since it can meet the challenge of a potential competitor by expanding its output at a lower average cost than before and thus can lower the price at which it can sell the product.

Network economies are cost savings that result from a situation in which a product is more valuable to buyers the more people use them. A prime example of network economies is computer operating systems. The fact that Microsoft's' Windows operating system is used on so many personal computers means that lots of applications are written for that operating system and competition among these applications keeps their prices low. The availability of many applications and low costs among applications encourage people to install Windows on their computers and thus gives Microsoft market power.

Learning Objective 3: Analyze how high start-up costs affect economies of scale. Discuss why this can lead to natural monopoly.

Start-up costs are a form of fixed costs and are thus spread out over the number of units of output a firm produces. This means that, if marginal cost is low, average total cost will be falling and this is simply another way of saying that there are economies of scale. High start-up costs can act as a barrier to entry and thus prevent other firms from entering an industry. The resulting monopoly is known as a **natural monopoly.**

> **Hint: You should review the material in Chapter 6 on different types of costs if these concepts are not clear.**

Learning Objective 4: Explain how a monopolist chooses an output level that maximizes its profit. Do this both in words and using a graph.

This is a direct application of the Cost-Benefit Principle. Suppose that a monopolist produces one unit of a good. It will earn additional revenue when it sells this unit; this is the **marginal revenue** it gains from producing the good. It will incur additional cost equal to the marginal cost. The Cost-Benefit Principle implies that the firm should produce additional units of the good as long as the marginal revenue (the marginal benefit) is at least as great as the marginal cost.

Figure 10.7 in the text illustrates how the profit maximizing level of output is determined for a monopolist. There is a simple, 2-step rubric for using this graph:

1. Find where the marginal revenue and marginal cost curves intersect and mark this quantity on the graph. This is the profit maximizing output level of output.

2. Draw up from the quantity you marked on the graph to the demand curve. The price associated with this quantity is the profit maximizing price that the monopolist should charge for this good.

> **Note: Being a monopolist does not guarantee that a firm will earn positive economic profits. Figure 10.8 in the text illustrates this fact.**

Learning Objective 5: Analyze the effects of monopoly on consumer surplus, producer surplus and total economic surplus.

A monopolist charges a price that is higher than the marginal cost of a good. This has three effects. First, in a perfectly competitive market, the price buyers pay is equal to the marginal cost; thus, buyers pay a higher price under monopoly than they do under perfect competition and consumer surplus is therefore lower. Second, buyers purchase fewer units of the good and thus total economic surplus is reduced; this is another example of the Equilibrium Principle. Third, since the price the seller receives on the units sold is higher than their marginal cost, producer surplus rises. Thus, monopoly reduces consumer surplus, increases producer surplus and reduces total economic surplus. Figure 10.10 in the text illustrates these effects.

Hint: You should review Chapter 7 if you do not remember the concepts of consumer surplus, producer surplus and total economic surplus.

Learning Objective 6: Define price discrimination. Discuss particular methods of price discrimination. Analyze the effects of price discrimination on consumer surplus, producer surplus and total economic surplus.

Price discrimination is the practice of charging different prices for essentially the same good. The word "discrimination" may lead you to think that this is an obviously bad practice but this is not necessarily the case. Remember that monopoly reduces output below the perfectly competitive level; this means that there are still buyers who would like to purchase the good at a price above the firm's marginal cost. If the firm could figure out a way to sell the good to these customers and still charge its profit maximizing price to its original customers, it will both increase its producer surplus *and* increase consumer surplus.

A monopolist that can actually charge each customer a price equal to that person's reservation price is called a **perfectly discriminating monopolist**. This obviously requires a great deal of information and so other types of price discrimination are more common. For example, the **hurdle method** of price discrimination is the practice by which a seller offers a discount to all buyers who overcome some obstacle. A **perfect hurdle** is a price that completely segregates buyers whose reservation price is above it from those whose reservation price is below it. Rebates in which customers have to fill out forms and return them are good examples of perfect hurdles.

Learning Objective 7: Discuss public policies applied to natural monopolies.

Natural monopolies exist due to economies of scale. Public policy should theoretically encourage economies of scale since this can potentially reduce the prices buyers pay and increase both consumer surplus and total economic surplus.

A number of policies have been developed to both reap the benefits of scale economies and prevent monopolists from reducing total economic surplus. **State ownership and management**, **state regulation of private monopolies**, and **exclusive contracting for natural monopoly** are commonly applied to utilities such as electric power, water supplies and cable television. **Antitrust laws** consist of regulations that prevent the formation of cartels and monopolies and that allow governments to monitor the prices charged by corporations for certain products. Enforcing these laws can also work to regulate the actions of natural monopolies.

Learning Objective 8 (Appendix): Analyze the effects of monopoly on the equilibrium price and quantity of a good using equations for the demand curve, the marginal revenue curve and the marginal cost curve.

The Appendix to Chapter 3 showed how supply and demand curves can be expressed as linear equations and then solved to find the equilibrium price and equilibrium quantity. This is an extension of that skill; here, you need to be able to find the quantity at which marginal cost equals marginal revenue, and then use this quantity to find the price the monopolist will charge.

Hint: You should review the Appendix to Chapter 3 if you do not remember these concepts.

III. Self-Test

<u>Key Terms</u>
Match the term in the right-hand column with the appropriate definition in the left-hand column by placing the letter of the term in the blank in front of its definition. (Answers are given at the end of the chapter.)

1. _____ The additional revenue a firm gains by selling one additional unit of output.

2. _____ A price that completely segregates buyers whose reservation price is above it from those whose reservation price is below it.

3. _____ A market in which a large number of firms produce slightly differentiated products that are reasonably close substitutes for one another.

4. _____ A firm's ability to raise the price of a good without losing all of its sales.

5. _____ A proportional increase in all factors of production leads to a greater than proportional increase in output.

6. _____ The practice of charging different prices for essentially the same good.

7. _____ A public policy in which a firm is permitted to charge a price equal to its explicit costs of production plus a markup to cover implicit costs.

a. constant returns to scale

b. cost-plus regulation

c. economies of scale

d. hurdle method of price discrimination

e. imperfectly competitive firm

f. increasing returns to scale

g. marginal revenue

8. _____ The only supplier of a unique product with no close substitutes.

h. market power

9. _____ A monopoly that results from economies of scale.

i. monopolistic competition

10. _____ A firm that charges each buyer exactly his or her reservation price.

j. natural monopoly

11. _____ A synonym for economies of scale.

k. oligopoly

12. _____ A proportional increase in all factors of production leads to an increase in output of the same proportion.

l. perfect hurdle

13. _____ The practice by which a seller offers a discount to all buyers who overcome some obstacle.

m. perfectly discriminating monopolist

14. _____ A market in which a small number of large firms produce products that are either close or perfect substitutes.

n. price discrimination

15. _____ A firm with at least some ability to set its own price.

o. price setter

16. _____ A synonym for a price setter.

p. price monopoly

Multiple-Choice Questions
Circle the letter that corresponds to the best answer. (Answers are given at the end of the chapter.)

1.   An imperfectly competitive firm is one
   A.   that attempts but fails to compete perfectly.
   B.   with complete control over how much it produces.
   C.   with the ability to set price at any level it wishes.
   D.   that possesses some degree of control over its price.
   E.   that faces a perfectly elastic demand curve.

2.   A price setters faces a
   A.   perfectly elastic demand curve.   D.   unit elastic demand curve.
   B.   constantly varying price.   E.   perfectly inelastic demand curve.
   C.   less than perfectly elastic demand curve.

3.   Market power refers to a firm's ability to
   A.   destroy its competitors.
   B.   prevent unionization of its workforce.
   C.   raise its price without losing all of its sales.
   D.   influence the price charged by its competitors.
   E.   force its customers to pay prices above their reservation prices.

4.   Eli Lilly had a monopoly in the production of the anti-depressant Prozac because
   A.   it had exclusive ownership of the necessary ingredients.
   B.   it was the only company that had the knowledge to make anti-depressants.
   C.   there was a perfectly elastic demand for Prozac.
   D.   it had a patent on the production of Prozac.
   E.   there was a perfectly inelastic supply of Prozac.

5.   Increasing returns to scale is a situation where doubling all inputs leads to
      A.   a doubling in the price of inputs.
      B.   more than doubling in the amount of output produced.
      C.   a doubling in the price of outputs.
      D.   doubling the amount of output produced.
      E.   less than doubling the amount of output produced.

6.   A situation in which a product is more valuable to buyers the more people use them is a
      A.   network economy.
      B.   market economy.
      C.   variable cost.
      D.   perfectly elastic demand curve.
      E.   theoretically impossible situation.

7.   Suppose that the total cost curve for a firm is given by $TC = a + b*Q$ with a and b both
      being positive numbers. This means that the firm's average total costs will be
      A.   constant.
      B.   rise and fall in a regular pattern.
      C.   fall as output increases.
      D.   rise as output increases.
      E.   shaped like a U.

8.   A hot dog vendor advertises that the first hot dog is $1 but that you can buy two for
      $1.50. this implies that the vendor's marginal revenue for the second hot dog is
      A.   zero
      B. $0.50
      C. $1.00
      D. $1.50
      E. $2.50

9.   Perfectly competitive firms and monopolists both produce where
      A.   marginal revenue equals to marginal cost.
      B.   price equals marginal cost.   D.   marginal revenue equals zero.
      C.   price equals marginal revenue.   E.   marginal cost is declining.

Use the following information for problems 10, 11 and 12: the demand curve for a monopolist is
given in the table below:

Quantity Demanded	Price
1	10
2	9
3	8
4	7
5	6
6	5
5	4

10.   The marginal revenue of the first unit sold is
        A.   zero
        B.   4
        C.   18
        D.   10
        E.   indeterminate

11.   If the marginal cost is constant at 4, then this firm should produce _____ units.
        A.   2
        B.   3
        C.   4
        D.   5
        E.   6

12.   If the marginal cost is constant at 4, then this firm should charge a price of _____.
        A.   3
        B.   4
        C.   5
        D.   6
        E.   7

13.   Economists consider monopoly socially undesirable because a monopolist
        A.   always earns positive economic profits.
        B.   can charge any price he wants.
        C.   exploits the inelastic nature of demand.
        D.   produces less than the socially efficient amount.
        E.   produces more than the socially efficient amount.

14.   A monopolist will create _____ compared to a perfectly competitive market.
        A.   more consumer surplus
        B.   less producer surplus
        C.   a deadweight loss
        D.   more total economic surplus
        E.   the same total economic surplus

15.   Perfect competition is efficient and monopoly in not because in perfect competition
                _____ while in monopoly _____.
        A. $P = MC$; $P > MC$ D. $P = MC$; $P < MC$
        B. $P < MR$; $P = MR$ E. $P = MR$; $P = MC$
        C. $P = MR$; $P < MR$

16.   Price discrimination means a firm charges
       A.   all consumers the same price.
       B.   different prices to different consumers because of transportation costs.
       C.   the same price to all consumers despite differences in transportation costs.
       D.   different prices to different consumers when all production costs are the same.
       E.   higher prices to women and members of racial minorities.

17.   A customer purchases a new computer that is advertised for $500. As she is paying for
       the computer at the check-out counter, the clerks tells her that there is a $50 rebate on the
       computer if she fills out a form, attaches her receipt and mails them in within 30 days.
       This is an example of
       A.   a barrier to entry.
       B.   the hurdle method of price discrimination.
       C.   the perfect hurdle method of price discrimination.
       D.   falling average costs.
       E.   perfectly elastic demand.

18.   Economies of scale are a defining feature of a natural monopoly. This means that
       A.   marginal cost equals marginal revenue.
       B.   marginal cost will always be less than average total cost.
       C.   marginal cost will always be less than average variable cost.
       D.   marginal cost will always be greater than average total cost.
       E.   marginal cost will always be greater than average variable cost.

19.   Which one of the following is an example of exclusive contracting for natural monopoly?
       A.   Municipal garbage collection through a single private company.
       B.   A state-owned electric power company.
       C.   Satellite television service.
       D.   A bookstore in a small town.
       E.   An oil well in Alaska.

20.   Cost-plus regulation of a natural monopoly involves
       A.   letting the firm set their price and then reducing that by a fixed amount.
       B.   insuring that the firm charges a price equal to its explicit costs of production plus
             a markup to cover implicit costs.
       C.   granting the firm a patent.
       D.   keeping other firms from entering.
       E.   creating a government-owned corporation.

Short Answer Problems
(Answers and solutions are given at the end of the chapter.)

1. Profit maximization for a monopoly

The table below contains the information available to a monopolist:

Output	Price ($)	Total Revenue	Marginal revenue	Total cost ($)	Marginal cost
10	9.00			100.00	
15	8.50			105.00	
20	8.00			115.00	
25	7.50			135.00	
30	7.00			157.50	
35	6.50			185.00	

A. Fill in the data for total revenue and marginal revenue. Is marginal revenue constant or decreasing? _____

B. The monopolist (should/should not) _____ produce 20 units of output because (marginal revenue / marginal cost) _____ exceeds (marginal revenue / marginal cost).

C. The monopolist (should/should not) _____ produce 35 units of output because (marginal revenue / marginal cost) _____ exceeds (marginal revenue / marginal cost).

D. The profit maximizing level of output is _____. The monopolist should charge a price of _____.

2. Natural monopoly

The graph below represents the information available to a monopolist:

A. The graph suggests that this is a natural monopoly because: _____.

B. The monopolist will maximize its profit at an output of _____ and charge a price of _____.

C. At the profit maximizing output level, the monopolist will have a (profit/loss) per unit equal to _____.

D. If the government ordered the monopolist to sell the product at a price equal to its marginal cost, it produces at an output of _____ and earns a (profit/loss) _____ of _____.

IV. Becoming an Economic Naturalist: Case Study

"Although the chemical ingredients for each mass-manufactured pill cost only pennies, retail prices are hundreds -- even thousands -- of times greater. Drug companies argue that the high prices reflect the costs of the years of research and development necessary before a new drug makes it to market. According to industry spokesperson Marjorie Powell, it costs an average of $800 million and takes 12 to 15 years before a new medicine makes it to drug store shelves." (Quotation is from an episode of the PBS program *Frontline* entitled "The Other Drug Wars" and is available at http://www.pbs.org/wgbh/pages/frontline/shows/other/etc/faqs.html:

What do you think the average total cost curve for a particular pharmaceutical would look like? What about the marginal cost curve? Suppose the government told drug companies that they had to charge a price per pill equal to its marginal cost. What would this do to drug companies' profits? How does this relate to public policy towards natural monopolies?

Answer:

V. Self-Test Solutions

Key Terms

1. g	5. f	9. j	13. d
2. l	6. n	10. m	14. k
3. i	7. b	11. c	15. o
4. h	8. p	12. a	16. e

Multiple-Choice Questions

1. D	6. A	11. C	16. D
2. C	7. C	12. E	17. B
3. C	8. B	13. D	18. B
4. D	9. A	14. C	19. A
5. B	10. D	15. A	20. B

Short Answer Problems

1.   A.

Output	Price ($)	Total Revenue	Marginal revenue	Total cost ($)	Marginal cost
10	9.00	90.00	9	100.00	10
15	8.50	127.50	7.50	105.00	1
20	8.00	160.00	6.50	115.00	2
25	7.50	187.50	5.50	135.00	4
30	7.00	210.00	4.50	157.50	4.50
35	6.50	227.50	3.50	185.00	5.50

    B.   should not; marginal revenue; marginal cost
    C.   should not; marginal cost; marginal revenue
    D.   30; $7

2.   A.   ATC lies above MC at all levels of output.
    B.   3.5; $22.50
    C. $11 ($33.50 - $22.50)
    D.   7; $65.10, which is equal to $(14.30 - 5)*7$

Chapter 11
Strategic Choice in Oligopoly, Monopolistic Competition, and Everyday Life

I. Pretest: What Do You Really Know?
Circle the letter that corresponds to the best answer. (Answers appear immediately after the final question).

1. Game theory is useful because it helps us understand
   A. how perfectly competitive markets operate.
   B. the demand curve.
   C. how oligopolists and monopolistic competitors behave.
   D. how monopolists behave.
   E. how to develop board games.

2. Which of the following is a basic element of a game:
   A. the number of players.
   B. the players' strategies.
   C. payoffs.
   D. (A), (B) and (C) are all basic elements of a game.
   E. none of (A), (B) or (C) is basic element of a game.

3. When both players of a game choose the best strategy available to them given the other player's strategies,
   A. the game collapses.
   B. the players have both played dominated strategies.
   C. the result is a Nash equilibrium.
   D. neither player has a dominant strategy available to them.
   E. we can then write down the payoff matrix.

4. The prisoner's dilemma is a game in which
   A. each player has a dominant strategy.
   B. each player has a dominant strategy that results in a lower payoff than their dominated strategies.
   C. each player has a dominant strategy that results in the largest payoff to all players.
   D. neither player has a dominant strategy.
   E. only one player has a dominant strategy.

5. The prisoner's dilemma is a good description of the behavior of
   A. cartels.
   B. a monopolist.
   C. a perfectly competitive firm.
   D. a prisoner who can coordinate actions with an accomplice.
   E. no one; it is just a theoretical possibility.

6. Tit-for-tat strategy is a strategy employed in
   A. a Nash equilibrium.
   B. a prisoner's dilemma played a single time.
   C. a repeated prisoner's dilemma.
   D. a payoff matrix.
   E. a dominated strategy.

7. A decision tree is useful for representing
   A. a game in which players choose their strategies sequentially.
   B. a game in which players choose their strategies simultaneously.
   C. a repeated prisoner's dilemma.
   D. a prisoner's dilemma game played a single time
   E. a game in which the players are arborists.

8. A credible threat or credible promise draws its credibility from the fact that
   A. there are potential legal sanctions against the players.
   B. there is uncertainty about payoffs.
   C. the players know each other well.
   D. there are no dominant strategies.
   E. it is in the threatener's or promiser's interest to act on the threat or promise.

9. A commitment problem exists when
   A. players cannot make either credible threats or credible promises.
   B. players can make credible threats but not credible promises.
   C. players can make credible promises but not credible threats.
   D. players make decisions sequentially.
   E. players make decisions simultaneously.

10. The strategic use of preferences is a way of dealing with
    A. decision trees.
    B. commitment problems.
    C. dominant strategies.
    D. dominated strategies.
    E. the Nash equilibrium.

Solutions and Feedback to Pretest
The answers to the pretest are provided below along with the relevant Learning Objective from the Key Point Review. We strongly recommend that you take the time to review the appropriate material for each question you answered incorrectly.

Correct Answer	Learning Objective
1. C	1
2. D	1
3. C	1
4. B	2
5. A	3
6. C	3
7. A	4
8. E	4
9. A	4
10. B	4

II. Key Point Review
The Forest

This chapter focuses on game theory and applies this tool to monopolistic competition and oligopoly. This is the second of two chapters on imperfect competition and continues the discussion of this topic begun in Chapter 10.

The central questions you need to be able to answer are:
- What are the basic elements of a game?
- What is the Prisoner's Dilemma and how does it apply to real-world situations?
- How do games in which timing matters differ from games in which it does not?
- What are commitment problems and how do they affect games?
- How can altering preferences solve commitment problems?

The Trees

Learning Objective 1: Describe the basic elements of a game. Define a payoff matrix and then discuss the meaning of the terms dominant strategy, dominated strategy and Nash equilibrium.

The **basic elements of a game** are the (1) **players**, (2) the list of possible actions available to the players, called **strategies**, and (3) the **payoffs** each player receives for each possible combination of strategies.

Game theory allows for many players but this chapter only considers games with two players. This is handy because we can then describe the payoffs for each possible combination of strategies in a table called a **payoff matrix**.

Hint: You should work with Example 11.1 in the textbook while reviewing these ideas. Table 11.1 shows the basic elements of a game.

The players are trying to do the best that they can for themselves, so each player looks at their strategies and evaluates them in light of what the other player will do. There are two possible strategies that are of particular interest. First, a **dominant strategy** is a strategy that yields a higher payoff no matter what strategies the other player chooses. Second, a **dominated strategy** is a strategy that leads to a lower payoff than an alternative choice, regardless of what the other player chooses.

A game is at a **Nash equilibrium** if each player's strategy is the best he or she can choose given the other player's strategies.

Hint: If both players have dominant strategies, then a Nash equilibrium has to exist for the game. However, the reverse does not have to be the case, i.e. there can be a Nash equilibrium for a game even one player does not have a dominant strategy.

Note: Sylvia Nassar's book *A Beautiful Mind* is the story of John Nash, the mathematician who developed this particular definition of equilibrium. (The 2002 movie of the same name won the Academy Award for Best Picture.) Nash shared the 1994 Nobel Prize in economics for this concept; see http://nobelprize.org/economics/laureates/1994/index.html

Learning Objective 2: Define and explain the prisoner's dilemma.

The **prisoner's dilemma** is a game in which each player has a dominant strategy, but when each player executes that strategy the resulting payoffs are smaller than if each had played a dominated strategy.

Hint: Remember the Equilibrium Principle from Chapter 3. Here is a situation where collective action (such as the prisoners being able to talk with one another) would improve the situation but since they are acting individually there are no unexploited gains and they have come to an equilibrium.

You have probably experienced a non-economic example of the prisoner's dilemma. For example, suppose that you are a spectator at a rock concert. If everyone sits in their place then everyone can see the performers; however, an individual can get an even better view by standing up. If someone does this in front of you, he blocks your view, so you have stand up to see. You are now are blocking another concertgoer and they have to stand up. Soon most if not all of the spectators are standing up and not seeing the performers any better than they did when they were seated.

Learning Objective 3: Apply the prisoner's dilemma to cartels. Extend this idea to the repeated prisoner's dilemma and tit-for-tat strategies.

A **cartel** is a coalition of firms that agrees to restrict output in order to earn a positive economic profit and is a particular form of oligopoly. The strategies for members of a cartel are simple: restrict output as agreed or cheat on the agreement and sell more than you agreed to. If all firms in the cartel restrict output together they earn economic profits. However, it usually turns out that if everyone sticks to the agreement except for one firm, that firm can earn bigger profits by cheating than by obeying the agreement. This is therefore a dominant strategy for that firm. This is true for any particular firm so this is a dominant strategy on the part of *all* the firms, which leads to a collapse of the cartel. The prisoner's dilemma is therefore a good model of a cartel.

The Organization of Petroleum Exporting Countries (OPEC) "coordinate their oil production policies in order to help stabilize the oil market and to help oil producers achieve a reasonable rate of return on their investments;" that is, they are a cartel. (Quote is from http://www.opec.org/aboutus/functions/functions.htm). OPEC began in 1960 and has had to deal with cheating and other problems since then. The standard prisoner's dilemma is a good model of a particular year in OPEC's history but is not a good model of the organization over time. A **repeated prisoner's dilemma** is a standard prisoner's dilemma that is played repeatedly and more accurately reflects cartel behavior over time, such as that of OPEC since 1960. A strategy that prevents cheating in the repeated prisoner's dilemma is called the **tit-for-tat** strategy: players cooperate on the first move and then mimic their partner's move on each successive more.

Learning Objective 4: Explain what a decision tree is. Use a decision tree to discuss the concepts of a credible promise and a credible threat.

The players in the games discussed in Learning Objectives 2 and 3 choose their strategies simultaneously. However, there are many games in which this is not the case and players choose their strategies sequentially. In this case, a payoff matrix cannot be used to represent the players, strategies and payoffs.

A **decision tree** (also called a **game tree**) is a diagram that describes the possible moves for a game in sequence and lists the payoffs that correspond to each possible combination of moves. This diagram shows the basic elements of a *sequential* game.

> **Note: Examples of decision trees are given in the text, Figures 11.3 and 11.4**

Sequential games involve actions that will take place in the future and so players can make threats against or promises to the other players regarding their future actions. A **credible**

promise is a promise to take an action that is in the promiser's interest to keep. Similarly, a **credible threat** is a threat to take an action that is in the threatener's interest to carry out. Only credible promises and threats will affect other players' actions.

> Note: Robert J. Aumann and Thomas C. Schelling shared the 2005 Nobel Prize in economics for their work on credible threats and promises; see http://nobelprize.org/economics/laureates/2005/index.html

Learning Objective 5: Define the commitment problem. Explain how commitment devices are used to overcome the commitment problem. Extend this idea to the strategic role of preferences.

There are many situations where the players cannot make credible promises or threats in order to reach desired outcomes; this is known as a **commitment problem**. The solution to this problem is to develop **commitment devices**: ways of changing incentives so that otherwise empty promises or threats become credible. There are many types of commitment devices. One device that is discussed in the text is to use preferences themselves as a way of making promises and threats credible. For example, social norms and concerns about fairness can be introduced into players' preferences so that rather than simply caring about their own payoffs they are concerned with those of other players.

III. Self-Test

Key Terms
Match the term in the right-hand column with the appropriate definition in the left-hand column by placing the letter of the term in the blank in front of its definition. (Answers are given at the end of the chapter.)

1. _____ A situation in which people cannot achieve their goals because of an inability to make credible threats or promises.

    a. basic elements of a game

2. _____ A game in which each player has a dominant strategy, and when each plays it, the resulting payoffs are smaller than if each had played a dominated strategy.

    b. cartel

3. _____ Any combination of strategies in which each player's strategy is his or her best choice, given the other player's strategies.

    c. commitment device

4. _____ A table that describes the payoffs in a game for each possible combination of strategies.

    d. commitment problem

5. _____ A strategy for the repeated prisoner's dilemma in which players cooperate on the first move and then mimic their partner's previous move on each successive more.

    e. credible promise

6. _____ A promise to take an action that is in the promiser's interest to keep.

    f. credible threat

7. _____ A way of changing incentives so as to make otherwise empty threats or promises credible.

    g. decision tree

8. _____ The players, strategies available to each player and the

    h. dominant strategy

payoffs each player receives for each possible combination of strategies.

9. ____ A coalition of firms that agrees to restrict output in order to earn a positive economic profit.

i. dominated strategy

10. ____ A standard prisoner's dilemma that confronts the same players repeatedly.

j. game tree

11. ____ A diagram that describes the possible moves in a game in sequence and lists the payoffs that correspond to each possible combination of moves.

k. Nash equilibrium

12. ____ A threat to take an action that is in the threatener's interest to carry out.

l. payoff matrix

13. ____ The other strategies available to a player who has a dominant strategy.

m. prisoner's dilemma

14. ____ A synonym for a decision tree.

n. repeated prisoner's dilemma

o. tit-for-tat

15. ____ A strategy that yields a higher payoff no matter what strategies the other players in a game choose.

Multiple-Choice Questions
Circle the letter that corresponds to the best answer. (Answers are given at the end of the chapter.)

1. Game theory is useful in studying imperfect competition because, unlike the tools developed previously in the text, it incorporates
    A. profit maximization.   D.   utility maximization.
    B. more than one good.   E.   interdependency.
    C. time.

2. A payoff matrix presents
    A. the number of players.   D.   (A), (B) and (C).
    B. the players' strategies.   E.   neither (A) nor (B) nor (C).
    C. payoffs.

3. A player has a dominant strategy when
    A. that player has a strategy that will yield the highest payoff no matter what strategy the other player chooses.
    B. that player has a strategy that leads to a lower payoff than an alternative choice, regardless of what the other player chooses.
    C. both players choose identical strategies.
    D. the payoff to a strategy is dependent on the strategy chosen by the other player.
    E. both players have only one strategy available to them.

4. A player has a dominated strategy when
    A. that player has a strategy that will yield the highest payoff no matter what strategy the other player chooses.

B.   that player has a strategy that leads to a lower payoff than an alternative choice, regardless of what the other player chooses.
C.   both players choose identical strategies.
D.   the payoff to a strategy is dependent on the strategy chosen by the other player.
E.   both players have only one strategy available to them.

Use the following information for problems 5, 6, 7 and 8: Joan and John are watching a movie at home and neither of them likes it. Each is thinking, "maybe we should just stop watching it now." They have been together for 40 years so they know each other well. Here is the payoff matrix for their situation:

		Joan	
		Keep watching	Stop watching
John	Keep watching	Joan: 30 John: 5	Joan: 12 John: 10
	Stop watching	Joan: 10 John: -2	Joan: 15 John: 8

5.   John has _____ dominant strategy/strategies in this game.
       A. 0   B. 1   C. 2   D. 3   E. 4

6.   Joan has _____ dominant strategy/strategies in this game.
       A. 0   B. 1   C. 2   D. 3   E. 4

7.   This game has _____ Nash equilibrium/equilibria.
       A. 0   B. 1   C. 2   D. 3   E. 4

8.   This game
       A.   might be a prisoner's dilemma but we do not have enough information to judge.
       B.   is not a prisoner's dilemma since there is no crime involved.
       C.   is a prisoner's dilemma because both players have dominated strategies.
       D.   is not a prisoner's dilemma because both players do not have dominated strategies.
       E.   is a prisoner's dilemma because the equilibrium payoffs are smaller than other payoffs.

9.   When a group of firms agrees to restrict production with the goal of earning economic profits, this group is called
       A.   a pure monopoly.   D.   a group of monopolistic competitors.
       B.   an oligopoly.   E.   imperfect competition.
       C.   a cartel.

10.   The tit-for-tat strategy applies only applies to a prisoner's dilemma that
       A.   is played one time.
       B.   is repeated.

C.   involves small children.
D.   has no Nash equilibrium.
E.   has more than one Nash equilibrium.

11.   Two children are accused of breaking a window. If they adhere to a tit-for-tat strategy, when the first child _____ breaking the window the first time she is asked then the other child will _____ breaking the window the second time he is asked.
    A.   denies; confess to   D.   confesses to; confess to
    B.   confesses to; deny   E.   accuses the other child of; confess to
    C.   denies; accuses the other child of

12.   A game in which two players choose their strategies sequentially is best represented by a
    A.   supply and demand diagram.   D.   strategic possibilities curve.
    B.   payoff matrix.   E.   decision tree.
    C.   production possibilities curve.

Use the following information for problems 13, 14, 15 and 16: Harry and Sally are at a diner and are about to order. Harry is either going to order a sandwich and coffee or just coffee. Sally is going to have pie with ice cream or pie without ice cream. They will give their orders to the server in sequence, and since they know each other well the following decision tree represents the utility they will receive given their possible choices:

X:
Harry orders a sandwich and coffee

Y:
Sally orders pie with ice cream

Z:
Sally orders pie without ice cream

25 for Harry
225 for Sally

300 for Harry
200 for Sally

75 for Harry
150 for Sally

125 for Harry
125 for Sally

13.   Given these payoffs, we can predict that
    A.   Harry will always choose the upper branch.
    B.   Sally will always pick the lower branch of X.
    C.   Harry will always choose the lower branch.
    D.   Sally will always pick the lower branch of Z.
    E.   Harry does not know whether to order a sandwich or not.
14.   Given these payoffs, we can predict that
    A.   Sally will always pick the lower branch of either Y or Z.
    B.   Harry will quit the game.

C.   Sally will pick the lower branch of Y.
D.   Harry comes out the same regardless of what Sally does.
E.   Sally will pick the upper branch of Z.

15.   Given this decision tree, the equilibrium outcome of this game will be for Harry to
       choose the _____ and Sally to choose _____.
       A.   lower branch of Y; Y   D.   upper branch of Z; Z
       B.   upper branch of Y; Z   E.   upper branch of Y; X
       C.   lower branch of Z; Y

16.   If, before Harry chose, Sally could make a credible commitment to choose either the top
       or bottom branch when her turn came, Harry would choose the _____ and Sally would
       choose the _____.
       A.   top branch at X; bottom branch at Y
       B.   top branch at X; top branch at Y
       C.   bottom branch at X; bottom branch at Z
       D.   bottom branch at X; top branch at Z
       E.   bottom branch at X; bottom branch at X

17.   Suppose that two players cannot achieve their goals because they are unable to make a
       credible threat or promise. This situation is called
       A.   the prisoner's dilemma.   D.   a Nash equilibrium.
       B.   a commitment problem.   E.   a payoff.
       C.   a dominant strategy.

18.   To solve a commitment problem,
       A.   there must be a change in the players' material incentives.
       B.   it is impossible to use changes in the players' psychological incentives.
       C.   there must be a change in the players' psychological incentives.
       D.   there can be a change in the players' material incentives, their psychological
             incentives or both.
       E.   there can be either a change in the players' material incentives or their
             psychological incentives but never both.

19.   Which of the following actions is consistent with the assumption of narrowly self
       interested individuals?
       A.   Leaving a tip at a restaurant in which you will never eat ever again.
       B.   Spending $5000 to sue someone over a $500 accident.
       C.   Holding the door open for someone you never meet again.
       D.   Buying a car at the sticker price because the salesperson is a friend of yours.
       E.   Negotiating for the lowest price on a home.

20.   Using psychological incentives to solve a commitment problem will not be very effective
       in a game that is played
       A.   repeatedly between two strangers.
       B.   only once between two family members who live in the same home.

C. repeatedly between two family members who live in the same home.
D. only once between two strangers.
E. repeatedly between friends who live in the same apartment.

Short Answer Problems
(Answers and solutions are given at the end of the chapter.)

1. Understanding the basic elements of a game

A town has two donut shops, Mr. Donut and Ms. Donut. They currently sell donuts for 50 cents per donut and each shop earns revenue of $1,000 per week. Mr. Donut is thinking about charging 45 cents per donut, which he figures will increase his revenue to $1,200 per week. If Ms. Donut's price stays at 50 cents per donut after Mr. Donut cuts his price, she will earn $500 per week. If Ms. Donut cuts her price to 45 cents, her total revenue will rise to $1,200 per week if Mr. Donut continues to charge 50 cents. Mr. Donut will collect $500 in revenue if he keeps his price at 50 cents while Ms. Donut lowers hers to 45 cents. Mr. Donut and Ms. Donut will receive $900 each in total revenue if they both lower their price to 45 cents.

Use the payoff matrix given below to construct the basic elements of this game:

A. Write the names of the two players in the payoff matrix.
B. Write the two strategies available to each player in the payoff matrix.
C. Write the payoffs for each player given the strategy of the other in the proper cells of the payoff matrix.

2. Working with a payoff matrix to find dominant strategies, dominated strategies and Nash equilibrium.

St. Benedict and St. Scholastica were brother and sister and each had their own monastery. Once a year Benedict would bring his monks to Scholastica's monastery and the monks and nuns would spend the day discussing the splendors and mysteries of their faith. On one of these occasions the conversation was going so well that Scholastica asked Benedict and his monks to stay through the night and talk. Benedict was horrified; he felt that he had to return to his monastery! Scholastica considers praying for rain to keep Benedict from leaving. Here is the payoff matrix for this situation; numbers are measures of happiness:

		Scholastica	
		Pray for rain	Do not pray for rain
Benedict	Monks stay overnight:	Benedict: 100 Scholastica: 100	Benedict: 0 Scholastica: 50
	Monks leave immediately:	Benedict: 50 Scholastica: 0	Benedict: 50 Scholastica: 50

A. If Scholastica prays for rain but the monks leave then she receives (0/100) _____ and Benedict receives (50/100) _____.

B. Benedict concludes that staying is (a dominant/a dominated/neither a dominant nor dominated) _____ strategy and that leaving is a (a dominant / a dominated neither a dominant nor dominated) _____ strategy.

C. Scholastica concludes that praying for rain is (a dominant/a dominated/neither a dominant nor dominated) _____ strategy and that leaving is a (a dominant / a dominated /neither a dominant nor dominated) _____ strategy.

D. Does this game have at least one equilibrium? _____ Does this game have two equilibria? _____ If yes, what are they? _____.

IV. Becoming an Economic Naturalist: Case Study

You have probably played the game "Rock, paper scissors." Suppose that you eat dinner with a friend and then play this game in order to decide who will pay the $25 bill for your two meals. Construct a payoff matrix for this game. Is there a dominant strategy for this game? Is there a Nash equilibrium?

(Game theory appears in many areas of popular culture; see the examples at www.gametheory.net, developed and maintained by Professor Mike Shor of the Owen Graduate School of Management at Vanderbilt University.)

Answer:

V. Self-Test Solutions
Key Terms

1. d	6. e	11. g
2. m	7. c	12. f
3. k	8. a	13. i
4. l	9. b	14. j
5. o	10. n	15. h

Multiple-Choice Questions

1. E	6. A	11. D	16. A
2. D	7. B	12. E	17. B
3. A	8. D	13. E	18. D
4. B	9. C	14. C	19. E
5. B	10. B	15. D	20. D

Short Answer Problems

1.

		Mr. Donut	
		Keep price at 50 cents	Cut price to 45 cents
Ms. Donut	Keep price at 50 cents	Mr. Donut: $1000 Ms. Donut: $1000	Mr. Donut: $1350 Ms. Donut: $500
	Cut price to 45 cents	Mr. Donut: $1350 Ms. Donut: $500	Mr. Donut: $900 Ms. Donut: $900

2. A.   0; 50
   B.   neither a dominant nor dominated; neither a dominant nor dominated
   C.   neither a dominant nor dominated; neither a dominant nor dominated
   B.   yes; yes, {Pray for rain, Stay} and {Do not pray for rain, Leave}

Chapter 12
Externalities and Property Rights

I. Pretest: What Do You Really Know?
Circle the letter that corresponds to the best answer. (Answers appear immediately after the final question).

1. An external benefit from an activity
   A. is reaped only by those who directly participate in the activity.
   B. is reaped only by those who do not directly participate in the activity.
   C. ensures that the social demand curve and the private demand curve are the same.
   D. happens only outdoors.
   E. happens only outside of a company, not within it.

2. Which of the following is an example of an activity with an external cost?
   A. You own cats and you let them run free in a neighborhood that has a problem with mice.
   B. You have a roommate and you keep your area of the apartment clean.
   C. You listen to music using headphones.
   D. You buy a new computer and you have to buy a case to carry it in.
   E. Smoking with a group of friends who do not smoke and do not like smoking.

3. A market that is subject to an externality will produce an output level that is
   A. greater than the optimal level.   B. exactly equal to the optimal level.
   C. lower than the optimal level.
   D. either greater or lower than the optimal level depending on whether the externality is an external cost or an external benefit.
   E. exactly equal to the optimal level but at a price higher than the market equilibrium price.

4. The Coase theorem states that
   A. Government action is needed to remedy externalities.
   B. Markets are unaffected by externalities.
   C. If negotiations are very costly, people will come to an agreement about reducing an externality.
   D. If negotiations are costless, people will come to an agreement about reducing an externality.
   E. Government actions are ineffective in remedying externalities.

5. Speed limits on roads are a _____ the external costs of driving.
    A. private, non-governmental solution to
    B. legal remedy for
    C. unnecessary in order to deal with
    D. mix of (A), (B) and (C) for dealing with
    E. policy that creates

6. A company dumps waste into a river and kills fish. If the waste generates an external cost of $10 per gallon of water discharged, then
    A. the external cost can be remedied by a $10 per gallon subsidy on discharges.
    B. the external cost can be remedied by doing nothing since the invisible hand will take care of it.
    C. the price of fish will rise by an amount to offset the external cost and this will compensate the fishing industry.
    D. the external cost can be remedied by a $10 per gallon tax on discharges.
    E. the company will compensate the fishing industry if negotiations are costly.

7. A compensating subsidy used to rectify an external benefit from consuming a good will
    A. cause the supply curve to shift up and reduce the quantity of the good produced.
    B. cause the demand curve to shift up and increase the quantity of the good produced.
    C. cause the supply curve to shift down and increase the quantity of the good produced.
    D. cause the demand curve to shift down and decrease the quantity of the good produced.
    E. have no effect on the quantity of the good produced.

8. The tragedy of the commons refers to
    A. the tendency for a resource that has no price to be used until its marginal benefit rises to infinity.
    B. the tendency for a resource that has no price to be used until its marginal benefit falls to zero.
    C. the tendency of private ownership to cause marginal benefits and marginal costs to be greater than zero.
    D. the tendency for really bad lunches to be served in the student commons.
    E. the tendency for markets without externalities to produce too little of a good.

9. Positional externalities
    A. only occur in professional sports.
    B. arise in situations where absolute performance is the criteria for success.
    C. cause people to invest too little in performance enhancement.
    D. arise when an increase is one person's performance reduces the expected reward of the other participants.
    E. arise when one person is taller than another person.

10. Social norms are
    A. completely ineffectual in solving positional arms races.
    B. requirements that people wear certain types of clothing.
    C. sometimes an informal solution to positional arms races.
    D. Synonyms for positional externalities.

E. Rarely obeyed in most societies.

Solutions and Feedback to Pretest

The answers to the pretest are provided below along with the relevant Learning Objective from the Key Point Review. We strongly recommend that you take the time to review the appropriate material for each question you answered incorrectly.

Correct Answer	Learning Objective
1. B	1
2. E	1
3. D	1
4. D	2
5. B	2
6. D	3
7. B	3
8. B	4
9. D	5
10. C	5

II. Key Point Review
The Forest

This chapter focuses on an issue that has been in the background since Chapter 1: externalities. The Efficiency Principle states that market equilibrium is efficient, *assuming that all of the relevant benefits from consumption and all of the relevant costs of production are included.* We now analyze market equilibria in which this assumption is not true.

The central questions you need to be able to answer are:
- What are externalities and how do they affect resource allocation?
- How can externalities and their effects be remedied?
- What is the optimal amount of an externality?
- What is the Tragedy of the Commons and how is private ownership a way of preventing this?
- What are positional externalities, what are their effects and how can they be remedied?

The Trees

Learning Objective 1: Define the terms external cost, external benefit and externality. Analyze how externalities affect resource allocation.

An **external cost** a cost from an activity that falls on those who do not pursue the activity. Watery eyes from being in a smoky restaurant even though you do not smoke are an example of this. An **external benefit** is a benefit from an activity received by people who do not pursue the activity. If you avoid getting a cold because the people around you wash their hands and do other things to keep from getting a cold, and not because of anything you did to prevent a cold from coming on, you have received an external benefit. We say that an activity generates an **externality** when it creates an external benefit or external cost.

> Note: The text uses the term "activity" to mean any action that someone might take; this includes producing a good or buying a good. The authors are trying to be as general as possible in their discussion.

Externalities affect resource allocation by encouraging people to either carry out too much of an activity or too little. This is because the people affected by the externalities will not be able to accurately apply the Cost-Benefit Principle; either the costs or the benefits or both will be inaccurate and the decision reached will be incorrect.

We can easily add external costs and benefits to the supply and demand model to analyze how externalities affect market equilibrium. External costs cause the private supply curve to be below the social supply curve (i.e. the supply curve that includes the external cost) and thus the market produces too much of a good and generates a deadweight loss. (See Figure 12.1 in the text for the relevant graphs.) Similarly, an external benefit will cause the market to produce too little of a good because the social demand curve (i.e. the demand curve that includes the external benefit) is above the private demand curve. This too generates a deadweight loss; see Figure 12.2 in the text for an illustration.

Learning Objective 2: Understand how externalities can be remedied either through private agreements or through formal, legal means.
The presence of externalities means that market equilibrium is not efficient. How then can resources be allocated efficiently? The **Coase theorem** is the proposition that a group of people can always arrive at efficient solutions to the problems caused by externalities if at no cost individuals can negotiate the purchase and sale of the right to perform activities that cause externalities.

> Note: Ronald H. Coase was awarded the 1991 Nobel Prize in economics for this concept. Coase writes the idea was "named and formulated by [George] Stigler, although it is based on work of mine." See http://nobelprize.org/economics/laureates/1991/coase-lecture.html for this quotation and Coase's discussion of the Coase theorem.

The central assumption of the Coase theorem is, of course, that there are no costs of negotiating. This is clearly not the case in many situations and thus formal, legal remedies such as laws and regulations must be employed. Examples of these are myriad and include environmental laws, and traffic regulations.

Learning Objective 3: Show how externalities can be remedied using compensatory taxes and subsidies. Analyze why the optimal quantity of a negative externality is rarely zero.

The dollar value of external costs and benefits can often be measured even when there are costs to negotiating that keep the Coase theorem from ameliorating the externality. This information *can* be used to levy taxes or furnish subsidies in order to use the market to create a social optimum. This provides an alternative to law and regulations as a solution to externalities.

For example: suppose that burning gasoline in cars and trucks generates an external cost of $1 per gallon. A $1 per gallon tax on gasoline will shift the supply of gasoline up by $1 and make the market equilibrium quantity equal to the socially optimal quantity of gasoline. See Figure 12.3 for a graphical presentation of this type of policy and Figure 12.4 for a compensatory subsidy.

Hint: The effects of taxes on equilibrium prices and quantities were discussed in Chapter 7. You should review this material if you do not remember it.

An important implication of this analysis is that to remedy an externality does not mean that the activity producing the externality must be eliminated entirely nor does the externality itself have to be completely eliminated. Rather, the costs or benefits of the externality need to be properly included in the supply and demand curves for the good or service being produced. This flies in the face of many people's preconceptions, perhaps even your own.

Learning Objective 4: Discuss the tragedy of the commons and how private ownership helps solve this problem. Understand why private ownership is sometimes impractical and what the implications of this will be.

The **tragedy of the commons** is the tendency for a resource that has no price to be used until its marginal benefit falls to zero. You can clearly understand the tragedy of the commons by applying the Cost-Benefit Principle and the Scarcity Principle. The Cost-Benefit Principle implies that a person will use a resource that has no price until marginal benefit is driven to zero. The "tragedy" arises because people forget or ignore the Scarcity Principle, i.e. the idea that to have more of one thing usually means having less of another.

Note: Garret J. Hardin formulated the idea of the tragedy of the commons in an article published in 1968. You can learn more about Hardin and his writings (including the original article "The Tragedy of the Commons") at http://www.garretthardinsociety.org/index.html

Private ownership can help solve this problem; if someone has clear title to a resource they have an incentive to accurately measure the costs of using a resource and will thus charge a price that is not equal to zero. The amount of the resources that is used will fall as the price rises above zero and the marginal benefit will rise above zero as well.

Unfortunately, assigning property rights (i.e. clear title to ownership of a resource) is often difficult and thus the tragedy of the commons becomes a reality. Codfish, for example, have been over fished in the North Atlantic since it is almost impossible to say who "owns" a school of fish.

Learning Objective 5: Explain what positional externalities are and give examples. Discuss the need for positional arms control agreements and how social norms can be used in these situations.

A **positional externality** is an externality that comes about in situations where rewards depend on relative performance and when an increase in one person's performance reduces the expected reward to another person. Track events, for example, are susceptible to positional externalities since the winner of a race is simply the first person to cross the finish line. This means that an athlete who uses a new training technique or a new performance enhancing drug will cause a positional externality.

To keep up with the first athlete, the other runners will need to embrace the new training technique or start taking the new performance enhancing drug. This "keeping up with the Joneses" effect is known as a **positional arms race**. More formally, a positional arms race is a series of mutually offsetting investments in performance enhancement induced by a positional externality. The participants can stop this arms race by agreeing to a **positional arms control agreement** in which contestants attempt to limit mutually offsetting investments in performance enhancement. So, for example, the International Olympic Committee has banned the use of certain performance enhancing drugs in an attempt to stop a positional arms race involving these substances.

Social norms can also play a role in solving positional externalities. For example, you may be able to buy a more expensive car but that might encourage your friends to buy one too and they cannot afford it. So, a feeling of concern towards your friends might prevent you to from creating the positional externality (i.e. buying the better car).

III. Self-Test

Key Terms
Match the term in the right-hand column with the appropriate definition in the left-hand column by placing the letter of the term in the blank in front of its definition. (Answers are given at the end of the chapter.)

1. ____ The tendency for a resource that has no price to be used until its marginal benefit falls to zero

a. Coase theorem

2. ____ A series of mutually offsetting investments in performance enhancement induced by a positional externality.

b. external benefit

3. ____ A benefit from an activity received by people who do not pursue the activity.

c. external cost

4. ____ A synonym for an external benefit.

d. externality

5. ____ An agreement in which contestants attempt to limit mutually offsetting investments in performance enhancement.

e. negative externality

6. ____ The proposition that a group of people can always arrive at efficient solutions to the problems caused by externalities if at no cost individuals can negotiate the purchase and sale of the right to perform activities that cause externalities.

f. positional arms control agreement

7. _____ An external cost or benefit of an activity.   g. positional arms race

8. _____ An externality that comes about in situations in which   h. positional externality
reward depends on relative performance and an increase in one
person's performance reduces the expected reward of another.

9. _____ A cost from an activity that falls on those who do not   i. positive externality
pursue the activity.

10. _____ A synonym for an external cost.   j. tragedy of the commons

Multiple-Choice Questions
Circle the letter that corresponds to the best answer. (Answers are given at the end of the chapter.)

1.   If you hear music that you enjoy playing from your neighbor's apartment, this is a(n)
      A.   positional externality to you.   D.   external benefit to your neighbor.
      B.   external benefit to you.   E.   external cost to your neighbor.
      C.   external cost to you.

2.   An externality is
      A.   an external cost only.   D.   something that happens outside.
      B.   an external benefit only.   E.   a theoretical curiosity.
      C.   either an external cost or an external benefit.

Use the following information for problems 3, 4 and 5: vaccinating children against polio reduces the incidence of polio in two ways: by protecting the child who is vaccinated and by reducing the chance that someone who is not vaccinated will contract the disease from those around them.

3.   If you are someone who is vaccinated against polio, then you
      A.   create an external benefit.   D.   must bear an external cost.
      B.   generate an external cost.   E.   will not create any externalities.
      C.   receive an external benefit.

4.   If you are someone who is not vaccinated against polio and live with people who are, then you
      A.   create an external benefit.   D.   must bear an external cost.
      B.   generate an external cost.   E.   will not create any externalities.
      C.   receive an external benefit.

5.   This situation will lead to
      A.   too many people being vaccinated compared to the social optimum.
      B.   too few people being vaccinated compared to the social optimum.
      C.   the socially optimal number of people being vaccinated.
      D.   a price of vaccine that is too high.
      E.   none of (A), (B), (C) nor (D) happening.

6.   Suppose that generating electricity produces a negative externality when coal is burned to produce it. This will lead to a situation in which the
   A.   price of electricity is too high.
   B.   equilibrium quantity of electricity produced is below the socially optimal quantity.
   C.   equilibrium quantity of electricity produced is at the socially optimal quantity.
   D.   equilibrium quantity of electricity produced is above the socially optimal quantity.
   E.   the private supply curve for electricity is above the social supply curve.

7.   Suppose that after an externality is corrected you observe the equilibrium price and equilibrium quantity of the good that generated the externality both increase. The externality must have been a(n)
   A.   external cost.
   B.   positional externality.
   C.   example of the Coase theorem.
   D.   external benefit.
   E.   insufficient information to determine.

8.   Which of the following factors would make it easier to apply the Coase Theorem to solve an externality?
   A.   The market supply and demand curves reflect all relevant costs and benefits.
   B.   The gains from reducing the externality are small compared to the costs of negotiating a solution.
   C.   The gains from reducing the externality are high compared to the costs of negotiating a solution.
   D.   The people involved cannot monitor each others actions to ensure they obey an agreement.
   E.   None of these factors make it easier to apply the Coase Theorem.

9.   Most states require public school districts to offer kindergarten to young children. If there is a belief that attending kindergarten generates an externality, then this mandate is an example of
   A.   intrusive state government mandates.
   B.   a legal remedy for an externality.
   C.   a private solution for an externality, as suggested by the Coase theorem.
   D.   a government solution of an externality along the lines of the Coase theorem.
   E.   an external benefit.

Use the graph below for problems 10, 11 and 12: the graph below represents a market in which an external cost is generated by the good being bought and sold.

10.   _____ is caused by the external cost.
   A.   Supply B
   B.   The demand curve
   C.   The difference between Supply A and Supply B
   D.   The slope of the demand curve
   E.   The slope of the supply curves

11.   The external cost will result in a market quantity of _____ and a socially optimal quantity of _____.
   A. Q_A; Q_B B. Q_B; Q_A C. Q_B, Q_B D. Q_A, Q_A E. can't tell; can't tell

12.   The effects of the externality can be remedied by
   A.   waiting for the invisible hand to appear.
   B.   imposing a per-unit subsidy equal to the vertical distance between Supply A and Supply B.
   C.   imposing a per-unit subsidy equal to the horizontal distance between Supply A and Supply B.
   D.   imposing a per-unit tax equal to the horizontal distance between Supply A and Supply B.
   E.   imposing a per-unit tax equal to the vertical distance between Supply A and Supply B.

Use the graph below for problems 13, 14 and 15: the graph below represents a market in which an external benefit is generated by the good being bought and sold.

13. _____ is caused by the external cost.
    A.   Demand A
    B.   The supply curve
    C.   The difference between Demand A and Demand B
    D.   The slope of the demand curves
    E.   The slope of the supply curve

14. The external cost will result in a market quantity of _____ and a socially optimal quantity of _____.
    A. Q_A; Q_B B. Q_B; Q_A C. Q_B, Q_B D. Q_A, Q_A E. can't tell; can't tell

15. The effects of the externality can be remedied by
    A.   creating an external cost.
    B.   imposing a per-unit subsidy equal to the vertical distance between Demand A and Demand B.
    C.   imposing a per-unit subsidy equal to the horizontal distance between Demand A and Demand B.
    D.   imposing a per-unit tax equal to the horizontal distance between Demand A and Demand B.
    E.   imposing a per-unit tax equal to the vertical distance between Demand A and Demand B.

16.   Suppose that the noise generated by a grocery store is quite loud and bothers the people living nearby. If the marginal cost of reducing the noise is positive, then
        A.   the store should be required to eliminate the noise.
        B.   the optimal amount of noise will be greater than zero.
        C.   the optimal amount of noise is zero.
        D.   the Coase theorem is not applicable.
        E.   there is no means of reducing the noise and the neighbors will have to live with it.

Use the following information for problems 17 and 18: You observe that public land near your home is being ruined due to excessive recreational use.

17.   This is an example of
        A.   an external benefit to you.
        B.   an external cost that you are generating.
        C.   a positional externality.
        D.   the tragedy of the commons.
        E.   a legal remedy for an externality.

18.   A solution to this problem would be:
        A.   private ownership by a group of concerned citizens.
        B.   public ownership with a fee charged for recreational use.
        C.   either (A) or (B).
        D.   neither (A) nor (B).
        E.   leave things alone and they will take care of themselves.

Use the following information for problems 19 and 20: Suppose that an employer announces that he will henceforth judge his employees' abilities by who arrives for work the earliest.

19.   Suppose that the day after the announcement one person arrives 10 minutes earlier than she is required to do so by the employer. This will generate
        A.   a tragedy of the commons.
        B.   a positional externality.
        C.   a positional arms control agreement.
        D.   an externality of unknown type.
        E.   no further change in behavior by any employee.

20.   An example of a positional arms race touched off by the announcement would be
        A.   employees arriving earlier and earlier to work.
        B.   employees arriving later and later to work.
        C.   employees bringing arms to work.
        D.   the employer arriving later and later to work.
        E.   none of the above.

Short Answer Problems
(Answers and solutions are given at the end of the chapter.)

1. External costs and external benefits in the same market.
The supply and demand curves below show the private demand and private supply for a good.

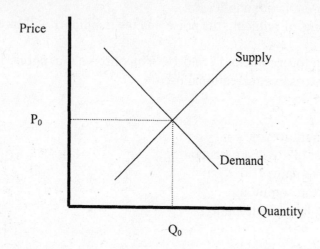

A. Suppose that there is an external cost to the production of this good. Show how this affects the demand curve, the supply curve or both.

B. Suppose that there is an external benefit to the production of this good. Show how this affects the demand curve, the supply curve or both.

C. The existence of both an external cost and an external benefit will lead to a market quantity that is (higher than / lower than / indeterminate relative to) _____ the socially optimal quantity.

D. The existence of both an external cost and an external benefit will lead to a market price that is (higher than / lower than / indeterminate relative to) _____ the socially optimal price.

E. Describe two methods for dealing with these externalities: _____
_____
_____
_____
_____

2. Externalities and deadweight loss

The table below provides information on the private demand and supply curves for a good:

Price	Quantity demanded	Quantity supplied
0	300	0
50	250	100
100	200	200
150	150	300
200	100	400
250	50	500
300	0	600

A. The equilibrium price in this market is _____ and the equilibrium quantity is _____.

B. Suppose that the production of this good creates an external cost of 150 per unit. Construct the social supply curve by filling in the two empty columns in the table below.

Quantity supplied	Price without external cost	External cost per unit	Price with external cost
0	0		
100	50		
200	100		
300	150		
400	200		
500	250		
600	300		

C. Using the supply curve in part (A) and the demand curve given in the first part of the problem, find the socially optimal price _____ and socially optimal quantity

_____.

D. The deadweight loss caused by the externality is _____.

IV. Becoming an Economic Naturalist: Case Study

An economic naturalist wrote:

The only practical remedy [to the huge increase in SUVs being driven], given the undeniable fact that driving bulky, polluting vehicles causes damage to others, is to give ourselves an incentive to take this damage into account when deciding what vehicles to buy.

No one complains of intrusive government regulations when we tax trucks according to weight, because a truck's weight is a good indicator of how much damage it does to our roads. Pegging passenger vehicle taxes to weight, emission levels and fuel economy can be recommended on similar practical grounds ("Feeling Crash-Resistant in an S.U.V." *New York Times*, May 16, 2000.)

What kind of externality is discussed in this passage? Is it a positional externality? To what types of solutions, in general, is the writer appealing? For example, is the writer appealing to the Coase Theorem? Legal remedies? Positional arms control agreements? Social norms?

Answer:

V. Self-Test Solutions

Key Terms

1. j	6. a
2. g	7. d
3. b	8. h
4. i	9. c
5. f	10. e

Multiple-Choice Questions

1. A	6. D	11. B	16. B
2. C	7. D	12. E	17. D
3. A	8. C	13. C	18. C
4. C	9. B	14. A	19. B
5. B	10. C	15. B	20. A

Short Answer Problems

1.

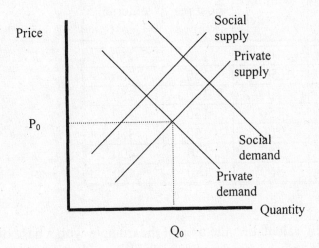

A. Shifts the supply curve to the left as shown above.
B. Shifts the demand curve to the right as shown above.
C. Note first that the way this graph is drawn the socially optimal quantity is above the equilibrium quantity; however, if the social demand were shifted out less and the social supply were shifted back more the opposite would be true. Second, no matter how far the social demand and social supply are shifted the socially optimal price is above the equilibrium price.
D. One method for dealing with this problem would be to have the producers voluntarily subsidize the buyers for each unit they buy. They could do this by including this subsidy as a cost of production. A second way to address these externalities is for the government to levy a tax on the producers and use the proceeds (and more money if needed) to subsidize the buyers.

2.   A.   100; 200
     B.

Quantity supplied	Price without external cost	External cost per unit	Price with external cost
0	0	150	150
100	50	150	200
200	100	150	250
300	150	150	300
400	200	150	350
500	250	150	400
600	300	150	450

     C.   200; 100
     D.   7,500; this is found by calculating the area of the triangle with a base of 150 (the size of the externality) times a height of 100 (the difference between the socially optimal quantity and the equilibrium quantity.

Chapter 13
The Economics of Information

I. Pretest: What Do You Really Know?
Circle the letter that corresponds to the best answer. (Answers appear immediately after the final question).

1. Intermediaries play an important role in markets because they
   A. offer jobs to lots of college graduates.
   B. convey information to buyers but not sellers.
   C. collect information on buyers for sellers and not vice versa.
   D. collect and convey information to buyers and sellers.
   E. allow buyers and sellers to hide information from one another.

2. A person engaged in rational search will gather information until
   A. the marginal cost of gathering information is zero.
   B. the marginal benefit of gathering information is zero.
   C. the total benefit of gathering information is equal to the total cost of gathering information.
   D. the total benefit of gathering information exceeds the total cost of gathering information.
   E. the marginal benefit of gathering information is equal to the marginal cost of gather information.

3. The free-rider problem refers to an incentive problem in which
   A. too little of a good is produced because those who do not pay for it cannot be excluded from using it.
   B. too much of a good is produced because those who do not pay for it cannot be excluded from using it.
   C. too little of a good is produced because those who pay for it are excluded from using it.
   D. too much of a good is produced because those who pay for it are excluded from using it.
   E. too much of a good is produced because people are willing to pay too high of a price.

4. Suppose that you buy a lottery ticket. "You have a 5% chance of winning $100" is printed on each ticket. If you purchase a ticket and tickets cost $1 each, the expected value of this gamble is
   A. $1   B. $2   C. $3   D. $4   E. $5

5. A fair gamble is a gamble in which
   A. everyone who accepts the gamble wins.
   B. only one person who accepts the gamble wins.
   C. the expected value of the gamble is zero.
   D. the expected value of the gamble is greater than zero.
   E. the probabilities of the gamble are all equal.

6. Lester is searching for an apartment. He works at a job that pays $15 per hour and he will have to take one hour off from work to visit an apartment. He is a risk-averse person. To make it worth his while, the expected value of the benefit of seeing another apartment must be
   A. greater than $15.   D. greater than zero.
   B. equal to $15.   E. equal to zero.
   C. less than $15.

7. Billie is at shopping at the farmers' market for fresh vegetables. If she has less information about the quality of the vegetables than those who are selling them, we call this a situation in which there is
   A. risk neutrality.
   B. risk aversion.
   C. a fair gamble.
   D. a rational search.
   E. asymmetric information.

8. The example of good quality cars not being offered by sellers in the used car market due to asymmetric information is known as
   A. a fair gamble.
   B. a rational search.
   C. the lemons problem.
   D. the costly-to-fake principle.
   E. the problem of disappearing political discourse.

9. Wearing clothes that are known to be expensive in order to send a signal to others is known as
   A. the lemons problem.
   B. conspicuous consumption.
   C. statistical discrimination.
   D. risk-neutrality.
   E. moral hazard.

10. Marshall has flood insurance and takes no special precautions to prevent flood damage when he hears that there is a high chance of a flood in his area. This is an example of
   A. adverse selection.
   B. conspicuous consumption.
   C. risk-neutrality.
   D. statistical discrimination.
   E. moral hazard.

Solutions and Feedback to Pretest
The answers to the pretest are provided below along with the relevant Learning Objective from the Key Point Review. We strongly recommend that you take the time to review the appropriate material for each question you answered incorrectly.

Correct Answer	Learning Objective
1. D	1
2. E	2
3. A	2
4. D	3
5. C	3
6. A	3
7. E	4
8. C	4
9. B	5
10. E	6

II. Key Point Review
The Forest

This chapter focuses on the economics of information. The economics of information is the study of information itself as a resource. As in the previous chapter, you will use tools that you have already studied (in this case, the Cost-Benefit Principle) and develop new skills.

The central questions you need to be able to answer are:
- What role in a market is played by information?
- What is rational search and how is it applied to finding the optimal amount of information?
- What is asymmetric information and how does it lead to the lemons problem?
- How are conspicuous consumption and statistical discrimination responses to asymmetric information?
- What are the causes and effects of adverse selection and moral hazard in insurance markets?

The Trees

Learning Objective 1: Understand the role information plays in markets.
We have assumed, up to this point, that buyers and sellers have all the information that they need to operate in a market and that no one agent has more information than any other agent. This is

not, however, the case in many real-world situations. Information itself is thus a resource that buyers and sellers must acquire and use.

An important source of information for buyers and sellers is a person or firm that specializes in gathering and disseminating useful information. These agents are known as **middlemen** or **intermediaries**. Recent estimates put the value of the amount of output produced by intermediaries at roughly 25% of total U.S. production.[1] Intermediaries increase total economic surplus by allowing buyers and sellers to make transactions that they might not otherwise be able to complete.

Learning Objective 2: Explain the concept of rational search. Use this concept to define the optimal amount of information. Define the free-rider problem and how it applies to information. Discuss two guidelines for rational search.

The process of finding information is called **search** by economists. A person engages in **rational search** when they apply the Cost-Benefit Principle to search. The person has obtained the **optimal amount of information** when the marginal benefit of acquiring additional information is equal to the marginal cost of acquiring additional information. This process can be illustrated with a graph; see Figure 13.1 in the text.

> Hint: You may want to review the Cost-Benefit Principle (in Chapter 1) at this point since you will be applying it often in this chapter.

The **free-rider problem** is an incentive problem in which too little of a good is produced because those who do not pay for it cannot be excluded from using it. Information is especially susceptible to this problem; once an optimal amount of information has been gathered it usually becomes available to others and they have no incentive to pay for it when they have received it for little or no cost. For example, specialty electronics stores often provide knowledgeable service to customers about their products but sell their products at higher prices than large national chain stores. There is an incentive for customers to browse specialty electronics stores and learn what they need to know about a particular piece of equipment (a stereo receiver or MP3 player, for example) and then buy it for a lower price at the national chain store. This leads to too few people providing intelligent service since there is no profit to be made from it.

The Cost-Benefit Principle suggests two general guidelines for rational search. First, it will be rational to search longer for more expensive items since the benefits of search will be relatively high. (If they were not, then the searcher would not be willing to pay a high price for the item!) Second, a rational search will be shorter the higher is the opportunity cost of the information. If an agent spends too long searching the opportunity cost will get so high that the benefit will never exceed the cost at the margin.

Learning Objective 3: Define the following terms: expected value of a gamble, fair gamble, risk-neutral person, risk-averse person. Apply these concepts to the gamble inherent in search and the commitment problem.

---

[1] This was originally pointed out in Daniel F. Spulber, "Market Microstructure and Intermediation." *Journal of Economic Perspectives* 10 (Summer 1996): 135-152.

Rational search inherently involves uncertain outcomes. We can examine this problem systematically by framing search in terms of a gamble. A **gamble** involves specifying all of the possible outcomes of some activity along with the probability of each possible outcome. The value of the gamble is given by the **expected value of a gamble,** which is equal to taking each possible outcome of a gamble, multiplying it by its probability of occurring and then summing all of these together over all possible outcomes.

For example: "A bird in the hand is worth two in the bush" is an old aphorism that expresses the conundrum of rational search. Suppose that you are bird watcher and you can either go to a place where you will see a particular bird with complete certainty, or you can go to another place where you might see two birds. The probability of seeing the two birds is ½; suppose further that if you do not see two birds you will see none and thus the probability of seeing no birds is ½.

The gamble is whether or not to go to the place where you can see two birds with uncertainty. If we multiply each event (seeing two birds, seeing no birds) by their respective probabilities (½ and ½), and add them together and then subtract the bird that were not able to see we have the expected value of the gamble: $(½)*2 + (½)*(0) - 1 = 0$. This is an example of a **fair gamble** since the expected value is exactly zero. That is, on average a person will see one bird regardless of which place they choose to go.

A person who accepts a gamble that is fair or better is called a **risk-neutral person**. However, there are people who will not accept a fair gamble and must receive an expected value greater than zero in order to accept a gamble; such a person is called a **risk-averse person**. In the bird watching example, a risk-averse person would want a better than 50-50 chance of seeing two birds in order to forsake the certain single bird. A risk-neutral person would be willing to take the gamble with the 50-50 probability.

The **commitment problem** arises in this context because of uncertainty. The idea is that in the future a gamble with better odds might appear and this leads to agents breaking agreements that they have made in the past. One way to deal with this problem is to write contracts in which there are large penalties for breaking the agreements, large enough that they outweigh any benefit from breaking the contract.

Learning Objective 4: Define the term asymmetric information. Explain how this notion is the basis for the lemons model.
Asymmetric information refers to situations where buyers and sellers are not equally well informed about the characteristics of the goods they are trading.

The **lemons model** is built on a particular example of asymmetric information in which buyers have less information than sellers regarding the good they are trading. This means there is a probability that the buyer will end up with a good of lower quality (a "lemon"). A risk-averse buyer can compensate for this possibility by offering a lower price than they would have had there been no possibility of buying a lemon. But, if they lower the price they are willing to pay this means that those units that have a marginal cost above this price (i.e. a good that is not a lemon) will not be offered for sale! The good quality units are driven out of the market and buyers are left only with the lemons.

Hint: The best example of the lemons model is the used car market. Examples 13.7 and 13.8 in the text explain this very well and to test your understanding be sure to work through Exercise 13.4 in the text as well.

Note: George Akerlof, Michael Spence and Joseph Stiglitz shared the 2001 Nobel Prize in economics for developing and applying the idea of asymmetric information; see http://nobelprize.org/economics/laureates/2001/index.html

Learning Objective 5: Discuss the credibility problem in trading. Analyze and discuss the costly-to-fake principle, conspicuous consumption and statistical discrimination as responses to asymmetric information.

The lemons model suggests that a solution to the asymmetric information is for the seller of high-quality goods to communicate this fact credibly to the buyers. This is known more generally as the **credibility problem in trading** since there is a need for buyers and sellers to communicate or "signal" the true quality of the goods and services they are trading.

Hint: Recall from Chapter 11 that a credible signal is a threat or a promise that is in the signaler's interest to keep.

The chapter discusses three examples of credible signals that are used to overcome specific asymmetric information problems. In the case of goods where the quality is unknown to the buyer, a solution is to send a signal that is costly or difficult to fake; this is called **costly-to-fake principle**. For example, in the 1980s Korean cars earned a reputation for low quality. The Korean car manufacturers responded by offering 10-year, 100,000 mile warranties on their cars. This was a signal that was costly to the manufacturers and in their interest to fulfill.

A common predicament faced by job seekers and salespeople is the need to send signals to potential employers and customers that distinguish them from others. One way to do this is through **conspicuous consumption**, which is through buying and consuming certain types of goods and *making sure that others see* that you are buying and consuming those goods. In the movie *Tin Men*, for example, Danny DeVito plays an aluminum siding salesman living in Baltimore in 1963. Aluminum siding salesmen were not held in high repute. He and his wife have an argument about how much money he is spending and she suggests that he get rid of his Cadillac; he replies that he can't do that because driving a Cadillac is important to maintaining his customers' trust.

Firms hiring workers face a problem of not being able to distinguish between low quality and high quality job applicants similar to that of used car buyers. A solution to this problem, both for firms hiring workers or for a consumer making a purchase, is to make judgments about the quality of people, goods or services based on the characteristics of the groups to which the people or goods belong. This is known as **statistical discrimination**. A specific instance of statistical discrimination that is discussed in the text is called **disappearing political discourse**. In this theory, people who support a position may remain silent because speaking out would create a risk of being misunderstood. That is, a person might be classified into the wrong group and, by being identified as a member of that group, will be subject to statistical discrimination.

Learning Objective 6: Define the terms adverse selection and moral hazard. Apply these ideas to insurance markets and the general concept of asymmetric information .
Statistical discrimination is a response to asymmetric information, but it also has role in creating other asymmetric information problems. Suppose, for example, that an insurance company gives discounts to people who do not smoke. The health of those who do not smoke is not uniformly good, however, and thus people who are less healthy yet are not smokers are more likely to buy insurance than those who are healthier and are not smokers. This is known as **adverse selection** and in general refers to a pattern in which insurance tends to be purchased disproportionately by those who are most costly for companies to insure.

Another asymmetric information problem in insurance markets is that an insurer has no prior information about how likely a given person is to take precautions against the event being insured. This is called **moral hazard**. For example, the person who is given the non-smoker discount may not do other things such as eat right and exercise.

A solution to the adverse selection and moral hazard problems in insurance is to include deductible provisions in policies. This makes the person more likely to take precautions (since they will bear some of the cost) and will lower the price of policies (making those who are less costly insure more likely to buy insurance.)

III. Self-Test

Key Terms
Match the term in the right-hand column with the appropriate definition in the left-hand column by placing the letter of the term in the blank in front of its definition. (Answers are given at the end of the chapter.)

1. ____ A person who would accept any gamble that is fair or better.

2. ____ A model in which asymmetric information tends to reduce the average quality of goods offered for sale.

3. ____ The pattern in which insurance tends to be purchased disproportionately by those who are most costly for companies to insure.

4. ____ The theory that people who support a position may remain silent because speaking out would create a risk of being misunderstood.

a. adverse selection

b. asymmetric information

c. better-than-fair gamble

d. costly-to-fake principle

5. _____ An incentive problem in which too little of a good is produced because those who do not pay for it cannot be excluded from using it.

e. disappearing political discourse

6. _____ The result of taking each possible outcome of a gamble, multiplying it by its probability of occurring and then summing all of these together over all possible outcomes.

f. expected value of a gamble

7. _____ A person who would refuse any gamble that is fair.

g. fair gamble

8. _____ A situation in which buyers and sellers are not equally well informed about the characteristics of the goods for sale in the market place.

h. free-rider problem

9. _____ The tendency of people to expend less effort protecting those goods that are insured against theft or damage.

i. lemons model

10. _____ The practice of making judgments about the quality of people, goods or services based on the characteristics of the groups to which they belong.

j. moral hazard

11. _____ The notion that a signal must be costly or difficult to fake in order to communicate information credibly to a potential rival.

k. risk-averse person

12. _____ A gamble with an expected value greater than zero.

l. risk-neutral person

13. _____ A gamble with an expected value equal to zero.

m. statistical discrimination

Multiple-Choice Questions
Circle the letter that corresponds to the best answer. (Answers are given at the end of the chapter.)

1.   A person engaged in rational search should acquire information until
   A.   the marginal benefit of the additional information is zero.
   B.   the marginal benefit of the additional information at a maximum.
   C.   the total cost of acquiring information equals the total benefit.
   D.   the total benefit of acquiring information exceeds the total cost.
   E.   the marginal cost of acquiring information equals the marginal benefit.

Use the graph below for problems 2, 3 and 4: the graph below represents the marginal benefit and marginal cost of information for a person who is searching for a used book.

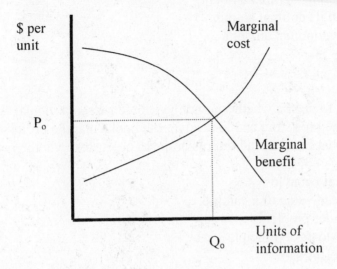

2.   The marginal benefit curve slopes down because
    A.   additional information on a used book provides no value to the person engaged in search.
    B.   additional information on a used book provides infinite value to the person engaged in search.
    C.   information on a used book is a resource and is subject to the law of diminishing returns.
    D.   information on a used book is free.
    E.   the book buyer will begin with the least expensive sources of information and only after these are exhausted move to expensive sources.

3.   The marginal cost curve for information about used books is upward sloping because
    A.   information on a used book is a resource and is subject to the law of diminishing returns.
    B.   the book buyer will begin with the least expensive sources of information and only after these are exhausted move to expensive sources.
    C.   the more information the book buyer acquires the happier she will be.
    D.   the book buyer will begin with the most expensive sources of information and only after these are exhausted move to cheaper sources.
    E.   the less information the book buyer acquires the happier she will be.

4.   Suppose that the buyer decides that she wants to give this book as a gift in the next week rather than just buying it for herself. The equilibrium value of information will
    A.   fall because the marginal benefit curve for information will shift down.
    B.   fall because the marginal cost curve for information will shift down.
    C.   not be affected.
    D.   rise because the marginal benefit curve for information will shift up.
    E.   rise because the marginal cost curve for information will shift up.

5.   The free-rider problem will cause the equilibrium amount of information to be
      A.   greater than its optimal amount
      B.   lower than its optimal amount.
      C.   equal to its optimal amount
      D.   zero.
      E.   unknown.

6.   Wynton is trying to decide whether or not he should take a particular college course. He
      goes to the college bookstore and looks over the books that the professor has ordered for
      the class, likes what he sees, and returns home to order them via the internet. This is an
      example of
      A.   risk-neutral behavior.
      B.   the expected value of a gamble.
      C.   the free-rider problem.
      D.   the costly-to-fake principle
      E.   adverse selection

7.   Erica is trying to decide whether to stay with his current job or quit and move to another
      city. She thinks that there is a 70% chance that her net earnings will be $1000 more in
      another city and a 30% chance they will be $1000 less. The expected value of her
      gamble is
      A. $1000   B. -$1000   C. $300   D. $700   E. $400

8.   Benny is driving on the freeway and notices that he is almost out of gas. He can take the
      first exit he finds and fill up with gas; that way, he will definitely not run out of gas. He
      can skip that exit and proceed to the next one and fill up with gas there since he will save
      $10 on gas compared with stopping at the first exit. However, there is a 20% chance that
      he won't make it that far and will have to pay $50 for a service station to bring him fuel.
      He will pass this exit and go on to the next if he is
      A.   a risk-averse person.
      B.   a rise-neutral person.
      C.   engaged in rational search.
      D.   a free-rider.
      E.   engaged in statistical discrimination.

9.   Tim is a risk-averse person while Jacqui is a risk-neutral person. They are faced with the
      following gamble: win $5,000 with the probability of 65% or lose $9,000 with a
      probability of 35%. In this case,
      A.   both Tim and Jacqui will accept this gamble.
      B.   only Tim will accept this gamble.
      C.   only Jacqui will accept this gamble.
      D.   neither Tim nor Jacqui will accept this gamble.
      E.   there is not enough information to determine whether either or both will accept or
            reject this gamble.

10.   Ron is searching for an accountant to prepare his income taxes. The cost of talking to
       another accountant is zero. Ron is risk-neutral; this means that he will
       A.   talk with all of the accountants in his town.
       B.   hire the first accountant he talks with.
       C.   use conspicuous consumption as a way of sorting through accountants.
       D.   continue talking to accountants even if the expected value of another interview is
             zero.
       E.   continue talking to accountants only if the expected value of another interview is
             positive.

11.   A situation in which buyers and sellers are not equally well-informed about some or all
       characteristics of a good they are trading is
       A.   impossible.
       B.   known as symmetric information.
       C.   called the free-rider problem
       D.   known as asymmetric information.
       E.   risk-aversion

Use the following information for problems 12, 13 and 14: Suppose that market research reveals
that consumers will pay $4 per pound for high-quality fish and $2 per pound for low-quality fish.
Buyers cannot tell by looking at the fish in a display case whether they are high- or low-quality
fish.

12.   If the chance of buying high-quality fish is 75% and the chance of buying low-quality
       fish is 25%, buyers will be willing to pay _____ per pound of fish if they are
       risk-neutral.
       A. $1.50   B. $2   C. $3   D. $3.50   E. $4

13.   Suppose that high-quality fish cost $3.75 per pound to produce. Given the information
       on buyers, we can expect
       A.   both high- and low-quality fish will be offered for sale.
       B.   only low-quality fish will be offered for sale.
       C.   only high-quality fish will be offered for sale.
       D.   no fish of either quality will be offered for sale.
       E.   nothing since we do not have enough information to answer this question.

14.   If the fish-seller were to offer a "money-back plus 10%" guarantee on the fish, this would
       be an example of
       A.   risk-neutrality.
       B.   the lemons problem.
       C.   the costly-to-fake principle.
       D.   asymmetric information.
       E.   the expected value of the gamble.

15.   Which of the following is not an example of a solution to the commitment problem inherent in search?
      A.   A borrower signs a loan agreement at a bank.
      B.   A tenant and a landlord enter into a lease.
      C.   A basketball player signs a contract with professional basketball team.
      D.   A college student signs a letter agreeing to attend a particular college.
      E.   A bibliophile buys a book via the internet rather than at his local bookstore.

16.   Being seen driving an expensive car is a good indication of the abilities of a
      A.   realtor.
      B.   carpenter.
      C.   college professor
      D.   political officeholder.
      E.   engineer.

17.   Suppose that you are offered a low-interest rate credit card because you live in a high-income neighborhood. This is an example of
      A.   adverse selection.   D.   the costly-to-fake principle.
      B.   statistical discrimination.   E.   the equilibrium principle.
      C.   conspicuous consumption.

18.   Suppose that a person who holds a particular viewpoint on an issue remains silent during a debate on the issue in order to minimize the risk of being misunderstood. This is known as
      A.   moral hazard.
      B.   risk neutrality.
      C.   disappearing political discourse.
      D.   political courage.
      E.   adverse selection.

19.   _____ is the notion that insurance tends to be purchased disproportionately by those who are most costly for companies to insure.
      A.   moral hazard.
      B.   risk neutrality.
      C.   disappearing political discourse.
      D.   political courage.
      E.   adverse selection.

20.   Clark just bought a new car and was required by state law to purchase full insurance coverage. The moral hazard problem suggests that Clark will
      A.   usually try to find a safe place to park his car to avoid break-ins.
      B.   be careful to lock his car whenever he parks it.
      C.   drive especially carefully in traffic.
      D.   park his car in his garage when bad weather is approaching.
      E.   keep his car outside regardless of what the weather is.

Short Answer Problems
(Answers and solutions are given at the end of the chapter.)

1. Understanding expected values and risk aversion
Suppose that you are booking an airline reservation on the internet. You find that you can fly to your destination and back for $300. You then have to decide: should I look at other websites? If you do, you will lose the $300 fare. Suppose that you have a 50% chance of finding a fare of $200 and a 50% chance of ending up with a $400 ticket.

    A. The expected value of this gamble is equal to _____. This tells you that it (is / is not) _____ a fair gamble.

    B. If you are a risk-neutral person, you (will / will not) _____ continue to search.

    C. If you are a risk-averse person, you (will / will not) _____ continue to search.

    D. Suppose your friend stops by and says that you are wrong regarding your probabilities and that there is a 75% chance of finding a fare of $200 and a 25% chance of a $400 ticket. Will that affect your decision as to whether you will continue to search? Explain:

    _____

    _____

    _____

2. Rational search and the optimal quantity of information
Let's continue searching for airfares. You find that you can fly to your destination and back for $300. You then have to decide: should I look at other websites? Ignoring what your friend said in the previous problem, suppose that you have a 50% chance of finding a fare of $200 and a 50% chance of ending up with another $300 ticket.

    A.   The marginal benefit of continuing to search for a lower airfare is ($100 / $50)

        _____.

    B.   Suppose that you can pick up extra hours at your job at $10 per hour and that it will take you one hour to search for other fares. Should you continue to search? Why or why not? _____

        _____

    C.   Suppose that you have a consulting business and can earn $75 per hour and that it will take you one hour to search for other fares. Should you continue to search? Why or why not? _____

        _____

        _____

3. Understanding the lemons model

(Adapted from a story in John McMillan, *Reinventing The Bazaar: A Natural History of Markets*. New York: Norton, 2002.) Sales of adulterated milk were a major problem in India until the 1970s; suppliers could supply high-quality milk or low-quality milk and buyers could not tell the difference. Suppose that buyers are willing to pay $1 per quart for high-quality milk and $0.50 per quart for low-quality milk. There is a 40% chance that the milk will be of high-quality and a 60% chance that it will be low-quality. Further, suppose that sellers are willing to sell high-quality milk for $0.80 per quart and low-quality milk for $0.40 per quart.

      A.   Assume that the buyers are risk-neutral people. How much would they be willing to pay per quart of milk? _____

      B.   At the price you found in (A), will sellers be willing to offer high-quality milk for sale? Why or why not? _____

_____

      C.   Explain how the costly-to-fake principle can be used to find a solution to this problem. _____

_____

_____

IV. Becoming an Economic Naturalist: Case Study

Consider the names of people you know well. If you didn't know them, would you have been able to tell anything about their background (education, where they were born, for example) from their name? Do you judge people by their name if you hear it before you meet them?

Certain names are more or less likely to be chosen by certain groups than others. For example, Roland G. Fryer, Jr. and Steven D. Levitt, in "The Causes and Consequences of Distinctively Black Names," (*Quarterly Journal of Economics*, August 2004, pp. 767-805) tested the hypothesis that types of names might be used as a method of statistical discrimination. They found "no negative relationship between having a distinctively Black name and later life outcomes after controlling for a child's circumstances at birth." Further examples of this phenomenon are provided in Levitt's book *Freakonomics* (William Morrow, 2005; co-authored with Stephen J. Dubner.)

Answer:

V. Self-Test Solutions

Key Terms

1. l	6. f	10. m
2. i	7. k	11. d
3. a	8. b	12. c
4. e	9. j	13. g
5. h		

Multiple-Choice Questions

1. E	6. C	11. D	16. A
2. C	7. E	12. D	17. B
3. B	8. B	13. B	18. C
4. D	9. A	14. C	19. E
5. B	10. E	15. E	20. E

Short Answer Problems

1.
   A. zero ($(0.5)*(400)+(0.5)*(200) - 300 = 200 + 100 - 300 = 0$); this is a fair gamble.
   B. will, since this is a fair gamble.
   C. will not, since they need better than a fair gamble.
   D. the expected value of the new gamble is: $(0.75)*(400)+(0.25)*(200) - 300 = 300 + 50 = 350$. This is better than a fair gamble so even a risk-averse person will accept this gamble.

2.
   A. $100 since you have a 50% chance of saving $200.
   B. continue searching since the marginal benefit of searching ($100) is greater than the marginal cost ($10).
   C. do not continue searching since the marginal benefit of searching ($100) is less than the marginal cost ($150).

3.
   A. $0.70 per quart, since the expected value of the gamble is $(0.4)*(1) + (0.6)*(0.5) = 0.40 + 0.30 = 0.70$
   B. No, since sellers need a price of $0.80 per quart to offer high-quality milk.
   C. The costly-to-fake principle suggests solutions such as branded milk or warranties under which buyers can return milk for a refund (or a refund plus a premium).

Chapter 14
Labor Markets, Poverty, and Income Distribution

I. Pretest: What Do You Really Know?
Circle the letter that corresponds to the best answer. (Answers appear immediately after the final question).

1. The value of marginal product is
   A. a synonym for marginal product.
   B. equal to the price at which the good being produced is sold.
   C. equal to the age of a worker.
   D. equal to the marginal product multiplied by the price at which the good being produced is sold.
   E. a synonym for the supply of labor.

2. For a given labor demand curve, shifts in labor supply affect
   A. the equilibrium wage only
   B. the equilibrium level of employment only.
   C. both the equilibrium wage and the equilibrium level of employment.
   D. the marginal product of labor curve.
   E. none of the above.

3. An increase in the demand for website designers will cause
   A. an increase in the wage and a decrease in employment for website designers.
   B. an increase in the wage and an increase in employment for website designers.
   C. a decrease in the wage and an increase in employment for website designers.
   D. a decrease in the wage and a decrease in employment for website designers.
   E. An increase the wage and have no effect on the employment of website designers.

4. _____ is a combination of factors including education, training and experience.
   A. Statistical discrimination
   B. Customer discrimination
   C. A labor union
   D. An in-kind transfer
   E. Human capital

5. Labor unions typically do not _____.
   A. avoid controlling the supply of labor.
   B. seek to increase members' wages.
   C. work to secure medical benefits paid to members.
   D. bargain for safer working conditions.
   E. negotiate for shorter work weeks or more paid vacation.

6. According to the theory of compensating wage differentials,
   A. an occupation in which there is a lower risk of injury will pay more than an occupation with a higher risk.
   B. an occupation in which there is a higher risk of injury will pay more than an occupation with a lower risk.
   C. there will be no earnings differentials across occupations with different risks of injury.
   D. if someone is injured on the job they will receive an insurance settlement.
   E. if someone is injured on the job they will receive a pay increase after they return from the hospital.

7. Discrimination in the labor market is a result of
   A. Employer decisions.
   B. Customer decisions.
   C. Employee decisions.
   D. Both (A) and (B).
   E. (A), (B) and (C).

8. Which of the following best describes changes in the U.S. income distribution since 1980?
   A. Income in all groups has grown at roughly the same rate.
   B. Income in the middle quintiles has grown at the fastest rate.
   C. Income in the bottom quintiles has grown at the fastest rate.
   D. Income among the top 5% of all recipients has growth at the fastest rate.
   E. Income in the bottom quintiles has fallen in absolute terms.

9. The Earned-Income Tax Credit (EITC) differs from a Negative Income Tax (NIT) in that
   A. The EITC does not seek to provide a minimum income level for a person or family.
   B. The EITC is paid in cash while the NIT is paid in-kind.
   C. The NIT is paid in cash while the EITC is paid in-kind.
   D. The NIT operates through the income tax system while the EITC does not.
   E. The EITC is managed by state governments but the NIT would be managed through the federal government.

10. A minimum wage is similar to a _____ in a market for a good or service.
    A. price ceiling
    B. price floor
    C. monopoly
    D. normal good
    E. price elasticity

Solutions and Feedback to Pretest
The answers to the pretest are provided below along with the relevant Learning Objective from the Key Point Review. We strongly recommend that you take the time to review the appropriate material for each question you answered incorrectly.

Correct Answer	Learning Objective
1. D	1
2. C	2
3. B	2
4. E	3
5. A	3
6. B	3
7. D	3
8. D	4
9. A	5
10. B	5

II. Key Point Review
The Forest

This chapter focuses on the labor market and labor market outcomes such as wages and the distribution of income. This is the first of three chapters on the Economics of Public Policy; all three chapters apply the tools developed in Chapters 1 through 13 to a series of public policy issues.

The central questions you need to be able to answer are
- What is the economic value of work?
- How are wage and employment determined in competitive labor markets?
- What are the causes of earnings differences?
- What are the recent trends in U.S. income inequality and what are the causes?
- What are some of the methods used to redistribute income in the U.S.?

The Trees

Learning Objective 1: Discuss the economic value of work.
Society and individuals value work for many reasons. The **economic value of work** centers on the monetary value of the goods and services that a worker can produce. The additional output that an additional worker can produce is the **marginal product (MP)** of a worker. (This is sometimes called the **marginal physical product** of a worker.) The **value of marginal product (VMP)** is equal to the MP times the price at which the good the worker is producing can be sold; this is how economists measure the economic value of work.

Note: Example 14.1 in the text uses a pottery to illustrate MP and VMP. To see a real pottery in action, visit the webpage of the St. John's Pottery at www.csbsju.edu/pottery

Learning Objective 2: Analyze how the equilibrium wage and employment level is determined in a competitive labor market.

Equilibrium wages and employment levels are determined in **labor markets**. This means that to analyze why wages and employment vary you we must understand the reasoning behind the demand curve for labor and the supply curve for labor.

The **demand curve for labor** is a result of the law of diminishing returns. Suppose that a firm is hiring workers. At a certain number of workers, the marginal product of labor (and hence the value of marginal product) will begin to decline. A firm will only hire a worker if their value of marginal product is greater than or equal to the wage; thus, as the number of workers hired increases the wage that the firm will offer falls.

Hint: You studied the law of diminishing returns in Chapter 3. If you do not remember this concept or are still unsure about it, you should review it now.

The **supply curve of labor** is a result of individual choices regarding working for pay. Specifically, the opportunity cost of working for pay generally rises; this means that in order to induce a person to supply a larger quantity of labor the wage must rise. Hence the supply curve of labor, like supply curves for goods and services, will generally be upward sloping.

The equilibrium wage and employment level is found where the demand curve for labor and the supply curve for labor intersect. Shifts in labor demand and labor supply will cause wages and employment to change; see Figure 14.2 in the text for an example.

Learning Objective 3: Analyze differences in earnings using the five models proposed in the text.

Five models that explain differences in earnings are presented in the text. The **human capital theory** builds on the basic supply and demand model presented above. It posits that a worker's marginal productivity is directly related to his or her **human capital** and differences in human capital create differences in the demand for labor and hence differences in wages. Human capital itself is a blend of factors that affect a worker's value of marginal product and includes both intentional actions (e.g. going to school) and unintentional effects (e.g. on-the-job training and experience.)

Note: Gary S. Becker was awarded the 1992 Nobel Prize in economics for his work in developing and applying the human capital theory; see http://nobelprize.org/economics/laureates/1992/press.html

Labor unions are organizations that workers join in order to bargain collectively with their employers for better wages and working conditions. Labor unions can affect wages in two ways. First, they can negotiate contracts with firms that will pay union members wages that are above the market equilibrium wage. (See Figure 14.4 in the text for an example.) Second, unions can directly affect the supply of labor by negotiating contracts in which firms agree to hire only members of the union.

A third hypothesis regarding earnings differences is the theory of **compensating wage differentials**. Differences in wages are, according to this theory, caused by differences in the attractiveness of working conditions in various jobs. For example, the heat, cold, physical strain and other conditions of a job on a loading dock might mean that a firm has to pay people more to work at this job than for people to work in an office answering customer calls. This is the case even if the two jobs require the same human capital and are no different in terms of unionization.

Discrimination in various forms is the fourth explanation of earnings differences presented in the text. **Employer discrimination** is clearly a possibility; if firms choose to hire one group of people over another or pay different people different wages for arbitrary reasons (race, ethnicity, gender for example) then earnings will differ across workers. Another form of discrimination, **customer discrimination**, is more subtle; here, consumers are willing to pay more for a product produced by members of a favored group, even if there is no difference in quality. For example, Sandra Day O'Connor, the first woman appointed to the U.S. Supreme Court, said in an interview that she could not get a job as a lawyer after graduating from Stanford Law School because, as one law partner said to her, "our clients would not approve" of a woman lawyer.

Note: The quote from Justice O'Connor is from an interview available at http://news.minnesota.publicradio.org/play/audio.php?media=/midday/2005/07/01_midday2. **She discusses employer discrimination against women in the legal profession as well and how this also prevented her from finding a position after law school.**

The final explanation involves **winner-take-all labor markets**. Winner-take-all labor markets are markets in which small differences in human capital translate into large differences in pay. The earnings of famous professional athletes and musicians are good examples of this phenomenon. Technologies such as television and recorded music allow well-known performers to sell their services in larger markets and earn greater rewards. At the same time, performers in smaller markets must compete with recorded music or sports broadcasts and thus cannot earn wages that are as high as they would be without such competition.

Learning Objective 4: Discuss recent trends in U.S. income inequality. Consider the ethical and moral aspects of income inequality.
Table 14.2 in the text provides data on income received by quintile, i.e. by the lowest 20%l, the next lowest 20%, and so on. The data show that income inequality has been growing since 1980 and that this trend is especially pronounced at the top of the income distribution.

Are these trends a cause for concern? The late John Rawls, a moral philosopher at Harvard University, argued that they are and proposed a way of thinking about a just distribution of income. He argued that risk-averse people who did not know what their talents were or the talents of others would divide all income earned equally. Clearly this is not what happens in the U.S. economy, but Rawls used this thought experiment to argue that people in general will not want to leave untouched the results of purely competitive labor markets interacting with discrimination and winner-take-all markets. Rather, they will consider notions of fairness and consider ways to redistribute income in ways that are fairer.

Learning Objective 5: Discuss the methods of income redistribution presented in the text. Welfare payments and **in-kind transfers** (that is, payments made in the form of goods and services rather than in cash) are direct methods of income redistribution. Governments collect taxes from citizens and then send cash or in-kind payments to those who meet certain income requirements. These programs are usually **means-tested**; this involves providing benefits that decline as a recipient earns additional income. The **Personal Responsibility Act**, enacted in 1996 and sometimes known simply as "welfare reform," changed these types of programs dramatically. First, the responsibility for welfare programs was shifted from the federal government to state governments. This allowed variation across the states in terms of minimum payments, whether payments would be in cash or in-kind and other program details. Second, the law set a nationwide five-year lifetime limit on payment of welfare benefits to any given recipient.

A **Negative Income Tax** (NIT) is often proposed by economists as an alternative to welfare payments. An NIT is a system under which the government would grant every citizen a cash payment each year that would bring that citizen up to a minimum level of income. These payments would be made via the income tax system and financed through additional taxes on earned income. The **Earned-Income Tax Credit** (EITC) works much like an NIT in that low-income workers receive credits on their federal income tax and thus can receive refunds on their income tax returns even if they pay no income tax. The EITC differs from an NIT in that there is no minimum level to which individual incomes are raised. There is therefore no guarantee that a worker who receives the EITC will meet a given level such as the **poverty threshold**, the level of income below which the federal government classifies a family as poor.

Minimum wages and **public employment for the poor** are often proposed as part of the solution to income inequality. A minimum wage is a price floor in a labor market and thus sets a level below which employers cannot lower wages. Economists point out that both of these polices suffer from a problem: they violate the Efficiency Principle. A minimum wage, for example, does this by preventing a labor market in which the minimum wage is above the equilibrium wage from reaching equilibrium; this prevents some employers and potential employees from making agreements that would allow some workers to work at below-minimum wages thus increasing total economic surplus. This is why many economists who support efforts to redistribute income lean towards a combination of methods (for example, combining minimum wages with an expanded EITC and increased public employment) rather than using only one method that might reduce economic efficiency greatly.

III. Self-Test

Key Terms
Match the term in the right-hand column with the appropriate definition in the left-hand column by placing the letter of the term in the blank in front of its definition. (Answers are given at the end of the chapter.)

1. ____ The dollar value of the additional output a firm produces by employing one additional unit of labor.

2. ____ A group of workers bargaining collectively with their employers for better wages and working conditions.

3. ____ A theory of wage determination positing that a worker's wage will be proportional to her or his stock of human capital.

4. ____ The willingness of consumers to pay more for a product produced by members of a favored group, even if there is no difference in quality.

5. ____ The 1996 federal law that shifted responsibility for welfare programs from the federal government to state governments and placed a five-year lifetime limit on payment of welfare benefits to any given recipient.

6. ____ A policy under which low-income workers receive credits on their federal income tax.

7. ____ A payment made in the form of a good or service rather than in cash.

8. ____ The additional output a firm produces by employing one additional unit of labor.

9. ____ The difference in a wage that reflects the attractiveness of a job's working conditions.

10. ____ An arbitrary preference by an employer for one group of workers over another.

11. ____ A market in which small differences in human capital translate into large differences in pay.

12. ____ A benefit program in which the benefit level declines as the recipient earns additional income.

13. ____ The level of income below which the federal government classifies a family as poor.

14. ____ A blend of factors (for example, education, training, experience) that affect a worker's value of marginal product.

15. ____ A system under which the government would grant every citizen a cash payment each year financed through additional taxes on earned income.

a. compensating wage differential

b. customer discrimination

c. earned-income tax credit

d. employer discrimination

e. human capital

f. human capital theory

g. in-kind transfer

h. labor union

i. marginal product (MP)

j. means-tested

k. negative income tax (NIT)

l. Personal Responsibility Act

m. poverty threshold

n. value of marginal product (VMP)

o. winner-take-all market

Multiple-Choice Questions
Circle the letter that corresponds to the best answer. (Answers are given at the end of the chapter.)
Use the following information for problems 1, 2, 3 and 4: the table below contains information on a dry-cleaning shop. Suppose that the shop charges a flat fee of $5 per pound to dry-clean clothes.

Number of workers	Pounds of clothes cleaned per week
0	0
1	160
2	310
3	450
4	580
5	700
6	810

1. The marginal product of the third worker is
    A. 110   B. 130   C. 140   D. 145   E. 150

2. The value of marginal product for the fourth worker is
    A. 800   B. 750   C. 700   D. 650   E. 600

3. Suppose that the going wage for workers is $725 per week. How many workers will this firm hire?
    A. 1   B. 2   C. 3   D. 4   E. 5

4. Suppose that the going wage for workers falls from $725 per week to $600 per week. The firm will hire _____ additional workers.
    A. 0   B. 1   C. 2   D. 3   E. 4

5. An increase in workers' marginal productivity will result in
    A. an increase in the equilibrium wage.
    B. an increase in the equilibrium level of employment.
    C. an increase in labor supply.
    D. none of the effects given in (A), (B) or (C).
    E. both (A) and (B).

6. You are observing a competitive labor market and find that the equilibrium wage has risen and the equilibrium level of employment has risen. You can infer from this that
    A. the supply of labor has increased.
    B. the demand for labor has decreased.
    C. the price at which firms sell their output has decreased.
    D. the supply of labor has decreased.
    E. the demand for labor has increased.

7. Judy makes sports trophies and the average price of sports trophies is falling. She should expect
    A.   her wage to rise because her value of marginal product is rising.
    B.   her wage to fall because her value of marginal product is falling.
    C.   her wage to rise because her value of marginal product is falling.
    D.   her wage to fall because her value of marginal product is rising.
    E.   her wage to be unaffected by the price of sports trophies.

8. One reason why many people will go back to school and take more classes is
    A.   to create a compensating wage differential.
    B.   to increase their stock of human capital.
    C.   to decrease their marginal productivity.
    D.   to increase the supply of labor in their chosen occupation.
    E.   to take advantage of the Earned-Income Tax Credit.

9. Suppose that a firm and a union reach an agreement whereby only members of the union will be hired by the firm. This will allow for an increase in wages because
    A.   the union can reduce the supply of labor by controlling union membership.
    B.   the firm can reduce the supply of labor by controlling union membership.
    C.   the firm can reduce the demand for labor by controlling union membership.
    D.   the union can increase the demand for labor by controlling union membership.
    E.   of factors not given in (A), (B), (C) or (D).

10. A mining company hires two women with exactly the same levels of human capital. One woman is assigned to work in the mine on a blasting crew and the other is assigned to work in the office. If the woman on the blasting crew earns a higher wage than the woman working in the office, a possible hypothesis that explains this is
    A.   statistical discrimination.   D.   sexism.
    B.   winner-take-all markets.   E.   customer discrimination.
    C.   compensating wage differentials.

11. An arbitrary preference by an employer for one group of workers over another is called _____ discrimination.
    A.   price   D.   employer
    B.   customer   E.   justified
    C.   statistical

12. In a winner-take-all labor market,
    A.   large differences in human capital translate into small differences in wages.
    B.   small differences in human capital are converted into large differences in wages.
    C.   small differences in human capital result in small differences in wages.
    D.   one worker receives all of the labor income and the rest receive nothing.
    E.   one employer hires all workers.

13.   Which of the following best describes changes in the U.S. income distribution between
       1945 and 1980?
       A.   Income in all groups grew at roughly the same rate.
       B.   Income in the middle quintiles grew at the fastest rate.
       C.   Income in the bottom quintiles grew at the fastest rate.
       D.   Income among the top 5% of all recipients grew at the fastest rate.
       E.   Income in the bottom quintiles fell in absolute terms.

14.   John Rawls argued that the degree of income inequality produced by competitive markets
       is
       A.   minor due to greed on the part of most workers.
       B.   greater than the amount people would prefer given their beliefs about fairness.
       C.   about right.
       D.   acceptable to most people given their beliefs about fairness.
       E.   too small and removes incentives for workers to work hard.

15.   The food stamp program issues stamps to individuals who can then use them to purchase
       groceries. This is an example of
       A.   a cash payment.   D.   a negative income tax.
       B.   a compensating wage differential.   E.   a minimum wage.
       C.   an in-kind payment.

16.   The Personal Responsibility Act of 1996
       A.   removed the five-year limit on receiving welfare payments.
       B.   shifted responsibility for welfare programs from state governments to the federal
             government.
       C.   eliminated all welfare payments.
       D.   reduced incentives to work for pay in order to encourage women to stay home
             with their children.
       E.   shifted responsibility for welfare programs from the federal government to state
             governments.

17.   The state of Minnesota provides cash assistance to households to help pay for heating
       bills. The amount of assistance a household receives is based on the household's income.
       This is an example of a
       A.   means-tested program.
       B.   in-kind payment.
       C.   price ceiling.
       D.   minimum wage.
       E.   compensating wage differential.

18.   A minimum wage that is above the equilibrium wage in a market results in a
       _____ wage for those who have a job and _____ in total economic
       surplus.
       A.   lower; an increase   C.   lower; a decrease   E.   higher; no change
       B.   higher; a decrease   D.   higher; an increase

19.   A Negative Income Tax
       A.   provides a tax cut for everyone who pays taxes.
       B.   eliminates tax withholding.
       C.   provides a minimum level of income for a taxpayer using the income tax system.
       D.   provides a minimum level of income for a taxpayer using the sales tax system.
       E.   implies that tax rates fall as a person's income rises.

20.   The _____ reduces or eliminates entirely the taxes paid by a low income family.
       A.   minimum wage
       B.   poverty threshold
       C.   demand for labor
       D.   creation of public employment programs
       E.   Earned-Income Tax Credit

Short Answer Problems
(Answers and solutions are given at the end of the chapter.)
1. You are given the following information on the hourly operations of a sandwich shop that
    sells sandwiches for $5 each:

Labor (Number of workers)	Output (Number of sandwiches produced)	Marginal product of labor	Value of marginal product
0	0	N/A	N/A
5	25		
10	65		
15	95		
20	115		
25	125		
30	130		

A. Fill in the column for the marginal product of labor. In what units is the marginal product
    expressed? _____   Explain why: _____
    _____

B. Do the data in the table obey the law of diminishing returns? _____ Explain
    your reasoning: _____
    _____

C. Fill in the column for the value of marginal product. In what units is the value of
    marginal product expressed? _____   Explain why: _____
    _____

D. Suppose that this sandwich shop has to pay $10 per hour to its workers in order to
    compete with other employers. How many workers will they hire per hour?
    _____   Explain your reasoning: _____
    _____

E. Suppose that the local wage falls to $5 per hour. Will this affect the number of workers this shop will hire per hour? _____ Explain why or why not: _____
_____

F. Ignore part (E) and suppose that the wage remains at $10 per hour. If the price at which the store can sell sandwiches falls to $4 each, Will this affect the number of workers this shop will hire per hour? _____ Explain why or why not: _____
_____

2. Supply and demand in labor markets

Suppose that the labor market for workers at ice cream shops in St. Cloud, Minnesota, is represented by the demand and supply curves below:

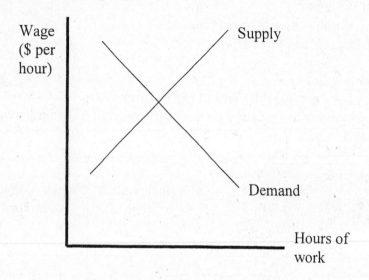

A. Label the equilibrium price and equilibrium quantity on the graph above.
B. A heat wave will (increase/decrease) _____ the demand for ice cream cones. This will cause the (supply of /demand for) _____ labor to (increase/decrease) _____. Draw this on the graph above.
C. As a result of part (B), the equilibrium wage will (rise/fall) _____ and the equilibrium quantity of labor will (rise/fall) _____. Label the new equilibrium wage and new equilibrium quantity of labor on your graph.
D. Suppose that the heat wave also encourages people to stop looking for work and go to the beach. This will (increase/decrease) _____ the (demand for/supply of) _____ labor. Draw this on the graph above.
E. Compared to the original equilibrium, the action you analyzed in part (D) will cause the equilibrium wage to (rise/fall/either rise or fall depending on the size of the change) _____ and the equilibrium quantity of labor to (rise/fall/either rise or fall depending on the size of the change) _____.

3. Applying hypotheses regarding earnings

Analyze how each of the following would affect the demand for or the supply of labor (if relevant), the equilibrium wage and the equilibrium quantity of employment. Consider each scenario separately, i.e. for each action, begin from an initial equilibrium and trace out its effects ignoring the previous questions.

A. The average level of human capital for a group of workers increases.

_____

_____

B. A labor union and a firm agree to a contract in which workers will be paid a wage above the local average wage.

_____

_____

C. The level of danger involved in an occupation falls.

_____

_____

_____

IV. Becoming an Economic Naturalist: Case Study

In her book *Understanding the Gender Gap: An Economic History of American Women* (Oxford University Press, 1990), Harvard economist Claudia Goldin uses the labor market models developed in this chapter to analyze the evolution of women's participation and earnings in U.S. labor markets. She reports that in 1950, 21 percent of white, married women participated in the paid labor market; by 1980, 56 percent participated. Use shifts in the demand for and supply of labor to analyze why this happened. What might be the roles of changing sex roles? Increased college attendance of women? Other factors?

Answer:

V. Self Test Solutions

Key Terms

1. n	6. c	11. o
2. h	7. g	12. j
3. f	8. i	13. m
4. b	9. a	14. e
5. l	10. d	15. k

Multiple-Choice Questions

1. C	6. A	11. D	16. E
2. D	7. B	12. B	17. A
3. B	8. B	13. A	18. B
4. D	9. A	14. B	19. C
5. E	10. C	15. C	20. E

Short Answer Problems
1.   Data for answers:

Labor (Number of workers)	Output (Number of sandwiches produced)	Marginal product of labor	Value of marginal product (Price of a sandwich = $5)	Value of marginal product (Price of a sandwich = $4)
0	0	N/A	N/A	N/A
5	25	5	$ 25	$ 20
10	65	8	$ 40	$ 32
15	95	6	$ 30	$ 24
20	115	4	$ 20	$ 16
25	125	2	$ 10	$ 8
30	130	1	$ 5	$ 4

A.   sandwiches per worker; see 3rd column of table.

B.   Yes, since the marginal product of labor decreases after 10 workers.

C.   dollars per worker; see 4th column of table.

D.   25 workers since this is where the value of marginal product equals the wage.

E.   30 workers since this is where the value of marginal product equals the new wage.

F.   The value of marginal product changes to the data in the 5th column of the table. At a wage of $10 per hour it makes sense to hire 20 workers because the wage is less than the value of marginal product. It does not make sense to hire 25 workers because at this point the wage is greater than the value of marginal product.

2.   A.   The equilibrium wage and employment level are where the supply and demand curves intersect.

B.   increase; demand for; increase.

C.   rise; rise

D.   decrease; supply of

E.   rise; either rise or fall depending on the size of the shifts in demand and supply.

3.   A.   An increase in the average level of human capital will shift up the value of marginal product curve since an increase in human capital increases marginal product at every level of employment. The value of marginal product curve is the labor demand curve and thus it shift up as well leading to an increase in the equilibrium wage and the equilibrium level of employment.

B.   This type of contract will not affect either labor demand or labor supply; rather, it imposes a price floor in the labor market. This leads to an increase in the wage paid to those who have jobs but a decrease in the level of employment.

C.   A decrease in the level of danger will reduce the compensating wage differential paid to that occupation. The differential is offered by employers and thus constitutes a shift down in the labor demand curve. This will cause the equilibrium wage to fall and the equilibrium level of employment to fall.

Chapter 15
The Environment, Health, and Safety

I. Pretest: What Do You Really Know?

Circle the letter that corresponds to the best answer. (Answers appear immediately after the final question).

1. _____ pays all expenses generated by the insured party's activity.
   A. Insurance with a large deductible provision
   B. Last-dollar insurance coverage
   C. First-dollar insurance coverage
   D. Adverse selection
   E. Moral hazard

2. If a consumer is paying for all of her medical care, she will purchase medical services until
   A. the marginal cost equals the marginal benefit.
   B. the marginal cost exceeds the marginal benefit.
   C. the marginal benefit far exceeds the marginal cost.
   D. the marginal cost equals zero.
   E. the marginal benefit equals zero.

3. Which of the following is a distinguishing feature of health maintenance organizations (HMOs)?
   A. HMOs emphasize emergency treatment.
   B. All HMOs are non-profit organizations.
   C. Consumers who belong to HMOs can get as much medical treatment as they want with no restrictions.
   D. Health care professionals employed by HMOs make decisions about the amount of medical care each member is allowed to receive.
   E. Consumers who belong to HMOs pay for all of their own medical expenses, no matter how high they are.

4. Economists argue that many legal restrictions on pollution
   A. are unfair.
   B. are unconstitutional.
   C. do not cost enough.
   D. do not restrict polluters enough.
   E. are not efficient.

5. The advantage of the tax approach to pollution abatement is that pollution is reduced by those firms that
   A. can do it at the lowest marginal cost.   D. emit the smallest amount of pollutants.
   B. can do it at the highest marginal cost.   E. emit the largest amount of pollutants.
   C. are the biggest taxpayers and thus can afford it.

6. Which of the following is *not* true of tradable pollution permits?
   A. Groups of private citizens can purchase permits in order to reduce pollution below the amount allowed when all permits are purchased by polluters.
   B. Firms purchase permits that allow them to emit a fixed amount of pollutants.
   C. The price of tradable permits can be determined through an auction.
   D. Rich firms can pollute to their hearts' content.
   E. A firm can sell pollution permits that it owns to other firms.

7. _____ is often cited as a reason why governments enact workplace regulations.
   A. The ease with which workers change jobs
   B. The inability of firms to control their workers' behavior.
   C. The ability of firms to exploit workers
   D. The fact that workers are well-informed about safety devices
   E. Excessive spending on safety equipment by firms

8. A serious flaw with the current workers' compensation system is that the premiums paid by firms
   A. are collected only from firms with high injury rates.
   B. cover the full social cost of workplace injuries.
   C. cause wages to be excessively high.
   D. are inversely related to a firm's size.
   E. are not directly related to a firm's injury rate.

9. A community that used the Cost-Benefit Principle to decide how much police protection it should have would
   A. hire as many police officers as necessary to reduce the crime rate to zero.
   B. hire less than the socially optimal number of police officers.
   C. hire police officers until the marginal cost of an additional officer is equal to the marginal benefit of the crime prevention the officer would provide.
   D. hire more than the socially optimal number of police officers.
   E. not be able to come to a decision regarding the number of police officers it should hire.

10. Vaccinations against infectious diseases are required by law rather than left to private decisions because of
    A. the Cost-Benefit Principle.
    B. drug companies that want to make big profits from vaccinations.
    C. a desire not to allow anyone to avoid vaccinations on religious grounds.
    D. individual decision makers failing to take adequate account of the costs they would impose on others if they became infected.
    E. reasons not covered by (A), (B), (C) or (D).

Solutions and Feedback to Pretest

The answers to the pretest are provided below along with the relevant Learning Objective from the Key Point Review. We strongly recommend that you take the time to review the appropriate material for each question you answered incorrectly.

Correct Answer	Learning Objective
1. C	1
2. A	1
3. D	1
4. E	2
5. A	2
6. D	2
7. C	3
8. E	3
9. C	4
10. D	4

II. Key Point Review
The Forest

This chapter focuses on how economic concepts can be used to analyze health care finance, environmental policy and workplace safety issues. This is the second of three chapters on the Economics of Public Policy; all three chapters apply the tools developed in Chapters 1 through 13 to a series of public policy issues. The Cost-Benefit Principle, in particular, is used throughout this chapter.

The central questions you need to be able to answer are
- What improvements to health care financing are suggested by economic analysis?
- How can taxes and tradable permits be used to reduce pollution?
- In what ways can workplace safety be improved by altering the costs and benefits of investing in risk reduction?
- Does economic analysis have anything to contribute to debates regarding public health and domestic security spending?

The Trees

Learning Objective 1: Analyze the economics of health care finance using the Cost-Benefit Principle.

Hint: You may want to review the Cost-Benefit Principle (in Chapter 1) at this point since you will be applying it often in this chapter.

Real health care expenditures per person in the U.S. have risen rapidly since World War II. An important cause of this increase has been the diffusion of health insurance, both private and public.

First-dollar insurance coverage is insurance that pays all expenses generated by an insured activity. Consumers who have first-dollar health insurance have an incentive to over use medical services since the marginal cost to them of medical services is zero. That is, a rational consumer will use the service until the marginal benefit is equal to the marginal cost; since at some point the marginal benefit of medical services diminishes the person with this type of coverage will utilize the service until the marginal benefit is driven to zero. This is a level of service that is greater than if the marginal cost were greater than zero.

> **Hint: Examples 15.1 and 15.2 in the text explain this very well. You should test your understanding by working through Exercises 15.1 and 15.2 in the text as well.**

Health insurance that has deductible provisions is one solution to the problems created by first-dollar coverage. The need to pay for the first $1000 of medical services, for example, raises the marginal cost a person faces and thus encourages them to choose a level of service that is lower than they would choose with first-dollar coverage.

A second solution to the overuse of medical services has been the development of **health maintenance organizations (HMOs)**. An HMO is a group of health care professionals that provides health services to individuals for a fixed annual fee. In return for the fixed fee, the doctors, nurses and other professionals have the power to decide the quantity of health services a person will be allowed to consume. A problem that results from this particular solution is that there is now an incentive for the HMO to minimize the amount of services provided in order to maximize their profits.

A consequence of the overuse of medical services is that the cost of basic health insurance has risen greatly. Applying the Cost-Benefit Principle, this means that consumers will purchase less medical care than they would if the cost were lower. In fact, may people cannot afford basic health insurance. A solution to this problem would be for the government to reimburse each family (up to a certain amount) for health insurance in order to lower its cost.

> **Note: The discussion of health insurance in this chapter complements the discussion of insurance in Chapter 13. The concepts of adverse selection and moral hazard were presented in that chapter and you may want to review them in order to get a complete picture of the problems facing health insurance provision in the U.S.**

Learning Objective 2: Discuss the use of taxes and tradable permits in environmental regulation.

Hint: You may want to review the concepts of external costs and benefits presented in Chapter 12.

The Cost-Benefit Principle suggests that one way to get a firm to pollute less is to increase the cost to them. A simple way to do this is to impose a tax proportional to the external cost per unit of output produced; we discussed this policy in Chapter 12. Example 15.3 adds an important point to the previous discussion: a tax will not only reduce production of the good that is creating the external cost, it will do so by giving an incentive to use the least cost method of pollution reduction.

Another way to achieve the same result is to set a target level of pollution and then auction off permits to emit the pollution. A company would only be allowed to pollute if they had a permit and then only the amount specified by the permit. This forces the firm to ask, how much is it worth to me to pollute a given amount? This sets the price at which permits will trade and ensures that those who want to pollute more will have to pay more for the privilege and those who reduce their emissions can sell their permits and be rewarded for their behavior. This has the further benefit of citizens being able to directly participate in the process by buying permits. A group that wants to stop reduce an emission to zero can, for example, prevent the pollution from taking place by purchasing all of the permits.

Learning Objective 3: Provide an economic analysis of workplace safety regulation. Discus the economics of workers' compensation.
Workplace safety is an important topic since most (probably all!) of us will work for a living. Currently, safety is regulated directly through rules and laws established by local, state and federal governments. These regulations are often defended as a necessary check on employer power. Conversely, they are often attacked as unnecessary in a world where workers can leave unsafe jobs and where employers have an incentive to provide the necessary degree of safety in order to attract and keep workers.

Compensating wage differentials (discussed in Chapter 14) are a market response to safety risks. However, there is the possibility of a positional arms race (discussed in Chapter 13). For example, if particularly dangerous jobs pay relatively high wages, and if the income a person earns relative to another person is important, then people may accept more risky occupations than they would otherwise.

Workers' compensation is a government insurance system that provides benefits to workers who are injured on the job and thus provides another incentive for people to accept risky positions. Like compensating wage differentials, however, this system may encourage too much risk-taking since current rates for workers' compensation are not tied directly to injury rates. The incentive to create a safe workplace is not high enough for firms and they will allow injuries to occur since it is cheaper to simply let workers' compensation pay for the injury.

Learning Objective 4: Discuss the economics of public health and security policies.
Terrorist attacks, hurricanes that devastated the Gulf Coast of the U.S. and concerns about flu pandemics have stimulated increased expenditures on public health and public safety. The Cost-Benefit Principle can be fruitfully applied to these areas just as they were to health care, environmental regulation and workplace safety.

For example, the Cost-Benefit Principle suggests that the optimal amount a society should spend on public health is that amount which equates the marginal benefit and the marginal cost of public health. The difficulty is that this spending cannot be left solely to the market because public health measures such as vaccinations carry external benefits and thus will be under produced unless measures are taken to "internalize" the external benefits.

III. Self-Test

Key Terms
Match the term in the right-hand column with the appropriate definition in the left-hand column by placing the letter of the term in the blank in front of its definition. (Answers are given at the end of the chapter.)

1. _____ A government insurance system that provides benefits to workers who are injured on the job.

2. _____ Insurance that pays all expenses generated by an insured activity.

3. _____ A group of health care professionals that provides services to individuals and families for a fixed annual fee.

a. first-dollar insurance coverage

b. health maintenance organization (HMO)

c. workers' compensation

Multiple-Choice Questions
Circle the letter that corresponds to the best answer. (Answers are given at the end of the chapter.)

Use the following information for problems 1, 2, 3 and 4: Tony has a sinus problem and is going to the doctor for treatment. Suppose that the doctor charges her patients $50 per visit. Tony's demand curve for visiting the doctor is given by the following table:

Number of visits	1	2	3	4
Marginal benefit	75	50	25	0

1. If Tony has first-dollar health insurance coverage, he will visit the doctor _____ time(s) to treat his sinus problem.
    A. 0   B. 1   C. 2   D. 3   E. 4

2. If Tony has no health insurance and must pay for his visits to the doctor himself, he will visit the doctor _____ time(s) to treat his sinus problem.
    A. 0   B. 1   C. 2   D. 3   E. 4

3.   Suppose Tony purchases a health insurance plan before visiting the doctor. The plan
      reimburses Tony $25 for each visit to the doctor. Under this plan, he will visit the doctor
      _____ time(s) to treat his sinus problem.
      A. 0   B. 1   C. 2   D. 3   E. 4

4.   Suppose that when Tony has a sinus problem he starts to sneeze, causing his family and
      co-workers to get sick. If Tony has a health plan that reimburses Tony $25 for each visit
      to the doctor, then the number of visits that Tony chooses will be
      A.   less than the socially optimal number of visits.
      B.   equal to the socially optimal number of visits.
      C.   more than the socially optimal number of visits.
      D.   the number of visits that drives his marginal benefit to zero.
      E.   indeterminate given the information provided.

5.   In terms of economic efficiency, first-dollar insurance coverage often encourages
      consumers to use _____ medical treatment. By contrast, HMOs tend to provide
      _____ medical treatment.
      A.   far too inexpensive; far too expensive
      B.   preventative; emergency
      C.   too much; too little
      D.   too little; too much
      E.   too little; just the right amount.

6.   A serious problem in the U.S. today is that the cost of health insurance is _____
      causing _____ to purchase it.
      A.   too low; too few
      B.   too low; too many
      C.   too high; too many
      D.   too high; too few
      E.   too high; no one

7.   An advantage of _____, when compared to other types of environmental
      programs, is that this program is economically efficient yet it does not require a detailed
      knowledge of the marginal cost of pollution on the part of the government.
      A.   a pollution tax
      B.   tradable pollution permits
      C.   fining polluters
      D.   government clean-ups of polluted sites
      E.   requiring across-the-board reductions in emissions

8.   The most efficient distribution of pollution abatement is the one for which
      A.   each polluter's total cost of abatement is the same.
      B.   each polluter's average cost of abatement is the same.
      C.   each polluter's marginal cost of abatement is the same.
      D.   each polluter reduces their amount of pollution by the same quantity.
      E.   each polluter reduces their amount of pollution to zero.

Use the following information for problems 9, 10, 11 and 12: Suppose that two paper companies are releasing harmful chemicals into a river as part of their production process. Each firm is currently releasing 5 tons of chemicals per day. There are 6 different technologies the firms can use to produce paper; the table below identifies the technologies (labeled #1 through #6), the quantity of chemicals that will be emitted by each technology, and the total cost (in dollars) to each firm of using that technology:

Firm	#1 5 tons/day	#2 4 tons/day	#3 3 tons/day	#4 2 tons/day	#5 1 ton/day	#6 0 tons/day
Acme	200	400	700	1300	2100	3100
Elmco	500	540	620	730	1000	1400

9.   Suppose that the local government enacted a regulation that required each firm to reduce its emissions by 40%. The two companies would choose technology _____ and their total private costs of using this technology would be _____.
A. #2; $940   B. #3; $1,320   C. #4; $2,030   D. #5; $3,100   E. #6; $4,500

10.   Suppose that as an alternative to a regulation, the local government considers levying a pollution tax. To reduce emissions by 40%, the lowest tax that would accomplish this goal would be _____ per ton of chemicals emitted.
A. $1000   B. $540   C. $400   D. $200   E. $40

11.   A local economist proposes tradable pollution permits as an alternative to both the regulation and the pollution tax. Each permit would allow the holder to release 1 ton of chemicals into the river. She suggests that the government auction 5 permits at an opening price of $100. The ultimate equilibrium price of a permit would be _____ and Acme would purchase _____ permits.
A. $1000; 5   B. $800; 5   C. $500; 4   D. $300; 4   E. $100; 3

12.   A local environmental organization decides that it is in favor of tradable pollution permits. They would like to see all of the pollution eliminated; to do this, their staff economist suggests that they purchase _____ permits at a price of _____ for each permit.
A. 2; $40   B. 3; $200   C. 4; $400   D. 5; $500   E. 5; $1100

13.   The workers' compensation system will act as a tax on workplace injuries if
A.   firms reduce their workforces.
B.   the premium accurately reflects the private costs of workplace injuries.
C.   firms reduce their spending on safety equipment.
D.   the premium accurately reflects the social costs of workplace injuries.
E.   the premium is a flat-rate amount for each firm.

Use the following information for problems 14, 15, 16 and 17: suppose that all workers in a small town prefer a safe job to a risky job. They prefer safe jobs to risky jobs so much that they would accept a salary that is $2000 less per year to have a safe job instead of a risky one.

Suppose that the marginal cost of providing safety is $700 per worker. Firms in the town currently pay $35,000 per year to workers and do not make any effort to improve the safety of their workplaces. A new firm is considering whether or not they should set up an office in this town; they plan to offer workers a salary of $34,000 per year and safe jobs.

14.   When the new firm announces that they are accepting job applications, they will find
        A.   no one willing to apply for a job.
        B.   only poorly qualified workers applying for jobs.
        C.   only the least safety conscious workers applying for jobs.
        D.   many workers applying for jobs.
        E.   they will lose money.

15.   The total cost of hiring a worker is _____ for the existing firms in the town and _____ for the new firm.
        A. $35,700; $33,700   D. $34,300; $35,700
        B. $35,000; $34,700   E. $34,300; $33,300
        C. $34,700; $35,000

16.   Workers employed at the existing firms receive a total benefit of _____ from their work and workers who choose to work at the new firm receive a total benefit of _____ from their work.
        A. $0; $1,000   D. $35,000; $34,000
        B. $1,000; $1,000   E. $35,000; $36,000
        C. $33,000; $34,000

17.   Bob works for one of the existing firms and Ray decides to take a job with the new firm. Which of the following statements best describes Bob and Ray's situation?
        A.   Bob will have more income and Ray will have the benefit of safety.
        B.   Ray will have more income and Bob will have the benefit of safety.
        C.   They will both earn the same income.
        D.   They will both earn more income.
        E.   They will both be worse off in terms of total benefits.

Use the following information for problems 18 and 19: suppose that the owners of a store in a mall are in the process of deciding whether or not to buy an additional security camera.

18.   The Cost-Benefit Principle suggests that the store should buy the camera
        A.   if the marginal cost equals the marginal benefit.
        B.   if the marginal cost exceeds the marginal benefit.
        C.   only if the marginal benefit far exceeds the marginal cost.
        D.   if the marginal cost equals zero.
        E.   if the marginal benefit equals zero.

19.   Suppose that the store owners decide to install the camera. If all of the costs and benefits of the security camera are accurately measured, then
        A.   There will no longer be any shoplifting in the store.

238

B.   The amount of shoplifting will increase.

C.   The amount of shoplifting will be lower than before the camera was installed but not eliminated entirely.

D.   The amount of shoplifting will be about the same as before the camera was installed.

E.   none of the actions in (A), (B), (C) or (D) will occur.

20.   Governments require children to be vaccinated against infectious diseases because
A.   parents typically take account of all the social costs and benefits of vaccinations.
B.   parents typically take account of all the private costs and benefits of vaccinations.
C.   parents typically do not take account of all the private costs and benefits of vaccinations.
D.   adults who do not need to be vaccinated will go ahead and get vaccinated anyway.
E.   parents typically do not take account of all the social costs and benefits of vaccinations.

Short Answer Problems
(Answers and solutions are given at the end of the chapter.)

1. How long should David stay in the hospital?
Let's dig deeper into Example 15.1 in the text. Suppose that David's demand curve for hospital care is given in the graph below:

A. David will stay _____ day(s) in the hospital at a price of $300 and _____ day(s) in the hospital at a price of $150 dollars.
B. Suppose David has first-dollar health insurance. In this case, he will choose to stay _____ day(s) in the hospital.
C. Suppose that marginal cost of a day in the hospital is $300 and David stays for 3 days rather than 1 day. David's additional consumer surplus is equal to _____, the

hospital's additional total cost is _____, and the change in total economic surplus is equal to _____.

D. Suppose that David's insurance policy were changed so that hospital expenses are reimbursed at the rate of $75 per day rather than $300 per day. In this case, the price to David is _____ per day and he will choose to stay _____ day(s) in the hospital. Compared to staying for one day, David's additional consumer surplus is equal to _____, the hospital's additional total cost is _____, and the change in total economic surplus is equal to _____.

E. Suppose that there is an external benefit generated when David goes to the hospital. How would this affect your answers to parts (C) and (D)? _____

_____

_____

2. Environmental regulations versus tradable permits

Suppose that two companies are emitting carbon dioxide into the atmosphere. Each firm is currently emitting 4 tons per day. There are 5 different technologies the firms can use to produce their product; the table below identifies the technologies (labeled A through E), the quantity of carbon dioxide that will be emitted by each technology, and the total cost (in dollars) to each firm of using that technology:

Firm	A	B	C	D	E
	4 tons/day	3 tons/day	2 tons/day	1 ton/day	0 tons/day
Lexacorp	350	400	500	700	1000
Jokerinc	225	250	290	400	600

A. Suppose that the government enacts a law requiring a 50% reduction in emissions from each company. Both firms will choose technology _____ and the total cost to these companies will be _____.

B. Suppose that instead of enacting the law described in (A), the government decides to issue 4 permits to emit carbon dioxide, with each permit worth 1 ton of emissions. The government auctions off the permits with an opening price of $75 each. The equilibrium price of permits will be _____ each, with Lexacorp buying _____ permits and Jokerinc buying _____ permits. The revenue raised by the government will be _____.

C. Suppose that a local environmental group does not like the idea of 4 tons of carbon dioxide emissions and would prefer only 3 tons of emissions. If they offer to (buy/sell) _____ (0/1/2/3/4) permit(s) they will accomplish their goal. The reasoning for this is: _____

_____

_____

IV. Becoming an Economic Naturalist: Case Study

How much is your life worth? That is, how much money would you need to leave to your survivors in order to compensate them for your death or for a serious injury? Are you paid a high enough wage to compensate for the risks you must endure? Are the costs of safety rules and regulations promulgated by governments worth the benefits you receive as a worker?

These may seem like impertinent questions but economists and regulators often ask them with regard to health and safety regulations. The monetary values put on a single life range between $3 million to $7 million per person according to W. Kip Viscusi, a professor of law and economics at Harvard University. In his article "Economic Foundations of the Current Regulatory Reform Efforts" (*Journal of Economic Perspectives* 10 (Summer 1996): 119-134) he reports that regulations on passive restraints and seat belts in cars pass a cost-benefit test since they cost only $300,000 per life saved. On the other hand, regulations on the use of formaldehyde do not pass this test because they cost $72 billion dollars per life saved. (All dollar amounts in constant 1984 dollars.)

Answer:

V. Self Test Solutions

Key Terms
1. c
2. a
3. b

Multiple-Choice Questions

1. E	6. D	11. D	16. E
2. C	7. B	12. E	17. A
3. D	8. C	13. D	18. A
4. A	9. A	14. D	19. C
5. C	10. D	15. B	20.

Short Answer Problems
1.   A.   1; 2
       B.   3

C.   300; 600; -300, i.e. total economic surplus falls by 300 compared to 1 day in the hospital.
D. $225; 1.5 days; $18.75, which is computed as $(1/2)*(\$75)*(1/2$ day); $37.50, which is computed as $(1/2$ day)$*(\$300)$ minus the $225 that David pays to the hospital; total economic surplus falls by $18.75 compared to 1 day in the hospital.
E.   An external benefit would mean that the social demand curve is above the private demand curve. This means that the private benefits calculated in parts (C) and (D) are smaller than the social benefits and that a one-day stay is shorter than the socially optimal length of a hospital stay. There is therefore is a case to be made for subsidizing David's health care in order to encourage him to stay in the hospital longer

2.   A.   C; $790
       B. $110; 2; 2; $440
       C.   1; by purchasing a permit, the environmental group leaves only three permits available to polluters and thus only allows them to emit a total of 3 tons of carbon dioxide.

Chapter 16
Public Goods and Tax Policy

I. Pretest: What Do You Really Know?
Circle the letter that corresponds to the best answer. (Answers appear immediately after the final question).

1. A good that can be consumed by one person yet not reduce the availability of the good to others is a(n) _____ good.
   A. nonexcludable
   B. pure public
   C. pure private
   D. nonrival
   E. common

2. A good that is highly nonrival and highly nonexcludable is a _____ good.
   A. public   B. private   C. commons   D. collective   E. inferior

3. Karl pays $12,000 in taxes and earns $150,000. Jenni earns $50,000. Under a proportional tax system, Jenni will pay _____ in taxes.
   A. $12,000   B. $4000   C. $1200   D. $400   E. $120

4. A government that levies a head tax collects
   A. the same proportion of income in taxes from each taxpayer.
   B. a higher proportion of income in taxes the higher is the taxpayer's income.
   C. a lower proportion of income in taxes the higher is the taxpayer's income.
   D. rhe same dollar amount of income in taxes from each taxpayer.
   E. taxes only from those designated as heads of households.

5. Which of the following statements about public goods provision is true?
   A. Public goods are always produced by government.
   B. The optimal amount of a public good is always produced when the marginal cost is zero.
   C. More of a public good should be provided if the marginal benefit exceeds the marginal cost.
   D. More of a public good should be provided if the marginal cost exceeds the marginal benefit.
   E. The optimal amount of a public good is always produced when the marginal benefit is zero.

6. The market demand curve for a public good is
   A. always vertical.
   B. found by vertically summing the individual demand curves for the good.
   C. found by choosing one individual demand curve and using it as a representative for the market demand curve.
   D. found by horizontally summing the individual demand curves for the good.
   E. always horizontal.

7. Private provision of public goods can be done through
   A. donations.
   B. new technologies that exclude nonpayers.
   C. private contracting.
   D. the sale of byproducts generated by the public good.
   E. (A), (B), (C) and (D).

8. Regulating externalities and property rights are
   A. functions that governments carry out in addition to providing public goods.
   B. usually carried out by private firms with no prompting by government.
   C. functions that governments carry out only when they do not provide public goods.
   D. contracted out to the private sector by governments.
   E. only done by the federal government.

9. Rent-seeking and pork barrel spending are
   A. theoretical curiosities but not important to actual government spending.
   B. synonyms for public goods.
   C. inefficiencies associated with government provision of public goods.
   D. only observed in developing countries such as those in sub-Saharan Africa.
   E. not described by (A), (B), (C) or (D).

10. If the federal government must borrow to pay for public goods and other spending, then
    A. interest rates rise but this has no effect on private firms.
    B. interest rates fall and private investment increases.
    C. interest rates are unaffected.
    D. interest rates rise and private investment increases.
    E. interest rates rise and private investment decreases.

Solutions and Feedback to Pretest
The answers to the pretest are provided below along with the relevant Learning Objective from the Key Point Review. We strongly recommend that you take the time to review the appropriate material for each question you answered incorrectly.

Correct Answer	Learning Objective
1. D	1
2. A	1
3. B	2

4. D	2
5. C	3
6. B	3
7. E	4
8. A	5
9. C	6
10. E	7

II. Key Point Review
The Forest

This chapter focuses on the economics of government spending and tax policy. This is the third of three chapters on the Economics of Public Policy; all three chapters apply the tools developed in Chapters 1 through 13 to a series of public policy issues.

The central questions you need to be able to answer are:
- What distinguishes a public good from a private good?
- What is the optimal quantity of a public good?
- What options are available to private firms that provide public goods?
- What kinds of inefficiencies are associated with public provision of public goods?
- What criteria should be applied to taxation in order to promote efficiency?

The Trees

Learning Objective 1: Define the terms nonrival good and nonexcludable good. Use these terms to discuss the following concepts: pure public good, collective good, pure private good, pure commons good
The goods and services we have discussed so far have always had two properties:
- once a person consumes a unit of the good the amount available to others is reduced by one unit;
- to consume a good, a person must pay for it.

However, there are many goods and services where one or both of these conditions are not met. For example, some goods are **nonrival;** that is they are goods that are available in the same quantity to others even after a person consumes some of it. Further, there are goods for which it is difficult, or costly, to exclude those who do not pay for them; these are called **nonexcludable goods.**

Nonrival and nonexcludable are not absolute categories; rather, economists think about goods as being located along two continuums:

We can put these two continuums together as a table that describes four basic types of goods:

		Nonrival	
		Low	High
Nonexcludable	Low	Private good	Collective good
	High	Commons good	Public good

Note: The table above is NOT identical to Table 16.1 in the text. Compare the two tables and use which ever version helps you understand these concepts.

The four extreme versions of these goods are

- a **pure private good:** a good that is excludable and has the property that when one unit is consumed there is one less unit available for others. This is the type of good we have focused on up to this point.
- a **collective good**: a good that is completely nonrival but is excludable. High-speed, wired internet access is an example of this type of good.
- a **pure public good**: a good that is nonexcludable and nonrival. National defense is the classic example of a pure public good.
- a **pure commons good**: a good that is nonexcludable and has the property that when one unit is consumed there is one less unit available for others. Common resources such as fish are good examples of pure commons goods.

Governments usually focus on providing public goods, though sometimes they produce collective goods and even private goods.

Learning Objective 2: Analyze how public goods can be financed. Describe the following types of taxes: head tax, regressive tax, proportional income tax, progressive tax.
If citizens determine that a public good should be produced, they then need to determine how to pay for it. Ideally, everyone would pay for a public good in the way that they pay for a private good, i.e. they would pay an amount equal to what their willingness to pay for the good is. This is not usually possible since the good is nonexcludable. Further, since public goods are nonexcludable they are subject to the free-rider problem.

Hint: The free-rider problem was discussed in Chapter 13. You should review this concept if you do not remember it.

Governments typically get around these problems by levying taxes on citizens to pay for public goods. One method is to impose a **head tax**, i.e. a tax in which the government collects the same amount of money from each taxpayer. Notice that a head tax implies that people with low incomes pay a higher proportion of their income in tax than do people with high incomes. This means that a head tax is a **regressive tax**.

A method of avoiding regressive taxes is to collect the same proportion of income in taxes from each taxpayer. A tax under which all taxpayers pay the same proportion of their income in taxes is a **proportional income tax**. Further, since the willingness to pay for public goods is generally an increasing function of a taxpayer's income, most industrialized countries such as the U.S. have a **progressive tax** system in which the proportion of income paid in taxes rises as taxpayer income rises.

Learning Objective 3: Analyze how a government determines the optimal quantity of a public good.
Suppose citizens have determined that government will produce a public good and that they have decided on a method of financing. The next question the public must address is how much of the good should be produced?

The Cost-Benefit Principle is, as usual, the place to begin. The government should produce a quantity of the public good where the marginal cost of producing the good is equal to the marginal benefit of the good to those who want it. It is usually no more difficult to determine the marginal cost of a public good than it is for a private good. The difficulty comes from determining the marginal benefits and, in particular, the market demand curve for a public good.

A market demand curve for a private good is the "horizontal summation" of all the individual demand curves for that good. We cannot do this for a public good because it is nonrival. Changing the price and seeing how quantity demanded reacts will not provide us any information about marginal benefits since the quantity demanded will not change when prices change.

> **Hint: The market demand curve for a private good and its relationship to individual demand curves was discussed in Chapter 5. You should review this concept if you do not remember it.**

There is, however, another way to interpret a demand curve: we can start with a quantity and ask each person what their reservation price is for that quantity. We can do this for every taxpayer and then sum all of their reservation prices. This gives us one point on the market demand curve for a public good since we have a quantity demanded and the total amount that taxpayers are willing to pay for that quantity of the public good. This is shown graphically in Figure 16.2 in the text.

> **Hint: The vertical and horizontal interpretations of the demand curve were discussed in Chapter 3. You should review these concepts if you do not remember them.**

The optimal quantity of the public good is found where the market demand curve and the marginal cost curve intersect; see Figure 16.3 in the text.

Learning Objective 4: Discuss the private provision of public goods.
Public goods are often provided by private entities. Just as with government provision, private provision involves determining the optimal amount to be produced and developing a funding

mechanism. The optimal amount to be produced is determined in the same way for a private provider as for a public provider; it is the same method discussed in Learning Objective 3.

There are many ways that private groups can provide public goods. The text presents five possibilities. **Funding by donation** is just that: individuals contribute money to pay for a public good. For example, public radio stations (e.g. Minnesota Public Radio) ask people to become members and contribute money in order to pay for programming. Private charities are also good examples of this type of provision. Another possible funding source is to develop ways to **exclude** (or reduce the number of) **nonpayers**. Those who want the good can then be charged for it just as with a private good. A variation of excluding nonpayers is to provide the good through **private contracting**. For example, a group of citizens could contract for a snow-removal service to plow their street rather than have the city do it.

Finally, the **sale of byproducts** can be a rich source of financing for privately produced public goods. For example, commercial radio stations, unlike public radio, do not solicit donations. Rather, they sell on-air time to advertisers and then use the revenue generated to pay for programming.

Learning Objective 5: Discuss additional functions of government besides public goods provision.
"We hold these truths to be self-evident, that all men are created equal, that they are endowed by their Creator with certain unalienable Rights, that among these are Life, Liberty and the pursuit of Happiness.--That to secure these rights, Governments are instituted among Men, deriving their just powers from the consent of the governed." This is the second sentence of the Declaration of Independence and reminds us that governments do much more than provide public goods.

Two important functions of governments are to **regulate externalities and property rights**. One question arises immediately when citizens try to make this general notion concrete: what level of government should be doing the regulation? The federal government? State governments? Local government? If local governments, which ones? Cities? Counties? Region-wide bodies? There are entire courses and books devoted to these questions. Here, the point to remember is that like everything else we have examined the Scarcity Principle holds. For example, if the federal government takes on more responsibility for dealing with pollution, this means that state and local governments will have less power over their own land-use policies, air-quality standards and the like.

Learning Objective 6: Discuss pork barrel spending and rent seeking. Consider the idea of "starving the government" and why some advocate this course of action.
The authors discuss three sources of inefficiency in the political process. The first is **pork barrel spending**, i.e. government spending that benefits local areas but are of questionable value from a broader perspective. For example, suppose that a local government wants to build a road and they ask for state government money to help pay for it. The road may only benefit the residents of the town but by getting state money they spread the cost among all of the state's taxpayers. This makes the local legislator more popular since he or she can tell constituents that they "brought home the bacon" (hence the term "pork barrel.") An important reason why such

programs are enacted is the fact that legislators will support pork barrel projects in other areas in return for the others supporting their projects. This is known as **logrolling**.

A second source of inefficiency is **rent seeking**. Rent-seeking is the socially unproductive efforts of people or firms to win a prize. Government contracts are a good example of this process. Firms spend far more to win a contract and then produce a good than the benefits are to society; yet it is in the interest of the firms to do this because the private benefits they receive are large.

The waste generated by these and other inefficiencies has led some people to call for "**starving the government**." This is usually interpreted to mean keeping low the amount of taxes that a government can collect in order to force the government to use efficiently what revenue it does collect. This solution ignores the Cost-Benefit Principle by calling for less government across the board rather than asking whether the benefits we receive as citizens from individual programs are equal to or less than the costs of running them. As the authors put it, the question is "how much of our money do *we* want to spend on public services?" The answer economists give to this question is, "apply the Cost-Benefit Principle."

Learning Objective 7: Address the question, "what should we tax?"
The answer to this question is that there are two effects of taxation that should be minimized in order to efficiently generate revenue for the government. First, enough taxes should be collected to **minimize crowding out**. Crowding out is a phenomenon in which government borrowing leads to higher interest rates and thus reduces private investment spending. This means that governments should try to decide whether or not to borrow using (what else) the Cost-Benefit Principle: do the additional benefits generated by the borrowing equal the additional costs created by the borrowing, including the costs imposed by higher interest rates on private firms?

Second, governments should **avoid taxes that distort incentives**. For example, taxes that are imposed on inelastically supplied and/or demanded goods will have little effect on the quantities bought and sold.

Hint: The effects of taxes on equilibrium quantities and the role played by price elasticities of demand and supply were discussed in Chapter 7. You should review these concepts if you do not remember them.

III. Self-Test

Key Terms
Match the term in the right-hand column with the appropriate definition in the left-hand column by placing the letter of the term in the blank in front of its definition. (Answers are given at the end of the chapter.)

1. ____ A good that is difficult, or costly, to exclude nonpayers from consuming.

2. ____ A tax in which the proportion of income paid in taxes declines as income rises.

3. ____ A public expenditure that is larger than the total benefit it creates but that is favored by a legislator because constituents benefit from the expenditure by more than their share of the resulting extra taxes.

4. ____ The socially unproductive efforts of people or firms to win a prize.

5. ____ A good or service that, to at least some degree, is both nonrival and nonexcludable.

6. ____ A good or service that, to at least some degree, is nonrival but excludable.

7. ____ A tax in which the proportion of income paid in taxes rises as income rises.

8. ____ A tax that collects the same amount from every taxpayer.

9. ____ The practice whereby one legislator supports another's legislative proposals in return for the other legislator's support.

10. ____ Government borrowing that leads to higher interest rates thus causing private firms to cancel planned investment projects.

11. ____ A good whose consumption by one person does not diminish its availability for others.

12. ____ A tax under which all taxpayers pay the same proportion of their incomes in taxes.

13. ____ A good or service that, to a high degree, is both nonrival and nonexcludable.

14. ____ A good for which nonpayers can easily be excluded and for which each unit consumed by one person means one less unit available for others.

15. ____ A good for which non payers cannot be easily excluded and for which each unit consumed by one person means one less unit available for others.

a. collective good

b. crowding out

c. head tax

d. logrolling

e. nonexcludable good

f. nonrival good

g. pork barrel spending

h. progressive tax

i. proportional income tax

j. public good

k. pure common good

l. pure private good

m. pure public good

n. regressive tax

o. rent-seeking

Multiple-Choice Questions
Circle the letter that corresponds to the best answer. (Answers are given at the end of the chapter.)

1.   A(n) _____ good is impossible or highly costly to prevent consumers from consuming when they have not paid for it.
      A. nonexcludable   B. pure public   C. private   D. nonrival   E. normal

2.   Police patrols funded by taxes are an example of a good that is
      A.   neither nonrival nor nonexcludable.   D.   nonrival only.
      B.   both nonrival and nonexcludable.   E.   private.
      C.   nonexcludable only.

3.   A number of countries allow whales to be hunted. Pods of whales are an example of a(n)
      A.   public good.   D.   commons good.
      B.   pure public good.   E.   private good.
      C.   collective good.

4.   A(n) _____ good is nonrival but *is* excludable.
      A.   public good.   D.   commons good.
      B.   pure public good.   E.   private good.
      C.   collective good.

Use the following information for problems 5, 6, and 7: the table below shows the annual incomes of three people:

	Ralph	Clayton	Doug
Annual income:	$150,000	$100,000	$75,000

5.   Suppose that the government decides to levy a head tax to pay for a public good. This means that each person will pay
      A.   the same proportion of their income in taxes.
      B.   the same dollar amount in taxes.
      C.   a share based on their income.
      D.   taxes only if they are classified as a "head of household."
      E.   taxes only if they are not classified as a "head of household."

6.   Suppose that instead of head tax the government decides to levy a proportional income tax to pay for a public good. Which of the following lists of tax payments would result from a proportional income tax?
      A.   Ralph pays $15,000; Clayton pays $10,000; Doug pays $7,500
      B.   Ralph pays $7,500; Clayton pays $10,000; Doug pays $15,000
      C.   Ralph pays $7,500; Clayton pays $7,500; Doug pays $7,500
      D.   Ralph pays $22,500; Clayton pays $10,000; Doug pays $3,750
      E.   Ralph pays $15,000, Clayton pays nothing; Doug pays nothing.

7.   Suppose that instead of either a head tax or a proportional income tax, the government
      decides to levy a progressive income tax to pay for a public good. Which of the
      following lists of tax payments would result from a progressive income tax?
      A.   Ralph pays $15,000; Clayton pays $10,000; Doug pays $7,500
      B.   Ralph pays $7,500; Clayton pays $10,000; Doug pays $15,000
      C.   Ralph pays $7,500; Clayton pays $7,500; Doug pays $7,500
      D.   Ralph pays $22,500; Clayton pays $10,000; Doug pays $3,750
      E.   Ralph pays $15,000, Clayton pays nothing; Doug pays nothing.

8.   One problem with a head tax is that it is a(n) _____ tax.
      A.   regressive   D.   low
      B.   progressive   E.   optional
      C.   high

Use the following information for problems 9, 10, and 11: Jack and Rita are the only two
residents on a private, suburban street in Minnesota. It snows a bit in Minnesota so the streets
need to be plowed for people to drive their cars. The city in which Jack and Rita live does not
plow private streets and so they need to hire someone to plow the street. Having the street
plowed is worth $1500 to Jack and $1000 to Rita.

9   What is the most a contractor can charge for plowing the street and still be hired by at
      least one of these people?
      A. $1000   B. $1500   C. $2000   D. $2250   E. $2500

10.   Suppose the cost of plowing the street is $2000. It is _____ for them to share the
      cost of plowing because they will have a total economic _____.
      A.   inefficient; loss of $500.   D. efficient; surplus of $1000.
      B.   efficient; loss of $500.   E. inefficient; loss of $1000.
      C.   efficient; surplus of $500.

11.   Suppose the cost of plowing the street is $3000. It is _____ for them to share the
      cost of plowing because they will have a total economic _____.
      A.   inefficient; loss of $500.   D. efficient; surplus of $1000.
      B.   efficient; loss of $500.   E. inefficient; loss of $1000.
      C.   efficient; surplus of $500.

12.   A market demand curve for a private good is derived by summing the _____. By
      contrast, a market demand for a public good is constructed by the _____.
      A.   individual quantities at given prices; individual quantities at given prices
      B.   individual prices at given quantities; individual quantities at given prices
      C.   individual quantities at given prices; individual prices at given quantities
      D.   individual prices at given quantities; individual prices at given quantities
      E.   individual demand curves vertically; individual demand curves horizontally

13. A public radio station that conducts a pledge drive is _____ to fund a
     _____ good.
     A.   using donations; private
     B.   using donations; public
     C.   selling by-products; public
     D.   excluding non-payers; private
     E.   private contracting; public

14. Pay-per-view technology allows firms to convert a _____ good into a
     _____ good.
     A.   public; private   D.   public; collective
     B.   commons; public   E.   collective; public
     C.   commons; private

15. The federal government offers loans and grants for college students because
     A.   a college education is a pure public good.
     B.   private firms will not provide loans and grants for college education.
     C.   a college education is a pure private good.
     D.   private firms will not provide college education without government support.
     E.   a college education often generates positive externalities.

16. North Dakota wants to construct a canal to reduce the water level in Devils Lake. The
     water from the canal will flow from North Dakota and through Minnesota and into
     Canada. This is an example in which
     A.   local regulation is clearly the best approach.
     B.   state regulation is clearly the best approach.
     C.   federal regulation is clearly the best approach.
     D.   a mix of local, state and federal regulation is clearly the best approach.
     E.   none of (A), (B), (C) or (D) is the best approach.

17. Federal government spending on roads that benefit only a particular district or state but
     cost more than the total benefits to the all citizens is an example of
     A.   logrolling.   D.   an inferior good.
     B.   pork barrel spending.   E.   a normal good.
     C.   a public good.

18. Which of the following is a way to prevent rent-seeking by firms who are competing for a
     government contract?
     A.   Pass a law that bans lobbying.
     B.   Require complete disclosure of all lobbying expenses.
     C.   Award the contract only to firms who have never done business with the
          government.
     D.   Award the contract on the basis of price, quality of service, or other performance
          related measures.

E.   Award the contract only to firms who have done business with the government previously.

19. _____ is a situation in which government borrowing causes interest rates to rise and leads to private firms reducing their investment spending.
   A.   Rent-seeking   D.   Regressive taxation
   B.   Logrolling   E.   Excludability
   C.   Crowding out

20. A government that needs to collect revenue should
   A.   avoid taxes that distort incentives.
   B.   impose taxes that distort incentives.
   C.   levy taxes that reduce total economic surplus by the greatest amount.
   D.   put taxes on goods that have very high price elasticities of demand.
   E.   put taxes on goods that have very high price elasticities of supply.

Short Answer Problems
(Answers and solutions are given at the end of the chapter.)

1. Constructing and using the market demand curve for a public good.
Suppose that a community consists of four people. We have the following information on their reservation prices for a public good:

Quantity demanded	Freddie's reservation price	Bill's reservation price	Sonny's reservation price	Eddie's reservation price	Market reservation price
40	1	2	3	4	
30	2	3	4	5	
20	3	4	5	6	
10	4	5	6	7	

   A. Fill in the last column of the table.
   B. The market demand curve for this public good is given by two columns in this table: the (1st/2nd/3rd/4th/5th/6th) _____ column of the table and the (1st/2nd/3rd/4th/5th/6th) _____ column of the table.
   C. Suppose that the marginal cost of producing this good is $15. The government should produce _____ units of the good.
   D. Suppose that the marginal cost of producing this good is $20. The government should produce _____ units of the good.

2. Collecting taxes to pay for public goods
Let's continue with the example we worked with in question #1. Suppose that the marginal cost of producing this good is $15.
   A. At a marginal cost of $15 the group will choose a quantity demanded of _____ units of the good. This means that the government must collect ($18/$15) _____ to pay for the good.

B. If the government uses a head tax to pay for this, it should collect _____ from Freddie, _____ from Bill, _____ from Sonny and _____ from Eddie.

C. If the government uses a proportional income tax to pay for this, then it will collect (the same dollar amount / the same proportion of income) _____ from each member of the group.

D. Suppose that Freddie's income is less than Bill's, which is less than Sonny's, which is less than Eddie's. If the government uses a progressive income tax, then the (higher/lower) _____ income members of the group will pay a (higher/lower) _____ proportion of their income in taxes.

IV. Becoming an Economic Naturalist: Case Study

The proportion of total U.S. income spent by government on goods and services has fallen from 24% in 1953 to 19% in 2004. Over the same period, the proportion of total income collected in taxes has risen from 24% in 1953 to 27% in 2004. (Data are drawn from the National Income and Product Accounts, available at www.bea.gov.) What do these data say about the relative size of public goods provision versus transfer payments made by governments? Which measure, spending or taxation, is a better measure of the size of government? Would transfer payments be subject to more of the problems discussed in this chapter (e.g. rent-seeking, pork-barrel spending) than public goods?

Answer:

V. Self-Test Solutions

Key Terms

1. e	6. a	11. f
2. n	7. h	12. i
3. g	8. c	13. m
4. o	9. d	14. l
5. j	10. b	15. k

Multiple-Choice Questions

1. A	6. A	11. A	16. D
2. B	7. D	12. C	17. B
3. D	8. A	13. B	18. D
4. C	9. B	14. D	19. C
5. B	10. C	15. E	20. A

Short Answer Problems

1.   A.

Quantity demanded	Freddie's reservation price	Bill's reservation price	Sonny's reservation price	Eddie's reservation price	Market reservation price
40	1	2	3	4	10
30	2	3	4	5	14
20	3	4	5	6	18
10	4	5	6	7	22

        B. 1st; 6th
        C.   20
        D.   10

2.   A.   20; $18
        B. $4.50 for each person.
        C.   the same proportion of income
        D.   higher; higher

Chapter 17

Macroeconomics: The Bird's-Eye

View of the Economy

I. Pretest: What Do You Really Know?

Circle the letter that corresponds to the best answer. (Answers appear immediately after the final question).

1. Macroeconomic policies are government policies designed to affect
   A. the legal system of the whole country.
   B. the performance of the economy as a whole.
   C. particular sectors of the economy.
   D. the environmental impact of all industries.
   E. the economic activity of the government.

2. Average labor productivity equals
   A. average production per year.
   B. total output.
   C. output per person.
   D. output per employed worker.
   E. production per person.

3. The value of output was $400 billion in Northland and $500 billion in Southland. The population of Northland was 80 million and the population of Southland was 90 million. There were 40 million employed workers in Northland and 80 million employed workers in Southland. Average labor productivity was higher in _____ and the standard of living was _____.

A. Northland; the same in both countries
B. Northland; higher in Southland
C. Southland; higher in Northland
D. Southland; higher in Southland
E. Southland; the same in both countries

4. When jobs are hard to find, profits are low, few wage increases are given, and many companies go out of business, the economy is most likely in a(n)
  A. expansion.
  B. boom.
  C. recession.
  D. surplus.
  E. shortage.

5. The unemployment rate is the
  A. number of workers unemployed.
  B. number of workers in the labor force.
  C. number of workers minus those without a job.
  D. percentage of the labor force that is out of work.
  E. percentage of the population that is out of work.

6. The rate at which prices in general are increasing is called
  A. the inflation rate.
  B. the unemployment rate.
  C. average labor productivity.
  D. the standard of living.
  E. the trade balance.

7. A trade deficit occurs when
  A. government spending exceeds government revenue.
  B. government revenue exceeds government spending.
  C. exports equal imports.
  D. exports exceed imports.
  E. exports are less than imports.

8. Monetary policy refers to
  A. decisions to determine the government's budget.
  B. policy directed toward increasing exports and reducing imports.
  C. the determination of the nation's money supply.
  D. policies to reduce the power of unions and monopolies.
  E. government policies aimed at changing the underlying structure or institutions of the economy.

9. _____ analysis addresses the question of whether a policy should be used, while _____ analysis addresses the economic consequences of a particular policy.
   A. Normative; positive
   B. Positive; normative
   C. Structural; monetary
   D. Monetary; fiscal
   E. Fiscal; monetary

10. Which of the following statements is an example of positive analysis?
   A. If the Federal Reserve increases the money supply, interest rates decrease.
   B. Large budget deficits should be avoided.
   C. Higher taxes are needed to support education.
   D. A tax cut that benefits low-income households is acceptable.
   E. The Federal Reserve should increase interest rates to slow down the economy.

Solutions and Feedback to Pretest
For each question you incorrectly answered, we strongly recommend taking the time to review the appropriate material before continuing. In the table below is listed for each question the pertinent Learning Objective from the following Key Point Review.

Correct Answer	Learning Objective
1. B	7
2. D	2
3. B	1
4. C	3
5. D	4
6. A	5
7. E	6
8. C	7
9. A	8
10. A	8

II. Key Point Review
The Forest
This chapter focuses on introducing the subject matter of macroeconomics and the issues that are central to macroeconomics, as well as the basic tools of macroeconomics.
Macroeconomics is the study of the performance of national economies and the policies governments use to try to improve that performance. The central questions you need to be able to answer are as follows:
   • What are the central issues of macroeconomics?
   • What are the three types of macroeconomic policy?
   • How does normative macroeconomic analysis differ from positive macroeconomic analysis?
   • What are the strengths and weaknesses of aggregation?

The Trees

Learning Objective 1: Explain economic growth and standard of living

Among the issues macroeconomists study are the sources of long-run economic growth and living standards. By standard of living, economists mean the degree to which people have access to goods and services that make their lives easier, healthier, safer, and more enjoyable. People with a higher standard of living have more goods to consume, but even the wealthiest people are subject to the principle of scarcity. Standard of living is inextricably linked to economic growth because the more we produce, the more we can consume. The high standard of living that contemporary Americans enjoy, for example, is the result of several centuries of economic growth in the U.S. Economic growth is a process of increasing the quantity and quality of goods and services that an economy can produce. Two questions economists try to answer are, What causes economic growth to fluctuate over time? and Why does economic growth and the standard of living vary among countries?

Learning Objective 2: Calculate output per person and average labor productivity

One factor related to economic growth is the growth in population and hence the number of workers available to produce the goods and services. Increases in population allow the total output of goods and services to increase, but because the goods and services must be shared among a larger population it does not necessarily equate with a higher standard of living. Because of changes in population over time, output per person (output divided by the number of people in an economy) is a much better indicator of living standards than total output. Macroeconomists also study the relationship between average labor productivity, or output divided by the number of employed workers, and living standards. Because of the connection between production and consumption, average labor productivity is closely related to output per person and living standards.

Learning Objective 3: Define recession, depression, expansion and boom

Economies do not, however, always grow steadily; they go through periods of strength and weakness. Periods of rapid economic growth are called expansions, and when an expansion is particularly strong it is called a boom. Slowdowns in economic growth are called recessions, and particularly severe slowdowns (for example, during the 1930s) are referred to as depressions.

> Note: There is no consensus among economists as to specific rates of economic growth that demarcate when an expansion should be called a boom, nor when a recession should be considered a depression. The difference between expansion and boom, and recession and depression is more qualitative than quantitative.

Learning Objective 4: Define unemployment rate and explain its relationship to recessions and expansions.

These fluctuations in the rate of economic growth cause changes in the unemployment rate, the fraction of people who would like to be employed but can't find work. Unemployment tends to rise during recessions and fall during expansions. But even during the "good times" some people are unemployed. Questions that macroeconomists try to answer include: Why does unemployment rise during periods of recession; why are there always unemployed people, even when the economy is booming; and why do unemployment rates sometimes differ markedly from country to country.

Learning Objective 5: Define inflation and explain why macroeconomists study inflation.

Inflation is another important macroeconomic variable. Inflation is the rate at which prices in general are increasing over time. Inflation imposes a variety of costs on the economy and, as such, macroeconomists are interested in understanding its causes. Two questions that macroeconomists grapple with are why the rate of inflation varies from one period to another, and what causes the rate of inflation to differ markedly from country to country. Inflation and unemployment are often linked in policy discussions because it is often argued that unemployment can only be reduced if the inflation rate is allowed to rise. Macroeconomists have studied this issue to provide a better understanding of this policy debate.

Note: Inflation does **not** imply that all prices are rising. The prices of some goods will be rising, but the prices of other goods may be falling, while the prices of a third group of goods may be constant. You can think of inflation as essentially an increase in the average price of goods and services. The average may rise even though all prices are not rising.

Learning Objective 6: Define trade deficit and trade surplus.

While macroeconomics focuses on national economies, macroeconomists recognize that national economies do not exist in isolation. They are increasingly interdependent. The international flows of goods and services are both an economic issue and a political issue. Trade imbalances, which occur when the quantity of goods and services that a country sells abroad (its exports) differ significantly from the quantity of goods and services its citizens buy from abroad (its imports), often cause economic and political problems. When a nation exports more than it imports, it runs a trade surplus, while the reverse results in a trade deficit. Macroeconomists try to determine the causes of trade surpluses and deficits, and determine whether they are harmful or helpful.

Note: Because one country's exports are another country's imports, a trade surplus for one country implies a trade deficit for at least one other country.

Learning Objective 7: Identify the three types of macroeconomics policy: monetary, fiscal and structural policy.

In addition to analyzing the factors that affect the performance of the national economies, macroeconomists also study macroeconomic policy. Understanding the effects of various policies and helping government officials develop better policies are important objectives of macroeconomics. There are three major types of macroeconomic policy: monetary policy, fiscal policy, and structural policy. Monetary policy refers to the determination of the nation's money supply. In virtually all countries monetary policy is controlled by the central bank. Fiscal policy refers to decisions that determine the government's budget, including the amount and composition of government expenditures and government revenues. When government expenditures are greater than government revenues, the government runs a deficit, and when government revenues are greater than government expenditures, the government runs a surplus. The term structural policy includes government policies aimed at changing the underlying structure, or institutions, of the nation's economy.

Learning Objective 8: Explain the importance of normative and positive analyses.

Macroeconomists are often called upon to analyze the effects of a proposed policy. An objective analysis aimed at determining only the economic consequences of a particular policy is called positive analysis, while a normative analysis includes recommendations on whether a particular policy should be implemented. Positive analysis is objective and scientific, but normative analysis involves the values of the person or organization doing the analysis. Economists generally agree on issues related to positive analysis, but often disagree on normative analysis.

Learning Objective 9: Define aggregation and identify the strengths and weaknesses of aggregation.

Although macroeconomics take a "bird's eye" view of the economy and microeconomics work at the ground level, the basic tools of analysis are much the same. They apply the same core principles in their efforts to understand and predict economic behavior. Because the national economy is much bigger, however, macroeconomists use aggregation to link individual behavior to national economic performance. **Aggregation** is the adding up of individual economic variables to obtain economy-wide totals.

Note: While macroeconomists and microeconomists employ the same basic tools of analysis, it does not always follow that the conclusions of macroeconomic analyses are the same as those of microeconomic analyses. An analogy: if an individual stands up during a football game, s/he can see better. If all spectators stand up, not everyone can see better.

III. Self-Test

Key Terms
Match the term in the right-hand column with the appropriate definition in the left-hand column by placing the letter of the term in the blank in front of its' definition. (Answers are given at the end of the chapter.)

1. ____ Decisions that determine the government's budget, including the amount and composition of government expenditures and government revenues

a. aggregation

2. ____ Output per employed worker

b. average labor productivity

3. ____ Addresses the consequences of a particular event or policy, not whether those consequences are desirable

c. fiscal policy

4. ____ The adding up of individual economic variables to obtain economy-wide totals

d. macroeconomic policies

5. ____ Determines the nation's money supply

e. monetary policy

6. ____ Addresses the question of whether a policy should be used; involves the values of the person doing the analysis

f. normative analysis

7. ____ Government actions designed to affect the performance of the economy as a whole

g. positive analysis

8. ____ Government policies aimed at changing the underlying structure, or institutions, of the nation's economy

h. structural policy

Multiple-Choice Questions
Circle the letter that corresponds to the best answer. (Answers are given at the end of the chapter.)

1. Economic growth is defined as a process of
   A. steady increase in the price of goods and services produced in the economy.
   B. steady increase in the quantity and quality of goods and services the economy can produce.
   C. constant increase in the quantity and quality of goods and services the economy can produce.
   D. constant increase in the price and quality of goods and services the economy can produce.
   E. constant increase in the number of jobs needed to produce the goods and service in the economy.

2. Our standard of living is directly tied to economic growth because
   A. everyone in society shares equally in the fruits of economic growth.
   B. the two terms are synonymous.
   C. in most cases economic growth brings an improvement in the average person's standard of living.
   D. the government can only improve people's standard of living if the economy is growing.
   E. a higher standard of living causes an increase in economic growth.

3. Microland has a population of 50 people and 40 of them worked last year with a total output of $200,000. The average labor productivity of Microland equaled
   A. $200,000.
   B. $200.
   C. $4,000.
   D. $40,000.
   E. $5,000.

4. During the 1930s, economies around the world were in a(n)
   A. recession.
   B. depression.
   C. expansion.
   D. boom.
   E. aggregation.

5. The unemployment rate is the
   A. percentage of people who would like to be employed but can't find work.
   B. number of people who would like to be employed but can't find work.
   C. fraction of people who are not working.
   D. number of people who are not working.
   E. the number of unemployed people.

6. The unemployment rate increases during
   A. expansions and booms.
   B. expansions and recessions.
   C. booms and recessions.
   D. recessions and depressions.
   E. booms and depressions.

7. The inflation rate
   A. was higher in the 1990s than during the 1970s.
   B. increases the standard of living for people on fixed incomes.
   C. is the rate at which prices in general are increasing over time.
   D. is roughly equal in most countries.
   E. rises during recessions along with the unemployment rate.

8. If a country imports more than it exports, it has a
   A. trade balance.
   B. trade deficit.
   C. trade surplus.
   D. budget deficit.
   E. inflation.

9. Government policies that affect the performance of the economy as a whole are called
   A. positive analysis.
   B. normative analysis.
   C. aggregation.
   D. microeconomic policy.
   E. macroeconomic policy.

10. Monetary policy
    A. refers to decisions that determine the government's budget.
    B. is controlled by a government institution called the Congressional Budget Office.
    C. is aimed at changing the underlying structure, or institutions, of the nation's economy.
    D. refers to the determination of the nation's money supply.
    E. can result in a budget deficit or budget surplus.

11. The amount and composition of government expenditures and government revenues is determined by
    A. fiscal policy.
    B. monetary policy.
    C. structural policy.
    D. normative analysis.
    E. positive analysis.

12. When a government collects more in taxes than it spends, it runs a
    A. trade deficit.
    B. trade surplus.
    C. budget deficit.
    D. budget surplus.
    E. trade imbalance.

13. Supporters of structural policy argue that economic growth can be stimulated and living standards improved if
    A. the money supply is controlled by the central bank.
    B. the underlying structure, or institutions, of a nation's economy are changed.
    C. positive analysis is used to determine macroeconomic policy.
    D. normative analysis is used to determine macroeconomic policy.
    E. the federal budget is balanced.

14. Normative analysis differs from positive analysis in that
    A. normative analysis is limited to determining the consequences of a particular policy, while positive analysis includes recommendations on the desirability of the policy.
    B. positive analysis is limited to determining the consequences of a particular policy, while normative analysis includes recommendations on the desirability of the policy.
    C. normative analysis is supposed to be objective and scientific, while positive analysis involves values of the person or organization doing the analysis.
    D. economists typically agree on normative analysis, but often disagree on positive analysis.

  E. liberal economists use positive analysis, while conservative economists use normative analysis.

15. When macroeconomists add together the purchases of houses, cars, food, clothing, entertainment, and other goods and services by households in an economy, they are using
  A. normative analysis.
  B. positive analysis.
  C. aggregation.
  D. macroeconomic policy.
  E. fiscal policy.

16. The strength of aggregation is that it helps to reveal the "big picture," but its weakness is that it
  A. adds together "apples and oranges."
  B. involves the values of the person doing the analysis.
  C. gives excessive importance to the details.
  D. adds together data on different individuals.
  E. may obscure important details.

17. Microland has a population of 50 people and 40 of them worked last year with a total output of $200,000. The output per person of Microland equaled
  A. $200,000.
  B. $200.
  C. $4,000.
  D. $40,000.
  E. $5,000.

18. If Macroland sells more goods to foreign buyers than it purchases from them, it will have a
  A. trade balance.
  B. trade deficit.
  C. trade surplus.
  D. budget deficit.
  E. budget surplus.

19. When a government's expenditures are greater than its revenues, it has a
  A. budget deficit.
  B. budget surplus.
  C. trade deficit.
  D. trade surplus.
  E. trade imbalance.

20. In debating a government program for agriculture, Senator Agus from Kansas stated that the spending should be increased because many farmers have suffered crop losses in the last year. Senator Scrimp from New York replied that his analysis indicates that an increase in spending for the program will increase the budget deficit. Senator Agus' statement is based on

A. aggregation, while Senator Scrimp's statement is based on disaggregation.
B. disaggregation, while Senator Scrimp's statement is based on aggregation.
C. positive analysis, while Senator Scrimp's statement is based on normative analysis.
D. normative analysis, while Senator Scrimp's statement is based on positive analysis.
E. positive analysis, as is the statement of Senator Scrimp.

Short Answer Problems
(Answers and solutions are given at the end of the chapter.)

1. Economic Growth and Standard of Living
Use the data in the following table on output, employment, and population in the United States and Canada during 2003 to answer the questions below.

Economic variable	United States	Canada
Output (GDP)	$10,948,546,920,448	$856,522,817,536
Population	290,809,984	31,630,000
Employed persons	140,178,802	29,178,765

A. Output per person in the United States during 2003 equaled _____ and in Canada equaled _____ .
B. The average labor productivity in the United States during 2003 equaled _____ and in Canada equaled _____ .
C. Based on the data in the table above, which country had the highest standard of living during 2003? _____

2. Normative and Positive Analysis
In the blank following each statement, write an N if the statement is based on normative analysis, or a P if the statement is based on positive analysis.

A. The U.S. Energy Department stated that "increased production of oil in April and May 2000 will result in lower gasoline prices in the summer of 2000." _____
B. Alan Greenspan, Chairman of the Board of Governors of the Federal Reserve System, stated in March 2000 that "the stock prices should rise no faster than household income." _____
C. In April 2000, William Sullivan, chief economist at Morgan Stanley Dean Witter, stated, "the retrenchment in equity [stock] prices will undoubtedly affect the economy later in the year."

_____
D. On April 4, 2000 in an article published in *The Wall Street Journal*, Brian Blackstone and Jonathan Nicholson wrote, "The National Association of Purchasing Management monthly index, a broad measure of the health of the manufacturing sector, slipped a bit to 55.8 in March from 56.9 in February. That corresponds to a 4.8% annualized growth in gross domestic product." _____
E. In an article published on the Dismal Science web site, entitled, "Krugman vs. Republican Gas Tax Relief," Michael Boldin analyzed a tax policy proposed by the Republican Party congressional leaders. He states, "the Republican plan to immediately repeal the 4.3 cents per gallon federal surcharge that was added in 1993 and suspend the larger 18.4 cents per gallon federal tax if gasoline hits $2 per gallon is both untimely and unwise as a basic policy. For

one it would hurt the highway fund that is a direct beneficiary of the tax. Worse yet, it would encourage gas consumption at a time when OPEC is keeping to a tight supply schedule and domestic inventories are dwindling." _____

F. In response to the question, what is the best Fed monetary policy course at this time (March 2000), Kevin Hassett, Resident Scholar at the American Enterprise Institute, responded, "The best Fed move right now would be no move, but it is a close call." _____

G. In an article published on the Dismal Science web site, entitled, "The New Economy's Dark Side," Mark Zandi states, "Families in the top 20% of the wealth distribution own well over 80% of the nation's wealth, while the top 5% of families own 60% of the wealth."

_____

3. Aggregation
Use the data in the following table on production in Macrolandia to answer the questions below.

Product	Price per unit	Units produced in 2005	Units produced in 2006
Clothing	$5	1000	600
Food	$2	5000	4000
Houses	$100	25	80

A. The total value of Macrolandia's output in 2005 equaled _____ and in 2006 equaled _____.

B. Based on your answer to Question 3A, in 2006 Macrolandia produced (more/less) _____ output than in 2005.

C. The change in output from 2005 to 2006 would suggest the Macrolandia economy experienced _____ and, thus, one could deduce that the Macrolandian standard of living had (improved/worsened) _____ .

D. The workers of Macrolandia are equally divided into three groups who each specialize in producing a single good (i.e., clothing, food, or houses). Calculate the output produced by each group in 2005 and 2006. The clothing workers produced _____ output in 2005 and _____ in 2006, the food workers produced _____ output in 2005 and _____ in 2006, and the housing workers produced _____ output in 2005 and _____ in 2006.

E. Thus, the output and standard of living of the (clothing/food/housing) _____ workers of Macrolandia's increased, while the output and standard of living of (clothing/food/housing) _____ and (clothing/food/housing) _____ workers of Macrolandia's decreased .

F. Thus, the aggregation in Question 3A obscures the fact that a majority of Macrolandia workers output and standard of living (decreased/increased) _____ in 2006 compared to 2005.

IV. Economic Naturalist Application
{No Economic Naturalist examples in text}

V. Self-Test Solutions

Key Terms
1. c
2. b
3. g
4. a
5. e
6. f
7. d
8. h

Multiple-Choice Questions
1. B
2. C
3. E Average labor productivity = output/number of employed workers, (i.e., $200,000/40 = $5,000)
4. B
5. A
6. D
7. C
8. B
9. E
10. D
11. A
12. D
13. B
14. B
15. C
16. E
17. C Output per person = output/number of people in the economy, (i.e., $200,000/50 = $4,000)
18. C
19. A
20. D Senator Agus' statement refers to the desirability of the policy, while Senator Shrimps' statement only refers to the effect of the policy on the government's budget.

Short Answer Problems

1.
A. Output per person = Output divided by population $37,648.46; $27,079.44
B. Average labor productivity = Output divided by the number of employed persons $78,104.16; $54,979.32
C. The United States has the highest standard of living because both output per person and average labor productivity are higher than in Canada.

2.
A. P because the analysis is a prediction based on an application of the supply and demand model.
B. N because the analysis is based on his values (key word is "should")
C. P because the analysis is a statement of the effect of the change in stock market prices on the economy
D. P because it only indicates the statistical analysis
E. N because it is a statement of the desirability of the policy based on his values
F. N because it is a statement of the desirability of the policy based on his values
G. P because it only indicates the statistical findings of the economic analysis

3.
A. (1,000 x $5) + (5,000 x $2) + (25 x $100) = $17,500; (600 x $5) + (4,000 x $2) + (80 x $100) = $19,000
B. more
C. economic growth; improved
D. 1,000 x $5 = $5,000; 600 x $5 = $3,000; 5,000 x $2 = $10,000; 4,000 x $2 = $8,000; 25 x $100 = $2,500; 80 x $100 = $8,000
E. housing; clothing; food
F. decreased

Chapter 18

Measuring Economic Activity:
GDP and Unemployment

I. Pretest: What Do You Really Know?
Circle the letter that corresponds to the best answer. (Answers appear immediately after the final question).

1. Gross domestic product (GDP) equals the _____ of final _____ produced within a country during a given period of time.
   A. market value; goods
   B. market value; services
   C. market value; goods and services
   D. quantity; goods
   E. quantity; goods and services

2. Three equivalent ways to measure GDP are total _____, total _____, and total _____.
   A. profits; production; saving.
   B. expenditure; income; profits
   C. investment; consumption; saving
   D. production; income; expenditure
   E. revenue; profits; production

3. If Bountiful Orchard grows $200,000 worth of peaches, sells $50,000 worth of peaches to consumers and uses to rest to make jam that is sold to consumers for $200,000, Bountiful Orchard's contribution to GDP is:
   A. $50,000.
   B. $100,000.
   C. $200,000.
   D. $250,000.
   E. $450,000.

4. Goods and services that are used up in the production of other goods and services are called _____ goods and services.
   A. intermediate
   B. final

C. value added

D. nominal

E. real

5. Capital goods are treated as _____ goods and, therefore, _____ GDP.

   A. final; included in

   B. final; excluded from

   C. intermediate; included in

   D. intermediate; excluded from

   E. non-market; excluded from

6. Suppose a jar of DeLux popcorn, which is ultimately sold to a customer at Friendly Groceries, is produced by the following production process:

Name of Company	Revenues	Cost of Purchased Inputs
Fulton Family Farm	$1.00	0
DeLux Popcorn Co.	$2.50	$1.00
Friendly Groceries	$5.00	$2.50

What is the value added of Friendly Groceries?

   A. $1.00

   B. $2.50

   C. $5.00

   D. $7.50

   E. $8.50

7. Given the following data for an economy, compute the value of GDP.

Consumption expenditures	1,500
Imports	500
Government purchases of goods and services	800
Construction of new homes and apartments	600
Sales of existing homes and apartments	500
Exports	400
Government payments to retirees	300
Household purchases of durable goods	400
Beginning-of-year inventory	600
End-of-year inventory	700
Business fixed investment	400

   A. 2,800

   B. 2,900

   C. 3,300

   D. 3,400

   E. 6,700

8. Consumption spending includes spending on:

   A. durables, nondurables, and services.

   B. stocks, bonds, and other financial instruments.

C. capital goods, residential housing, and changes in inventories.

D. goods and services by federal, state, and local governments.

E. goods and services sold abroad minus goods and services produced abroad.

9. Which of the following would increase the investment component of U.S. GDP?
   A. You purchase a vacation at Disney World in Florida.
   B. You purchase shares of Disney stock.
   C. Disney World purchases tires for the monorail from a firm in Ohio.
   D. A French man purchases a vacation at a Disney theme park in France.
   E. A French child purchases mouse ears made in California at a Disney theme park in France.

10. Which of the following would increase the government purchases component of U.S. GDP?
    A. The U.S. federal government pays $3 billion in pensions to government workers.
    B. The U.S. federal government pays $3 billion in interest on the national debt.
    C. The U.S. federal government pays $3 billion in salaries to soldiers in the military.
    D. The U.S. federal government pays $3 billion in interest to foreign holders of U.S. government bonds.
    E. The U.S. federal government pays $3 billion to social security recipients.

Solutions and Feedback to Pretest

For each question you incorrectly answered, we strongly recommend taking the time to review the appropriate material before continuing. In the table below are listed for each question the pertinent Learning Objective from the following Key Point Review.

Correct Answer	Learning Objective
1. C	1
2. D	2
3. D	2
4. A	2
5. A	2
6. B	2
7. B	2
8. A	2
9. C	2
10. C	2

II. Key Point Review
The Forest

This chapter focuses on how economists measure two basic macroeconomic variables, gross domestic product (GDP) and the rate of unemployment. It also discusses how the measures are used, and provides some insight into the debates on the accuracy of the measurements. The central questions you need to be able to answer are

- How do economists define and measure an economy's output?
- What is the relationship between real GDP and economic well-being?

- How do economists define and measure the unemployment rate?
- What are the costs of unemployment and criticisms of the official unemployment rate?

The Trees

The **gross domestic product (GDP)** is the market value of the final goods and services produced in a country during a given period. To calculate GDP, economists aggregate, or add up, the market values of the different goods and services the economy produces. Economists, however, do not include the value of all goods and services in the calculation. Only the market values of **final goods and services**, the goods or services consumed by the ultimate user, are counted as part of GDP. The market values of **intermediate goods and services**, those used up in the production of final goods and services, are not included when calculating GDP because they are already included in the market value of the final goods and services.

> **Note**: The distinction between final and intermediate goods is difficult to determine for some goods, e.g., capital goods. **Capital goods** are long-lived goods that are used to produce other goods and, thus, are not exactly final goods but neither are they intermediate goods. To overcome this difficulty, economists have conventionally classified newly-produced capital goods as final goods for the purposes of calculating GDP.

Because GDP is a measure of domestic production, only goods and services produced within a nation's borders are included in its calculation. Similarly, because GDP is measured for a given period, only goods and services produced during the current year (or the portion of the value produced during the current year) are counted as part of the current year's GDP.

Learning Objective 2: Calculate GDP using the value-added, expenditure, or income methods

There are three methods for measuring GDP: (1) by aggregating the value added by each firm in the production process, (2) by adding up the total amount spent on final goods and services and subtracting the amount spent on imported goods and services, and (3) by adding labor income and capital income. The **value added** by any firm equals the market value of its product or service minus the cost of inputs purchased from other firms. The value added by each firm represents the portion of the value of the final good or service that the firm creates in its stage of the production process. Summing the value added by all firms in the economy yields the total value of final goods and service, or GDP. An advantage of the value-added method is that it eliminates the problem of dividing the value of a final good or service between two periods.

To calculate GDP using the expenditure method, economic statisticians add together consumption expenditures, investment, government purchases, and net exports. **Consumption expenditure (C)** is spending by households on goods and services. Consumption spending can be divided into three subcategories; (1) consumer durables, long-lived consumer goods such as cars and furniture; (2) consumer nondurables, shorter-lived goods like food and clothing; and (3) services, including everything from haircuts to taxi rides to legal, financial and educational services. **Investment (*I*)** is spending by firms on final goods and services, primarily capital goods and housing. Investment is also divided into three subcategories: (1) business fixed investment, the purchase of new capital goods such as machinery, factories and office buildings; (2) residential investment, the construction of new homes and apartment buildings; and (3) inventory investment, the addition of unsold goods to company inventories. **Government purchases (*G*)** are purchases of final goods by federal, state, and local governments. Government purchases do not include transfer payments (payments made by the government in which no current goods or services are received), or interest paid on the government debt. In the foreign sector, **net exports (*NX*)** equal exports minus imports. Exports are domestically produced final goods and services that are sold abroad. Imports are purchases by domestic buyers of goods and services that were produced abroad. Using symbols for each of the components, the algebraic equation for calculating GDP (*Y*) is written: $Y = C + I + G + NX$.

> **Hint:** When calculating GDP using the expenditure method, be careful to not include in the calculation an expenditure component and one or more of the subcategories. For example, if a dollar value is give for consumption expenditures and for consumer durables, only include the value of the consumption expenditures in your calculation. On the other hand, if no dollar value is given for consumption expenditures, then add together the value of consumer durables, consumer nondurables and services to calculate the consumption expenditures component of GDP.

The third method of calculating GDP is to sum total labor and capital incomes. Labor income, before taxes includes wages, salaries, and the income of the self-employed. It represents about 75% of GDP. Capital income is made up of payments to the owners of physical capital (factories, machines, and office buildings) and intangible capital (such as copyrights and patents), and it represents about 25% of GDP. The components of capital income include such items as pre-tax profits earned by business owners, the rents paid to owners of land or buildings, interest received by bondholders, and the royalties received by holders of copyrights or patents.

Learning Objective 3: Define nominal GDP and real GDP

As a measure of the total production of an economy during a given period, GDP is useful in comparisons of economic activity in different places, but cannot be used to make comparisons over time. To make comparisons of production in an economy over time, GDP must be adjusted for inflation. To adjust for inflation economists differentiate between nominal GDP and real GDP. **Nominal GDP** measures the current dollar value of production, in which the quantities of final goods and services produced are valued at current-year prices. **Real GDP** measures the actual physical volume of production, in which the quantities of final goods and services produced are valued at the prices in a base year.

Hint: Nominal GDP for different years is essentially calculated in two different units of measures (e.g., 2002 prices for 2002 GDP and 2003 prices for 2003 GDP). Because they are two different units of measure they are not comparable. Deriving conclusions about the state of the economy by comparing nominal GDP for two different periods is the equivalent of weighing yourself on two different scales to determine whether you had lost or gained weight.

Learning Objective 4: Explain the relationship between GDP and economic well-being
While economists and policymakers often assume that a higher GDP is better, real GDP is not the same as economic well-being. With the major exception of government-produced goods and services, real GDP captures only those goods and services that are priced and sold in markets. There are many factors that contribute to people's economic well-being that are not priced and sold in markets. Thus, at best, it is an imperfect measure of economic well-being. Some important factors that are excluded from real GDP are leisure time; environmental quality; resource depletion; nonmarket activities such as volunteer services, home-grown foods, homemaker services, and underground economic activities from informal babysitting to organized crime; "quality of life" issues such as crime, traffic congestion, civic organization, and open space; and income inequality. Nevertheless, real GDP per person does tend to be positively associated with many things people value, including a high material standard of living, better health and life expectancies, and better education.

Note: In evaluating the effects of a proposed economic policy, considering only the likely effects on GDP is not sufficient. The correct way is to apply the cost-benefit principle.

Learning Objective 5: Explain how the Bureau of Labor Statistics calculates unemployment
A second macroeconomic measure that receives a great deal of attention from economists and policymakers, as well as the general public, is the rate of unemployment. In the United States, the Bureau of Labor Statistics (BLS) conducts a monthly survey of approximately 60,000 households in order to calculate the official unemployment rate. Each person in those households who is 16 years or older is placed in one of three categories: employed, unemployed, or out of the labor force. A person is employed if he or she worked full time or part time during the week preceding the survey, or is on vacation or sick leave from a regular job. A person is unemployed if he or she did not work during the week preceding the survey, but made some effort to find work during the previous four weeks. All other persons are considered out of the labor force. In assessing the impact of unemployment on jobless people, economists estimate how long individual workers have been without work. The BLS asks respondents how long they have been continuously unemployed to determine the **unemployment spell**. The length of an unemployment spell is called its **duration**. The duration of unemployment rises during recessions and falls during expansions.

Learning Objective 6: Calculate the unemployment rate and participation rate
To calculate the unemployment rate, the BLS first adds the total number of employed and unemployed people in the economy to determine the size of the **labor force**. The **unemployment rate** is then calculated as the number of unemployed people divided by the labor force and expressed as a percentage. Another useful statistic calculated by the BLS is the **participation rate**, or the percentage of working-age population that is in the labor force.

Learning Objective 7: Discuss the costs of unemployment
Unemployment imposes economic, psychological, and social costs on a nation. The main economic cost, borne by both the unemployed individuals and society, is the output that is lost because the work force is not fully utilized. The psychological costs of unemployment are felt primarily by the unemployed workers and their families, and include a loss of self-esteem, feelings of loss of control over one's life, depression, and suicidal behavior. The social costs, borne by both the unemployed individuals and society, include increases in crime, domestic violence, drug abuse, and other social problems.

Learning Objective 8: Discuss the criticisms of the official unemployment rate
There are some criticisms of the techniques used by the BLS to measure the rate of unemployment. One criticism is that the official unemployment rate understates the true extent of unemployment because of so-called discouraged workers and involuntary part-time workers. **Discouraged workers** are people who say they would like to have a job, but have not made an effort to find one in the past four weeks. Some observers have suggested that treating discouraged workers as unemployed would provide a more accurate picture of the labor market. Involuntary part-time workers are people who say they would like to work full time but are able to find only part-time work.

III. Self-Test

Key Terms
Match the term in the right-hand column with the appropriate definition in the left-hand column by placing the letter of the term in the blank in front of its' definition. (Answers are given at the end of the chapter.)

1. ____Purchases by federal, state, and local governments of final goods and services

2. ____ The percentage of the working-age population in the labor force

3. ____ Exports minus imports

4. ____ A measure of GDP in which the quantities produced are valued at the prices in a base year rather than at current prices

5. ____ The length of an unemployment spell

6. ____ Goods or services consumed by the ultimate user

7. ____ The total number of employed and unemployed people in the economy

8. ____ The market value of any firm's product or service minus the cost of inputs purchased from other firms

a. capital good

b. consumption expenditure

c. discouraged workers

d. duration (of an unemployment spell)

e. final goods and services

f. government purchases

g. gross domestic product (GDP)

h. intermediate goods and services

9. ____ People who say they would like to have a job but have not
made an effort to find one in the past 4 weeks

i. investment

10.____ A measure of GDP in which the quantities produced are
valued at current-year prices

j. labor force

11.____ Spending by firms on final goods and services, primarily
capital goods and housing

k. net exports

12.____ A period during which an individual is continuously
unemployed

l. nominal GDP

13.____ Spending by households on goods and services, such as
food, clothing, and entertainment

m. participation rate

14.____ A long-lived good, which is itself produced and used to
produce other goods and services

n. real GDP

15.____The market value of the final goods and services produced
in a country during a given period

o. unemployment rate

16.____ The number of unemployed people divided by the labor
force

p. unemployment spell

17.____ Goods or services used up in the production of final goods
and services and therefore not counted as part of GDP

q. value added

Multiple-Choice Questions
Circle the letter that corresponds to the best answer. (Answers are given at the end of the chapter.)

1. Which of the following would be included in the calculation of GDP for 2006?
   A. the price of a home built in 2001 and sold in 2006
   B. the price of 100 shares of Exxon stock purchased in 2006
   C. the price of a classic 1960 Thunderbird purchased in 2006
   D. the price of a new punch press built and purchased in 2006 to replace a worn out machine
   E. the price of a used bicycle purchased at a garage sale in 2006

2. Which of the following is an intermediate good and, therefore, would be excluded from the calculation of GDP?
   A. a new set of tires sold to a car owner
   B. a new set of tires purchased by Ford to install on a new Explorer
   C. 100 shares of stock in Microsoft
   D. a new home
   E. a pre-owned automobile

3. The value-added method eliminates the problem of
   A. differentiating between final and intermediate goods and services.
   B. inflation when comparing GDP over time.
   C. determining whether capital is a final good or intermediate good.
   D. dividing the value of a final good or service between two periods.
   E. aggregation.

4. Consumption expenditure is subdivided into three categories, including
   A. consumer durables, consumer nondurables, and new homes.
   B. consumer services, consumer durables and new homes.
   C. consumer durables, consumer nondurables, and services.
   D. exports, imports, and services.
   E. consumer durables, consumer nondurables, and net exports.

5. Which of the following is included when using the expenditure method to measure GDP?
   A. corporate profits
   B. gross private domestic investment
   C. capital income
   D. net interest on the government debt
   E. labor income

6. Which of the following is included when using the labor and capital income method to measure GDP?
   A. government purchases of goods and services
   B. net exports of goods and services
   C. household consumption expenditures
   D. gross private domestic investment
   E. business profits

7. If the value of imports is greater than the value of exports, then
   A. net exports are negative.
   B. net exports are positive.
   C. net exports are zero.
   D. net exports are not, under such circumstances, included in the calculation of GDP.
   E. net exports cannot be determined from the information provided.

8. To calculate nominal GDP, the quantities of goods and services are valued at prices in the
   _____ year, but to calculate real GDP they are valued at _____-year prices.
   A. current, base
   B. base; current
   C. current; current
   D. base; base
   E. current; last

9. Real GDP is GDP adjusted for
   A. changes in the quality of goods and services.
   B. value added during a previous year.
   C. inflation.
   D. imports.
   E. changes in the cost of intermediate goods and services.

10. One shortcoming of GDP as an indicator of economic well-being is that it fails to measure the
    A. growth in productivity.

B. increase in the quantity of goods.

C. nonmarket production.

D. change in the price level.

E. increase in the number of imported goods.

11. GDP would be a better measure of economic well-being if it included

A. the costs of education.

B. the total value of intermediate goods.

C. the market value of final goods.

D. the sales of corporate stock.

E. leisure.

12. Despite some problems with equating GDP with economic well-being, real GDP per person does imply greater economic well-being because it tends to be positively associated with

A. crime, pollution, and economic inequality.

B. better education, health, and life expectancy.

C. poverty, depletion of nonrenewable resources, and congestion.

D. unemployment, availability of goods and services, and better education.

E. the total quantity of goods and services available.

13. The official unemployment rate is calculated as

A. the number of working-age people 16 years or older who are employed divided by the number of people in the labor force.

B. all people 18 years of age or older who are employed, plus all those unemployed who are actively seeking work.

C. the percentage of the working-age population 16 years or older who are not working but are actively seeking work.

D. the number of people 16 years or older who are not employed and are actively seeking work divided by the number of people in the labor force.

E. all people 16 years of age or older who are employed, plus all those unemployed who are actively seeking work, divided by the number of people in the labor force.

14. In the monthly survey conducted by the Bureau of Labor Statistics, a person who was not working during the previous week and was not actively seeking work during the last four weeks is classified as

A. employed.

B. unemployed.

C. underemployed.

D. part-time employed.

E. not a member of the labor force.

15. From an economic perspective, the main cost of unemployment is

A. increased crime, domestic violence, alcoholism, and drug abuse.

B. a loss of output and income because the labor force is not fully employed.

C. increased stress, loss of self-esteem and deterioration in the workers skills from lack of use.

D. workers' loss of income and control over their lives.

E. the increase in the cost of social programs to combat increased crime, alcoholism, drug abuse, and other social problems.

16. The cost of unemployment that is almost exclusively borne by workers and their families is the _____ cost.
    A. economic
    B. social
    C. psychological
    D. historical
    E. total

17. An unemployment spell begins when a worker
    A. losses his/her job and ends when he/she finds a new job.
    B. losses his/her job and ends when he/she finds a new job or leaves the labor force.
    C. starts to actively look for employment and ends when he/she finds a new job.
    D. is not working and starts to actively look for employment and ends when he/she finds a new job or leaves the labor force.
    E. becomes discouraged and stops seeking employment and ends when he/she begins to actively look for employment.

18. The duration of unemployment
    A. rises during recessions.
    B. falls during recessions.
    C. is a period during which an individual is continuously unemployed.
    D. is shorter for the chronically unemployed than it is for the long-term unemployed.
    E. is of less importance to macroeconomics than the costs of unemployment.

19. The accuracy of the official unemployment rate is criticized because
    A. unemployed homemakers and students who are not actively seeking employment are not included in the number of unemployed people.
    B. people who would like to work but have given up trying to find work are not included in the number of unemployed people.
    C. it fails to indicate how many people work at more than one job.
    D. people less than 16 years of age and over 70 years of age are excluded from the data.
    E. the BLS survey does not include all the households in the United States.

20. In recent years, the Bureau of Labor Statistics has released special unemployment rates that include estimates of the number of discouraged and part-time workers that indicate the number of
    A. discouraged workers is insignificant, but the number of part-time workers is significant.
    B. part-time workers is insignificant, but the number of discouraged workers is significant.
    C. part-time workers and discouraged workers is insignificant.
    D. discouraged workers and part-time workers is fairly significant.
    E. discouraged workers and part-time workers is decreasing

Short Answer Problems
(Answers and solutions are given at the end of the chapter.)

1. The Expenditure Approach to GDP
This problem will give you practice calculating GDP using the expenditure method. Use the data in following table to answer the questions below.

Expenditure Components	1st Quarter, 2005 ($ Bil.)
Business fixed investment	1,305.9
Durable Goods	1,023.6
Exports	1,244.5
Federal government purchases	842.0
Imports	1,938.1
Inventory investment	69.4
Nondurable goods	2,490.0
Residential investment	709.3
Services	5,029.2
State and local government purchases	1,415.9

Source: U.S. Department of Commerce, Bureau of Economic Analysis. BEA News Release (Gross Domestic Product and Related Measures, Table 3), May 26, 2005.

A. Total consumption spending in the U.S. economy during the third quarter of 2002 equaled $_____ billion.

B. Total investment spending in the U.S. economy during the third quarter of 2002 equaled $_____ billion.

C. Net export spending in the U.S. economy during the third quarter of 2002 equaled $_____ billion.

D. Total government purchases in the U.S. economy during the third quarter of 2002 equaled $_____ billion.

E. The expenditure method of calculating indicates that gross domestic product for the U.S. economy during the third quarter of 2002 equaled $_____ billion.

2. The Income Approach to GDP
This problem will give you practice calculating GDP using the labor and capital income method. Use the data in following table to answer the questions below.

Income Components	3rd Quarter, 2002 ($ Bil.)
Compensation of employees	6967.0
Corporate profits	2,243.5
Net interest	557.4
Proprietor's income	962.0
Rental income	153.7

Source: U.S. Department of Commerce, Bureau of Economic Analysis. BEA News Release (Relation of GDP, GNP and NI, Table 9), May 26, 2005.

A. Total incomes received by the owners of capital during the third quarter of 2002 equaled $_____ billion.
B. Total incomes received by labor during the third quarter of 2002 equaled $_____ billion.
C. The income method of calculating indicates that gross domestic product for the U.S. economy during the third quarter of 2002 equaled $_____ billion.

3. Nominal and Real GDP

This problem will give you practice calculating GDP using the value-added method and adjusting nominal GDP to calculate real GDP.

A. Mr. Jones harvested logs (with no inputs from other companies) from his property in Northern California that he sold to a Nevada Mill for $1,500. The Nevada Mill cut and planed the logs into lumber and sold it for $4,000 to the Mesa Company, to be used to build tables. The Mesa Company used the lumber in producing 100 tables that they sold to customers for $70 each. Complete the table below to calculate the value added by each firm.

Company	Revenues	Cost of purchased inputs	Value added
Mr. Jones			
Nevada Mill			
Mesa Company			

B. The total value added in the production of the tables equals $_____ . This is equal to the _____ of the 100 tables.
C. If Mr. Jones had harvested the logs in October of 2000 but did not sell them to the Nevada Mill until January 2001, which then sold the lumber to Mesa Company that produced the tables in June 2001, the contribution to GDP in 2000 would equal $_____ and in 2001 would equal $_____ .
D. The nation of Mandar specializes in the production of vehicles. The table below provides data on the prices and quantities of the vehicles produced in 2001 and in 2005. Assume that 2001 is the base year. In 2001, nominal GDP equals $_____ and in 2005 it equals $_____ . In 2001, real GDP equals $_____ and in 2005 it equals $_____ .

	Bicycles		Automobiles		Trucks	
Year	Quantity	Price	Quantity	Price	Quantity	Price
2001	1,000	$50	100	$10,000	400	$15,000
2005	1,500	$60	50	$12,500	500	$15,000

4. Measures of Employment

This problem will give you practice in calculating employment measures. Use the data in following table to answer the questions below.

Year	Employed	Unemployed	Not in Labor Force	Working Age Population	Labor Force	Unemployment rate (%)	Participation rate (%)
2000	136,891	5,692	69,994				

2001	136,933	6,801	71,359				
2002	136,485	8,378	72,707				
2003	137,736	8,774	74,658				
2004	139,252	8,149	75,956				

Source: 2005 *Economic Report of the President,* February 2005, Table B-35.--Civilian population and labor force, 1929-2004

A. Calculate the working age population for 2000 through 2004 to complete column 5 of the table.
B. Calculate the size of the labor force for 2000 through 2004 to complete column 6 of the table.
C. Calculate the official unemployment rate for 2000 through 2004 to complete column 7 of the table. (Round your answers to the nearest tenth of a percent.)

Calculate the participation rate for 2000 through 2004 to complete column 8 of the table. (Round your answers to the nearest tenth of a percent.)

IV. Becoming an Economic Naturalist: Case Study

The Economic Naturalist 18.5 states that opportunity cost of sending children to school is higher in low-income agrarian societies the than in high-income non-agricultural countries. The following data from the United Nations Department of Economic and Social Indicators give the per capita income in 2003 (in the equivalent of U.S. dollars) and expected number of years of formal schooling, respectively: Canada $27,097, 16; Denmark $34,497, 17; Ethiopia $91, 5; Greece $15,690, 15; Lesotho $594, 11. Is the Economic Naturalist statement supported by the data? Explain your answer.
Answer

V. Self -Test Solutions

Key Terms
1. f
2. m
3. k
4. n
5. d
6. e
7. j
8. q
9. c
10. l
11. i
12. p
13. b
14. a
15. g

16. o
17. h

Multiple-Choice Questions
1. D The punch press is newly produced capital.
2. B The set of tires is an intermediate good and, therefore, is not included in GDP.
3. D
4. C
5. B
6. E Profit is a component of capital income.
7. A
8. A
9. C
10. C
11. E
12. B
13. D
14. E
15. B
16. C
17. D An unemployment spell begins when a person becomes unemployed (i.e., is not working and is actively seeking paid employment) and ends when s/he either becomes employed or leaves the labor force (ceases to actively seek paid employment).
18. A
19. B
20. C

Short Answer Problems
1.
A. $1,023.6 + $2,490.0 + $5,029.2 = $8,542.8 billion
B. $1,305.9 + $709.3 + 69.4 = $2.084.6 billion
C. $1,244.5 − $1,938.1 = $-693.6 billion
D. $842.0+ $1,415.9= $2,257.9 billion
E. $8,542.8 + $2.084.6 + $2,257.9 + ($-693.6) = $12,191.7 billion

2.
A. $2,243.5+ 557.4+ 153.7= $2,954.6 billion
B. $6967.0+ 962.0 = $7,929.0 billion
C. $2,954.6 + 7,929.0 = $ 10,883.6 billion [The difference between the answer in 2C and 1E is attributable to some technical adjustments that are not covered in the textbook.]

3.A.

Company	Revenues	Cost of purchased inputs	Value added
Mr. Jones	$1,500	$0	1,500
Nevada Mill	$4,000	$1,500	$2,500
Mesa Company	$7,000	$4,000	$3,000

B. $7,000; total market value

C. $1,500; $2,500 + $3,000 = $5,500

D. 1,000 x $50 + 100 x $10,000 + 400 x $15,000 = $7,050,000; 1,500 x $60 + 50 x $12,500 + 500 x $15,000 = $8,215,000; 1,000 x $50 + 100 x $10,000 + 400 x $15,000 = $7,050,000; 1,500 x $50 + 50 x $10,000 + 500 x $15,000 = $8,075,000

4.

A. Working age population = number of persons employed + number of persons unemployed + number of persons not in the labor force (2000: 136,891+ 5,692+ 69,994= 212,577)

B. Labor force = number of persons employed + number of persons unemployed (for example, 2000: 136,891+ 5,692= 142,583)

C. Unemployment rate = (number of persons unemployed divided by number of persons not in the labor force) times 100 (for example, 2000: (5,692/ 142,583) x 100 = 4.0%)

D. Participation rate = (number of persons in the labor force divided by Working age population) times 100 (for example, 2000: (142,583/212,577) x 100 = 67.1%)

Year	Employed	Unemployed	Not in Labor Force	Working Age Population	Labor Force	Unemployment rate (%)	Participation rate (%)
2000	136,891	5,692	69,994	212,577	142,583	4.0	67.1
2001	136,933	6,801	71,359	215,093	143,734	4.7	66.8
2002	136,485	8,378	72,707	217,570	144,863	5.8	66.6
2003	137,736	8,774	74,658	221,168	146,510	6.0	66.2
2004	139,252	8,149	75,956	223,357	147,401	5.5	66.0

Chapter 19
Measuring the Price Level and Inflation

I. Pretest: What Do You Really Know?
Circle the letter that corresponds to the best answer. (Answers appear immediately after the final question).

1. A measure of the average price of a given class of goods or services relative to the price of the same goods and services in a base year is called a
   A. real price.
   B. real quantity.
   C. rate of inflation.
   D. price level.
   E. price index.

2. The consumer price index for Planet Econ consists of only two items: books and hamburgers. In 1999, the base year, the typical consumer purchased 5 books for $20 each and 30 hamburgers for $1 each. In 2000, the typical consumer purchased 8 books for $22 each and 36 hamburgers for $1.50 each. The consumer price index for 2000 on Planet Econ equals
   A. 1.00
   B. 1.08
   C. 1.15
   D. 1.23
   E. 1.77

3. The CPI in year one equaled 1.45. The CPI in year two equaled 1.53. The rate of inflation between years one and two was _____ percent.
   A. 4.0
   B. 4.5
   C. 5.3
   D. 5.5
   E. 8.0

4. The situation when the price of most goods and services are falling over time is called
   A. inflation.
   B. disinflation.
   C. a boom.
   D. deflation.
   E. an expansion.

5. A quantity measured in terms of current dollar value is called a _____ quantity.
   A. nominal
   B. real
   C. deflated
   D. indexed
   E. relative

6. All of the following are real quantities EXCEPT the
   A. number of new cars produced in one year.
   B. tons of steel shipped to South America.
   C. millions of computer chips shipped to computer makers.
   D. billions of dollars invested in stocks.
   E. truckloads of oranges used to manufacture juice.

7. A college graduate in 1972 found a job paying $10,000. The CPI was 0.418 in 1972. A college graduate in 2000 found a job paying $30,000. The CPI was 1.68 in 2000. The 1972 graduate's job paid ____ in nominal terms and _____ in real terms than the 2000 graduate's job.
   A. more; less
   B. more; more
   C. less; the same
   D. less, more
   E. less, less

8. The real wage is the wage
   A. measured in current dollars.
   B. required to maintain a minimum standard of living.
   C. employers are required to pay workers.
   D. measured in terms of purchasing power.
   E. the federal government sets as the minimum wage.

9. The CPI equals 1.00 in year one and 1.20 in year two. If the nominal wage is $15 in year one and a contract calls for the wage to be indexed to the CPI, what will be the nominal wage in year two?
   A. $12.50
   B. $15.00
   C. $15.20
   D. $17.25
   E. $18.00

10. If the Boskin Commission's conclusion that the CPI _____ the "true" inflation rate is correct, then indexing Social Security benefits to the CPI is ____ the federal government billions of dollars.
    A. understates; costing
    B. understates; saving
    C. measures; saving
    D. overstates; costing
    E. overstates; saving

Solutions and Feedback to Pretest
For each question you incorrectly answered, we strongly recommend taking the time to review the appropriate material before continuing. In the table below is listed for each question the pertinent Learning Objective from the following Key Point Review.

Correct Answer	Learning Objective
1. E	1
2. E	1
3. D	2
4. D	1
5. A	3
6. D	3
7. D	3
8. D	3
9. E	3
10. D	5

II. Key Point Review
The Forest

This chapter focuses on measuring the aggregate price level and inflation, adjusting dollar amounts to eliminate the effects of inflation, using a price index to maintain the constant real value of a variable, the costs of inflation, and the relationship between inflation and interest rates. The central questions you need to be able to answer are
- How is the Consumer Price Index (CPI) constructed and used to calculate inflation?
- How is the CPI used to adjust economic data to eliminate the effects of inflation?
- To what extent does the CPI measure "true" inflation?
- What are the costs of inflation?
- What is the effect of inflation on interest rates?

The Trees

Learning Objective 1: Define price index, inflation and deflation, and explain how the Bureaus of Labor Statistics estimates the Consumer Price Index

The basic tool economists use to measure the price level and inflation in the U.S. economy is the consumer price index, or CPI. The CPI is a **price index**, a measure of the average price of a given class of goods or services relative to the price of the same goods and services in a base year. The **consumer price index** measures the cost, for any period, of a standard basket of goods and services relative to the cost of the same basket of goods and services in a fixed year, called the base year. The Bureaus of Labor Statistics (BLS) determines the goods and services to include in the standard basket through the Consumer Expenditure Survey. Then each month the BLS employees survey thousands of stores to determine the current prices of the goods and services. The formula for calculating the CPI is "cost of the base-year basket of goods and services in the current year" divided by the "cost of the base-year basket of goods and services in the base year."

> **Note**: When calculating consumer price indices for a multi-year period, the denominator will be the **same** value (the cost of the base-year basket of goods and services) for each calculation.

Inflation measures how fast the average price level is changing over time. The rate of **inflation** is defined as the annual percentage rate of change in the price level, as measured, for example, by the CPI. **Deflation** is a situation in which the prices of most goods and services are falling over time, so that the rate of inflation is negative.

Learning Objective 2: Use the CPI to calculate the rate of inflation and explain why using the CPI to calculate the inflation rate may overstate the true inflation

The inflation rate is calculated for a specific time period (e.g., a year) by subtracting the price index of an earlier time period from the price index of a more recent time period (e.g., CPI in 2002 minus the CPI in 2001) and dividing the change in the price index by the price index in the earlier time period (e.g., CPI in 2001).

> **Hint**: When calculating the inflation rate for different years, the denominator will **NOT** be the same value for each calculation. The inflation rate is calculated by dividing the change in the price index by the price index at the end of the previous year. Students sometimes confuse the calculation of inflation rates with calculating the CPI and mistakenly use the base year price index to calculate a series of inflation rates.

Using the CPI to measure inflation has not been without controversy. Because the CPI has been used to index Social Security benefits, the U.S. government commissioned a report on the subject. The Boskin Commission concluded that the official CPI inflation overstates the true inflation rate by as much as one to two percent per year. The CPI may overstate inflation because of the quality adjustment bias and the substitution bias. Quality adjustment bias refers to the inability of government statisticians to adequately adjust the data for changes in product quality. The substitution bias arises from the fact that the CPI is calculated from a fixed basket of goods and services and, thus, does not allow for the possibility that consumers can switch from products whose prices are rising to those whose prices are stable or falling.

Learning Objective 3: Define indexing and deflating

The CPI not only allows us to measure changes in the cost of living, but can also be used to adjust economic data to eliminate the effects of inflation, a process called **deflating**. To adjust a **nominal quantity**, a quantity that is measured at its current dollar value, we divide the nominal quantity by a price index for the period. The adjusted value is called a **real quantity**, that is, a quantity measured in physical terms. Such real quantities are also sometimes referred to as inflation-adjusted quantities. For example, nominal wages for two different periods can be adjusted using the CPI to determine the change in real wages over time. The **real wage** is the wage paid to workers measured in terms of real purchasing power. To calculate the real wage we divide the nominal (dollar) wage by the CPI for that period. The CPI can also be used to convert real quantities to nominal quantities. The practice of increasing a nominal quantity according to changes in a price index in order to prevent inflation from eroding purchasing power is called **indexing**. For example, some labor contracts provide for indexing of wages, using the CPI, in later years of a contract period.

Note: Deflating and indexing are essentially opposite means of compensating for inflation. Deflating removes the monetary value of past inflation, while indexing adds in the monetary value of potential future inflation.

Learning Objective 4: Distinguish between price level and relative price

The **price level** is a measure of the overall level of prices in the economy at a particular point in time, as measured by a price index (e.g., the CPI). The **relative price** of a specific good or service is its price in comparison to the prices of other goods and services. Inflation is an increase in the overall price level, not an increase in the relative price of a good or service. Understanding the difference between the price level and the relative price of a good or service is necessary in order to explain the costs of inflation.

Note: Changes in the price level are generally believed to impose costs on society with little or no benefits, while changes in relative prices are generally believed to be beneficial to the economy with little or no costs.

Learning Objective 5: Explain the five costs of inflation

When an economy suffers from inflation, the cost of holding cash increases and causes consumers and businesses to make more frequent trips to the bank, and to purchase cash-management systems. Banks will, therefore, hire more employees to handle the increased transactions. These costs of economizing on cash have been called shoe-leather costs. Inflation also creates "noise" in the price system that obscures the information transmitted by prices, reduces the efficiency of the market system, and imposes costs on the economy. Similarly, inflation produces unintended changes in the tax people pay and distorts the incentives in the tax system that may encourage people to work, save, and invest. Another concern about inflation is that, if it is unanticipated, it arbitrarily redistributes wealth from one group to another (e.g., between lenders and borrowers, and workers and employers). As a result, a high inflation economy encourages people to use resources in trying to anticipate inflation to protect themselves against losses of wealth. The fifth cost of inflation is its tendency to interfere with the long-run planning of households and firms. While any inflation imposes some costs on the economy, **hyperinflation**, a situation in which the inflation rate is extremely high, greatly magnifies the costs.

Learning Objective 5: Explain the relationship between the inflation rate and interest rates
An important aspect of inflation is its effect on interest rates. To understand the relationship between inflation and interest rates, economists differentiate between the **nominal interest rate** and the **real interest rate.** The nominal interest rate (also called the market interest rate) is the annual percentage increase in the nominal value of a financial asset. The real interest rate is the annual percentage increase in the purchasing power of a financial asset, and is equal to the nominal interest rate minus the inflation rate. To obtain a given real interest rate, lenders must charge a higher nominal interest rate as the inflation rate rises. This tendency for nominal interest rates to rise when the inflation rate increases is called the **Fisher effect**.

> **Hint:** In order to correctly understand the relationship between the inflation rate and interest rates, it is important to recognize that the inflation rate is the independent variable (the causal factor) and the interest rate is the dependent variable (the effect). Thus, it is **not** correct to say that an increase in interest rates causes higher inflation rates.

III. Self-Test

Key Terms
Match the term in the right-hand column with the appropriate definition in the left-hand column by placing the letter of the term in the blank in front of its definition. (Answers are given at the end of the chapter.)

1. _____ The wage paid to workers measured in terms of real purchasing power.

2. _____ The tendency for nominal interest rates to be high when inflation is high and low when inflation is low.

3. _____ A measure of the overall level of prices at a particular point in time as measured by a price index such as the CPI.

4. _____ A situation in which the prices of most goods and services are falling over time so that inflation is negative.

5. _____ The practice of increasing a nominal quantity each period

a. consumer price index (CPI)

b. deflating (a nominal quantity)

c. deflation

d. Fisher effect

e. hyperinflation

by an amount equal to the percentage increase in a specified price index.

6. ____ A quantity that is measured in physical terms – for example, in terms of quantities of goods and services.

7. ____ The annual percentage increase in the nominal value of a financial asset.

8. ____ A situation in which the inflation rate is extremely high.

9. ____ For any period, measures the cost in that period of a standard basket of goods and services relative to the cost of the same basket of goods and services in a fixed year, called the base year.

10. ____ The annual percentage rate of change in the price level, as measured, for example by the CPI.

11. ____ A quantity that is measured in terms of its current dollar value.

12. ____ The process of dividing a nominal quantity by a price index (such as the CPI) to express the quantity in real terms.

13. ____ The annual percentage increase in the purchasing power of a financial asset.

14. ____ A measure of the average price of a given class of goods and services relative to the price of the same goods and services in a base year.

15. ____ The price of a specific good or service in comparison to the prices of other goods and services.

16. ____ A financial assets that pays the holder a nominal interest rate equal to the fixed real interest rate plus the actual rate of inflation each year.

f. indexing

g. inflation-protected bonds

h. nominal interest rate
i. nominal quantity

j. price index

k. price level

l. rate of inflation

m. real interest rate

n. real quantity

o. real wage

p. relative price

Multiple-Choice Questions
Circle the letter that corresponds to the best answer. (Answers are given at the end of the chapter.)

1. Inflation exists when
   A) and only when the prices of all goods and services are rising.
   B) the purchasing power of money is increasing.
   C) the average price level is rising, although some prices may be falling.
   D) the prices of basic necessities are increasing.
   E) wages and the price of oil are rising.

2. If the CPI is 125 at the end of 2004 and equals 150 at the end of 2005, then the inflation rate for 2005 would equal
   A) 15 percent.
   B) 20 percent.
   C) 25 percent
   D) 125 percent.
   E) 150 percent.

3. If the Consumer Price Index (CPI) overstates the true rate of inflation, the use of the CPI to adjust nominal incomes results in
    A) understating gains in real incomes.
    B) overstating gains in real incomes.
    C) an accurate statement of gains in real incomes.
    D) nominal values equaling real values.
    E) an arbitrary redistribution of income.

4. Which of the following statements is true about the relationship between a nominal quantity and a real quantity?
    A) A real quantity indicates the amount of money received, while a nominal quantity indicates the real quantity's purchasing power.
    B) A nominal quantity is measured in current dollar values, but a real quantity is measured in terms of physical quantity.
    C) A nominal quantity is adjusted for inflation; a real quantity is not.
    D) A real quantity minus a nominal quantity equals purchasing power.
    E) There is no difference; nominal quantity and real quantity are two different terms for the purchasing power of money.

5. If the Consumer Price Index (CPI) decreases
    A) the purchasing power of money decreases.
    B) a dollar will buy fewer goods and services.
    C) real income equals nominal income.
    D) there is inflation.
    E) there is deflation.

6. If you borrow money at what you believe is an appropriate interest rate for the level of expected inflation, but the actual inflation rate turns out to be much higher than you had expected, the
    A) loan will be paid back with dollars that have much higher purchasing power than you had expected.
    B) loan will be paid back with dollars that have the same purchasing power as the dollars you borrowed.
    C) borrower's and lender's wealth will have been destroyed by the higher inflation.
    D) borrower will gain from an intended redistribution of wealth.
    E) borrower will unintentionally redistribute wealth to the lender.

7. If, in a given period, the rate of inflation turns out to be lower than lenders and borrowers anticipated, the effect is that
    A) the real payments by the borrowers will be lower than expected.
    B) the nominal income of lenders will be higher than expected, but their real income will be lower than expected.
    C) the nominal income of the lenders will be as expected, but their real income will be higher than expected.
    D) both the nominal and real income of lenders will be higher than expected.

    E) the real income of lenders will be higher than expected, but their nominal income will be lower than expected.

8. The Consumer Price Index is a measure of the change in prices of
    A) a standard basket of all goods and services.
    B) a standard basket of goods determined by the Consumer Expenditure Survey.
    C) a standard basket of agricultural goods determined by the Consumer Expenditure Survey.
    D) a standard basket of selected items in wholesale markets.
    E) a standard basket of machinery, tools, and new plant.

9. "Shoe leather" costs of inflation refer to the
    A) difficulty of interpreting the price signals in an inflationary environment.
    B) unintended changes in taxes caused by inflation.
    C) arbitrary redistribution of wealth from one group to another.
    D) costs of economizing on holding cash.
    E) interference of inflation on the long-run planning of households and businesses.

10. The CPI for a given year measures the cost of living in that year relative to
    A) what it was in the base year.
    B) what it was in the previous year.
    C) the cost of the basic goods and services need to sustain a typical household.
    D) the amount spent on goods and services by the randomly selected families in the Consumer Expenditure Survey.
    E) the cost of the basic goods and services in the base year.

11. When comparing the money wages of today's workers to money wages workers earned 10 years ago, it is necessary to adjust the nominal wages by
    A) indexing the money wages in each period to today's price index.
    B) deflating the money wages in each period with today's price index.
    C) indexing the money wages in each period with the price indexes of the respective periods.
    D) deflating the money wages in each period with the price indexes of the respective periods.
    E) deflating the money wages in each period with the price index of the past period.

12. The Boskin Commission reported that the official inflation rate, based on the CPI, might overstate true inflation. It identified two reasons, including the
    A) quality adjustment bias and the indexing bias
    B) quality adjustment bias and the substitution bias.
    C) substitution bias and the indexing bias.
    D) quality adjustment bias and the deflation bias.
    E) indexing bias and deflation bias.

13. During the last half of 1999 and first quarter of 2000, the members of the Organization of Petroleum Exporting Countries (OPEC) negotiated reductions in the global production of oil. As a result, the price of heating oil and gasoline increased dramatically in the United States

during that period. This led some analysts to predict an increase in the inflation rate in the United States. Drawing such a conclusion results from confusing
A) inflation with indexing.
B) inflation with deflation.
C) a change in the relative price of a good with a change in the price level.
D) a change in the relative price level with a change in the absolute price level.
E) indexing with deflating.

14. Inflation creates static or "noise" in the price system, making it difficult for
A) businesses and households to make long-term plans.
B) lenders and borrowers to determine an appropriate level of nominal interest rate on loans.
C) employers and workers to determine the appropriate level of money wages to be paid.
D) businesses to interpret the information being transmitted by price changes.
E) households and businesses to hold cash.

15. The real interest rate can be written in mathematical terms as
A) $r = i - \pi$
B) $r = \pi - i$
C) $r = i + \pi$
D) $r = \pi + i$
E) $r = i / \pi$

16. In the United States during the 1970s, nominal interest rates were
A) falling and real interest rates were falling.
B) rising and real interest rates were rising.
C) falling and real interest rates were rising.
D) rising and real interest rates were falling.
E) rising and real interest rates became negative.

17. If the Consumer Price Index is 135 at the end of 2004 and at the end of 2005 it is 142, then during 2005 the economy experienced
A) deflation
B) inflation
C) hyperinflation
D) indexing
E) deflating

18. Mr. Long is considering the purchase of a corporate bond with a yield (interest rate) of 6% per year, and he expects the inflation rate will average 4% per year during the period that he would hold the bond. Mr. Long has decided to purchase the bond only if the real rate of return is positive on the investment. If the tax rate on the interest income is
A) greater than 33.3%, he should buy the bond.
B) greater than 50%, he should buy the bond.
C) less than 33.3%, he should buy the bond.
D) less than 50%, he should buy the bond.
E) less than 33.3%, he should not buy the bond.

19. Ms. Savior bought 300 shares of stock in the Dot.com Company in 2000 for $1,000. In 2002 she sold the shares for $1,050, earning $50 in capital gains. She must pay a 20% capital gains tax, leaving her with a net gain of $40. During the two years that she held the stock the price level rose by 4%. As a result her real return on the stock was

A) positive.
B) negative.
C) zero.
D) greater than the nominal yield (interest rate).
E) equal to the nominal yield (interest rate).

20. According to the Fisher Effect

A) high interest rates will cause high inflation rates.
B) high inflation rates will cause high interest rates.
C) low interest rates will cause high inflation rates.
D) low interest rates will cause low inflation rates.
E) low inflation rates will cause high interest rates.

Short Answer Problems
(Answers and solutions are given at the end of the chapter.)

1. Consumer Price Index and Inflation

The data in the following table are taken from the U.S. Consumer Expenditure Survey conducted by the Bureau of Labor Statistics. The "Average Annual Expenditure" refers to the cost of purchasing the standard market basket of goods and services by the typical household in the United States in each year.

Year	Average Annual Expenditure	Consumer Price Index	Inflation rate (%)	After-tax Income	After-tax Real Income
2003	$40,817			$48,596	
2002	40,677			46,934	
2001	39,518			44,587	
2000	38,045			41,532	
1999	36,995			40,652	
1998	35,535			38,358	

A. Using 1998 as the base year, complete column 3 of the table by calculating the Consumer Price Index for 1997-2003.

B. Complete column 4 of the table by calculating the inflation rates for 1998-2003.

C. In the same survey, the BLS provides the average nominal income after paying taxes of the typical household, shown in column 5 of the table. Using the CPI to adjust the nominal income, complete column 6 of the table by calculating the after-tax real income of the typical household for 1997-2003.

D. In which of the years from 1997-2003 was the typical household in the United States economically best off? _____ .

E. In which of the years from 1997-2003 was the typical household in the United States economically worst off? _____

2. Costs of Higher Education

Deloitte and Touche, LLP (an accounting firm) estimated the average cost of college during 1994-95 for four-year public and private institutions. The data is shown in the table below.

Categories	Public Colleges	Private Colleges
Tuition and fees	$2,686	$11,709
Books and Supplies	578	585
Room and Board	3,826	4,976
Transportation	592	523
Other	1,308	991
Total Cost	**$8,990**	**$18,784**

A. In the year 2000-01, it has also estimated that the total cost of attending a public college was $14,266 and a private college was $33,277. Using 1994-95 as the base year, calculate the price index for attending public and private colleges. Price index for public college 1994-95 _____ ; price index for private college 1994-95 _____; price index for public college 2000-01_____ ; price index for public college 2000-01 _____ .

B. What was the percentage increase in the cost of attending a public college between 1994-95 and 2000-01? _____ percent. What was the percentage increase in the cost of attending a private college between 1994-95 and 2000-01? _____ percent.

C. Sam attended a public college in his home state beginning in 1994-95 and graduated in 2000-01. He paid the cost of his college education by working part time and summers as a firefighter. When he entered college his nominal (money) income was $13,000 and the year he graduated his nominal income had risen to $15,500. Because the cost of college includes all his living expenses, the price index for attending a public college represents his cost of living index. Thus, his real income (measured in 1994-95 dollars) in 1994-95 was $_____ and in 2000-01 it was $_____ .

D. Was Sam economically better off during the year he graduated or the first year he entered college? Explain your answer. _____

E. Sue attended a private college outside of her home state beginning in 1994-95 and she also graduated in 2000-01. She paid the cost of her college education by working part time and summers as a consultant to businesses designing web pages. When she entered college her nominal (money) income was $40,000. Because the cost of college includes all her living expenses, the price index for attending a private college represents her cost of living index. If her real income was to remain constant from 1994-95 through 2000-01, her nominal income in 2000-01 would have had to rise to $_____ .

3. Nominal and Real Interest Rates

Answer the questions below based on the data in the following table. The table shows the inflation rate in the United States, measured by the CPI, and nominal interest rate, measured by the yield on the 10-year Treasury bond.

Year	Inflation rate	Interest rate
2004	2.68	4.27
2000	3.38	6.03
1996	1.88	6.44
1992	2.75	7.01
1988	3.65	8.85

A. In what year was the real interest rate on the 10-year Treasury bond the highest? _____
B. In what year did the financial investors who bought the 10-year Treasury bonds get the best deal? _____
C. In what year was the real interest rate on the 10-year Treasury bond the lowest, but still positive? _____
D. In what year did the financial investors who bought the 10-year Treasury bonds get the worst deal? _____
E. What was the real interest rate on the 10-year Treasury bond in 1996? _____ %

IV. Becoming an Economic Naturalist: Case Study

In Economic Naturalist 19.1, the textbook authors discuss the political implications of the minimum wage not being indexed to inflation. The table below shows the historical nominal minimum wage and the CPI from 1960 to 2000. Answer the questions below using the data in the table to determine the economic implications of the minimum wage not being indexed to inflation.

Year	Nominal Minimum Wage	CPI ('82-84=100)	Year	Nominal Minimum Wage	CPI ('82-84=100)
1960	$1.00	29.6	1985	$3.35	107.6
1965	$1.25	31.5	1990	$3.80	130.7
1970	$1.60	38.8	1995	$4.25	152.4
1975	$2.10	53.8	2000	$5.15	172.2
1980	$3.10	82.4	2004	$5.15	188.9

In which of the years shown in the table was the real value of the minimum wage highest? In which of the years shown in the table was the real value of the minimum wage lowest? During which two periods was the real value of the minimum wage rising? During which time period was the real value of the minimum wage rising? In which year, 1960 or 2004, did minimum wage earners have the highest purchasing power?
Answer:

V. Self-Test Solutions

Key Terms
1. o
2. d
3. k
4. c
5. f
6. n
7. h
8. e
9. a
10. l
11. i
12. b
13. m
14. j

15. p
16. g

Multiple-Choice Questions

1. C
2. B The inflation rate = (150 – 125)/125 = 25/125 = .20 or 20%
3. A If the true inflation rate is less than the official measure of inflation, then the real income would be greater than the official data would suggest.
4. B
5. E
6. D The borrower gains from being able to pay back the loan in less valuable dollars.
7. C
8. B
9. D
10. A
11. D
12. B
13. C The changes in the prices of gasoline and heating oil are changes in relative prices, not changes in the price level that would indicate inflation.
14. D
15. A r = real interest rate; i = nominal, or market, interest rate; and π = inflation rate
16. E
17. B
18. C If the tax rate is 33.3% or greater, Mr. Long will pay the equivalent of 2% or more in income taxes, leaving him an after-tax nominal return of 4% or less. Subtracting the 4% expected inflation would result in a zero or negative real return on the investment. Since he decided to only invest if the real return was positive he should only buy the bond if the tax rate is less than 33.3%.
19. C The $40 after-tax return divided by the $1,000 price of the bond equals a nominal rate of return of 4%. Subtracting the inflation rate of 4% would give her a real return of zero.
20. B

Short Answer Problems

1.
A. CPI = (cost of the base-year basket of goods and services in the current year) divided by (cost of the base-year basket of goods and services in the base year) . For example, 2001 CPI = $39,518 / $35,535 = 1.11
B. inflation rate = (CPI in year – CPI in previous year) / CPI in previous year. For example, 2001 inflation rate = (1.11 – 1.07) / 1.07 = 3.74%
C. real income = nominal income / price index. For example, 2001 After tax real income = $44,587/ 1.11= $40,168.47

Year	Average Annual Expenditure	Consumer Price Index	Inflation rate (%)	After-tax Income	After-tax Real Income
2003	$40,817	1.15	0.88	$48,596	$42,257.39
2002	40,677	1.14	2.70	46,934	$41,170.18

2001	39,518	1.11	3.74	44,587	$40,168.47
2000	38,045	1.07	2.88	41,532	$38,814.95
1999	36,995	1.04	4.00	40,652	$39,088.46
1998	35,535	1.00	NA	38,358	$38,358.00

D. 2003
E. 1998

2.
A. price index = $8.990/$8,990 = 1.00; 1.00; $14,266/$8,990 = 1.59; 1.77
B. percentage change = ($14,266- $8,990)/ $8,990 =58.7%; 77.2%
C. real income = $13,000 / 1.00 = $13,000; ($15,500/1.59 =) $9,748.43
D. during his first year
E. To determine how much her income would need to rise by, you need to index her income during the first year of school by multiplying it times the price index for private college during year she graduated, (i.e., $40,000 x 1.77 = $70,800.00).

3.
A. 1988
B. 1988
C. 2004
D. 2004
E. 4.56% (= 6.4 – 1.88)

Chapter 20
Economic Growth, Productivity, and Living Standards

I. Pretest: What Do You Really Know?

Circle the letter that corresponds to the best answer. (Answers appear immediately after the final question).

1. The key indicator of a country's living standard and economic well being is
   A. the unemployment rate.
   B. the inflation rate.
   C. real GDP.
   D. real GDP per person.
   E. average labor productivity.

2. Real GDP per person in Westland is $15,000, while real GDP in Eastland is $20,000, However, Westland's real GDP per person is growing at 2.5 % per year and Eastland's is growing at 1.5% per year. If these growth rates persist indefinitely, then
   A. Westland's real GDP per person will increase until it equals, but does not exceed, Eastland's.
   B. Westland's real GDP per person will eventually be greater than Eastland's.
   C. Eastland's real GDP per person will always be greater than Westland's.
   D. Eastland's real GDP per person will decline until it equals Westland's.
   E. Eastland's real GDP per person will decline, but never be less than Westland's.

3. If real GDP per person equaled $1,000 in 1900 and grew at a 4 percent annual rate, what would real GDP equal 100 years later?
   A. $4,040
   B. $5,100
   C. $8,705
   D. $50,505
   E. $4,780,612

304

4. The payment of interest not only on the original deposit, but on all previously accumulated interest is called
   A. the real interest rate
   B. the nominal interest rate
   C. simple interest
   D. conflict of interest
   E. compound interest

5. If when you are 21 you put $1,000 in a bank deposit promising to pay 8 percent annual compound interest, how much will be in the account 45 years later when you retire at age 66?
   A. $4,600
   B. $13,765
   C. $31,920
   D. $48,600
   E. $86,962

6. Growth of real GDP per person is totally determined by the growth of average
   A. labor productivity and the proportion of the population employed.
   B. labor productivity and the proportion of the population in the labor force.
   C. labor force participation and the share of income going to capital.
   D. labor force participation and the share of the population employed.
   E. number of employed workers and population.

7. In Macroland 400,000 of the 1 million people in the country are employed. Average labor productivity in Macroland is $30,000 per worker. Real GDP per person in Macroland totals
   A. $1,000
   B. $12,000
   C. $15,000
   D. $30,000
   E. $42,000

8. Average labor productivity is determined by
   A. consumption, investment, government spending, and net exports.
   B. the number employed, unemployed, and the labor force participation rate.
   C. the quantity and quality of human capital, physical capital, technology, natural resources, entrpreneurship, and the legal and political environment.
   D. the real interest rate, the nominal interest rate, and the rate of inflation.
   E. the difference between government spending and revenues.

9. Mike and Tom debone chicken breasts for Ted's Chicken Co. Mike is new and can only debone 20 chicken breasts per hour, while Tom's experience allows him to debone 50 chicken breasts per hour. Both Mike and Tom work 40 hours per week. Their average hourly productivity as a team is _____ chicken breasts.
   A. 30
   B. 35
   C. 70

D. 90

E. 140

10. Countries with large amounts of capital per worker tend to have _____ levels of real GDP per person and _____ levels of average labor productivity.
   A. high; high
   B. high; low
   C. low; low
   D. low; average
   E. low; high

Solutions and Feedback to Pretest

For each question you incorrectly answered, we strongly recommend taking the time to review the appropriate material before continuing. In the table below are listed for each question the pertinent Learning Objective from the following Key Point Review.

Correct Answer	Learning Objective
1. D	1
2. B	2
3. D	2
4. E	2
5. C	2
6. A	3
7. B	3
8. C	4
9. B	3
10. A	4

II. Key Point Review
The Forest

This chapter focuses on the sources of economic growth and rising standards of living in the modern world. Secondary issues discussed include government policies to promote economic growth, the costs of rapid economic growth, and whether there may be limits to economic growth. The central questions you need to be able to answer are

- How does compound interest relate to living standards?
- GDP per person can be expressed as the product of what two variables?
- What determines the productivity of the average worker in a particular country?
- What are the costs of economic growth?
- What are some of the policies that promote economic growth?
- What are the arguments for and against indefinitely sustainable economic growth?

The Trees

Learning Objective 1: Compare rates of growth in real GDP per person among countries during the 19th and 20th centuries

Despite the recognition that it is an imperfect measure, economists have focused on real GDP per person as a key measure of a country's living standard and stage of economic development. As discussed in Chapter 18, real GDP per person is positively related to a number of pertinent variables, such as life expectancy, infant health, and literacy. During the 19th century, the annual percentage change in real GDP per person began to increase in a number of industrializing countries, and during the latter half of the 20th century the rate of economic growth increased again. While there was a noticeable slowdown in their growth rates during the 1970s and 1980s, since 1995 they have rebounded largely because of advances in information and communication technology. As a result of the power of compound interest, real GDP per person in these countries is anywhere from 5 to 28 times greater than it was a century and a third ago.

Learning Objective 2: Define compound interest and explain the effects of compound interest on living standards

The increases in the growth rates of real GDP during the last half of the 20th century were relatively small in comparison to the previous 80 years, but the power of compound interest resulted in large changes in real GDP over time. **Compound interest** is the payment of interest not only on the original deposit, but also on all previously accumulated interest. This is distinguished from simple interest in which interest is paid only on the original deposit. When interest is compounded, small differences in interest rates or growth rates matter a lot. As in the case of the industrializing countries during the late 19th and 20th centuries, relatively small differences in growth rates, among the countries and during different time periods, ultimately produced very different living standards.

> **Note:** One way of grasping the power of compound interest is to apply what is often referred to as the "rule of 72." The rule of 72 is a quick way of estimating how long it will take for a country's real GDP to double as a result of a country's economic growth. For example, if GDP is growing at an average annual rate of two percent, by dividing 2 into 72 we find that the GDP will double in approximately 36 years. If growth increases to 3 percent, GDP will double in only 24 years.

Learning Objective 3: Discuss the relationship of real GDP per person to average labor productivity and share of working population

Real GDP per person can be expressed as the product of two terms: average labor productivity and the share of the population that is working. Real GDP per person can only grow if there is growth in worker productivity and/or the fraction of the population that is employed. In the United States, for example, during 1960-99 the fraction of the population employed increased as women entered the labor force in greater proportions, and as the coming of age of the "baby boomers" increased the share of the population that was of working age. This contributed to the increased growth in real GDP per capita in the United States during that time. In the long run, however, it is unlikely that this trend will continue as demographic changes take place. Average labor productivity is, therefore, the more important determinant of increases in living standards in the long run. In simple terms, the more people produce, the more they can consume.

Learning Objective 4: Discuss the determinants of average labor productivity
There are six factors that appear to account for the major differences in average labor productivity between countries and between generations. Human capital, i.e., the talents, education, training and skills of workers, is the *first* factor that affects average labor productivity. In general, people acquire additional education and skills when the difference in the additional wages paid (marginal benefit) to skilled workers is greater than the marginal cost of acquiring the skills. A *second* determinant of average labor productivity is physical capital, machines, equipment and buildings. More capital generally increases average labor productivity. There are, however, **diminishing returns to capital** (i.e., if the amount of labor and other inputs employed is held constant, then the greater the amount of capital already in use, the less an additional unit of capital adds to production).

Note: Diminishing returns to capital is an illustration of the principle of increasing opportunity cost, or the low-hanging fruit principle. Capital will first be applied to the most productive activities available. Thus, as additional capital is applied the marginal return will eventually begin to decline.

The *third* determinant of average labor productivity is the availability of land and other resources. In general, an abundance of natural resources increases the productivity of the workers who use them. Because resources can be obtained through trade, countries need not possess large quantities of them within their own border to achieve economic growth. A *fourth* determinant is technology. A country's ability to develop and apply new, more productive, technologies will increase its workers' productivity.

Note: Most economists would probably agree that new technologies are the single most important source of productivity improvements. Although a stable political and legal environment may be considered a prerequisite for a country to take advantage of the other five sources of productivity improvements.

Entrepreneurship and management are a *fifth* determinant of average labor productivity. **Entrepreneurs** are people who create new enterprises and who are critical to the introduction of new technologies into the production of goods and services. Managers also play an important role in determining average labor productivity as they work to introduce new technologies to better satisfy customers, organize production, obtain financing, assign workers to jobs and motivate them to work hard and effectively. Government, a *sixth* determinant, also has a role to play in fostering improved productivity. A key contribution of government is to provide a political and legal environment that encourages people to behave in economically productive ways. A stable government and well-defined property rights and free markets are important determinants of a nation's average labor productivity.

Learning Objective 5: Identify the costs of economic growth

While economic growth provides substantial benefits to society, it is not without costs. The high rate of investment in new physical and human capital requires that people save and, thus, consume less in the present. Also, reduced leisure time and, possibly, reduced workers' health and safety must be sacrificed in the present for workers to acquire the education and skills to build the capital infrastructure.

> **Note**: The fact that a higher living standard tomorrow must be purchased at the cost of current sacrifices is an example of the scarcity principle. The cost-benefit principle suggests that a nation should pursue additional growth only if the marginal benefits outweigh the marginal costs.

Learning Objective 6: Discuss potential government policies that may promote economic growth

If a society decides to try to increase its rate of economic growth, policymakers can help to achieve the goal by providing education and training programs or by subsidizing the provision of such programs by the private sector. In addition, governments can encourage high rates of saving and investment in the private sector through tax incentives. Governments can also directly contribute to capital formation through public investment in infrastructure. Government financing of research and development activities, especially in the area of basic scientific knowledge, and sharing the fruits of applied research in military and space applications can promote a higher rate of economic growth. Government also plays an essential role in providing the framework within which the private sector can operate productively, an area in which the poorest countries of the world lack adequate structural macroeconomic policies.

Learning Objective 7: Identify the issues raised in *The Limits to Growth*

While economic growth accelerated during the 19th and 20th centuries, an influential book, *The Limits to Growth*, published in 1972 reported the results of computer simulations that suggested continued growth would deplete natural resources, drinkable water, and breathable air. Critics of the limits to growth thesis point out that its underlying assumption is that growth implies producing more of the same type of goods. A second criticism is that it overlooks the fact that increased wealth expands a society's capacity to safeguard the environment. Additionally, it is argued that markets and government action can deal with the depletion of natural resources through new sources and conservation. Despite these shortcomings of the "limits to growth" perspective, most economists would agree that not all the problems created by economic growth can be dealt with effectively. Global environmental pollution will remain a problem unless international mechanisms are developed to deal with them. In particular, given that the relationship between pollution and real GDP per person is shaped like an inverted **U**, it is likely that as poorer countries become middle-income countries they will continue to pollute more until they become sufficiently wealthy to have the luxury of a clean environment.

III. Self-Test

Key Terms
Match the term in the right-hand column with the appropriate definition in the left-hand column by placing the letter of the term in the blank in front of its' definition. (Answers are given at the end of the chapter.)

1. ____ If the amount of labor and other inputs employed is held constant, then the greater the amount of capital already in use, the less an additional unit of capital adds to production.

a. compound interest

2. ____ People who create new economic enterprises.

b. diminishing returns to capital

3. ____ The payment of interest not only on the original deposit but on all previously accumulated interest.

c. entrepreneur

Multiple-Choice Questions
Circle the letter that corresponds to the best answer. (Answers are given at the end of the chapter.)

1. Which country had the highest rate of growth in real GDP per person during 1870-2003 and 1950- 2003?
    A. Australia
    B. Canada
    C. Japan
    D. United Kingdom
    E. United States

2. Compound interest differs from simple interest in that compound interest is interest paid on
    A. the original deposit only, whereas simple interest is interest paid on not only on the original deposit but also on all previously accumulated interest.
    B. all previously accumulated interest, whereas simple interest is interest paid not only on the original deposit but also on all previously accumulated interest.
    C. the original deposit only, whereas simple interest is interest paid only on all previously accumulated interest.
    D. the original deposit and on all previously accumulated interest, whereas simple interest is interest paid on all previously accumulated interest .
    E. the original deposit and on all previously accumulated interest, whereas simple interest is interest paid on the original deposit only.

3. If on the day you were born, your parents deposited $1,000 into a savings account that would earn an annual compound interest rate of 5 percent, what would the value of the account be on your 20th birthday?
    A. $1,100.00
    B. $2,653.30
    C. $3,325,256.73
    D. $1,500.00
    E. $1,050.00

4. The increase in average labor productivity is important to the economy because
   A. without it, real GDP per person cannot increase.
   B. without it, real GDP per person must decrease.
   C. it is a key to improving living standards in the long run.
   D. the fraction of the total population that is employed is constant over time and, thus, real GDP per person is solely dependent upon average labor productivity.
   E. it implies more resources are being employed to produce less output.

5. International data on the relationship between the amount of capital per worker and average labor productivity indicate that there is a
   A. positive relationship between the two variables.
   B. negative relationship between the two variables.
   C. no relationship between the two variables.
   D. positive relationship between the two variables for some countries, but a negative relationship between the two variables for other countries.
   E. positive relationship between the two variables for some countries, but no relationship between the two variables for other countries.

6. An abundance of natural resources, such as arable land, raw materials, and energy,
   A. within a country's borders is necessary to achieve economic growth.
   B. increases the productivity of workers who use them.
   C. results in economic growth only if the population increases at least as rapidly.
   D. results in economic growth only if an economy obtains them through international trade.
   E. seldom contribute to economic growth, as measured by percentage increases in real GDP per person.

7. The investment in human capital that contributed to the rapid economic recovery in Germany and Japan after World War II was mainly achieved through
   A. a superior system of higher education.
   B. public education.
   C. an apprentice system and on-the-job training.
   D. subsidies provided by the U.S.-funded Marshall Plan.
   E. a large wage differential paid to skilled versus unskilled workers.

8. The faster the rate of technological change, the
   A. lower the rate of growth in productivity.
   B. lower the rate of economic growth.
   C. higher the rate of unemployment.
   D. higher the rate of productivity.
   E. higher the rate of capital accumulation.

9. For a given number of workers, as the amount of capital is increased output will
   A. increase at a diminishing rate.
   B. increase at an increasing rate.
   C. increase at a constant rate.

   D. decrease at a diminishing rate.
   E. decrease at an increasing rate.

10. Entrepreneurship is
   A. easy to teach in schools and colleges.
   B. not affected by government policies.
   C. more important than management in determining average labor productivity.
   D. mainly affected by individual factors rather than sociological factors.
   E. believed to have been largely absent in medieval China.

11. Using production function $Y = K^{1/2}L^{1/2}$, if K increases from 4 to 8, and L increases from 25
    to 50, then Y will
   A. increase from 100 to 200.
   B. decrease from 200 to 100
   C. increase from 32 to 1250.
   D. increase from 10 to 20.
   E. be indeterminate (as there is not sufficient information to calculate the change in Y).

12. The scarcity principle implies that the cost of a higher economic growth rate is
   A. less future capital accumulation.
   B. less current consumption.
   C. greater future capital consumption.
   D. greater current consumption.
   E. greater future consumption.

13. The cost-benefit principle suggests that higher economic growth
   A. is always desirable.
   B. is seldom desirable.
   C. should be pursued only if the marginal benefits outweigh the marginal costs.
   D. should be pursued only if the marginal costs outweigh the marginal benefits.
   E. should be pursued only if the marginal benefits equal the marginal costs.

14. Most countries provide their citizens free public education through high school because
   A. the supply curve for education does not include all the social benefits of education.
   B. a market in equilibrium exploits all the gains achievable from collective action.
   C. the demand curve for education does not include all the social benefits of education.
   D. educational vouchers that help citizens purchase educational services in the private sector
      have not proven to increase human capital.
   E. direct government control over the standards and quality of education is necessary to
      increase human capital.

15. The U. S. government has promoted saving or investment in the economy by
   A. increasing the tax rates on Individual Retirement Accounts (IRAs).
   B. providing subsidies to the private sector to build infrastructure.
   C. reducing the amount of public investment in government-owned capital.
   D. providing funding during the early stages of the development of the internet.

E. eliminating all subsidies on Individual Retirement Accounts (IRAs).

16. In order to increase their rate of economic growth, most poor countries need to
    A. establish political stability and the rule of law.
    B. obtain greater financial support from the rich countries.
    C. extract more of the natural resources that lie within their borders.
    D. maintain the structural macroeconomic policies that they began to implement after World War II.
    E. increase regulation of private sector monopolies.

17. The general thesis of the book, *The Limits to Growth*, is that continued pursuit of economic growth will soon
    A. cease when all the workers are employed.
    B. consume all available natural resources, drinkable water, and breathable air.
    C. cause the principle of scarcity to no longer be an issue.
    D. increase the living standard of the poorest nations to that of the richest nations.
    E. limit our desire to increase the production of goods and services.

18. Critics of the "limits to growth" thesis argue that
    A. economic growth will always take the form of more of what we have now, rather than newer, better, and cleaner goods and services.
    B. the market is not capable of adjusting to shortages of resources.
    C. clean air and water are luxury goods and the more economically developed a country becomes the more resources there are to keep the environment clean.
    D. government action spurred by political pressure is the best way to avoid the depletion of natural resources and pollution of the environment that results from economic growth.
    E. *all* the problems created by economic growth can be dealt with effectively through the market or the political process.

19. One criticism of the "limits to growth" thesis is that the market can deal with shortages of natural resources that may result from economic growth through price changes that induce
    A. consumers to consume more and suppliers to produce less of the resources.
    B. consumers to consume less and suppliers to produce more of the resources.
    C. a slowdown in the rate of economic growth.
    D. government actions to allocate public funds to preserve open space and reduce air pollution.
    E. an optimal level of environmental quality on a global scale.

20. Empirical studies show that the relationship between pollution and real GDP per person takes the shape of an inverted **U**. This suggests that as countries move from very low levels of real GDP per person the level of pollution
    A. tends to continuously worsen.
    B. tends to continuously improve.
    C. improves, but from middle-income to high-income levels pollution worsens.
    D. worsens, but from middle-income to high-income levels pollution levels stabilize.
    E. worsens at middle-income levels, but improves at high-income levels.

Short Answer Problems
(Answers and solutions are given at the end of the chapter.)

1. Compounding Economic Growth Rates

The table below shows the output per person for selected countries in 1998 and the economic growth rates of the countries for 1990-98. Use the data in the table to answer the following questions.

Country	1998 GNP per capita[1]	1990 - 1998 Growth Rate	2008 GNP per capita
Canada	$24,050	2.2%	
France	22,320	1.5%	
Germany	20,810	1.6%	
Italy	20,200	1.2%	
Mexico	8,190	2.5%	
New Zealand	15,840	3.2%	

Source: *World Development Report, 1999/2000*, Tables 1 and 11.

[1] Calculated in 1998 dollars and using the purchasing power parity method to adjust the value of output across countries.

A. Assuming that each countrys' economy continues to grow at the same rate that it did during 1990-98, complete column 4 of the table by calculating the GNP per capita (person) for 2008.

B. On the graph below, plot the level of GNP per capita for the remaining countries for 10, 20, 50, and 100 years later, assuming a compound growth rate equal to that of 1990-98,

Compound Economic Growth

C. Approximately how many decades would it take for New Zealand's output per person to equal that of Canada's output per person? _____ decades.

D. Approximately how many decades would it take for Germany's output per person to equal that of France's output per person? _____ decades.

E. Approximately how many decades would it take for Mexico's output per person to equal that of Italy's output per person? _____ decades.

2. Why Nations Become Rich

This problem will help you understand the relationship between how much workers produce, how many people are working and the quantity of goods and services available to consume. The following table is comprised from data published by the U.S. Department of Labor' Bureau of Labor Statistics/ Office of Productivity and Technology. All data are for 1998 and the Real GDP and productivity are measured in 1998 dollars.

Country	Real GDP per person	Average Labor Productivity	Share of the population Employed
United States		$65,888	49.2
Canada	$25,496		47.5
France	$22,255	$56,722	
Japan	$24,170		51.2
Norway		$54,007	51.1

A. Complete the table above by calculating the value of real GDP per person for the United States and Norway, average labor productivity for Canada and Japan, and the share of the population employed in France during 1998.

B. The data indicate that workers in France produce considerable more output per year than do the workers in Norway, yet the average Norwegian has a higher standard of living. Explain why.

_____

C. A larger share of the population in Japan is employed than in the United States, yet the average American has a higher standard of living than the Japanese do. Explain why.

_____

D. The population in Japan is aging faster than the population in Canada and, thus, by the early 21st century the share of the population employed in Japan will decline as the elderly retire. If the share of the population employed in Japan falls to the level of Canada, which country would have the higher real GDP per capita, assuming no other changes? _____
Explain your answer. _____

IV. Becoming an Economic Naturalist: Case Study

The Economic Naturalist 20.5 discusses relationship between a country's level of income (real GDP per person) and the amount of air pollution in the country. The following table shows the classification by level of Real GDP per person of a limited number of countries in the *World Development Report 1999/2000*, and the graph shows the empirical relationship between air pollution and Real GDP per person.

Country	Ranking
Australia	High income
China	Low income
Mexico	Upper middle income
Namibia	Lower middle income

Real GDP per person

Identify each of the four countries listed in the table with one of the lettered points on the inverted U-shaped curve on the following graph. If the level of real GDP per person in Mexico increases so that it moves up to the next classification in future World Development Reports, will the amount of pollution likely increase or decrease? If the level of real GDP per person in China increases so that it moves up to the next classification in future World Development Reports, will the amount of pollution likely increase or decrease?

Answer:

V. Self-Test Solutions

Key Terms
1. b
2. c
3. a

Multiple-Choice Questions
1. C Compare the average annual growth rates for the countries in Table 20.1
2. E
3. B $1,000 x 1.05^{20} = $2,653.30
4. C
5. A See Figure 20.4
6. B
7. C See Economic Naturalist 20.1
8. D
9. A
10. E
11. D $Y=\sqrt{100} = 10$ vs. $Y= \sqrt{400} = 20$
12. B
13. C
14. C
15. D
16. A
17. B
18. C
19. B
20. E

Short Answer Problems
(Answers and solutions are given at the end of the chapter.)
1.

A.

Country	1998 GNP per capita[1]	1990 - 1998 Growth Rate	2008 GNP per capita
Canada	$24,050.00	2.2%	$37,164.90
France	$22,320.00	1.5%	$30,061.80
Germany	$20,810.00	1.6%	$28,585.53
Italy	$20,200.00	1.2%	$25,642.57
Mexico	$8,190.00	2.5%	$13,420.27
New Zealand	$15,840.00	3.2%	$29,740.56

B.

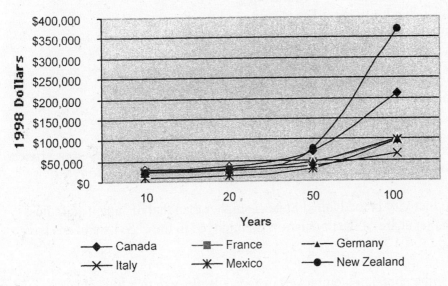

Compound Economic Growth

- Canada
- France
- Germany
- Italy
- Mexico
- New Zealand

C. 5
D. 5
E. 6

2.
A.

Country	Real GDP per person	Average Labor Productivity	Share of the population Employed
US	$32,417	$65,888	49.2
Canada	$25,496	$53,676	47.5
France	$22,255	$56,722	39.2
Japan	$24,170	$47,207	51.2
Norway	$27,598	$54,007	51.1

B. Because a larger share of the population is employed in Norway than is employed in France, the average person in Norway has a higher standard of living than the French.

C. The average labor productivity in the United States is higher than that of Japan, and, thus, despite the fact that a smaller share of the population is employed in the U.S. its citizens have a higher standard of living.

D. Canada. If the share of the population employed in Japan declines to that of Canada, the standard of living for the average Canadian will be higher than that of the Japanese because of its higher average labor productivity.

2.

A.

Country	Real GDP per person	Average Labor Productivity	Share of the population Employed
US	$32,413	$65,888	49.2
Canada	$25,496	$53,702	47.5
France	$22,255	$56,722	39.2
Japan	$24,170	$47,232	51.2
Norway	$27,581	$54,007	51.1

B. Because a larger share of the population is employed in Norway than is employed in France, the average person in Norway has a higher standard of living than the French.

C. The average labor productivity in the United States is higher than that of Japan, and, thus, despite the fact that a smaller share of the population is employed in the U.S. its citizens have a higher standard of living.

D. Canada. If the share of the population employed in Japan declines to that of Canada, the standard of living for the average Canadian will be higher than that of the Japanese because of its higher average labor productivity.

Chapter 21
Workers, Wages, and Unemployment in the Modern Economy

I. Pretest: What Do You Really Know?
Circle the letter that corresponds to the best answer. (Answers appear immediately after the final question).

1. In the twentieth century, average real wages have risen substantially
   A. only in the United States.
   B. in industrial countries excluding the United States
   C. in industrial countries including the United States
   D. in neither the United States nor other industrial countries.
   E. in the United States, but not in other industrial countries.

2. In the United States the real wages of the least-skilled, least educated workers have _____ and the wages of best-educated, highest skilled workers have _____.
   A. increased; increased
   B. declined; increased
   C. increased; declined
   D. declined; declined
   E. declined; remained constant

3. In the last two decades of the twentieth century, the number of people with jobs in the United States:
   A. declined more rapidly than the population over sixteen.
   B. declined more slowly than the population over sixteen.
   C. remained approximately constant.
   D. grew more rapidly than the population over sixteen.
   E. grew more slowly than the population over sixteen.

4. According to the principle of diminishing returns to labor, if the amount of capital and other inputs are held constant, employing additional workers
   A. increases output at an increasing rate.
   B. increases output at a constant rate.
   C. increases output at a decreasing rate.
   D. decreases output at an increasing rate.
   E. decreases output at a decreasing rate.

5. High Tech, Inc. produces plastic chairs that sell for $10 each. The following table provides information about how many plastic chairs can be produced per hour. For simplicity assume that labor is the only input. How many workers will be hired, if the hourly wage for workers is $50?

Number of Workers	Chairs Produced per Hour
0	0
1	12
2	22
3	30
4	36
5	40

   A. 1
   B. 2
   C. 3
   D. 4
   E. 5

6. As the real wage increases the quantity of labor demanded _____ and the quantity of labor supplied _____.
   A. increases; increases
   B. increases; decreases
   C. decreases; decreases
   D. decreases; increases
   E. does not change; does not change

7. The slowdown in the growth of real wages in the United States since 1973, accompanied with job growth is consistent with _____ growth of labor demand and _____ growth of labor supply.
   A. slower; slower
   B. slower; faster
   C. slower; no change in
   D. faster; faster
   E. faster; slower

8. Initially workers in the shoe industry and the computer industry earn the same wage. Reductions in trade barriers give domestic consumers access to cheaper shoes produced abroad, so domestic shoe prices fall. At the same time foreign consumers purchase more computers, raising the relative price of computers. As a result of these changes, employment in the shoe industry ____ and employment in the computer industry _____.

A. increases; increases
B. increases; decreases
C. decreases; increases
D. decreases; does not change
E. decreases; decreases

9. Worker mobility is the
   A. demand for labor in different industries and firms.
   B. movement of workers between job, firms, and industries.
   C. process of increasing the size of the working-age population.
   D. attempt to increase workers' reservation prices.
   E. way to end globalization.

10. Skill-biased technological change affects the marginal products of _____ workers differently from those of _____ workers.
    A. male; female
    B. union; nonunion
    C. government; private-sector
    D. retail-industry; service-sector
    E. highly trained; low-skilled

Solutions and Feedback to Pretest

For each question you incorrectly answered, we strongly recommend taking the time to review the appropriate material before continuing. In the table below are listed for each question the pertinent Learning Objective from the following Key Point Review.

Correct Answer	Learning Objective
1. C	1
2. B	1
3. D	1
4. C	2
5. D	2
6. D	2, 4
7. B	3, 4
8. C	5
9. B	5
10. E	5

II. Key Point Review
The Forest

This chapter focuses on some important trends in the labor markets of industrialized countries, using supply and demand model to explain trends in real wages and employment. In addition, problems of unemployment, especially long-term unemployment, are discussed. The central questions you need to be able to answer are

- What are the five trends that have characterized the labor markets of industrialized countries during the 20th century?
- What factors determine the demand and supply of labor?
- What changes in the factors of supply and demand for labor explain the trends in real wages and employment in industrialized countries?
- What are the three types of unemployment?
- What are the major impediments to full employment?

The Trees

Learning Objective 1: Discuss international patterns in employment
The higher unemployment rates experienced by Western Europe over the past 20 years can be understood as a product of the structural features. Western European labor markets have a much higher degree of both government regulation and unionization compared to the United States. Globalization and skill-biased technological change, which caused low wage workers in the United States to see their wages fall, resulted in Western European employers permanently laying off workers *because wages could not fall*.

Learning Objective 2: Identify the factors that affect the demand for labor
The demand for labor is based on the two notions: how productive a given worker is and the value of the worker's production. As the firm hires additional workers, it is able to produce a greater amount of output. The key measure for labor demand analysis is not the total amount produced by 5 employees but the extra production associated with the hiring of the fifth worker. The extra output obtained by hiring an extra worker defines the marginal product of labor. The principle of **diminishing returns to labor** states that if other inputs like capital are fixed, the extra output from hiring an extra worker will decline at some point. However, knowing the marginal product of one's workers is not enough information to render a judgment about the optimal number to hire. Ultimately, the firm cares less about the amount each worker produces than about the additional revenue the extra production will generate. The benefit of hiring an extra worker is calculated as price of the product multiplied by the worker's marginal product, and is referred to as the value of marginal product. In fact, the value of marginal product is the firm's demand curve for labor.

> **Note**: The economic basis for the principle of diminishing returns to labor is related to the principle of increasing opportunity cost. A firm will use its available workers in the most productive way possible and, thus, will assign its first worker employed to its most productive job.

Learning Objective 3: Identify the factors that shift the labor demand curve

Two factors cause the labor demand curve to shift to the right or left. First, if the price of the firm's output increases, then the value to the firm of a given worker's marginal product grows, thus shifting labor demand to the right. Second, if the marginal productivity of workers rises due to technological change or training, then labor demand will increase, shifting to the right. Reductions in output price or marginal productivity cause decreases in labor demand. A decrease in the wage rate does not cause an increase in labor demand; it causes an increase in the quantity of labor demanded or a movement along the labor demand curve.

Learning Objective 4: Discuss the nature of labor supply and identify the factors that cause the labor supply curve to shift

The supply of labor shows the total number of people willing to work at each real wage rate. The real wage rate represents the opportunity cost of not working, for example, if the wage is $5 and one chooses to work one less hour, one has given up $5. The plausible assumption is made that the higher the real wage rate, the greater the number of people who will be willing to work. Increases and decreases in the supply of labor stem from changes in the size of the working age population and the percentage of working-age people who seek employment.

> **Note**: The decision of whether to work at any given wage is an application of the cost-benefit principle. In applying the cost-benefit principle to the employment decision, an additional worker should be employed only if the marginal benefit is at least equal to the marginal cost of employing the worker.

Learning Objective 5: Explain domestic and international patterns in real wages

The first trend, significant real wage growth over the entire twentieth century, has resulted from sustained productivity growth. For the industrial countries, technological progress and large increases in the stock of capital caused the productivity growth. Of course, the size of the working-age population expanded (a labor supply increase), but the increase in labor demand due to greater productivity was large enough to absorb the new entrants and to drive the real wage up.

The second trend, a distinct slowdown in real wage growth during the past 30 years, comes from a slowdown in productivity growth coupled with continued growth in the working-age population, particularly the rising participation of women. Unlike the first 70 years of the century, the increases in labor demand were large enough to accommodate the new entrants but not large enough to drive the real wage up markedly.

The third trend, increased wage inequality, is caused by two factors: globalization and technological change. Greater international trade has encouraged countries to further specialize in producing the goods for which they possess a comparative advantage, benefiting all consumers in all countries. When domestic markets are opened to trade, some markets will see an increase in demand for their output (the ones with a comparative advantage), while others will see a decrease in demand (those without a comparative advantage). As demand goes, so goes price. Thus, in the markets *lacking* a comparative advantage, the decrease in demand results in a lower price, translating into a decrease in the value for marginal product and, in turn, lower wages. In the markets *with* a comparative advantage, the reverse occurs, driving wages up. The United States enjoys comparative advantage in goods produced by highly skilled, high-wage workers but has difficulty competing with other countries in the production of goods requiring low-skilled, low-wage workers. The effects of trade then tend to drive the high-wage workers' wage up further while lowering the wages of low-wage workers, making wage inequality more pronounced. The free market solution involves **worker mobility**, the movement of worker's between jobs, firms, and industries. The higher wages in the high-skilled labor markets should draw new workers in while the lower wages in the low-skilled labor markets should cause workers to exit. However, the transition from one labor market to another, particularly from low skilled to high skilled, does not happen instantly, so government assistance to aid the process may be justified. The other issue propelling greater wage inequality is the nature of technological progress. While technological progress expands the size of the economic pie, it is not neutral in its influences. Unfortunately, it appears that skill-biased technological change – technological change favoring the marginal productivity of high skilled workers – characterizes recent decades. The effect of skill-biased technological change serves to increase the demand for high-skilled workers, resulting in higher wages for workers already receiving high wages. As a consequence, wage inequality worsens.

Learning Objective 6: Define frictional, structural, and cyclical unemployment

Economists have separated unemployment into three categories. **Frictional unemployment** results from the matching of workers and jobs and lasts for a relatively short period. Because workers and jobs are dissimilar or heterogeneous and the labor market is ever changing or dynamic, the process of matching workers and jobs takes time. So when a person quits one job, he or she may spend a few weeks or months finding the next one. Frictional unemployment is considered beneficial to the economy when a better match of worker and job occurs. Long-term and chronic unemployment that exists despite the normal operation of the economy is termed **structural unemployment**. The causes of structural unemployment take several forms: lack of skills, language barriers, or discrimination. Changes in the nature of the economy can also produce long-term unemployment. For example, the United States steel industry is in decline and many former steelworkers will never again work in the steel industry. Finally, structural features of the economy can cause chronic unemployment. Government programs may also contribute to structural unemployment. The minimum wage, as with any price floor, generates a surplus of workers, more commonly called unemployment. Unemployment insurance is a government transfer to unemployed workers, designed to lessen the burden of unemployment while searching for a new job. However, it may also lengthen the period of search and/or reduce the intensity of the search. Government regulations for workplace health and safety or discrimination tend to raise the cost of employing workers and reduce their productivity. Thus, firms wish to hire fewer workers than they would have in the absence of the regulations. Finally, labor unions "cause" unemployment by increasing the wage the firm must pay and hence the cost of hiring a worker. When the economy suffers a recession, the additional unemployment that results is called **cyclical unemployment**.

> **Note**: While government regulations impose costs (i.e., higher structural unemployment), there are also benefits of the regulations (e.g., fewer injured workers). In order to achieve maximum economic efficiency, legislators should use the cost-benefit criterion when deciding which regulations to impose on the labor markets.

Learning Objective 7: Explain the costs associated with the different types of unemployment

The psychological and financial costs of frictional unemployment are relatively minor because of its short in duration. In fact, frictional unemployment is considered beneficial to the economy when a better match of workers and jobs occur. Structural and cyclical unemployment, on the other hand, impose heavy economic costs on workers and society, as well as psychological costs on workers and their families.

III. Self-Test

Key Terms

Match the term in the right-hand column with the appropriate definition in the left-hand column by placing the letter of the term in the blank in front of its' definition. (Answers are given at the end of the chapter.)

1. _____Technological change that affects the marginal products of higher-skilled workers differently from those of lower-skilled workers.

a. cyclical unemployment

2. _____ The extra unemployment that occurs during periods of recession.

b. diminishing returns to labor

3. _____ The movement of workers between jobs, firms and industries.

c. frictional unemployment

4. _____ If the amount of capital and other inputs in use is held constant, then the greater the quantity of labor already employed, the less each additional worker adds to production.

d. skill-biased technological change

5. _____ The short-term unemployment associated with the process of matching workers with jobs.

e. structural unemployment

6. _____ The long-term and chronic unemployment that exists even when the economy is producing at normal rates.

f. worker mobility

Multiple-Choice Questions

Circle the letter that corresponds to the best answer. (Answers are given at the end of the chapter.)

1. Which of the following statements is *not* supported by the data presented in the textbook?
   A. During the twentieth century, the industrial nations have experienced sizable real-wage growth.
   B. Real wages for skilled workers have risen dramatically over the past 20 years.
   C. The differential between skilled and unskilled workers' real wages has remained constant over the twentieth century.
   D. Real-wage inequality is less pronounced in Western Europe than in the United States.
   E. The average worker in the United States in 1999 has four times the purchasing power of the average worker in 1929.

2. Which of the following statements is *not* supported by the data presented in the textbook?
    A. Over the past several decades, the United States economy has generated a significant number of new jobs.
    B. Western European countries have experienced lower levels of unemployment than the United States in recent years.
    C. Job creation in Western European countries has been meager over the past two decades.
    D. In 1999, more than two-thirds of the over-16 population in the United States held a job.
    E. Of late, the United States economy has created jobs at a rate exceeding the rate of growth of the over-16 population.

3. When a firm hires 3, 4, and 5 workers, it observes that total output is 15, 25, and 30 units, respectively. The marginal product of the fourth worker, therefore, is _____ units.
    A. 40
    B. 25
    C. 15
    D. 10
    E. 5

4. Suppose the marginal products of the fifth, sixth, and seventh workers are 7, 4, and 1, respectively. One can infer that the firm
    A. is experiencing diminishing returns to labor.
    B. has hired too many workers.
    C. is profit maximizing.
    D. has selected low skilled workers.
    E. is experiencing negative returns to labor.

5. In order for a firm to determine the value of a particular worker, the firm must know
    A. the average amount of output the worker will produce.
    B. the extra amount of output the worker will produce.
    C. the price at which the output can be sold.
    D. the average amount of output the worker will produce and the price at which the output can be sold.
    E. the extra amount of output the worker will produce and the price at which the output can be sold.

6. The _____ is the firm's demand curve for labor because it illustrates the _____ for each extra worker.
    A. marginal product curve; extra output
    B. value of marginal product curve; the extra revenue
    C. value of average product curve; the average revenue
    D. value of marginal product curve; the extra profit
    E. value of marginal product curve; the extra cost

7. Which of the following events would not cause the demand curve for labor to shift?
    A. An increase in the productivity of labor.
    B. A decrease in demand for the output produced by the labor.

C. A decrease in the wage rate paid to laborers.

D. Introduction of new, inexpensive capital equipment designed to replace laborers.

E. An increase in demand for the output produced by the labor.

8. The reason the labor supply curve is thought to be upward sloping is that as the real wage rate rises,

A. the opportunity cost of not working increases.

B. the attractiveness of working declines.

C. the alternatives to working become more attractive.

D. the greed of individuals becomes more obvious.

E. more individuals are seduced into working when they would rather not.

9. The most important factor that shifts the labor supply curve is the

A. size of the real wage rate.

B. growth of the real wage rate.

C. the size of the under-16 population.

D. social norms about work.

E. the size of the working-age population.

10. In terms of the model of labor markets, the growth of real wages in the industrial countries during the twentieth century is best explained as a(n)

A. decrease in labor supply due to declining working-age populations.

B. increase in labor demand due to higher prices for consumer goods.

C. result of unions and government regulation of labor markets.

D. increase in labor demand due to technological change and the growth of capital stocks.

E. increase in labor supply due to increasing availability of educational opportunities.

11. The slowdown in real-wage growth that characterizes the past 30 years of the twentieth century is best explained as a(n)

A. nearly total lack of productivity growth.

B. combination of less rapid productivity growth and increased labor supply.

C. increase in labor supply.

D. combination of higher prices for consumer goods and decreased labor supply.

E. increased government regulation of the labor market.

12. The increased wage inequality in the United States caused by increased international trade stems from

A. foreign countries "dumping" products on the United States.

B. increased demand for domestically produced goods requiring low-skilled labor.

C. increased demand for domestically produced goods requiring high-skilled labor.

D. decreased demand for domestically produced goods requiring high-skilled labor.

E. the productivity of foreign labor being higher than the productivity of American labor.

13. As wages in United States decline for low-skilled workers and rise for high-skilled workers,
    A. the incentive to become a high-skilled worker is stronger, pulling more workers to the high-skill sector.
    B. the United States government should enact legislation to protect low–skilled workers from international competition.
    C. the United States government should compensate low-skilled workers with cash payments for the rest of their working life.
    D. no effective solution exists, so the growing inequality must just be accepted.
    E. allowing low-skilled workers to unionize is the only possible avenue to greater wage equality.

14. The technological change of the past 30 years seems to have
    A. benefited all workers equally.
    B. predominantly benefited low-skilled workers.
    C. harmed both low- and high-skilled workers.
    D. only benefited workers in the computer industry.
    E. predominantly benefited high-skilled workers.

15. To counteract the negative effects of both international trade and skill-biased technological change on the wages of low-skilled workers, the textbook proposes
    A. an end to international trade.
    B. governmental review of technologies with a ban on those that favor the highly skilled.
    C. assistance to retrain low-skilled workers and ease their transition to new labor markets.
    D. a hike in the minimum wage.
    E. subsidies to the industries that employ large numbers of low-skilled workers.

16. Generally speaking, _____ unemployment is thought to be the least costly because _____.
    A. cyclical; it is just part of the business cycle
    B. structural; as economies grow, some sectors gain and others lose
    C. cyclical; most of the layoffs are short term
    D. frictional; it results in a better match of workers with jobs
    E. frictional; it tends to last the longest

17. Which of the following features of labor markets in the United States does *not* contribute to long-term, chronic unemployment?
    A. Minimum wage legislation.
    B. Labor unions.
    C. Job search engines on the Internet.
    D. Unemployment insurance.
    E. Health and safety regulations.

18. According to the textbook, the best explanation for the chronically higher unemployment rates in Western Europe is
    A. a lack of retraining programs.
    B. a decline in demand for low-skilled workers.

C. structural features of the labor market that retard worker mobility.

D. excessive international trade.

E. a combination of a decrease in demand for low-skilled workers and more limited worker mobility.

19. The combination of greater international trade and skill-biased technological change in the United States during the past 30 years has

A. harmed low- and high-skilled workers equally.

B. dramatically increased the degree of wage inequality because the United States has a comparative advantage in goods requiring high-skilled workers.

C. not intensified the degree of wage inequality since the United States has a comparative advantage in goods that require both low- and high-skilled workers.

D. harmed low-skilled workers without providing any tangible benefit to consumers.

E. harmed low-skilled workers less than if only one of the two factors was present.

20. Which of the following proposals to assist low-skilled workers deals with the effects of international trade and skill-biased technological change would be most economically efficient?

A. A program to setup and provide access to an Internet-based job bank aimed at all industries.

B. Extension of the coverage period for unemployment insurance.

C. Tariffs on foreign goods produced using inexpensive foreign labor.

D. A public relations campaign to encourage consumers to buy American-made goods.

E. Demands that foreign countries pay their low-skilled workers more.

Short Answer Problems
(Answers and solutions are given at the end of the chapter.)

1. Labor Markets

Calculation of marginal product, the value of marginal product, and determining the profit maximizing level of labor usage are reviewed in this question. The data below show the relationship between labor usage and total output for a firm.

Employee-hours	Output	Price	Marginal Product	Value of Marginal Product
0	0	$2		
1	65	$2		
2	105	$2		
3	125	$2		
4	135	$2		
5	140	$2		

A. Calculate the marginal product and the value of the marginal product for the different levels of employee-hours.

B. Suppose the price the firm receives for its output rises from $2 to $3. As a result, the (marginal product/value of marginal product) _____ increases, implying the firm's demand for labor has (increased/decreased) _____.

C. Suppose that the efficiency of labor increases such that all employee-hours generate 10% more output, e.g., the first employee-hours now results in 71.5 units of output. The impact is that (only the marginal product/both the marginal product and the value of marginal product) _____ increase, shifting the labor demand curve to the (left/right) _____.

D. If the firm must pay a wage of $40 per employee-hour, the profit maximizing level of labor usage is (3/4) _____. If the wage rate were to fall to $20, the firm would increase its (labor demand/ quantity of labor demanded) _____ to (3/4) _____ hours.

2. Labor Market Dynamics I

This question assesses your ability to use the labor market model to explain the trends in wage and employment data presented at the beginning of the chapter. The graphs below show the market for two types of labor in the United States: workers A produce good X while workers B produce good Z. Presently, both occupations pay the same real wage to workers. Suppose a new trade agreement is signed to ease trading with other countries. Suppose further that in the international market, the United States has a comparative advantage in producing Z, and other countries have a comparative advantage in X.

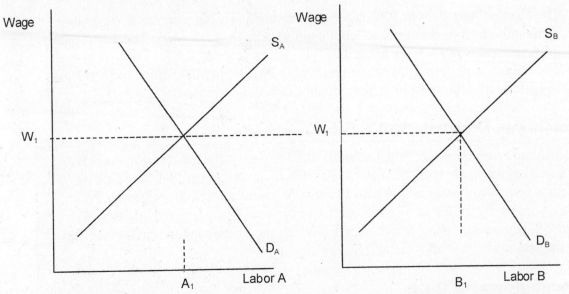

A. Illustrate the effects of the trade agreement on the wages of workers A and B.
B. Suppose that in addition to the trade agreement, recent technological innovations have favored workers B. Illustrate the effects, if any, on the wages of workers A and B.
C. A group, representing workers A, lobbies vigorously in opposition to the trade agreement on the grounds that workers would be harmed. Discuss who, if anyone, would be harmed by failing to sign the trade agreement.
D. Discuss an efficient way to assist workers A and have greater international trade.

3. Labor Market Dynamics II
This question also assesses your ability to use the labor market model to explain the trends in wage and employment, but rather than reasoning from the change to the effect, now the reasoning will run from effect to change. The table below presents hypothetical data on equilibrium real wages and employment for a national labor market.

Year	Real Wage	Employment
2002	$5.00	100
2003	$5.50	120
2004	$6.00	100
2005	$6.00	130
2006	$5.75	125

Hint: Draw a labor supply and demand graph that shows the equilibrium real wage and employment level for the initial year in each question. Then, identify the equilibrium real wage and employment level for the later year in the question and determine what type of change in supply or demand conditions would be necessary to achieve the change in equilibrium.

A. From 2002 to 2006, the data indicate that an (increase/decrease) _____ in the (supply of/demand for) _____ labor occurred.
B. Apparently, the (size of the working population/productivity of workers) _____ declined from 2003 to 2004, since the data are consistent with a decrease in the (supply of/demand for) _____ labor.

C. The change from 2004 to 2005 can best be explained as an increase in (just labor demand/both labor demand and labor supply) _____ because (employment grew/the real wage was unchanged) _____.

D. The reduction in both equilibrium real wages and employment from 2003 to 2004 suggests that (labor supply increased/labor demand decreased) _____.

IV. Becoming an Economic Naturalist: Case Study

In Economic Naturalist 21.5, the textbook authors discuss the causes of the relatively high rates of unemployment in Western Europe. In an article entitled "Curbing Unemployment in Europe: Are There Lessons from Ireland and the Netherlands?" published in *Current Issues in Economics and Finance* (Vol. 7, No. 5 – May 2001), Cédric Tille and Kei-Mu Yi present the following graph showing unemployment rates for Ireland, the Netherlands and the European Union.

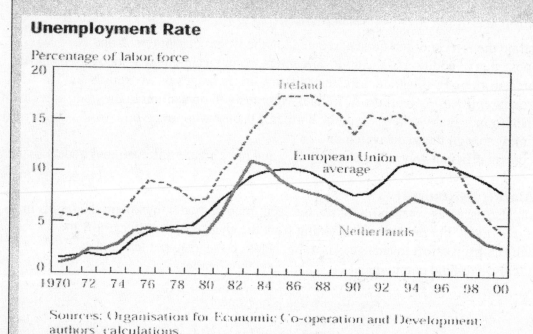

What conclusions can be drawn about the structural rigidities of the labor markets in these countries during 1970 through the mid-1980s compared to the mid-1980s through 2000?

Answer:

Self-Test Solutions

Key Terms
1. d
2. a
3. f
4. b
5. c
6. e

Multiple-Choice Questions
1. C
2. B
3. D Total output with 4 workers is 25 while total output with 3 workers is 15 so adding the fourth worker increases total output by 10 units.
4. A
5. E The firm need to know the value of the marginal product ($P*MP$) for each worker.
6. B
7. C A wage change would cause a movement along the labor demand curve.
8. A
9. E
10. D
11. B
12. C
13. A
14. E
15. C
16. D
17. C
18. E
19. B
20. A

Short Answer Problems
1.
   A. See table.

Employee-hours	Output	Price	Marginal Product	Value of Marginal Product
0	0	$2		
1	65	$2	65	$130
2	105	$2	40	$80
3	125	$2	20	$40
4	135	$2	10	$20
5	140	$2	5	$10

   A. value of marginal product; increased
   B. both the marginal product and the value of the marginal product; right
   C. 3; quantity of labor demanded; 4

2.

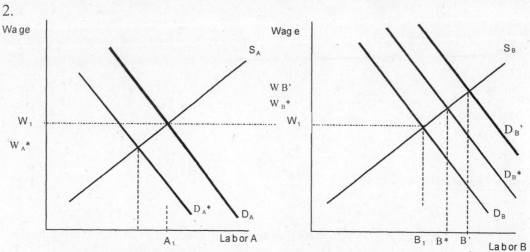

A. The demand for good X declines due to trade and, thus, the demand for labor A declines (D_A*), lowering employment and wages. Demand for Z increases with trade, which increases demand for B workers (D_B*) driving employment and wages up.

B. The technological change further stimulates demand for labor B (D_B'), causing an added increase in wages and employment.

C. Failing to sign the trade agreement harms consumers and workers producing good Z.

D. Sign the agreement and use tax revenues to assist the unemployed laborers in A to get new training and locate new jobs.

3.

A. increase; demand for

B. size of the working population; supply of

C. both labor demand and labor supply; the real wage was unchanged

D. labor demand decreased

Chapter 22
Saving and Capital Formation

I. Pretest: What Do You Really Know?
Circle the letter that corresponds to the best answer. (Answers appear immediately after the final question).

1. The saving rate equals saving divided by
   A. wealth.
   B. assets.
   C. liabilities.
   D. income.
   E. investment.

2. Charles has the following assets and liabilities:
Two cars	$10,000
House	$300,000
Mortgage	$100,000
Cash	$1,000
Car loans	$4,000
Checking account balance	$2,000
Credit card balance	$1,000

   What is Charles's wealth?
   A. $206,000
   B. $208,000
   C. $210,000
   D. $312,000
   E. $416,000

3. Which of the following is a stock?
   A. saving
   B. income
   C. consumption
   D. wealth
   E. investment

4. Saving is a(n) _____ and wealth is a(n) _____.
   A. flow; flow
   B. flow; stock
   C. asset; liability
   D. liability; asset
   E. stock; flow

5. Saving for protection against unexpected setbacks, such as the loss of a job or a medical emergency, is called _____ saving.
   A. public
   B. national
   C. precautionary
   D. life-cycle
   E. bequest

6. Saving done for the purpose of leaving an inheritance is called _____ saving.
   A. public
   B. national
   C. precautionary
   D. life-cycle
   E. bequest

7. Life-cycle saving is saving
   A. to meet long-term objectives, such as retirement, college attendance, or the purchase of a home.
   B. for protection against unexpected setbacks, such as the loss of a job or a medical emergency.
   C. for the purpose of leaving an inheritance.
   D. to pay life-insurance premiums.
   E. by older people to induce younger people to care for them.

8. Saving by households and businesses is called _____ saving.
   A. private
   B. public
   C. national
   D. aggregate
   E. bequest

9. _____ saving equals _____ saving plus _____ saving.
   A. National; private; public
   B. Public; national; private
   C. Private; national; public
   D. Life-cycle; bequest; precautionary
   E. Precautionary; bequest; life-cycle

10. Public saving is negative when
    A. there is a government budget surplus.
    B. there is a government budget deficit.
    C. the government's budget is balanced.
    D. after-tax income of households and businesses is greater than consumption expenditures.
    E. after-tax income of households and businesses is less than consumption expenditure.

Solutions and Feedback to Pretest
For each question you incorrectly answered, we strongly recommend taking the time to review the appropriate material before continuing. In the table below are listed for each question the pertinent Learning Objective from the following Key Point Review.

Correct Answer	Learning Objective
1. D	1
2. B	1
3. D	1
4. B	1
5. C	2
6. E	2
7. A	2
8. A	4
9. A	4
10. B	4

II. Key Point Review
The Forest

This chapter focuses on saving and its links to the formation of new capital. The central questions you need to be able to answer are

- How are saving and wealth related?
- Why do people save?
- What are the components of national saving?
- What is the relationship between national saving and investment?

The Trees

Learning Objective 1: Define saving, saving rate, wealth, assets, liabilities, stocks, flows, capital gains, capital losses, and explain the link between saving and wealth

Saving by an economic unit (e.g., a household, business, or nation) is its current income minus its spending on current needs. It can be expressed as a **saving rate** by dividing the amount of saving by the amount of income. Saving by an economic unit is closely related to its **wealth**, the value of its assets minus its liabilities. **Assets** are anything of value that is owned, while **liabilities** are the debts that are owed. Accountants list the assets and liabilities of an economic unit on a balance sheet to determine its net worth. Saving and wealth are related because saving contributes to wealth. This relationship is best understood by distinguishing between stocks and flows. A **flow** is a measure that is defined per unit of time, and a **stock** is a measure that is defined at a point in time. In many cases, a flow is the rate of change in a stock. For example, the flow of saving causes the stock of wealth to change at the same rate. Higher rates of saving, therefore, lead to faster accumulation of wealth and a higher standard of living. Although saving increases wealth, it is not the only factor that determines wealth. Wealth also changes because of changes in the values of the real and financial assets owed by an economic unit. If the value of an existing asset increases, the owner has a **capital gain**, but if the value of an existing asset decreases, then there is a **capital loss**. In summary, changes in wealth equal the amount of saving plus capital gains minus capital losses.

Hint: Use the bathtub analogy to help you remember the concepts of stock and flow. The amount of water in the bathtub at any specific moment is the "stock" of water, while turning on the tap adds a "flow" of water. The more water flowing in per minute, the higher the rate of change in the stock of water in the bathtub. Opening the drain will cause a flow of water out of the tub and, therefore, will reduce the stock of water in the tub.

Similarly, the stock and flow concepts can be applied to economic variables. For example, wealth is a stock of assets and saving is a flow of assets. If a family currently owns assets, say a house (valued at $100,000), a Picasso painting ($250,000) and $50,000 in certificates of deposit (CDs), its total wealth equals $400,000. If the family saves $10,000 during the next year, its wealth at the end of next year will be $410,000. The higher one's rate of saving (flow), the faster one's (stock of) wealth increases. If the family then takes $20,000 out of its CDs to pay for a vacation the following year, then its wealth at the end of that year would fall to $390,000.

Learning Objective 2: Identify the three broad reasons why people save and explain the relationship between the amount of saving and interest rates

People save part of their income rather than spending all they earn for three reasons. First, they save to meet certain long-term objectives, such as retirement or the purchase of a home. This is called **life-cycle saving**. A second reason people save is called **precautionary saving**, saving to protect against unexpected setbacks. The third reason for saving is **bequest saving**, saving for the purpose of leaving an inheritance. Although most people save for one of these three reasons, the amount that they save depends on the economic environment. The economic variable that is most important in saving decisions is the real interest rate, r. The real interest rate is the reward for saving. Because of the power of compound interest in the long run, a higher real interest rate causes a dramatic increase in the real value of a saver's wealth. On the other hand, a higher real interest rate reduces the amount people need to save each year to reach a given wealth target. Nonetheless, empirical evidence suggests people are willing to save more the higher the real interest rate, all else being equal.

Learning Objective 3: Discuss the reasons why U.S. household saving rate is low
There are some who argue that, despite these rational reasons for saving, some people lack the self-control to do what is in their own best interest. Despite having good intentions to save, for example, some lack the necessary self-control to put aside as much of their income as they would like. This so-called self-control hypothesis suggests that consumer credit arrangements that make borrowing and spending easier may reduce the amount that people save. Similarly, the demonstration effect suggests that additional spending by some people causes others to spend more to maintain a lifestyle commensurate with their peer group. These hypotheses, in addition to the generous government assistance for the elderly, may explain why household saving in the U.S. has declined recently.

Learning Objective 4: Define national saving, private saving, public saving, and government budget deficit and surplus.
The above discussion pertains to individual saving, but macroeconomists are interested primarily in saving and wealth for the country as a whole. Similar to any economic unit, a nation's saving equals its current income less its spending on current needs. The current income of a country is its GDP (Y), the value of the final goods and service produced within the country's borders during the year. Identifying the part of total expenditures that corresponds to a country's current needs is more difficult. Because investment spending is done to improve the future productive capacity, it is clearly not a part of spending on current needs. For consumption and government spending, some portion is for current needs while another portion is for future needs. Determining how much should be attributed to each portion is extremely difficult. For this reason, the U.S. government statistics has for some years treated all of consumption expenditures and government spending as spending on current needs. The textbook authors follow this convention, with the caveat that this will understate the true amount of national saving. **National saving** (S), therefore, equals GDP less consumption expenditures and government purchases of goods and services, or $S = Y - C - G$ (this excludes the international sector, which is discussed in a later chapter).

To better understand national saving, one can divide it into two major components: private saving by households and businesses, and public saving by the government. To distinguish these two components, the above equation is expanded to incorporate taxes and payments made by the government to the private sector. Government payments to the private sector include transfer payments and interest paid to individuals and institutions that hold government bonds. **Transfer payments** are payments the government makes to the public for which it receives no current goods or services in return (e.g., social security benefits). If T represents taxes paid by the private sector to the government less transfer payments and government interest payments, it can be called net taxes. **Private saving** can, thus, be expressed as $S_{private} = Y - T - C$, or private sector after-tax income minus its consumption spending. Private sector saving can be further broken down into household saving and business saving. **Public saving**, or saving of the government sector, is equal to net tax payments minus government purchases ($S_{public} = T - G$). A **government budget deficit**, the excess of government spending over tax collections ($G - T$), implies that public saving is negative, while a **government budget surplus**, the excess of government tax collections over spending ($T - G$), means public saving is positive.

> **Note:** To conclude that the adverse effects of low household saving on the family implies that low household saving is a problem for nation is to commit the "fallacy of composition." The fallacy of composition states, what is true for one part of a whole is not necessarily true for the whole. For example, if you alone stand up at a football game, you can see the game better. It does not follow, however, that if everyone at the game stands up, everyone can see better. Thus, while a low household saving rate may cause microeconomic problems for a family (such as insufficient funds to pay for college or to retire), it is not necessarily a macroeconomic problem for the nation.

Learning Objective 5: Discuss why low U.S. household saving is not a macroeconomic problem, but may be a microeconomic concern

In recent years, decreases in private household saving in the United States have been partially offset by increases in public saving. The relatively low U.S. household saving rate is not a problem from a macroeconomic perspective because national saving, not household saving, determines the capacity of an economy to invest in new capital goods and continue to improve its standard of living. Although U.S. household saving is low, saving by business firms is significant, and, during the 1990s, government budget surpluses have approximately offset the fall in household saving. Overall, despite the fact that it is low by international standards, the U.S. national saving rate has been reasonably stable and sufficient to allow it to become one of the most productive economies in the world. From a microeconomic perspective, however, the low household saving rate does exacerbate the problem of large and growing inequality in wealth among U.S. households. Saving patterns are increasing this inequality as better-off households not only save more, but, as business owners and stockholders, they also are the ultimate beneficiaries of the saving by businesses.

Learning Objective 6: Apply cost-benefit analysis to the investment decision and identify the factors that affect the costs and benefits of investment

From the point of view of the economy as a whole, the importance of national saving is that it provides the funds needed for investment. Investment is the creation of new capital goods and housing and is critical to increasing average labor productivity and improving standards of living. Firms' willingness to invest depends on the expected cost of using the capital and the expected benefit, measured as the marginal product, of the capital. On the cost side, two important factors are the price of capital goods and the real interest rate. The more expensive the capital goods, the less willing businesses are to invest in them. The real interest rate measures the opportunity cost of a capital investment. Since an increase in the real interest rate increases the opportunity cost of investing in new capital, it lowers the willingness of firms to invest. On the benefit side, the key factor in determining business investment is the value of the marginal product of the new capital, calculated net of operating costs, maintenance expenses, and taxes paid on the revenues the capital generates. The value of the marginal product of capital is affected by several factors, including technological improvement and the relative price of the good or service that the capital is used to produce. Technological improvements and increases in the price of the good or service raise the marginal product of capital and increase the willingness of businesses to invest.

Learning Objective 7: Apply the supply and demand model to analyze the issue of national saving

The factors that affect the costs and benefits of investment can be analyzed in a supply and demand model. In an economy without international borrowing and lending, national saving must equal investment. The supply of national savings and the demand for savings are equalized through the workings of financial markets. The supply of saving shows the relationship between the real interest rate and the quantity of national saving. It is an upward-sloping curve because empirical evidence suggests that increases in the real interest rate stimulate saving, all other things equal. The demand for saving shows the relationship between the real interest rate and the quantity of investment in new capital. It is a downward-sloping curve because higher real interest rates raise the opportunity cost of capital and reduce the willingness of firms to invest, all other things equal. Holding aside the possibility of borrowing from foreigners, a country can only invest those resources that its savers make available.

In equilibrium, desired investment (the quantity demanded of saving) and national saving (the quantity supplied of saving) must be equal. Desired saving is equated with desired investment through adjustments in the real interest rate, which functions as the price of saving. Changes in factors other than the real interest rate that affect the supply of or demand for saving will shift the curves, leading to a new equilibrium in the financial market. Technological improvements and changes in the price of the good or service produced by the capital will shift the demand for saving. The supply of saving is affected by changes in private and public saving. In particular, an increase in the government budget deficit shifts the supply of saving curve to the left and the equilibrium quantity of saving and investment will decrease. This tendency of government budget deficits to reduce investment spending is called **crowding out**.

Hint: The financial markets are a mechanism for rationing the limited national saving in an economy among the many possible investment opportunities. Essentially, markets ration the national savings first to those individual investors whose projects generate the greatest profits and, therefore, can afford to pay the highest price (i.e., the highest interest rate) to obtain the loans. When the government runs a budget deficit, it must borrow funds to cover the excess expenditures. It pays back the loans, however, with tax revenues rather than with profits.

You can think of the financial markets as a queue with private sector borrowers lined up to get their projects funded. The investors with the highest potential for earning profits are at the front of the line and those with lower profit potential behind. Then, the government representatives come along and they "cut" in line. As a result, they push further back in the queue some private sector investors. If some private sector investors fail to get to the front of the line before the national saving runs out, they will not get their projects funded. Thus, they are crowded out.

III. Self-Test

Key Terms
Match the term in the right-hand column with the appropriate definition in the left-hand column by placing the letter of the term in the blank in front of its' definition. (Answers are given at the end of the chapter.)

1. ____The excess of government spending over tax collections (G – T).

a. assets

2. ____The saving of the entire economy, equal to GDP less consumption expenditures and government purchases of goods and services, or Y – C – G.

b. balance sheet

3. ____The debts that one owes

c. bequest saving

4. ____Decreases in the value of existing assets.

d. capital gains

5. ____Saving that is identical to the government budget surplus.

e. capital losses

6. ____Payments the government makes to the public for which it receives no current goods or services in return.

f. crowding out

7. ____After-tax income of the private sector minus its consumption spending (Y – T – C).

g. flow

8. ____Saving done for the purpose of leaving an inheritance.

h. government budget deficit

9. ____A measure that is defined per unit of time.

i. government budget surplus

10. ___Saving divided by income.

j. liabilities

11. ___A measure that is defined at a point in time.

k. life-cycle saving.

12. ___Saving to meet long-term objectives, such as retirement, college attendance, or purchase of a home.

l. national saving

13. ___Current income minus spending on current needs.

m. precautionary saving

14. ___Saving to protect against unexpected setbacks, such as the loss of a job or a medical emergency.

n. private saving

15. ___The tendency of increased government deficits to reduce investment spending.

o. public saving

16. ___The value of assets minus liabilities.

p. saving

17. ___Anything of value that one owns.

q. saving rate

18. ___Increases in the value of existing assets.

r. stock

19. ___The excess of government tax collections over government spending (T – G).

s. transfer payments

20. ___A list of an economic units assets and liabilities on a specific date.

t. wealth

Multiple-Choice Questions
Circle the letter that corresponds to the best answer. (Answers are given at the end of the chapter.)

1. Luis had accumulated $5,000 in wealth at the end of a year. At the beginning of the next year he deposits $50 in a saving account that will earn 10% interest per year. If there are no changes in his liabilities, at the end of the next year his wealth will have
   A.   increased by $50.
   B.   decreased by $50.
   C.   increased by $55.
   D.   decreased by $55.
   E.   not changed.

2. The strong U.S. bull market of the late 1990s ended (at least temporarily) in early 2000, as the stock market indexes fell 25% or more during the second quarter of 2000. As a result, many Americans
   A.   suffered capital losses and increases in their wealth.
   B.   suffered capital losses and decreases in their wealth.
   C.   enjoyed capital gains and increases in their wealth.
   D.   enjoyed capital gains and decreases in their wealth.
   E.   suffered capital losses and decreases in their liabilities.

3. If the real interest rate on saving account increases from 3% to 5%, all other things equal
   A.   business investment spending for new capital will increase.
   B.   business investment spending for new capital will remain unchanged.
   C.   people will be less willing to save.
   D.   people will be more willing to save.
   E.   the amount people will save will remain unchanged.

4. Which of the following hypotheses is a plausible explanation for why U.S. households save so little?
   A.   Interest rates in the United States are typically lower than they are in the rest of the world.
   B.   Most American already own homes and, therefore, have less need for life-cycle saving.
   C.   The highly developed financial markets in the United States have reduced the need for precautionary saving by Americans.
   D.   Government assistance to low-income U.S. households has increased the demonstration effects on spending by the poor.
   E.   Government assistance to the elderly has reduced the need for life-cycle saving.

5. If net taxes paid by households increase,
   A.   private saving will decrease.
   B.   private saving will increase.
   C.   public saving will decrease.
   D.   transfer payments to households will decrease.
   E.   transfer payments to households will increase.

6. The low and declining U.S. household saving rate is
   A. a macroeconomic problem because it reduces the amount of funds available for investment and, thus, reduces the standard of living.
   B. not a macroeconomic problem because the national saving rate has been stable and sufficient.
   C. a microeconomic problem because it reduces the amount of funds available for investment and, thus, reduces the standard of living.
   D. not a microeconomic problem because the national saving rate has been stable and sufficient.
   E. not a microeconomic problem because the booming stock market has increased the wealth of Americans and reduced income inequality.

7. Joe's Taco Hut can purchase a delivery truck for $20,000 and Joe estimates it will generate a net income (i.e., after-taxes and maintenance and operating costs) of $2,000 per year. He should
   A. purchase the truck if the real interest rate is less than 2%.
   B. not purchase the truck if the real interest rate is greater than 2%.
   C. purchase the truck if the real interest rate is greater than 10%.
   D. purchase the truck if the real interest rate is less than 10%.
   E. purchase the truck if the real interest rate is less than 3%.

8. The investment demand curve indicates that there is a(n)
   A. positive relationship between the real interest rates and the level of investment spending, all other things equal.
   B. inverse relationship between the real interest rates and the level of investment spending, all other things equal.
   C. direct relationship between the real interest rates and the level of investment spending, all other things equal.
   D. inverse relationship between the determinants of investment and the level of investment spending, holding interest rates constant.
   E. positive relationship between the determinants of investment and the level of investment spending, holding interest rates constant.

9. Rafael's current income is $100 more per month than his current consumption needs. He decides to use the $100 to reduce his credit card debt. As a result, his
   A. liabilities will decrease and his wealth will increase.
   B. liabilities and his wealth will decrease.
   C. assets will decrease and his wealth will increase.
   D. assets and his wealth will decrease.
   E. assets and his wealth will increase.

10. If, in a given year, the saving rate in an economy decreases by an amount equal to the net capital gains, the economy's
   A. wealth will decrease.
   B. wealth will increase.

C. wealth will remain unchanged.

D. assets will decrease.

E. liabilities will decrease.

11. One reason that household saving in Japan is higher than household saving in the U.S. is

   A. that the average Japanese income is higher than it is in the United States.

   B. housing in the United States is more expensive and, therefore, Americans spend more of their income on housing and save less.

   C. because Japanese workers continue working until they are much older and, therefore, they can save more.

   D. the Japanese save more for precautionary reasons because they have, in general, less job security than American workers.

   E. the higher cost of housing and larger down payments required to purchase a house in Japan results in higher life-cycle saving.

12. During a conversation with her mother about her financial circumstances, Sylvia complained that she could not afford to save because she wanted to maintain a lifestyle similar to that of her friends. Her mother suggested that if she would save more now, she would not only have more wealth, but she would also have a higher standard of living than her friends in the future. Her mother's argument was

   A. incorrect, because if she saved her standard of living would be lower than that of her friends.

   B. incorrect, and probably an attempt to confuse her daughter in order to get her to begin saving some of her income.

   C. correct, because of the power of compound interest her income would increase to a level that would allow her to save and consume more.

   D. correct, because the more saving, the higher the standard of living.

   E. irrelevant, because daughters never listen to what their mother tells them.

13. Household saving in the United States

   A. is low relative to previous periods, but approximately equal to the rate in other countries.

   B. decreased through the 1990s and became negative in 1998.

   C. had decreased since the 1960s, but, because the economy was so strong during the 1990s, has recently increased.

   D. is low relative to other countries and has declined since the 1960s.

   E. is low relative to other countries, but has increased during the 1990s.

14. Private saving

   A. can be broken down into household saving and business saving.

   B. can be broken down into transfers and household saving.

   C. rises when net taxes increase.

   D. falls when income rises.

   E. rises when government spending decreases.

15. An increase in net taxes (i.e., taxes paid by the private sector to the government minus transfer payments and interest payments made by the government to the private sector) will
    A. increase private saving.
    B. decrease public saving.
    C. increase public saving.
    D. reduce investment in new capital equipment.
    E. cause crowding out.

16. Public saving is
    A. increased when the government budget deficit rises.
    B. identical to the government budget surplus.
    C. less important to national saving than private saving.
    D. more important to national saving than private saving.
    E. unimportant in determining the capacity of an economy to invest in new capital.

17. Samantha has $5,000 in a CD account paying 10% interest. It will mature in a few weeks and the bank told her that interest rates on CDs were decreasing. She is thinking of spending it on a new computer and software that she will use to start a bookkeeping service. If she were to do so, she would have to quit her job where she makes $15,000 per year in after-tax income. She has estimated that the bookkeeping service will earn a net income of $15, 250 after taxes, and maintenance and operating costs.
    A. Since the interest rate is declining, Samantha would be better off using the money to buy the computer.
    B. If the interest rate on the new CD is 7% or greater she should leave the money in the CD.
    C. If the interest rate on the new CD is 2.5% or greater she should buy the computer.
    D. If the interest rate on the new CD is 2% or less she should leave the money in the CD.
    E. If the interest rate on the new CD is 5% or greater she should leave the money in the CD.

18. As the cost of capital goods increases relative to other prices, the
    A. demand for investment in new capital will shift to the left.
    B. demand for investment in new capital will shift to the right.
    C. amount of investment in new capital will increase.
    D. amount of saving will rise.
    E. amount of saving will fall.

19. A decrease in the capital gains tax on income generated through investment in new capital will
    A. shift the demand for investment curve to the left.
    B. shift the demand for investment curve to the right.
    C. shift the supply of saving curve to the left.
    D. shift the supply of saving curve to the right.
    E. decrease real interest rates.

20. The introduction of a new technology that raises the marginal product of new capital will
   A. decrease real interest rates and increase the equilibrium quantity of saving supplied and demanded.
   B. decrease real interest rates and the equilibrium quantity of saving supplied and demanded.
   C. increase real interest rates and the equilibrium quantity of saving supplied and demanded.
   D. increase real interest rates and decrease the equilibrium quantity of saving supplied and demanded.
   E. decrease real interest rates and the equilibrium quantity of saving supplied and demanded will remain unchanged.

Short Answer Problems
(Answers and solutions are given at the end of the chapter.)

1. Savings and Wealth
In this problem you will identify an individual's assets and liabilities to determine his wealth. You will also calculate the effect of saving on wealth over time.

At the end of the year 2000, Franklin prepared for the new millenium by writing down all his assets and liabilities. His list included a car with a market value of $7,500, but with $6,000 left on the car loan; his home with a market value of $125,000 and a mortgage of $122,500; a checking account with a $750 balance; a credit card balance of $1,000; 8,000 shares of the ABC Corporation with a current price of $12 per share; and a debt of $2,500 on a student loan.

A. Construct Franklin's balance sheet below, and calculate his wealth.

Franklin's Balance Sheet

Assets	Liabilities
Total	Total
	Net Worth

B. Upon returning to work in January 2001, his boss informed him that he had been awarded a bonus of $1,000. He decided he would not spend it on consumption, but rather used it to increase his wealth. His alternatives were to put it into a CD account paying 7.5% annual interest, pay off his credit card debt that had an annual interest charge of 11%, or pay off his student loan that had a 7% annual interest charge. What would you recommend that he do with his bonus to maximize the increase in his wealth? _____
Why? _____

C. After reviewing his net worth, Franklin decided that he has insufficient wealth to achieve his goal of retiring in 20 years. He decided he would begin saving $500 per year in a 401K account (a retirement account that is not subject to taxes until after he retires). After investigating all the options, Franklin settled on depositing his 401K funds into a money market account paying 5% annual interest. Assume that Franklin deposits $500 on the 1st of January in each year, and calculate the value of his retirement account at the end of each of the following periods: 1 year _____, 2 years _____, 3 years _____ , 4 years _____, 5 years _____ .

D. At the end of the 5th year, Franklin reviews his retirement account and discovers that had he deposited the 401K funds in a stock fund rather than the money market account, he would have earned an average of 10% in capital gains each year. Recalculate the value that his retirement account would have reached, if he had chosen the stock fund, at the end of 1 year _____, 2 years _____ , 3 years _____ , 4 years _____ , and 5 years _____ .

2. Cost-Benefit Analysis for Investment Decisions

This problem focuses on the use of cost-benefit analysis in making investment decisions. You will calculate the marginal product of capital, determine the marginal benefit and marginal cost of capital, and decide whether to make an investment. You will also analyze the effects of changes in taxation, the cost of capital, and expected income on the investment decision.

Thelma is thinking of going into the business of translating documents for international businesses. In order to do so, she needs to borrow $5,000 to the buy computer equipment. She has estimated that she will earn a profit of $25,000 per year, after deducting operating and maintenance costs. The tax rate on her business profit each year would be 15%, and the annual interest rate on the loan would equal 12%. Her best job alternative would be teaching Spanish in high school with an after-tax income of $20,000.

A. Assume the computer equipment does not lose value over time. Calculate the marginal product of the computer equipment. $ _____

B. Calculate the amount of the annual interest that Thelma would have to pay on the loan. $_____

C. Should Thelma choose to invest in the computer equipment and start the translation business? _____ Why or why not? _____
_____

D. If the government increases the tax rate on business profits to 19%, and the computer equipment does not lose value over time, calculate the marginal product of the computer equipment. $ _____

E. After the tax increase in Question D, should Thelma to buy the computer equipment and start the translation business? _____ Why? _____
_____

F. If the cost of the computer equipment decreased to $2,000, should Thelma buy the computer equipment and start the translation business? _____ Why or why not? _____
_____

G. If the computer equipment was less productive than Thelma thought, so that her profit was $22,500 per year, should Thelma buy the computer equipment and start the translation business? _____ Why or why not? ? _____

_____

3. The Supply and Demand for Saving

In this problem you will use the supply and demand model to analyze the financial market for saving and investment. You will determine the equilibrium real interest rate and quantity of saving and determine the effects of changes in the government budget and technology on the market equilibrium.

Answer the questions below based on the following the supply and demand curves for saving.

Real Interest Rate (%)

($ billions)

A. The equilibrium real interest rate is _____ % and the equilibrium quantity of saving/investment is $_____ billion.

B. An increase in the government budget surplus would cause the (supply/demand) _____ curve for saving to (increase/decrease) _____ . On the above graph, draw a new curve that would reflect the change caused by the increased government budget surplus.

C. As a result of the increased government budget surplus, the equilibrium real interest rate _____ and the equilibrium quantity of saving/investment _____ .

D. The introduction of new technologies that increase the marginal product of new capital would cause the (supply/demand) _____ curve for saving to (increase/decrease) _____ . On the above graph, draw a new curve that would reflect the change caused by the new technologies.

E. As a result of the new technologies, the equilibrium real interest rate _____ and the equilibrium quantity of saving/investment _____ .

IV. Becoming an Economic Naturalist: Case Study

Economic Naturalist 22.5 discusses alternative tax mechanisms (income vs. consumption taxes) to increase national savings in the U.S. In 2001, the U.S. Congress legislated lower income tax rates on capital gains and dividends, in part, "to promote saving and economic growth." These lower tax rates, however, are temporary and will expire in 2008 without further legislation. President Bush has proposed in his 2006 budget to make the tax cuts permanent. But some oppose his proposal arguing that it will reduce our national saving. Discuss the implicit assumptions of those who support the President's proposal and those opposed regarding the impact of the tax cuts on the private and public components of national saving.

Answer:

V. Self-Test Solutions

Key Terms
1. h
2. l
3. j
4. e
5. o
6. s
7. n
8. c
9. g
10. q
11. r
12. k
13. p
14. m
15. f
16. t
17. a
18. d
19. i
20. b

Multiple-Choice Questions

1. C His wealth increases by an amount equal to the saving plus the interest earned on the saving. Thus, $50 + $5 ($50 x .10) = $55
2. B
3. D
4. E
5. A
6. B
7. D If the interest rate is less than 10%, then the financial cost of the capital (equal to the amount of the loan times the interest rate) will be less than the financial benefit of the capital (equal to the net income earned with the capital).
8. B
9. A Debt is a type of liability, and reducing liabilities increase wealth.
10. C
11. E
12. C
13. D
14. A
15. C
16. B
17. E The financial benefit of the computer is $250. If the interest rate on the CD were less than 5%, the financial cost of the capital ($5,000 times the interest rate) would be less than the financial benefit of the computer. Therefore, if the interest rate on the CD is less than 5%, she should buy the computer.
18. A
19. B
20. C

Short Answer Problems

1.

A.

Franklin's Balance Sheet

Assets		Liabilities	
Car	$7,500	Car loan	$6,000
Home	125,000	Mortgage	122,500
Checking account	750	Credit card balance	1,000
ABC Corp. shares	96,000	Student loan	2,500
Total	$ 229,250	Total	$132,000
		Net Worth	$ 97,250

B. He should pay off his credit card debt because it will reduce his liabilities and, thus, increase his wealth. The credit card debt has a higher opportunity cost (interest rate) than the student loan and he will save more in interest payments than he would earn on the CD account.

C. $525(= $500 + [$500 x.05]); $1,076.25 (= 525 + 500 + [1,025 x .05]); $1,655.06; $2,262.81; $2,900.95

D. $550; $1,155; $1,820.50; $2,552.55; $3,357.80

2.

A. $1,250 (Thelma would have to pay $3,750 [$25,000 x .15] in profit taxes, leaving her an after-tax income of $25,000 – $3,750 = $21,250. Subtracting the Spanish teacher salary [$20,000] that she must forego to start the translating business from the after-tax income [$21,250] equals the marginal product of the computer equipment.)

B. $600 (= $5,000 x .12)

C. Yes; Because the financial cost ($600 interest payment) is less than the financial benefit ($1,250 marginal product of the computer equipment).

D. $250 (The solution is the same as in 2A, except the tax rate is now .19.)

E. No; Because the financial cost ($600) is greater than the financial benefit ($250).

F. Yes; Because the financial cost ($240) is less than the financial benefit ($250).

G. No; Because the financial benefit ($ –1,775) is less than the financial cost.

3.

A. 4; $1,000 billion

B. supply; increase;

C. decreased; increased

D. demand; increase;

E. increased; increased

Chapter 23
Money, Prices and the Federal Reserve

I. Pretest: What Do You Really Know?

Circle the letter that corresponds to the best answer. (Answers appear immediately after the final question).

1. Money is
   A. the same as income.
   B. all financial assets.
   C. any asset used to make purchases.
   D. the sum of assets minus debts.
   E. the market value of all final goods and services produced in a country in a year.

2. The functions of money include
   A. medium of exchange, diversification of risk, and store of value.
   B. medium of exchange, unit of value, and store of account.
   C. medium of value, unit of exchange, and store of account.
   D. medium of account, store of value, and unit of exchange.
   E. medium of exchange, unit of account, and store of value.

3. M1 consists of
   A. all currency and balances held in checking accounts.
   B. currency outstanding and balances held in checking accounts.
   C. M2 plus savings deposits, small-denomination time deposits, and money market mutual funds.
   D. currency outstanding, balances in checking accounts plus savings deposits, small-denomination time deposits, and money market mutual funds.
   E. M2 minus balances in checking accounts, savings deposits, small-denomination time deposits, and money market mutual funds.

4. Banks reserves are
    A. cash or similar assets held for the purpose of meeting depositor withdrawals and payments.
    B. cash or similar assets held for the purpose of insuring bank deposits.
    C. cash or similar assets held for the purpose of making loans.
    D. cash or similar assets held for the purpose of ensuring that loans are repaid and depositors funds are not depleted.
    E. cash or similar assets held for the purpose of facilitating monetary policy.

5. A fractional-reserve banking system
    A. allows bank reserves to circulate as part of the money supply.
    B. requires banks to hold reserves equal to 100 percent of their deposits.
    C. allows banks to expand the money supply by lending some of their deposits.
    D. is illegal in most countries because banks are required to maintain reserves equal to their deposits.
    E. enables banks to lend 100 percent of their reserves.

6. The primary responsibility of the Federal Reserve System is to
    A. regulate the stock market.
    B. enable banks to make affordable mortgages.
    C. print currency.
    D. conduct monetary policy.
    E. insure bank deposits.

7. The most important, most convenient, and most flexible way in which the Federal Reserve affects the supply of bank reserves is through
    A. conducting open-market operations.
    B. changing the Federal Reserve discount rate.
    C. printing currency.
    D. changing interest rates.
    E. conducting bank examinations.

8. If the Federal Reserve wants to decrease the money supply, it should
    A. print more currency.
    B. print less currency.
    C. conduct open-market purchases.
    D. conduct open-market sales.
    E. decrease interest rates.

9. Deposit insurance is a system in which the government guarantees that
    A. depositors will not lose any money even if their bank goes bankrupt.
    B. people can have deposits at commercial banks.
    C. commercial banks will not go bankrupt.
    D. depositors of commercial banks can obtain low-cost life insurance.
    E. commercial banks will not lose any deposits.

10. In the long run, a higher rate of growth in the money supply will cause a higher rate of inflation
   A. if the velocity of money increases.
   B. because the larger amount of money in circulation will allow people to bid up the prices of goods and services.
   C. because the higher velocity of money will allow people to bid up the prices of goods and services.
   D. because the larger quantity of transactions will allow people to bid up the prices of goods and services.
   E. if the velocity of money increases and the quantity of transactions is constant.

Solutions and Feedback to Pretest

For each question you incorrectly answered, we strongly recommend taking the time to review the appropriate material before continuing. In the table below are listed for each question the pertinent Learning Objective from the following Key Point Review.

Correct Answer	Learning Objective
1. C	1
2. E	2
3. B	3
4. A	4
5. C	4
6. D	5
7. A	6
8. D	6
9. A	7
10. B	8

II. Key Point Review
The Forest

This chapter focuses on the role of money in modern economies. The central questions you need to be able to answer are:
- What is money and what are the functions of money?
- How is the money supply measured?
- How is money created?
- What is the structure and responsibilities of the Federal Reserve Banking System?
- What is the relationship between the money supply and inflation in the long run?

The Trees

Learning Objective 1: Define money and barter

Money is any asset that can be used in making purchases. Without money, all economic transactions would have to be in the form of **barter**, that is the direct trade of goods and services for other goods and services. Barter is inefficient because it requires that both parties to a trade have something the other party wants, a so-called double coincidence of wants. Money facilitates more efficient transactions and permits individuals to specialize in producing particular goods and services.

Learning Objective 2: Define the three functions of money

Money has three principal uses: it serves as a medium of exchange, a unit of account, and a store of value. Money serves as a **medium of exchange** when it is used to purchase goods and services. As a **unit of account**, money is the basic yardstick for measuring economic value. As a **store of value** money serves as a means of holding wealth.

Note: The store of value function of money is undermined by inflation because inflation erodes the purchasing power of money. When you hold some of your wealth in the form of money and the economy experiences inflation, what you can purchase with those dollars decreases over time. It make sense then that, as the purchase power of your money decreases, you will choose to hold less of your wealth in the form of money (and, thus, more of your wealth in some other form, e.g., land). During periods of hyperinflation (rapidly escalating inflation), the medium of exchange function of money can also be undermined. That is, people will prefer to not accept money in exchange for goods and services and may revert to a barter system, or give preference to some non-domestic currencies (e.g., dollars rather than rubles).

Learning Objective 3: Calculate the amount of M1 and M2

When measuring the quantity of money in the economy, economists vary as to how they define the concept of money. The narrowest definition of the amount of money in the United States is called **M1**, the sum of currency outstanding and balances held in checking accounts. A broader measure of the money supply is **M2**, which includes all the assets in M1 plus savings deposits, small-denomination time deposits, and money market mutual funds. Because the definition of the money supply includes both currency and bank deposits, the amount of money in the economy depends in part on the behavior of commercial banks and their depositors. When households or businesses deposit currency into a bank, the currency becomes a part of the bank reserves.

Hint: Because the money measures are cumulative, when calculating M2 be sure to remember to begin with the value of M1 (or the amounts of the components that make of M1) before adding in the value of the non-M1 components.

Learning Objective 4: Define bank reserves, 100% reserve banking, reserve/deposit ratio, and fractional reserve banking system
Bank reserves are cash or similar assets held by commercial banks for the purpose of meeting depositor withdrawals and payments. When banks must keep bank reserves equal to the amount of their deposits, it is referred to as a **100% reserve banking system**. If banks can maintain a **reserve/deposit ratio** (bank reserves divided by deposits) of less than 100%, then it is referred to as a **fractional-reserve banking system**. In a fractional-reserve banking system the amount of the money supply is expanded when banks make loans in the form of new deposits.

Learning Objective 5: Define the Federal Reserve System, Board of Governors, and Federal Open-Market Committee and discuss the structure of each component of the Fed
The **Federal Reserve System**, often called the Fed, is the central bank of the United States and is responsible for monetary policy, as well as oversight and regulation of financial markets. The leadership of the Fed is provided by its **Board of Governors**, consisting of seven members appointed by the President to staggered fourteen-year terms. Decisions about monetary policy are made by the **Federal Open Market Committee** (FOMC), which is made up of the seven members of the Board of Governors, the President of the Federal Reserve Bank of New York, and four of the presidents of the other Federal Reserve Banks. The Fed's primary responsibility is making monetary policy, which involves decisions about the appropriate size of the nation's money supply. The Fed controls the money supply indirectly by changing the amount of reserves held by commercial banks. The Fed affects the amount of reserves through open-market operations, discount window lending, and changing reserve requirements.

Learning Objective 6: Explain how the Fed uses open market operations to change the amount of bank reserves and the money supply
Open-market operations are the most important tool of monetary policy. When the Fed wants to increase the money supply, the Fed buys government bonds (an **open-market purchase)** from the public. The seller of the bond receives a check in exchange for its bonds and deposits some, or all, of the amount of the check in a bank account. As a result, the bank's reserves increase allowing the bank to make new loans and increase the money supply. **Open-market sales** of government bonds to the public are used to reduce bank reserves and the money supply. When the buyer writes a check to pay for the bond, banks reserves are decreased and, thus, the bank lending eventually is reduced.

Learning Objective 7: Explain the Fed's role in stabilizing financial markets
Besides controlling the money supply, the Fed has the responsibility (along with other government agencies) of ensuring that financial markets operate smoothly. Historically, in the United States, banking panics were the most disruptive type of recurrent financial crisis. A banking panic is an episode in which depositors, spurred by news or rumors of the imminent bankruptcy of one or more banks, rush to withdraw their deposits from the banking system. The Fed, established in 1913 in response to a particularly severe banking panic in 1907, was given the power to supervise and regulate banks to create greater confidence in banks, and was allowed to lend cash to banks to help them meet withdrawals during a bank panic. Following the creation of the Fed there were no bank panics until 1930. During 1930-33, however, the United States experienced the worst and most protracted series of bank panics in its history. The inability of

the Fed to stop the bank panics of the 1930s caused Congress to institute a system of deposit insurance. Under a system of deposit insurance, the government guarantees depositors that they will get their money back even if the bank goes bankrupt, eliminating the incentive of depositors to withdraw their deposits when rumors of financial trouble are circulating.

Learning Objective 8: Explain the relationship between money and prices in the long run
In the long run, the rate of growth of the money supply and the inflation rate are positively related. That is, a higher rate of growth in the money supply will cause a higher rate of inflation because the larger amount of money in circulation will allow people to bid up the prices of goods and services. Velocity measures the speed at which money circulates and is calculated as the value of transactions (or nominal GDP) divided by the supply of money. The definition of velocity can be rewritten as the quantity equation, or $M \times V = P \times Y$. The quantity equation shows that, if velocity and output are constant, a given percentage increase in the money supply will lead to the same percentage increase in the price level.

> **Hint:** The key to understanding the relationship between the change in the money supply and the inflation rate is to recognize that the quantity equation refers to **amounts** of money supply and price **level**, whereas the last sentence in the above paragraph refers to a **change** in the money supply and the **change** in the price level.

III. Self-Test

Key Terms
Match the term in the right-hand column with the appropriate definition in the left-hand column by placing the letter of the term in the blank in front of its' definition. (Answers are given at the end of the chapter.)

1. _____ A basic measure of economic value.

2. _____ Any asset that can be used in making purchases.

3. _____ Bank reserves divided by deposits.

4. _____ The sum of currency outstanding and balances held in checking accounts.

5. _____ A situation in which banks' reserves equal 100 percent of their deposits.

6. _____ Cash or similar assets held by commercial banks for the purpose of meeting depositor withdrawals and payments.

7. _____ An asset used in purchasing goods and services.

8. _____ An asset that services as a means of holding wealth.

9. _____ All the assets in M1 plus some additional assets that are usable in making payments but at greater cost or inconvenience than currency or checks.

10._____ The direct trade of goods or services for other goods or services.

a. bank reserves

b. banking panic

c. barter

d. Board of Governors

e. deposit insurance

f. Federal Open Market Committee (or FOMC)

g. Federal Reserve System (or Fed)

h. fractional-reserve banking system

i. M1

j. M2

11.____ The leadership of the Fed, consisting of seven governors appointed by the President to staggered 14-year terms.

12.____ A banking system in which bank reserves are less than deposits so that the reserve-deposit ration is less than 100 percent.

13.____ The committee that makes decisions concerning monetary policy.

14.____ The central bank of the United States.

15.____ Open-market purchases and open-market sales.

16.____ A system under which the government guarantees that depositors will not lose any money even if their bank goes bankrupt.

17.____ The sale by the Fed of government bonds to the public for the purpose of reducing bank reserves and the money supply.

18.____ A measure of the speed at which money circulates.

19.____ Money times velocity equals nominal GDP.

20.____ An episode in which depositors, spurred by news or rumors of the imminent bankruptcy of one or more banks, rsuh to withdraw their deposits from the banking system.

21.____ The purchase of government bonds from the public by the Fed for the purpose of increasing the supply of bank reserves and the money supply.

k. medium of exchange

l. money

m. 100 percent reserves banking

n. open-market operations

o. open-market purchases

p. open-market sale

q. quantity equation

r. reserve-deposit ratio

s. store of value

t. unit of account

u. velocity

Multiple-Choice Questions
Circle the letter that corresponds to the best answer. (Answers are given at the end of the chapter.)

1. Double coincidence of wants is avoided if money is used as a
   A. medium of exchange.
   B. measure of value.
   C. standard of deferred payment.
   D. store of value
   E. tool of monetary policy.

2. Money serves as a basic yardstick for measuring economic value (i.e., a unit of account), allowing
   A. people to hold their wealth in a liquid form.
   B. governments to restrict the issuance of private monies.
   C. easy comparison of the relative prices of goods and services.
   D. goods and services to be exchanged with a double coincidence of wants.
   E. private money to be issued for local use.

3. In the United States, money is issued
   A. only by the Fed.
   B. by the Fed and all commercial banks.
   C. mainly by the c Fed, but also is issued privately in some communities.
   D. once per year by the Fed.
   E. by the U.S. Congress

4. M1 differs from M2 in that
    A. M1 includes currency and balances held in checking accounts, which are not included in M2.
    B. M2 includes savings deposits, small-denomination time deposits, and money market mutual funds which are not included in M1
    C. M2 includes small savings accounts, large time deposits, and money market mutual funds that are not included in M1.
    D. M1 is a broader measure of the money supply than M2.
    E. the assets in M2 are more liquid than the assets in M1.

5. The difference between a fractional-reserve banking system and a 100 percent reserve banking system is that a fractional reserve banking system
    A. only allows banks to lend a fraction of their reserves, whereas a 100 percent banking system allows banks to lend 100 percent of their reserves.
    B. only allows the money supply to increase by a fraction of banks' reserves, whereas a 100 percent banking system allows the money supply to increase by 100 percent of their reserves.
    C. does not allow banks to lend their reserves, but a 100 percent reserve banking system does allow banks to lend their reserves.
    D. allows banks to lend some of their reserves, but a 100 percent reserve banking system does not allow banks to lend any of their reserves.
    E. does not allow for growth in the money supply through bank lending, while a 100 percent reserve banking system does allow for growth in the money supply through bank lending.

6. When a bank makes a loan by crediting the borrower's checking account balance with an amount equal to the loan
    A. money is created.
    B. the bank gains new reserves.
    C. the bank immediately loses reserves.
    D. money is destroyed.
    E. the Fed has made an open-market purchase.

7. If a bank's desired reserve/deposit ratio is .33 and it has deposit liabilities of $100 million and reserves of $50 million, it
    A. has too few reserves and will reduce its lending.
    B. has too many reserves and will increase its lending.
    C. has the correct amount of reserves and outstanding loans.
    D. should increase the amount of its reserves.
    E. should decrease the amount of its reserves.

8. If the reserve/deposit ratio is .25 and the banking system receives an additional $10 million in reserves, bank deposits can increase by a maximum of
    A. $10 million.
    B. $250 million.
    C. $400 million.
    D. $4 million.
    E. $40 million.

9. Decisions about the United States' monetary policy are made by the
   A. U.S. Congress.
   B. President of the United States.
   C. Fed's Board of Governors.
   D. Federal Open Market Committee (FOMC).
   E. 12 presidents of the regional Federal Reserve Banks.

10. The most important tool of monetary policy is
    A. reserve requirement ratios.
    B. the discount rate.
    C. open-market operations.
    D. the minimum net worth required of banks.
    E. market interest rates.

11. When the Fed sells government securities, the banks'
    A. reserves will increase and lending will expand, causing an increase in the money supply.
    B. reserves will decrease and lending will contract, causing a decrease in the money supply.
    C. reserve requirements will increase and lending will contract, causing a decrease in the money supply.
    D. reserves/deposit ratio will increase and lending will expand, causing an increase in the money supply.
    E. reserves/deposit ratio will decrease and lending will contract, causing an increase in the money supply.

12. An open-market purchase of government securities by the Fed will
    A. increase bank reserves, and the money supply will increase.
    B. decrease bank reserves, and the money supply will increase.
    C. increase bank reserves, and the money supply will decrease.
    D. decrease bank reserves, and the money supply will decrease.
    E. increase bank reserves, and the money supply will not change.

13. The FOMC consists of
    A. seven members appointed by the President of the United States, subject to confirmation by the Senate.
    B. 12 regional Federal Reserve Bank presidents.
    C. the seven Fed governors, the president of the Federal Reserve bank of New York, and four presidents of other regional Federal Reserve Banks.
    D. the Fed chairman, the secretary of the U.S. Treasury and 12 regional Federal Reserve Bank presidents.
    E. the President of the United States, the Fed chairman, and the secretary of the U.S. Treasury.

14. When an individual deposits currency into a checking account
    A. bank reserves increase, which allows banks to lend more and, ultimately, increases the money supply.
    B. bank reserves decrease, which reduces the amount banks can lend thereby reducing the growth of the money supply.
    C. bank reserves are unchanged.
    D. bank reserves decrease, which increases the amount banks can lend, thereby increasing the growth of the money supply.
    E. bank reserves increase, which reduces the amount banks can lend, thereby reducing the growth of the money supply.

15. Deposit insurance for banks
    A. helped the Fed combat the bank panics of 1930-33.
    B. was first legislated by the Federal Reserve Bank Act of 1913.
    C. may induce the managers of banks to take more risks.
    D. guarantees the interest payments on depositors' checking accounts.
    E. is a perfect solution to the problem of bank panics.

16. Holding money as a store of wealth has the advantage of being useful as a medium of exchange and being anonymous. The disadvantages of holding your wealth in the form of money are that it
    A. may be stolen or lost, and people may think you're a smuggler or drug dealer.
    B. is difficult to trace and may be lost or stolen.
    C. may be lost or stolen and usually pays no interest.
    D. pays no interest and is difficult to trace.
    E. pays no interest and people may think you're a smuggler or drug dealer.

17. During the bank panic of 1930-33, the public withdrew deposits from the bank preferring to hold currency. As a result,
    A. bank reserves decreased but were offset by an equal increase in currency, with no net effect on the money supply.
    B. bank reserves increased by less than the increase in currency, causing the money supply to decrease.
    C. bank reserves decreased by more than the increase in currency, causing the money supply to decrease.
    D. bank reserves decreased by less than the increase in currency, causing the money supply to increase.
    E. bank reserves decrease by an amount equal to the increase in currency, causing the money supply to decrease.

18. From a macroeconomic perspective, a major reason that control of the supply of money is important is that,
    A. in the long run, the higher the rate of inflation, the higher the rate of growth of the money supply.
    B. in the long run, the higher the rate of growth of the money supply, the higher the rate of inflation.

C. in the short run, the higher the rate of growth of the money supply, the higher the rate of inflation.
D. in the long run, the lower the rate of growth of the money supply, the higher the rate of inflation.
E. in the long run, the higher the rate of growth of the money supply, the higher velocity of money.

19. The measure of the speed at which money circulates, or velocity, is equivalent to
    A. value of transactions divided by nominal GDP.
    B. nominal GDP times price divided by money supply.
    C. price times money supply divided by nominal GDP.
    D. nominal GDP divided by money supply.
    E. total value of transactions divided by nominal GDP.

20. The quantity equation
    A. states that the velocity of money is equal to the money supply times nominal GDP.
    B. implies that if velocity and real output are constant, an increase in inflation will cause an equal increase in the money supply in the long run.
    C. implies that if velocity and real output are constant, an increase in the money supply will cause an equal increase in inflation in the long run.
    D. implies that if velocity and real output are constant, an increase in the money supply will cause an equal increase in inflation in the short run.
    E. implies that if velocity and real output are constant, an increase in inflation will cause an equal increase in the money supply in the short run.

Short Answer Problems
(Answers and solutions are given at the end of the chapter.)

1. Measuring the Money Supply
In this problem you will practice calculating the measures of the U.S. money supply—Ml and M2.

Month/Year	Currency	Savings deposits	Demand and other checkable deposits	Money market mutual funds	Small time deposits
Mar. '05	$703.9	$3.548.3	$667.6	$702.4	$850.2
Apr. '05	704.4	3,542.9	649.7	706.6	865.6
May '05	706.1	3,516.3	659.7	704.5	883.8
June '05	709.0	3,535.8	656.2	701.7	900.3

Source: Federal Reserve Board of Governors Statistical Release July 14, 2005. All figures are in billions of dollars.

A. Use the preceding data to complete the following table, calculating the amounts for Ml and M2 for January through April 2000.

Month/Year	M1	M2
Aug-02		
Sep-02		
Oct-02		
Nov-02		

B. If the public transfers funds from their (small) savings accounts at the Township Savings and Loan Association to their checking accounts at the Village Bank, this will (increase/decrease/leave unchanged)_____ M1, and (increase/decrease/leave unchanged) _____ M2.

C. If the public deposits currency into their checking accounts at Village Bank, this will (increase/decrease/leave unchanged) _____ M1, and (increase/ decrease/leave unchanged) _____ M2.

2. Reserve/Deposit Ratio, Open-Market Operations, and Money Creation

In this problem you will calculate reserve/deposit ratios, determine how much a bank can lend based on its reserves, deposit liabilities and reserve/deposit ratio, and determine the effect of open-market sales and purchases of government securities on a bank's ability to lend and create money. Each question refers back to balance sheet of The Bank of Haute Finance shown below (i.e., do not take into account the transaction indicated in Questions 3A-3C when answering Questions 3B-3D).

Balance Sheet of
The Bank of Haute Finance

Assets	Liabilities	
Currency (= reserves) $10,000	Deposits	$10,000

A. If The Bank of Haute Finance has a desired reserve/deposit ratio of 10%, it can make new loans of $_____ in the form of new _____. After making the new loans The Bank of Haute Finance will have total deposit liabilities of $_____, currency (= reserves) of $_____, and outstanding loans of $_____. Its total assets will then equal $_____ and its total liabilities will equal $_____.

B. If the Fed imposes a minimum reserve/deposit ratio in the form of a 20% reserve requirement, the maximum amount of new loans The Bank of Haute Finance could make would be $_____. After making the new loans The Bank of Haute Finance would have total deposit liabilities of $_____, currency (= reserves) of $_____ and outstanding loans of $_____. Its total assets would then equal $_____ and its total liabilities would equal $_____.

C. Assume the Federal Reserve System buys $3000 of government securities from Susan Slavin and she deposits the $3000 in her checking account at The Bank of Haute Finance. Following the deposit, The Bank of Haute Finance would have currency (= reserves) of $_____ and deposit liabilities of $_____. Assuming the Fed maintains a minimum reserve/deposit ratio of 20%, The Bank of Haute Finance could make new loans of $_____. By doing so it would (increase/decrease) _____ the money supply by $_____.

D. Assume the Federal Reserve System sells $3000 of government securities to The Bank of Haute Finance which it pays for out of its reserves. After the sale of the government securities, The Bank of Haute Finance would have currency (= reserves) of $_____ and deposit liabilities of $_____. Assuming the Fed maintains a minimum reserve/deposit ratio of 20%, The Bank of Haute Finance could make new loans of $_____. By doing so it would (increase/decrease) _____ the money supply by $_____.

E. In comparing the answers to Questions 3B and 3D, by selling $3,000 of government securities to The Bank of Haute Finance, the Fed would be able to reduce the growth in the supply of money by $_____ .

3. Quantity Equation

This problem focuses on the relationship between the rate of growth of the money supply and inflation rates. You will practice calculating velocity and analyzing the relationship between growth in the money supply and inflation rates.

Date	M1	M2	Nominal GDP	Velocity of M1	Velocity of M2
June 2004	$1,336.8	$6,276.5	$11,657.5		
Sept. 2004	$1,351.8	$6.334.4	$11,814.9		
Dec. 2004	$1,365.6	$6,422.1	$11,994.8		
Mar. 2005	$1,371.4	$6,472.3	$12,191.7		

Sources: M1 and M2 data are from the Federal Reserve Board of Governors Statistical Release July 14, 2005, and Nominal GDP data are from the web site of the Bureau of Economic Analysis at http://www.bea.gov/bea/dn/home/gdp.htm. All figures are in billions of dollars.

A. Complete the above table by calculating the velocity of M1 and M2 for June 2004, September 2004, December 2004, and March 2005 (round your answer to the nearest hundredth).

Dates	M1 Growth Rate	Inflation Rate
1961-70	51.9	33.6
1971-80	89.4	116.8
1981-90	100.6	53.8
1991-00	56.5	40.2

Source: The data were calculated from the Federal Reserve Economic Data (FRED II) available through the Federal Reserve Bank of St. Louis web site at http://research.stlouisfed.org/fred2/

B. Does the above data on the U.S. inflation rate and M1 growth rate support the conclusion that an increase in the supply of money will cause an exact increase the inflation rate in the long run.

_____

C. Does the above data support the weaker conclusion that higher rates of growth in the money supply will cause higher inflation rates_____

_____

IV. Becoming an Economic Naturalist: Case Study

In the Economic Naturalist 23.1, it is explained that privately issued monies, such as Ithaca Hours and LETS (local electronic trading system), are alternative media of exchange in some communities where the law allows. The common characteristic of Ithaca Hours and LETS is that they function as a medium of exchange and, thus, facilitate trade. Credit cards are also issued by privately owned companies, typically banks, and are used to facilitate the purchase of goods and services. Discuss whether credit cards are privately issued monies.

Answer:

V. Self-Test Solutions

Key Terms

1. t
2. l
3. r
4. i
5. m
6. a
7. k
8. s
9. j
10. c
11. d
12. h
13. f
14. g
15. n
16. e
17. p
18. u
19. q
20. b
21. o

Multiple-Choice Questions

1. A
2. C
3. C
4. B
5. D
6. A
7. B With $50 million in reserves and $100 million in deposits, its reserve/deposit ratio of 1/2 is greater than its desired ratio. It would, therefore, increase its deposits to $150 million by making new loans.
8. E $10 million in new reserves divided by $40 million in new deposits equals .25 (the reserve/deposit ratio)
9. D
10. C
11. B
12. A
13. C
14. A
15. C
16. C
17. E Because each dollar of bank reserves translates into several dollars of money supply, the decrease in bank reserves is equal to the increase in currency caused the money supply to decrease.
18. B
19. D
20. C

Short Answer Problems

1.
A.

Month/Year	M1	M2
Mar. '05	$1,371.50	$6,472.40
Apr. '05	$1,354.10	$6,469.20
May '05	$1,365.80	$6,470.40
June '05	$1,365.20	$6,503.00

B. increase; leave unchanged (because the components of M1 are also included in M2)
C. leave unchanged; leave unchanged (currency and checking deposits are included in both M1 and M2. Thus, depositing currency into a checking account does not change the amount of M1 or M2.)

2.
A. $90,000 (Because the desired reserve/deposit ratio is .10 the $10,000 in reserves can support $10,000/.10 = $100,000 in deposits. Thus, $100,000 minus the existing $10,000 in deposits = $90,000); checking deposits; $100,000; $10,000; $90,000; $100,000; $100,000

B. $40,000 (Now that the Fed has imposed a reserve requirements of .20, the $10,000 in reserves can support $10,000/.2 = $50,000. Thus, the bank can make new loan of $40,000); $50,000; $10,000; $40,000; $50,000; $50,000

C. $10,000 + $3,000 = $13,000; $13,000; $52,000 ($13,000/.2 = $65,000 from which the existing $13,000 is subtracted, allowing new loans of $52,000); increase; $52,000

D. $10,000 - $3,000 = $7,000; $7,000/.2 = $35,000 from which the existing $10,000 is subtracted, allowing new loans of $25,000; increase; $25,000

$50,000 - $25,000 = $25,000

3.

A.

Date	M1	M2	Nominal GDP	Velocity M1	Velocity M2
June 2004	$1,336.8	$6,276.5	$11,657.5	8.72	1.86
Sept. 2004	$1,351.8	$6.334.4	$11,814.9	8.74	1.87
Dec. 2004	$1,365.6	$6,422.1	$11,994.8	8.78	1.87
Mar. 2005	$1,371.4	$6,472.3	$12,191.7	8.89	1.88

B. No, the data does not support the extreme conclusion that an increase in the growth rate of money will lend to an exact increase in the inflation rate

C. With the exception of 1981-90, higher growth in M1 did lead to higher inflation in the U.S. Thus, the weaker conclusion that higher growth in the money supply will cause higher inflation is partially supported by the data.

Chapter 24
Financial Markets and
International Capital Flows

I. Pretest: What Do You Really Know?

Circle the letter that corresponds to the best answer. (Answers appear immediately after the final question).

1) Financial intermediaries are firms that
   A. extend credit to borrowers using funds from savers.
   B. match buyers and sellers of stocks.
   C. match buyers and sellers of bonds.
   D. conduct open market operations.
   E. issue currency in exchange for government debt.

2) A legal promise to repay a debt is called
   A. equity.
   B. stock.
   C. a bond.
   D. a dividend.
   E. the principal amount.

3) Stockholders receive returns on their financial investment in the form of _____ and _____.
   A. interest payments; dividends
   B. interest payments; deposits
   C. coupon payments; capital gains
   D. capital gains; interest payments
   E. capital gains; dividends

4) To the individual investor, a major advantage of mutual funds is
   A. increased interest income.
   B. increased diversification.
   C. increased riskiness.
   D. decreased diversification.
   E. increased dividends.

5) If domestic saving is greater than domestic investment, then a country will have a _____ and _____ net capital inflows.
   A. trade deficit; negative
   B. trade deficit; positive
   C. trade balance; zero
   D. trade surplus; negative
   E. trade surplus; positive

6) Purchases of foreign assets by domestic firms or households is called a(n)
   A. import.
   B. export.
   C. capital outflow.
   D. capital inflow.
   E. protectionism.

7) When a U.S. exporter sells software to France and uses the proceeds to buy stock in a French company, U.S. exports _____ and there is a capital _____ to/from the United States.
   A. increase; outflow
   B. increase; inflow
   C. do not change; outflow
   D. decrease; outflow
   E. decrease; inflow

8) In an open economy, a decrease in capital inflows _____ the equilibrium domestic real interest rate and _____ the quantity of domestic investment.
   A. increases; increases
   B. increases; decreases
   C. decreases; does not change
   D. decreases; increases
   E. decreases; decreases

9) If the United States has a $500 billion net capital inflow, then there must be a
   A. trade surplus of $500 billion.
   B. trade deficit of $500 billion.
   C. no trade surplus or trade deficit.
   D. net capital outflow of $1,000 billion.
   E. trade surplus of $1,000 billion.

10) At each value of the domestic interest rate, a decrease in the riskiness of domestic assets _____ capital inflows, _____ capital outflows, and _____ net capital inflows.
   A. increase; increase; increase
   B. increase; increase; decrease
   C. increase; decrease; increase
   D. decrease; decrease; decrease
   E. decrease; increase; decrease

Solutions and Feedback to Pretest

For each question you incorrectly answered, we strongly recommend taking the time to review the appropriate material before continuing. In the table below are listed for each question the pertinent Learning Objective from the following Key Point Review.

Correct Answer	Learning Objective
1. A	2
2. C	3
3. E	4
4. B	5
5. D	6, 7
6. C	7
7. A	7
8. B	7
9. B	7
10. C	8

II. Key Point Review
The Forest

This chapter focuses on the major financial markets and institutions, and their role in directing saving to productive uses, as well as the international dimension of capital and saving. The central questions you need to be able to answer are:

- What are the major financial institutions and how does the financial system allocate saving to alternative productive uses?
- What factors determine international capital flows and how are international capital flows related to net exports?
- What is the relationship between international capital flows and domestic saving and investment?

The Trees

Learning Objective 1: Explain how market-oriented financial systems improve the allocation of saving

A successful economy not only saves but also uses its' saving to invest in projects that are likely to be the most productive. In a market economy like that of the United States, savings are allocated by means of a decentralized, market-oriented financial system. A market-oriented financial system improves the allocation of savings by providing savers information about the uses of their funds that are most likely to prove productive, and by helping savers share the risks of individual investment projects. Three key components of a market-oriented financial system are discussed in this chapter: (1) the banking system, (2) the bond market, and (3) the stock market.

Learning Objective 2: Define financial intermediaries and explain the role of financial intermediaries in a market economy

Financial intermediaries are firms that extend credit to borrowers using funds raised from savers. The most important financial intermediaries in the banking system are the commercial banks. They are privately owned firms that accept deposits from individuals and businesses and use those deposits to make loans. Savers are willing to hold bank deposits because banks (and other financial intermediaries) have a comparative advantage in information-gathering about lending opportunities that results in lower costs and better results than individual savers could achieve on their own. Banks also make it easier for households and business to make payments for goods and services.

Note: Banks and other financial intermediaries have gained experience in evaluating potential borrowers and monitoring borrowers' activities. This not only benefits the banks and savers, but also helps the borrowers by providing access to credit that may otherwise not be provided.

Learning Objective 3: Explain how bond markets can be a source of funds for businesses; define bond, principal amount, maturity date, coupon rate and coupon payment

In addition to obtaining funds from banks, corporations and governments can obtain funds in the bond market. Corporations and governments frequently raise funds by issuing bonds and selling them to savers. A **bond** is a legal promise to repay a debt, usually including the **principal amount** (the amount originally lent), **maturity date** (the date at which the principal will be repaid) and regular interest payments. The promised interest rate when a bond is issued is called the **coupon rate**, which is paid to the bondholder in regular interest payments called **coupon payments**. The coupon rate must be sufficiently attractive to savers, depending upon the term, or length of time before the debt is fully repaid, and the risk that the borrower will not repay the debt. Bonds also differ in terms of their tax treatment. The interest on municipal bonds, issued by local governments, is exempt from federal income taxes and, thus, typically pays a lower coupon rate than do other comparable bonds. Bondholders do not have to hold bonds until they are to be repaid by the issuer because they can sell them in the bond market. The price (or market value) of a bond at any point in time is inversely related to interest rates being paid on comparable newly issued bonds.

Hint: Because bond prices and interest rates are inversely related, if interest rates on new bond issues rise, the price a bond holder will received for an outstanding bond will fall. That is, if you are holding a bond that pays an interest rate of six percent annually, and new bond issues are now paying seven percent annually, you will only be able to sell the bond to another investor if you price the bond sufficiently low to allow the investor to earn the seven percent rate of return that the investor could currently earn elsewhere. The price would be below what you paid for the bond and would result in a capital loss.

Learning Objective 4: Explain the role of the stock markets; define stock dividend and risk premium

Another important way of raising funds, but one that is restricted to corporations is issuing stock to the public. A share of **stock**, also called equity, is a claim to partial ownership of a firm. Stockholders receive returns on their financial investment in a firm through dividend payments and capital gains (the increase in the price of the stock). A **dividend** is a regular payment received by stockholders for each share that they own, as determined by the firm's management and is usually dependent on the firm's recent profits. The price of a share of stock at any point in time depends on the expected future dividends and capital gain, adjusted for the risk premium. **Risk premium** is the rate of return that financial investors require to hold risky assets minus the rate of return on safe assets.

Learning Objective 5: Define diversification and explain the role of mutual funds

Like banks, bond and stock markets provide a means of channeling funds from savers to borrowers with productive investment opportunities. Savers and their financial advisors search for high returns in the bond and stock markets and, thus, provide a powerful incentive to potential borrowers to use the funds productively. The markets also give savers a means to diversify their financial investments. **Diversification** is the practice of spreading one's wealth over a variety of different financial investments in order to reduce overall risk. From society's perspective, diversification makes it possible for risky but worthwhile projects to obtain funding without individual savers having to bear too much risk. For the typical saver, a convenient way to diversify is buy stocks and bonds indirectly through mutual funds. A **mutual fund** is a financial intermediary that sells shares to the public, then uses the funds raised to buy a wide variety of financial assets.

> **Note**: In the past, small investor with limited funds would find it very difficult to achieve a diversified portfolio of investments by directly purchasing individual stocks and bonds. Most small investors, therefore, did little more than put their wealth into saving accounts. But in recent years with the rapid growth in the number of stock and bond mutual funds, small investors have increasingly been able to reduce the risks of investing and simultaneously increase their rate of return by purchasing shares of stock and bond mutual funds.

Learning Objective 6: Define trade balance, trade surplus, and trade deficit and capital flows

When an economy is open to trade, its **trade balance**, the value of a country's exports minus the value of its imports in a particular period, may be positive or negative. A country is said to have a **trade surplus** for a period when the value of its exports exceeds the value of its imports. Alternatively, a country is said to have a **trade deficit** for a period, when the value of its imports exceeds the value of its exports. In addition to the trade of goods and services that is captured in the trade balance, trade among countries occurs in real and financial assets.

Learning Objective 7: Discuss the relationships among international capital flows, and domestic saving and investment
Purchases or sales of real and financial assets across international borders are known as **international capital flows**. From the perspective of a particular country, purchases of domestic assets by foreigners are called **capital inflows**, and purchases of foreign assets by domestic households and firms are called **capital outflows**. Capital inflows are related to real interest rates and investment risk in a country. The higher the real interest rate in a country, and the lower the risk of investing there, the higher its capital inflows. Capital inflows expand a country's pool of saving, allowing for more domestic investment and economic growth. A potential drawback, however, to using capital inflows to finance domestic investment is that the interest and dividends on the borrowed funds must be paid to foreign savers rather than domestic residents.

Learning Objective 8: Explain the link between the trade balance and capital flows
There is a precise link between the trade balance and international capital flows. In any given period, the trade balance and net capital inflows add up to zero, or NX (net exports) + KI (net capital inflows) = 0. This link suggests the primary cause of a trade deficit is a country's low rate of national saving. A low-saving, high-spending country is likely to import more and export less than a high-saving, low-spending country. A low-saving, high-spending country is also likely to have higher real interest rates in order to attract capital inflows. Because the sum of the trade balance and capital inflows is zero, a high level of net capital inflows is consistent with a large trade deficit.

> **Note:** In theory, it is impossible for a country to continuously run a trade deficit because the capital inflows will eventually decrease the value of its currency vis-à-vis other currencies. As this happens, the cost of imports will increase and it will import less, and its exports will become more competitive and its exports will grow. As a result, net exports will rise and its trade deficit will decline.

III. Self-Test

Key Terms
Match the term in the right-hand column with the appropriate definition in the left-hand column by placing the letter of the term in the blank in front of its' definition. (Answers are given at the end of the chapter.)

1. _____ Firms that extend credit to borrowers using funds raised from savers.

    a. bond

2. _____ A regular payment received by stockholders for each share that they own.

    b. capital inflows

3. _____ The value of a country's exports less the value of its imports in a particular period (quarter or year).

    c. capital outflows

4. _____ When imports exceed exports, the difference between the value of a country's imports and the value of its exports in a given period.

    d. coupon payment

5. _____ A legal promise to repay a debt, usually including both the

    e. coupon rate

principal amount and regular interest payments.

6. ____ the practice of spreading of one's wealth over a variety of different financial investments to reduce overall risk.

7. ____ When exports exceed imports, the difference between the value of a country's exports and the value of its imports in a given period.

8. ____ A financial intermediary that sells shares in itself to the public, then uses the funds raised to buy a wide variety of financial assets.

9. ____ The amount originally lent.

10. ____ A claim to a partial ownership of a firm.

11. ____ Purchases or sales of real and financial assets across international borders.

12. ____ The interest rate promised when a bond is issued.

13. ____ Purchases of foreign assets by domestic households and firms.

14. ____ The rate of return that financial investors require to hold risky assets minus the rate of return on safe assets.

15. ____ Regular interest payments made to the bondholder.

16. ____ The date at which the principal of a bond will be repaid.

17. ____ Equal to foreign purchases of domestic assets minus domestic purchases of foreign assets.

18. ____ Purchases of domestic assets by foreign households and firms.

f. diversification

g. dividend

h. financial intermediaries

i. international capital flows

j. maturation date

k. net capital inflows

l. mutual fund

m. principal amount

n. risk premium

o. stock

p. trade balance (or net exports)

q. trade deficit

r. trade surplus

Multiple-Choice Questions
Circle the letter that corresponds to the best answer. (Answers are given at the end of the chapter.)

1. A market-oriented financial system improves the allocation of savings by providing
    A. information about savers and helping savers share the risks of individual investment projects.
    B. information to savers about the risks of individual investment projects and helping investors reduce the risks of individual investment projects.
    C. information to savers about alternative productive uses for funds and helping savers share the risks of individual investment projects.
    D. banks with a comparative advantage over small savers in evaluating and monitoring prospective borrowers.
    E. information to financial intermediaries, stock and bond markets about alternative productive uses for funds and by reducing the risk to savers through diversification.

2. Banks and other financial intermediaries are necessary because they
   A. have a comparative advantage in evaluating the quality of borrowers.
   B. shift the risk of investing from borrowers to savers.
   C. facilitate the direct lending of funds by savers to borrowers.
   D. diversify the risk of saving.
   E. eliminate the need to gather information about borrowers.

3. A feature common to all financial intermediaries is that they
   A. buy and sell information about savers and borrowers.
   B. have a comparative advantage in gathering and evaluating information about borrowers.
   C. act as agents for buyers and sellers in the money market.
   D. shift the risk of investing from borrowers to savers.
   E. collect funds from a few savers and distribute the funds to many borrowers.

4. Which of the following sources of funds are available to large and well-established corporations but not to the typical small borrower?
   A. Financial intermediaries and bond markets
   B. Municipal bond and stock markets
   C. Financial intermediaries, stock and bond markets
   D. Stock and corporate bond markets
   E. All sources of funds are available to both large and well-established corporations and the typical small borrower.

5. In comparison to a corporate bond, a municipal bond of the same term and credit risk will have a
   A. higher risk premium.
   B. higher coupon payment.
   C. higher coupon rate.
   D. lower coupon rate.
   E. same coupon rate.

6. During the 1990s, the Japanese banking system
   A. experienced severe financial problems that contributed to a severe economic downturn in Japan.
   B. acquired corporate stocks and made loans to real estate developers that contributed to an economic boom in Japan.
   C. experienced severe financial problems that created a "credit crunch" for large corporations in Japan.
   D. experienced severe financial problems that created a global "credit crunch" for small- and medium-sized businesses.
   E. experienced severe financial problems that has forced the Japanese government to nationalize the banking system to return it to a healthy financial condition.

7. The price of a share of corporate stock varies over time depending upon stockholders' expectations about the future
   A. coupon rate, risk premium, and coupon payment.
   B. dividend, stock price, and coupon rate.
   C. coupon payment, dividend and risk premium.

    D. coupon rate, coupon premium and dividend.
    E. dividend, stock price, and risk premium

8. The informational role of the stock and bond markets provides incentives for savers and their financial advisors to
    A. direct funds to those borrowers that appear to have the safest investments.
    B. direct funds to those borrowers that appear to have the most productive investments.
    C. diversify their investments by purchasing mutual funds.
    D. shift the risk of investing to the borrowers.
    E. avoid the cost of paying the financial intermediaries by going directly to the borrowers to make loans.

9. Antonio holds a two-year bond issued by the Jetson Corporation with a principal amount of $10,000. The annual coupon rate is 6 percent. He considered selling it after receiving the first coupon payment a week ago at a price of $9,390. Since that time, the coupon rate on new bond issues has risen from 6.5% to 7.0%. If he were to sell the bond today, the price would be
    A. $10,000.
    B. higher than it was a week ago.
    C. the same at it was a week ago.
    D. lower than it was a week ago.
    E. impossible to determine from the information given.

10. When American investors pay cash for shares of stock in a French corporation, from the perspective of
    A. the United States, it is a capital inflow.
    B. France, it is a capital outflow.
    C. the United States, it is a capital outflow.
    D. France, it is a trade deficit.
    E. the United States, it is a trade deficit.

11. If interest rates in Japan increase relative to international interest rate levels, all else being equal, Japan's net capital
    A. inflows will tend to increase, and the pool of funds for domestic investment will tend to decrease.
    B. inflows will tend to increase, and the pool of funds for domestic investment will tend to increase.
    C. outflows will tend to increase, and the pool of funds for domestic investment will tend to decrease.
    D. outflows will tend to increase, and the pool of funds for domestic investment will tend to increase.
    E. inflows will tend to decrease, and the pool of funds for domestic investment will tend to decrease.

12. The sum of national saving and capital inflows from abroad must equal
    A. domestic investment in new capital goods.
    B. capital outflows.
    C. aggregate demand.
    D. the trade deficit.
    E. the trade surplus.

13. The U.S. trade deficit is mainly caused by
    A. production of inferior goods in the country.
    B. unfair trade restrictions imposed by other countries on imports.
    C. a low rate of national saving.
    D. cheap labor in other countries.
    E. inadequate safety and environmental protections in other countries.

14. Which of the following transactions would cause a capital inflow to a country?
    A. exports of goods or services
    B. import of goods or services
    C. purchasing financial assets (e.g., a corporate bond) from abroad
    D. purchasing real assets (e.g., a factory) abroad
    E. lending money abroad

15. The illegal drug trade has increased the political instability in Colombia and has
    A. reduced net capital outflows from Colombia.
    B. reduced net capital inflows to Colombia.
    C. increased net capital inflows to Colombia.
    D. increased Colombia's trade deficit.
    E. decreased Colombia's trade surplus.

16. An increase in net capital inflows to a country will
    A. increase its real interest rates.
    B. increase its imports.
    C. decrease its exports.
    D. decrease its real interest rates.
    E. decrease its investment in new capital.

17. During the 1960s and 1970s, the U.S. trade balance was close to zero, but during the 1980s
    the trade deficit ballooned to unprecedented levels due to
    A. an inability of U.S. companies to compete in the international market.
    B. a decline in private saving that resulted from an upsurge in consumption.
    C. a decline in national saving without a corresponding decrease in investment.
    D. a worldwide recession that made it difficult for U. S. companies to sell their products
    abroad.
    E. unfair protectionist policies imposed by the United State's major trade partners.

18. A country's trade balance and its net capital inflows
    A. Add up to zero.
    B. determine the size of the pool of saving available for capital investment.
    C. must always equal the sum of the four components of aggregate demand.
    D. must equal domestic investment in new capital goods.
    E. are identical in open and closed economies.

19. Capital inflows used to finance capital investment in some developing countries have
    A. decreased domestic saving.
    B. benefited domestic savers because of higher interest rates paid on saving accounts.
    C. caused debt crises because the returns on the investments were less than the interest cost of the capital.
    D. caused debt crises because the returns on the investments were greater than the interest cost of the capital.
    E. had economic benefits without costs.

20. The Argentine economic collapse in 2001-02 was caused by:
    A. an increase in domestic savings rates and a corresponding decline in domestic consumption spending that led to a collapse in production.
    B. an insufficient level of skilled and educated workers to work in the growing high tech industries.
    C. the International Monetary Fund's refusal to provide additional loans to the Argentine government to pay its foreign debt.
    D. Argentina defaulting on its foreign debt and the subsequent unwillingness of foreign lenders to make additional loans.
    E. Argentina defaulting on its foreign debt because the Argentine government's spending exceeded its tax revenues.

Short Answer Problems
(Answers and solutions are given at the end of the chapter.)

1. Bond and Stock Prices
This problem will require you to calculate the effects of various factors on the price of bonds and stocks.

A. Carley has purchased a newly issued bond from the SimonSays Corp. for $10,000. The SimonSays Corp. will pay the bondholder $750 at the end of years 1-4 and will pay $10,750 at the end of year 5. The bond has a principal amount of $_____, a term of _____ years, a coupon rate of _____ %, and a coupon payment of $_____ .
B. After receiving coupon payments 1 through 4, Carley has decided to sell the bond. What price should she expect to receive if the one-year interest rate on comparable financial assets is 5%? $_____ What price should she expect to receive if the one-year interest rate on comparable financial assets is 8%? $_____
C. Justin has decided to buy 100 shares of stock in The Boot Company. He expects the company to pay a dividend of $3 per share in one year and expects the price of the shares will be $40

at that time. How much should he be willing to pay today per share if the safe rate of interest is 7% and The Boot Company carries no risk? $_____

D. How much should Justin be willing to pay today per share if the safe rate of interest is 5% and The Boot Company carries no risk? $_____

E. How much should Justin be willing to pay today per share if the safe rate of interest is 5% and he requires a risk premium of 2%? $_____

2. International Capital Flows

This problem focuses on the determinants of international capital flows, including risks and domestic and international interest rates.

A. The graph below shows the net capital inflows to the United States for 2006. What level of domestic interest rate is necessary for net capital inflows to be positive? _____ percent

Net capital inflows _KI_

B. On the graph above, show the impact of increased riskiness of domestic assets (label the new curve KI₁).

C. On the graph above, show the impact of an increase in real interest rates abroad (label the new curve KI₂).

D. On the graph above, show the impact of an increase in riskiness of assets abroad (label the new curve KI₃).

3. Saving, Investment and Capital Flows in an Open Economy

This problem expands upon the saving-investment diagram for a closed economy by focusing on the effects of international capital flows on domestic interest rates and investment.

A. In an open economy the amount of investment must be equal to _____ plus _____ .

B. The graph below shows domestic saving (S) and domestic investment curves. Draw a new curve that would show the impact of opening the domestic financial markets to capital inflows (label the new curve S+KI).

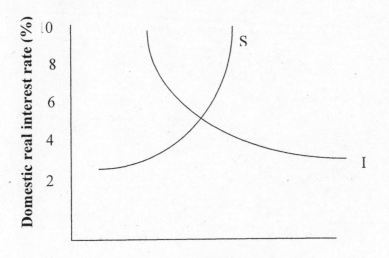

Saving and Investment

C. As a result of opening the domestic economy to capital inflows, the domestic equilibrium interest rate will (decrease/increase/remain unchanged) _____ and the equilibrium level of saving and investment will (decrease/increase/remain unchanged)

_____ .

D. As the economy is opened, if capital inflows allow the level of investment to exceed the amount of national saving, then the country must also have a trade (surplus/deficit)

_____ .

IV. Becoming an Economic Naturalist: Case Study

In Economic Naturalist 24.4, the relationship between the U.S. trade deficit and the level of national saving and investment is explained. It is noted that the large U.S. trade deficits since the late 1970s, particularly during the mid-1980s and the latter part of the 1990s, correspond to periods in which investment in the U.S. exceeded national saving. More recently, since the economic recovery began in 2002, investments in residential housing and business capital have grown rapidly, while national saving has been restrained by increases in the government budget deficit. Given these trends in U.S. investment and saving, what would you expect to find in terms of the U.S. trade balance during this period? Is the actual data on the U.S. trade balance during 2002-05 consistent with your prediction?
Answer:

V. Self-Test Solutions

Key Terms
1. h
2. g
3. p
4. q
5. a
6. f
7. r
8. l
9. m
10. o
11. i
12. e
13. c
14. n
15. d
16. j
17. k
18. b

Multiple-Choice Questions
1. C
2. A
3. B
4. D
5. D Because municipal bonds are exempt from federal income taxes, they have a lower coupon rate than comparable non-municipal bonds.
6. A
7. E
8. B
9. D
10. C
11. B
12. A
13. C
14. A
15. B
16. D
17. C
18. A
19. C
20. D

Short Answer Problems
1.
A. $10,000; 5; 7.5%; $750
B. $10,750 / 1.05 = $10, 238.10; $9,953.70
C. $43 / 1.07 = $40.19
D. $43 / 1.05 = $40.95
E. $43 / (1.05 + .02) = $40.19

2.
A. 4
B.

C.

D.

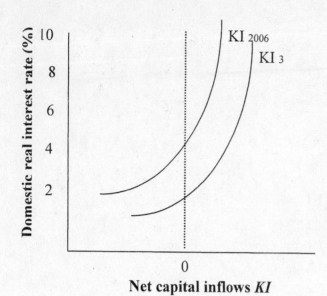

3.
A. saving; capital inflows
B.

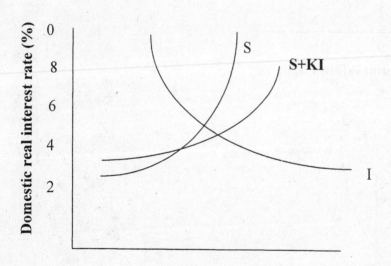

C. decrease; increase
D. deficit

Chapter 25
Short-term Economic Fluctuations:
An Introduction

I. Pretest: What Do You Really Know?
Circle the letter that corresponds to the best answer. (Answers appear immediately after the final question).

1) Since the end of World War II, recessions in the U.S have _____ than expansions.
   A. occurred more frequently
   B. been shorter in duration, on average,
   C. been longer in duration, on average,
   D. generated more inflation
   E. been more predictable

2) Economic activity moves from a trough into a period of _____ until it reaches a _____ and then into a period of _____.
   A. expansion; trough; recession.
   B. recession; trough; expansion
   C. expansion; peak; recession
   D. recession; peak; expansion
   E. expansion; trough; expansion

3) In reference to short-term economic fluctuations, the "peak" refers to
   A. a period in which the economy is growing at a rate significantly above normal.
   B. the high point of economic activity prior to a downturn.
   C. the low point of economic activity prior to a recovery.
   D. a particularly strong and protracted expansion.
   E. a particularly severe and protracted recession.

4) An expansion is
   A. a period in which the economy is growing at a rate significantly below normal.
   B. a period in which the economy is growing at a rate significantly above normal.
   C. the high point of economic activity prior to a downturn.
   D. the low point of economic activity prior to a recovery.

E. a particularly severe or protracted recession.

5) The following data give the dates of successive turning points in U.S. economic activity and the corresponding levels of real GDP at the time:

Turning Point	Date	Real GDP(1996 $ billions)
(A)	Jan. 1980	4958.9
(B)	July 1980	4850.3
(C)	July 1981	5056.8
(D)	Nov. 1982	4912.1
(E)	July 1990	6731.7

Which of the following periods is a recession?
A. Jan. 1980 through July 1980
B. Jan. 1980 through July 1981
C. July 1980 through July 1981
D. July 1980 though Nov. 1982
E. Nov. 1982 through July 1990

6) All of the following are characteristics of short-term economic fluctuations EXCEPT
A. expansions and recessions are felt throughout the economy.
B. expansions and recessions are irregular in length and severity
C. unemployment falls sharply during recessions.
D. durable-goods industries are more sensitive to short-term fluctuations than service and non-durable industries.
E. recessions tend to be followed by a decline in inflation.

7) Which of the following workers is most likely to lose his/her job during a recession?
A. construction worker
B. baker
C. farmer
D. barber
E. police officer

8) The difference between the economy's potential output and its actual output at a point in time is called the
A. budget deficit.
B. trade deficit.
C. output gap.
D. full-employment rate.
E. cyclical peak.

9) If potential output equals $5 billion and actual output equals $3.5 billion, then this economy has a(n)
A. budget deficit.
B. trade deficit.
C. expansionary gap.
D. recessionary gap.

E. value-added gap.

10) In Macroland potential GDP equals $8 trillion and real GDP equals $7.6 trillion. Macroland
    has a(n) _____ gap equal to _____ percent of potential GDP.
    A. expansionary; -5
    B. expansionary; 5
    C. recessionary; -5
    D. recessionary; 5
    E. recessionary; 6

Solutions and Feedback to Pretest
For each question you incorrectly answered, we strongly recommend taking the time to review
the appropriate material before continuing. In the table below are listed for each question the
pertinent Learning Objective from the following Key Point Review.

Correct Answer	Learning Objective
1. B	1
2. C	1
3. B	1
4. B	1
5. A	1
6. B	2
7. A	2
8. C	3
9. D	3
10. D	3

II. Key Point Review
The Forest

This chapter focuses on the history, characteristics and causes of short-run fluctuations in
economic conditions, and concludes with preview of the causes of recessions and expansions.
The central questions you need to be able to answer are
   - What are the four stages of the business cycle?
   - What are the primary characteristics of recessions and expansions?
   - What are the two types of output gaps and how are they measured?
   - How is the natural rate of unemployment defined and how is it related to cyclical
     unemployment?
   - What is Okun's Law?

The Trees

Learning Objective 1: Define recession, depression, expansion, boom, peak, and trough
The short-run fluctuations in economic conditions are commonly known as recessions and
expansions. A **recession**, or contraction, is a period in which the economy is growing at a rate
significantly below normal. An extremely severe or protracted recession is called a **depression**.

A more informal definition of a recession (often used by the mass media) is a period during which real GDP falls for at least two consecutive quarters. While the "two consecutive quarters" rule would not classify a slow-growth episode as a recession, many economists would argue that a period in which real GDP growth is significantly below normal should be counted as a recession. The beginning of a recession is called a **peak**, the high point of economic activity prior to a downturn. The end of a recession, marking the low point of economic activity prior to a recovery, is called the **trough**. By far the longest and most severe recession in the United States was during 1929-33. Since World War II, U.S. recessions have generally been short, lasting between six and sixteen months. The opposite of a recession is an **expansion**; a period in which the economy is growing at a rate that is significantly above normal. A particularly strong and protracted expansion is called a **boom**. On average, expansions have lasted longer than recessions. The two longest expansions were during 1961-69, and 1990-2001 (in February, 2000 this boom broke the all-time record for the duration of a U.S. expansion).

Learning Objective 2: Discuss the characteristics of short-term economic fluctuations
Expansions and recessions are not new, as they have been a feature of industrial economies since at least the late 18th century. Short-run economic fluctuations, although they are sometimes referred to as business cycles, or cyclical fluctuations, do not recur at predictable intervals but rather are quite irregular in their length and severity. This irregularity makes it extremely hard to predict the dates of peaks and troughs. Expansions and recessions are felt throughout the economy, and even globally. Unemployment is a key indicator of short-term fluctuations, typically rising during recessions and falling (although more slowly) during expansions. Cyclical unemployment is the type of unemployment associated with recessions. In addition to rising unemployment, labor market conditions become more unfavorable during recessions, with real wages growing more slowly and workers less likely to receive promotions or bonuses. Inflation also follows a typical pattern during recessions and expansions, though not as sharply defined. Recessions tend to be preceded by increases in inflation, and followed soon after by a decline in the rate of inflation. Durable goods industries tend to be more affected by recessions and expansions, while services and nondurable goods industries are less sensitive to short-term economic fluctuations.

Learning Objective 3: Define potential output, output gap, recessionary gap and expansionary gap
Economists measure expansions and recessions by determining how far actual output is from potential output. **Potential output** (also known as potential GDP or full-employment output) is the maximum sustainable amount of output (real GDP) that an economy can produce. Actual output (real GDP) may be below or above potential output at any point in time. The difference between potential output and actual output is called the **output gap**. The output gap is expressed in symbols as $Y^* - Y$. A positive output gap, when actual output is below potential output and resources are not fully utilized, is called a **recessionary gap**. A negative output gap, when actual output is above potential output and resources are utilized at above-normal rates, is called an **expansionary gap**.

Note: Be careful to not become confused by the terminology regarding output gaps. Sometimes students mistakenly think that because actual output is below potential the output gap should be negative. When actual output is below potential output there is a **positive** output gap. When actual output is above potential output there is a **negative** output gap.

Learning Objective 4: Define the natural rate of unemployment and explain its relationship to cyclical unemployment

Recessionary gaps are associated with below normal utilization of labor resources. This is another way of saying there is extra unemployment during recessions. Specifically, in addition to the frictional and structural unemployment, which are always present in the labor market, cyclical unemployment is present during recessions. Economists call that part of the total unemployment rate that is attributable to frictional and structural unemployment the **natural rate of unemployment**. The natural rate of unemployment can vary over time because of changes in frictional and/or structural unemployment. The natural rate of unemployment is the unemployment rate that prevails when cyclical unemployment is zero. Cyclical unemployment can, therefore, be calculated as the difference between the actual unemployment rate (u) and the natural rate of unemployment (u^*). During recessions cyclical unemployment is positive, and during expansions it is negative.

Hint: The concept of a "natural" rate of unemployment is intended to reflect the fact that there is always some amount of unemployment in the economy, i.e., it is a *natural* state of the economy. Thus, it is virtually impossible for the unemployment rate to ever equal zero.

Learning Objective 5: Define Okun's Law and explain its importance to understanding short-run fluctuations in the economy

A rule of thumb called Okun's Law helps economists quantify the relationship between the amount of cyclical unemployment and the output gap. **Okun's Law** states that each extra percentage point of cyclical unemployment is associated with about a two-percentage point increase in the output gap. The output losses calculated according to Okun's Law suggest that recessions have significant costs (which are reflected, for example, in the importance that short-run economic fluctuations have on presidential elections in the United States).

Note: Be careful to not mistakenly attribute Okun's Law to indicate that the change in unemployment causes the output gap. The cause-and-effect works in the opposite direction. That is, an increase in output gap causes unemployment to rise. It is, however, much easier to observe changes in unemployment than changes in output gaps. Thus, Okun's Law is more of a rule of thumb than an analytical theory.

Learning Objective 6: Explain why short-run fluctuations occur
In the short run, prices do not always adjust immediately to changing demand or supply as some producers vary the quantity of output rather than price, meeting the demand at a preset price. In the short run, therefore, changes in economy-wide spending are the primary cause of output gaps. In the long run, however, prices will adjust to their market-clearing levels, as producers better understand the information provided by the market, and output will equal potential output. The quantities of inputs, and the productivity with which they are used, are the primary determinants of economic activity in the long run. While total spending in the economy affects output in the short run, in the long run its main effects are on prices.

III. Self-Test

Key Terms
Match the term in the right-hand column with the appropriate definition in the left-hand column by placing the letter of the term in the blank in front of its' definition. (Answers are given at the end of the chapter.)

1. _____A particularly strong and protracted expansion.   a. boom

2. _____ The maximum sustainable amount of output (real GDP)   b. depression
that an economy can produce.

3. _____ Each extra percentage point of cyclical unemployment is   c. expansion
associated with about a 2 percentage point increase in the output
gap, measured in relation to potential output.

4. _____ An extremely severe or protracted recession.   d. expansionary gap

5. _____ A negative output gap, which occurs when actual output is   e. natural rate of
above potential output   unemployment

6. _____ The end of a recession, the low point of economic activity   f. Okun's Law
prior to a recovery.

7. _____The difference between the economy's potential output and   g. output gap
its actual output at some point in time.

8. _____ A period in which the economy is growing at a rate   h. peak
significantly below normal.

9. _____ The part of the total unemployment rate that is attributable   i. potential output
to frictional and structural unemployment.

10. _____ The beginning of a recession, (the high point of economic   j. recession
activity prior to a downturn).

11. _____ A period in which the economy is growing at a rate that is   k. recessionary gap
significantly above normal.

12. _____ A positive output gap, which occurs when potential output   l. trough
exceeds actual output.

Multiple-Choice Questions
Circle the letter that corresponds to the best answer. (Answers are given at the end of the chapter.)

1. The longest and most severe recession in the United States was during
   A. August 1957 to February 1961, initiating what became known as the Great Depression.
   B. November 1973 to March 1975, initiating what became known as the Great Depression.
   C. May 1937 to June 1938, initiating what became known as the Great Depression.
   D. January 1980 to November 1982, initiating what became known as the Great Depression.
   E. August 1929 to March 1933, initiating what became known as the Great Depression.

2. Short-term economic fluctuations
   A. recur at predictable intervals.
   B. have a limited impact on a few industries or regions.
   C. contain peaks and troughs that are easily predicted by the professional forecasters.
   D. are irregular in their length and severity.
   E. have little impact on unemployment and inflation.

3. Unemployment typically
   A. is unaffected by recessions and expansions.
   B. rises during recession and falls during expansions.
   C. falls during recessions and rises during expansions.
   D. rises during recessions and falls during expansions, as does inflation.
   E. falls during recessions and rises during expansions, as does inflation.

4. The Japanese economy slowed markedly during the 1990s due to
   A. faster growth in potential output combined with a significant output gap.
   B. slower growth in potential output, and actual output equal to potential output.
   C. slower growth in potential output combined with a significant output gap.
   D. faster growth in potential output, and actual output equal to potential output.
   E. normal growth in potential output combined with a significant output gap.

5. As the average age of U.S. workers has increased since 1980
   A. frictional unemployment has fallen and the natural rate of unemployment has decreased.
   B. cyclical unemployment has fallen and the natural rate of unemployment has decreased.
   C. structural unemployment has fallen and the natural rate of unemployment has decreased.
   D. frictional unemployment has risen and the natural rate of unemployment has increased.
   E. cyclical unemployment has risen and the natural rate of unemployment has increased.

6. If cyclical unemployment rises to 2.5% and potential output (GDP) equals $9,000 billion, the output gap would equal
   A. $22,500 billion.
   B. $225 billion.
   C. $9,000 billion.
   D. $8,775 billion.
   E. $9,225 billion.

7. The firm behavior known as "meeting the demand, " refers to
   A. firms adjusting prices from moment to moment in response to changes in demand.
   B. firms adjusting prices continuously in order to ensure that the quantity supplied equals the quantity demanded.
   C. changes in economy-wide spending as the primary cause of output gaps.
   D. price changes that eliminate output gaps in a self-correcting market.
   E. firms adjusting prices only periodically, while in the short run varying the quantity of output.

8. A recessionary gap occurs when
   A. total spending is abnormally high.
   B. total spending is at normal levels, but potential output is growing at abnormally high levels.
   C. total spending is low for some reason.
   D. potential output is less than actual output.
   E. actual output is greater than potential output.

9. The self-correcting market mechanism eliminates output gaps over time though price
   A. decreases if demand exceeds potential output.
   B. increases if demand is less than potential output.
   C. decreases if an expansionary gap exists.
   D. decreases if recessionary gap exists.
   E. increases if recessionary gap exists.

10. The longest expansion in the U.S. economy
    A. began in August 1929, at the trough of the Great Depression.
    B. lasted 106 months.
    C. began in March 1991, at the trough of the 1990-91 recession.
    D. lasted 92 months.
    E. began in February 1961, at the trough of the 1960-61 recession.

11. On average, recessions in the United States have been
    A. shorter than expansions.
    B. longer than expansions.
    C. longer and more severe during the post-WWII period than prior to WWII.
    D. shorter but more severe during the post-WWII period than prior to WWII.
    E. equal in duration to expansions.

12. During short-term economic fluctuations, inflation tends to
    A. rise following an economic peak and fall soon after the trough.
    B. fall following an economic peak and rise soon after the trough.
    C. rise following an economic peak and rise soon after the trough.
    D. fall following an economic peak and rise soon after the trough.
    E. move in the same direction as unemployment.

13. An economy grows significantly below its maximum sustainable output when
    A. actual output is above potential output.
    B. actual output equals potential output, but potential output is growing very slowly.
    C. actual output equals potential output, but potential output is growing very rapidly.
    D. actual output is below potential output and potential output is growing very rapidly.
    E. actual output is above potential output and potential output is growing very rapidly.

14. An expansionary gap implies that resources are
    A. not being fully utilized and the unemployment rate would be above the natural rate of unemployment.
    B. being utilized at above-normal rates and the unemployment rate would be above the natural rate of unemployment.
    C. not being fully utilized and the unemployment rate would be below the natural rate of unemployment.
    D. being utilized at above-normal rates and cyclical unemployment is positive.
    E. being utilized at above-normal rates and cyclical unemployment is negative.

15. In some markets, such as the market for grain, price-setting by auction occurs, but in other markets it does not because
    A. there are not enough auctioneers to announce prices for all the markets.
    B. auctions are inefficient when there are a small number of customers and low sales volume at any given time.
    C. auctions are inefficient when a market has a large number of buyers and sellers and a large volume of standardized goods.
    D. auctions are not feasible when the goods are perishable (e.g., ice cream).
    E. the economic benefits of auctions are less than the economic costs of auctions in markets for perishable goods.

16. In the long run
    A. prices adjust to market-clearing levels, and output equals potential output.
    B. prices adjust to market-clearing levels, and output is less than potential output.
    C. prices adjust to market-clearing levels, and output is greater than potential output.
    D. output is primarily determined by economy-wide spending.
    E. the main effect of total spending is on output.

17. During the period 1960-1999, inflation was at its highest level in the United States during the
    A. boom of 1961-69.
    B. expansion of 1982-90.
    C. expansion of 1990-99.
    D. recession of 1981-82.
    E. recession of 1973-75.

18. Recessions and expansions have a greater impact on
    A. inflation than on unemployment.
    B. frictional unemployment than on cyclical unemployment.
    C. structural unemployment than on cyclical unemployment.

D. industries that produce durable goods than on service and nondurable goods industries.

E. industries that produce services and nondurable goods than on durable goods industries.

19. The difference between the total unemployment rate and the natural rate of unemployment
    A. is positive during a recession.
    B. is negative during a recession.
    C. is positive during an expansion.
    D. represents that portion of total unemployment that economists call frictional unemployment.
    E. represents that portion of total unemployment that economists call structural unemployment.

20. Online job services have made labor markets more efficient and, thus, have contributed to
    A. a decline in cyclical unemployment.
    B. an increase in cyclical unemployment.
    C. a decline the natural rate of unemployment.
    D. an increase in the natural rate of unemployment.
    E. an increase in structural and frictional unemployment.

Short Answer Problems
(Answers and solutions are given at the end of the chapter.)

1. Actual Output and Potential Output

This problem utilizes data on real GDP and potential GDP for the United States for the years 1994-1999, in billions of 1992 dollars, and will help you become more familiar with the concept of output gaps (recessionary and expansionary gaps).

Year	Real GDP	Potential GDP	Output Gap	Expansionary or Recessionary Gap?
1998	$9,611	$9,777		
1999	9,762	9,955		
2000	9,995	10,138		
2001	10,720	10,325		
2002	10,553	10,517		
2003	10,883	10,714		

A. Complete column 4 of the above table by calculating the size of the output gap for 1998 through 2003 (be sure to include a plus sign if a positive gap, or a minus sign if negative gap).
B. In column 5 of the above table, identify whether the output gap was a recessionary gap or an expansionary gap for each year.

IV. Becoming an Economic Naturalist: Case Study

Economic Naturalist 25.3 discusses the monetary policy decisions of the Federal
Reserve during 1999-2000 to counteract the perceived threat of increasing inflation
brought on by a growing expansionary gap. By early 2001, the U.S. economy had
stalled and fell into a recession and the Fed reversed course, taking measures to
eliminate the recessionary gap. Go to the Federal Reserve web site at
http://www.federalreserve.gov/fomc/ and review the FOMC's policy decisions since
2001 to determine how long the Fed continued the policy begun in early 2001. What
does the most recent policy decisions indicate is the Fed's current economic concern,
expansionary or recessionary gap?
Answer:

V. Self-Test Solutions

Key Terms
1. a
2. i
3. f
4. b
5. d
6. l
7. g
8. j
9. e
10. h
11. c
12. k

Multiple-Choice Questions
1. E
2. D
3. B
4. C
5. A
6. B $9,000 billion times .025 = $225 billion
7. E
8. C
9. D
10. C
11. A
12. D
13. B
14. E
15. B
16. A

17. D
18. D
19. A
20. C

Short Answer Problems

1.

A. and B.

Year	Real GDP	Potential GDP	Output Gap	Expansionary or Recessionary Gap?
1998	$9,611	$9,777	+$166	Recessionary gap
1999	9,762	9,955	+$193	Recessionary gap
2000	9,995	10,138	+$143	Recessionary gap
2001	10,720	10,325	-$395	Expansionary gap
2002	10,553	10,517	-$36	Expansionary gap
2003	10,883	10,714	-$169	Expansionary gap

Chapter 26
Spending and Output
in the Short Run

I. Pretest: What Do You Really Know?

Circle the letter that corresponds to the best answer. (Answers appear immediately after the final question).

1. The two key assumptions of the basic Keynesian model are that aggregate demand _____ and that in the short run firms _____.
    A. is constant; meet demand at preset prices
    B. fluctuates; adjust prices to bring sales in line with capacity
    C. increases with the general level of prices; meet demand at preset prices
    D. is constant; adjust prices to bring sales in line with capacity
    E. fluctuates; meet demand at preset prices

2. Firms do not change prices frequently because
    A. there are legal prohibitions against doing so.
    B. it is easier to change the quantity of capital used in production.
    C. it is costly to do so.
    D. customers will refuse to patronize firms that change prices frequently.
    E. managers are lazy.

3. If firms sell more output than expected, planned investment
    A. is greater than actual investment.
    B. is less than actual investment.
    C. equals actual investment.
    D. equals zero.
    E. equals aggregate demand.

4. Dave's Mirror Company expects to sell $2,000,000 worth of mirrors and to produce $2,250,000 worth of mirrors in the coming year. The company purchases $500,000 of new equipment during the year. Sales for the year turn out to be $1,900,000. Actual investment by Dave's Mirror Company equals _____ and planned investment equals _____.
    A. $500,000; $500,000

B. $500,000; $750,000
C. $750,000; $850,000
D. $850,000; $500,000
E. $850,000; $750,000

5. The consumption function is relationship between consumption and
   A. aggregate demand.
   B. total spending.
   C. investment.
   D. its determinants, such as disposable income.
   E. unplanned changes in spending, particularly inventory investment.

6. If consumption increases by $90 when after-tax disposable income increases by $100, the marginal propensity to consume (mpc) equals
   A. 0.1
   B. 0.9
   C. 1.0
   D. 90
   E. 100

7. Autonomous expenditure is the portion of planned aggregate expenditure that
   A. equals aggregate output.
   B. equals planned spending.
   C. equals induced aggregate demand.
   D. is determined within the model.
   E. is determined outside the model.

8. In Macroland autonomous consumption equals 200, the marginal propensity to consume equals 0.6, net taxes are fixed at 50, planned investment is fixed at 100, government purchases are fixed at 200, and net exports are fixed at 30. Short-run equilibrium output in this economy equals
   A. 1,100
   B. 1,175
   C. 1,250
   D. 1,325
   E. 1,400

9. If planned aggregate expenditure in an economy can be written as: AD= 4000 + .8 Y, what is the short-run equilibrium level of output in this economy?
   A. 5,000
   B. 5,800
   C. 9,000
   D. 20,000
   E. 25,000

10. For an economy starting from potential output, a decrease in planned investment in the short run results in a(n)
    A. expansionary output gap.
    B. recessionary output gap.
    C. increase in potential output.
    D. decrease in potential output.
    E. increase in cyclical unemployment.

Solutions and Feedback to Pretest
For each question you incorrectly answered, we strongly recommend taking the time to review the appropriate material before continuing. In the table below are listed for each question as the pertinent Learning Objective from the following Key Point Review.

Correct Answer	Learning Objective
1. E	1
2. C	1
3. A	3
4. E	3
5. D	4
6. B	4
7. E	5
8. C	6
9. D	6
10. B	7

II. Key Point Review
The Forest

This chapter focuses on the basic Keynesian model (also known as the Keynesian Cross) showing how recessions and expansions may arise from fluctuations in aggregate spending. The central questions you need to be able to answer are
- What are the key assumptions of the Keynesian model and what are the four components of planned aggregate expenditure?
- What factors affect the consumption function and what is the relationship between the consumption function and planned aggregate expenditure?
- What determine the short-run equilibrium output?
- What is the income-expenditure multiplier and how can a change in planned spending can cause a change in the short-run equilibrium output?
- What stabilization policies are derived from the Keynesian analysis?

The Trees

Learning Objective 1: Identify the key assumption of the model
The Keynesian model is based on the ideas first developed by John Maynard Keynes (1883-1946) and published in *The General Theory of Employment, Interest and Money* (1936). The key assumption of the basic Keynesian model is that, in the short run, firms meet the demand for

their products at preset prices. Firms change prices only if the benefits of doing so outweigh the **menu costs**, (i.e., the costs of changing prices).

> **Note**: the decision by a firm whether to change price is an application of the cost-benefit principle. Firms will only change the price of a product if the marginal benefit is at least equal to the marginal cost.

Learning Objective 2: Define planned aggregate expenditure (PAE) and identify the four components of PAE

The most important concept of the basic Keynesian model is planned aggregate expenditure. **Planned aggregate expenditure** (PAE) is the total planned spending on final goods and services. PAE is composed of four components: (1) consumer expenditures, or simply consumption (C), is spending by domestic households on final goods and services; (2) investment (I) is spending by domestic firms on new capital goods, residential investment, and increases in inventories; (3) government purchases (G) is spending by domestic governments (federal, state and local) on goods and services; and (4) net exports (NX), or exports minus imports, is sales of domestically produced goods and services to foreigners less purchases by domestic residents of goods and services produced abroad which have been included in C, I, and G, but must be subtracted because they do not represent domestic production.

Learning Objective 3: Explain why planned spending may differ from actual spending

Planned spending (or PAE) may differ from actual spending. If, for example, a firm sells more of its output than it planned to sell, actual investment will be less than planned investment and total actual spending will be greater than total planned spending. Assuming that actual spending for consumption, government purchases, and net exports equals planned spending, but that actual investment may not equal planned investment, the equation for planned aggregate expenditure is $PAE = C + I^p + G + NX$, where I^p is planned investment spending.

> **Note:** If a firm's actual sales are greater than it's expected sales, actual investment will be less than planned investment because there will be an unexpected decrease in inventories. Since, changes in inventory are one component of investment, an unexpected decrease will reduce actual investment below the planned level of investment.

Learning Objective 4: Define consumption function and marginal propensity to consume

Consumption, the largest component of PAE, is affected by many factors, the most important being after-tax income, or disposable income. The relationship between consumption spending and its determinants, is referred to as the **consumption function** and is expressed by the equation $C = \overline{C} + c(Y - T)$, where $\overline{C}$ is a constant term intended to capture factors other than disposable income, and $(Y - T)$ represents disposable income, and mpc is a fixed number called the marginal propensity to consume. The **marginal propensity to consume**, or mpc, is the amount by which consumption rises when disposable income rises by one dollar, and is greater than 0 but less than 1 (i.e., $0 < c < 1$). The consumption function can also be show graphically, in which case $\overline{C}$

represents the intercept of the consumption function on the vertical axis and the mpc is the slope of the consumption function. The consumption function indicates that as disposable income rises, consumption spending will increase, but by a lesser amount.

Learning Objective 5: Explain the relationship between the consumption function and planned aggregate expenditure

Incorporating the consumption function into the equation for planned aggregate expenditure results in the expanded equation $PAE = [C + c(Y - T)] + I^p + G + NX$. Grouping together those terms that depend on output (Y), and those that do not, yields the equation $PAE = [C + cT + I^p + G + NX] + cY$. This equation captures the key idea that as planned aggregate expenditure changes real output changes with it, in the same direction. It also shows that planned aggregate expenditure can be divided into two parts, one portion that is determined outside the model called **autonomous expenditure** ($[C + cT + I^p + G + NX]$), and a second portion that is determined within the model (because it depends on output) called **induced expenditure** (cY).

> **Hint:** It will be important that you are able to calculate changes in the amount of autonomous expenditure because changes in autonomous expenditure cause changes in the equilibrium level of output. If you do not know the components of autonomous expenditure, you will not be able to calculate changes in autonomous expenditure and, thus, will not be able to determine the impact on the equilibrium level of output.

Learning Objective 6: Define short-run equilibrium output

In the basic Keynesian model, the **short-run equilibrium output** is the level at which output, Y, equals planned aggregate expenditure, PAE, and is the level of output that prevails during the period in which prices are predetermined. The short-run equilibrium output can be determined numerically by comparing possible levels for short-run equilibrium output to the value of planned aggregate expenditure at each level of output. The short-run equilibrium output is determined where $Y = PAE$, or equivalently $Y - PAE = 0$. The short-run equilibrium output can also be determined graphically where the 45° line intersects the expenditure line. If output is less (greater) than the equilibrium level in the short run, when prices are pre-set and firms are committed to meeting their customers' demand, output will rise (fall). Lastly, we can use algebra to determine the short-run equilibrium output (this is explained in detail in Appendix A of the textbook chapter).

Learning Objective 7: Explain how a decrease in planned spending can lead to a recession

A decrease in one or more of the components of autonomous planned aggregate expenditure will cause short-run equilibrium output to fall. When the short-run equilibrium output is less than the potential output, the result is a recessionary gap. According to the basic Keynesian model, inadequate spending is an important cause of recessions in the economy.

Learning Objective 8: Define the income-expenditure multiplier

A change in one or more of the components of autonomous planned aggregate expenditure will cause a larger change in the short-run equilibrium output. The impact on output is larger than the initial change in spending because of the multiplier effect. The effect of a one-unit increase or decrease in autonomous planned spending on the short-run equilibrium output is called the **income-expenditure multiplier,** or the multiplier for short. In the basic Keynesian model, the multiplier is inversely related to the marginal propensity to consume.

Learning Objective 9: Discuss the use of fiscal policy to stabilize planned spending
To fight recessions caused by insufficient planned aggregate expenditure, policymakers can use stabilization policies. **Stabilization policies** are government policies that are used to affect planned aggregate expenditure, with the objective of eliminating output gaps. There are two major types of stabilization policy, monetary policy and fiscal policy. This chapter focuses on fiscal policy, i.e., government spending and taxes. Keynes felt that changes in government spending were probably the most effective tool for reducing or eliminating output gaps. He argued that a recessionary gap could be eliminated by increases in government spending. Alternatively, a decrease in taxes (payments from the private sector to government) could eliminate a recessionary gap. Government spending can be in the form of government purchases of goods and services or transfer payments (payments from government to the private sector). Changes in government purchases directly change the amount of PAE, whereas transfer payments and taxes only indirectly change PAE by altering the amount of disposable income. The change in PAE is equal to the change in taxes (or transfer payments) times the mpc. Because the mpc is a fraction, the change in taxes or transfer payments must be larger than the change in government purchases to cause the same change in PAE.

Learning Objective 10: Discuss three qualifications related to the use of fiscal policy as a stabilization tool
While the basic Keynesian model suggests that fiscal policy can be used quite precisely to eliminate output gaps, in the real world it is more complicated than that. Using fiscal policy as a stabilization tool is complicated by the fact that fiscal policy may affect potential output as well as planned aggregate expenditure. Government spending, for example, on investments in public capital, (e.g., roads, airports, and schools) can play a major role in the growth of potential output. Taxes and transfer payments may affect the incentives, and thus the economic behavior, of households and firms that, in turn, affect potential output. A second qualification is the need to avoid large and persistent government budget deficits. The need to keep deficits under control may make it more difficult to increase government spending or cut taxes to fight a recession. The third qualification is that fiscal policy is not always flexible enough to be useful for stabilization. Changes in government spending or taxation must usually go through a lengthy legislative process making it difficult to respond in a timely way to economic conditions. In addition, policymakers have many objectives besides stabilizing planned aggregate expenditure.

III. Self-Test

<u>Key Terms</u>
Match the term in the right-hand column with the appropriate definition in the left-hand column by placing the letter of the term in the blank in front of its' definition. (Answers are given at the end of the chapter.)

1. ____ The tendency of changes in asset prices to affect households' wealth and thus their spending on consumption goods.

2. ____ The portion of planned aggregate expenditure that depends on output.

3. ____ The portion of planned aggregate expenditure that is independent of output.

4. ____ Government policies that are used to affect planned aggregate expenditure, with the objective of eliminating output gaps.

5. ____ The level of output at which output equals planned aggregate expenditure.

6. ____ Government policy actions designed to reduce planned spending and output.

7. ____ The costs of changing prices.

8. ____ The effect of a 1-unit increase in autonomous expenditure on short-run equilibrium output.

9. ____ Total planned spending on final goods and services.

10. ____ The relationship between consumption spending and its determinants, in particular, disposable (after-tax) income.

11. ____ The amount by which consumption rises when disposable income rise by one dollar.

12. ____ Provisions in law that imply automatic increases in government spending or decreases in taxes when real output declines.

13. ____ Government policy actions intended to increase planned spending and output.

a. automatic stabilizers

b. autonomous expenditure

c. consumption function

d. contractionary policies

e. expansionary policies

f. induced expenditure

g. income-expenditure multiplier

h. marginal propensity to consume (mpc)

i. menu costs

j. planned aggregate expenditure

k. short-run equilibrium output

l. stabilization policies

m. wealth effect

Multiple-Choice Questions
Circle the letter that corresponds to the best answer. (Answers are given at the end of the chapter.)

1. Which of the following is a key assumption of the basic Keynesian model?
   A. Total spending fluctuates.
   B. In the short run, firms meet the demand for their products at preset prices.
   C. In the long run, firms meet the demand for the products at preset prices.
   D. In the short run, firms adjust price to changes in planned aggregate expenditure so as to clear the market.
   E. In the long run, firms adjust price to changes in planned aggregate expenditure so as to clear the market.

2. When firms apply the core principle of cost-benefit analysis to price changing decisions, they change the prices of their goods if
   A. menu costs are greater than or equal to the benefits of changing prices.
   B. menu costs are greater than or equal to the additional revenue derived from changing prices.
   C. additional revenue derived from changing prices is less than the menu costs.
   D. additional revenue derived from changing prices is greater than the menu costs.

E. additional revenue derived from changing prices is less than or equal to the menu costs.

3. In *The General Theory of Employment, Interest, and Money*, John Maynard Keynes explained
   A. how economies always operate at the natural rate of employment.
   B. the causes of expansionary gaps and recommended the use of monetary policy to combat the resulting high inflation.
   C. how economies can remain at low levels of output for long periods and recommended increased government spending to combat the resulting high unemployment.
   D. that attempts to extract large reparation payments from Germany after World War I would prevent economic recovery of Germany and likely lead to another war.
   E. the key elements of the post-WWII international monetary and financial institutions.

4. Planned aggregate expenditure is the sum of desired or planned
   A. consumption expenditures, investment, government purchases, and net exports.
   B. consumption expenditures, investment, government purchases, and exports.
   C. consumption expenditures, investment, government purchases, and net imports.
   D. consumption expenditures, net investment, government purchasers, and net exports.
   E. consumption expenditures, net investment, government expenditures, and net exports.

5. If a firm's actual sales are greater than expected sales
   A. actual inventories will be greater than planned inventories, and actual investment will be greater than planned investment.
   B. actual inventories will be less than planned inventories, and actual investment will be less than planned investment.
   C. actual inventories will be greater than planned inventories, and actual investment will be less than planned investment.
   D. actual inventories will be less than planned inventories, and actual investment will be greater than planned investment.
   E. planned inventories will be less than actual inventories, and planned investment will be greater than actual investment.

6. A decrease in consumers' disposable income will cause a(n)
   A. decrease in the consumption function and an increase in output.
   B. increase in the consumption function and a decrease in output.
   C. decrease in the consumption function and an increase in planned aggregate expenditure.
   D. increase in the consumption function and an increase in planned aggregate expenditure.
   E. decrease in the consumption function and a decrease in planned aggregate expenditure.

7. If autonomous consumption equals $250 billion, the marginal propensity to consume (mpc) is .6, investment equals $180 billion, government purchases equal $75 billion, taxes equal $200, and net exports equal minus $40 billion, the planned aggregate expenditure equation is
   A. PAE = $250 billion + .6Y
   B. PAE = $585 billion + .6Y
   C. PAE = $505 billion + .6Y
   D. PAE = $625 billion + .6Y

E. PAE = $345 billion + .6Y

8. If, in the short run, real output is less than the equilibrium level of output, firms will respond by
   A. increasing the price of their products.
   B. decreasing the price of their products.
   C. increasing their production.
   D. decreasing their production.
   E. producing the same amount of output.

9. If the consumption function is C= $400 + .75Y, then the mpc equals
   A. $400.
   B. .25.
   C. $400 + .75.
   D. .75.
   E. 4.

10. John Maynard Keynes believed that the most effective stabilization policy was
    A. changes in government spending to reduce or eliminate output gaps.
    B. monetary policy to reduce or eliminate expansionary gaps.
    C. changes in government spending to reduce or eliminate recessionary gaps, but monetary policy to reduce or eliminate expansionary gaps.
    D. changes in taxes to reduce or eliminate output gaps.
    E. the self-correcting process of the market to reduce or eliminate output gaps.

11. The largest single component of planned aggregate expenditures is
    A. government spending
    B. consumption spending
    C. investment spending
    D. export spending
    E. import spending

12. The use of fiscal policy to eliminate output gaps is complicated by the fact that fiscal policy
    A. is more flexible than monetary policy.
    B. only affects planned aggregate expenditure, but has no effect on potential output.
    C. affects both planned aggregate expenditure and potential output.
    D. does not take into account the effects that automatic stabilizers have on potential output.
    E. includes not only government purchases, but also transfer payments and taxation.

13. If the marginal propensity to consume increases, the income-expenditure multiplier
    A. increases.
    B. decreases.
    C. remains unchanged.
    D. decreases by a smaller amount.
    E. increases by a larger amount.

14. Planned spending equals actual spending for households, governments, and foreigners in the basic Keynesian model, but for businesses
    A. planned spending equals actual inventories.
    B. planned spending equals planned inventories.
    C. actual investment may differ from planned investment.
    D. actual investment is always greater than planned investment.
    E. actual investment is always less than planned investment

15. The portion of planned aggregate expenditure that is determined within the model is called induced expenditure and includes
    A. that part of household consumption that is dependent upon income.
    B. all of household consumption.
    C. household consumption and investment spending.
    D. household consumption, investment spending, and government purchases.
    E. household consumption, investment spending, government purchases, and net exports.

16. The short-run equilibrium in the basic Keynesian model occurs where
    A. actual inventories are greater than the level planned by businesses.
    B. actual inventories are less than the level planned by businesses.
    C. planned aggregate expenditure equals the potential output.
    D. planned aggregate expenditure equals output.
    E. planned aggregate expenditure is greater than output.

17. In the basic Keynesian model, when planned aggregate expenditure equals output
    A. inventories are zero.
    B. consumption equals investment.
    C. unplanned changes in inventories are positive.
    D. unplanned changes in inventories equal zero.
    E. unplanned changes in inventories are negative.

18. If, in the short run, output is greater than the equilibrium level of output, firms will respond by
    A. increasing the price of their products.
    B. decreasing the price of their products.
    C. producing the same amount of output.
    D. increasing their production.
    E. decreasing their production.

19. A $100 increase in transfer payments or a $100 decrease in taxes will cause
    A. a smaller increase in planned aggregate expenditure than a $100 increase in government purchases.
    B. a larger increase in planned aggregate expenditure than a $100 increase in government purchases.
    C. the same increase in planned aggregate expenditure as would a $100 increase in government purchases.

D. a smaller decrease in planned aggregate expenditure than a $100 increase in government purchases.

E. a larger decrease in planned aggregate expenditure than a $100 increase in government purchases.

20. Fiscal policy is not always flexible enough to be useful for economic stabilization because
   A. automatic stabilizers counteract the stabilizing features of government spending and taxation.
   B. budget deficits are unconstitutional.
   C. the legislative process allows policymakers inadequate time to determine the appropriate level of government spending and taxation.
   D. it affects both planned aggregate expenditure and potential output.
   E. the only effects of fiscal policy that matter are its effects on potential output.

Short Answer Problems
(Answers and solutions are given at the end of the chapter.)

1. The Consumption Function and Planned Aggregate Expenditure
This problem is designed to help you understand the relationship between the consumption function and planned aggregate expenditure. You will be asked to graph the consumption function, write the algebraic equation for planned aggregate expenditure, and differentiate between autonomous and induced expenditure.

A. On the graph below, plot the consumption function curve (label it C) for disposable income levels $0 to $700, assuming C = $175 billion, the marginal propensity to consume (mpc) equals .75, and taxes equal $100 billion.

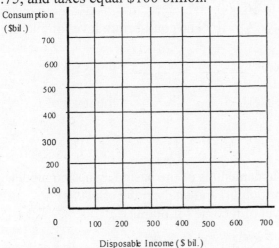

B. Assume that planned investment spending equals $50 billion, government purchases are $75 billion, and net exports equal –$75 billion. The algebraic equation for the planned aggregate expenditure curve would be PAE = $ _____ billion + _____ (Y - $ _____ billion) + $ _____ billion + $ _____ billion + $ _____ billion. Combining the autonomous portions of PAE would result in a simplified equation, PAE = $ _____ billion + _____ Y.

C. Plot the planned aggregate expenditure curve on the above graph and label it PAE.

D. Autonomous expenditure equals $_____ billion, and is graphically represented where the planned aggregate expenditure curve intersects the (vertical/ horizontal) _____ axis.

E. When disposable income equals $400 billion, the induced expenditure equals $_____ billion.

2. Numerical Determination of Short-run Equilibrium Output

The focus of this problem is the determination of the short-run equilibrium output within the framework of a numerical table.

(1) Output (Y)	(2) Planned aggregate expenditure	(3) Y– PAE	(4) Y = PAE?
$3,000			
3,500			
4,000			
4,500			
5,000			
5,500			
6,000			

A. Assume that planned aggregate expenditure is given by the equation PAE = $500 + .9 Y. Complete column 2 of the table by calculating the amount of planned aggregate expenditure when output equals $3,000 to $6,000.

B. Complete column 3 of the table by calculating the difference between output and planned aggregate expenditure when output equals $3,000 to $6,000.

C. Complete column 4 by determining whether or not Y = PAE. The equilibrium level of output equals $_____.

D. If output equals $ 3,500, firms will (increase/decrease) _____ the level of output.

E. If output equals $ 6,000, firms will (increase/decrease) _____ the level of output.

3. The Basic Keynesian Model

This problem is designed to help you understand the fundamentals of the basic Keynesian model. You will determine the equilibrium level of income (or output) and analyze the effects of changes in investment spending on the equilibrium level of income (or output).

A. Assume the consumption function is C = $200 billion + .8(Y-T), investment equals $ 150 billion, government purchases equal $200 billion, taxes equal $100 billion, and net exports equals minus $70 billion. Using this information, derive the aggregate expenditure function. PAE = $_____ billion + _____ Y.

B. On the graph below, plot the planned aggregate expenditure curve for level of output ranging from $0 billion to $5,000 billion (label the curve PAE).

C. The equilibrium level of output equals $ _____ billion.

D. If the potential output (Y*) equals $2,500, there would now be a (recessionary/ expansionary) _____ gap in the economy.

E. If firms produce $3,000 billion of output, planned aggregate expenditure would equal $_____ billion. As a result, firms would have $_____ billion of goods they intended to sell but didn't. This would cause firms (increase / decrease) _____ their level of output.

Note: Question 3F – 3H are based on information in Appendix B of the textbook chapter.

F. The mpc equals _____ and the multiplier equals _____.

G. If investment spending decreases by $100 billion, the planned aggregate expenditure curve will shift (upward / downward) _____ and the equilibrium output will (increase / decrease) _____ by an amount equal to the change in planned aggregate expenditure times the multiplier.

H. On the graph above, draw the planned aggregate expenditure curve after a $100-billion decrease in investment spending (label it PAE₁). The new equilibrium output would equal $_____ billion.

4. Solving the Basic Keynesian Model Numerically
(Based on material in Appendix A of the textbook chapter.)

This problem uses algebraic equations to determine the short-run equilibrium output. You will derive the planned aggregate expenditure equation and, employing the equation for the short-run equilibrium condition, calculate the short-run equilibrium output, and determine the effect of changes in government purchases, taxes, and transfer payments of the short-run equilibrium output.

Use the following set of equations to answer the questions below:

$C = \$400$ billion $+ .75(Y - T)$

$T = \$200$ billion

$I^p = \$250$ billion

$G = \$300$ billion

$NX = \$50$ billion

A. Using the information above, substitute into the equation the numerical values for each component of planned aggregate expenditure. Y= $_____ billion + _____(Y – $_____ billion) + $_____ billion + $_____ billion + $_____ billion.

B. After simplifying that equation yields the equation PAE = $_____ billion + _____ Y.

C. The definition of short-run equilibrium output implies that Y = PAE. Replacing PAE with the equation found in Question 4B yields Y = $_____ billion + _____ Y.

D. Now solve for Y in Y – ____ Y = $_____ billion, or Y = $_____ billion.

E. Thus, the equilibrium output equals $_____ billion.

F. If government purchases decrease by $100 billion the new short-run equilibrium output will equal $_____ billion.

G. Starting from the level of the short-run equilibrium output in Question 4E, an increase in taxation of $100 will result in a new short-run equilibrium output of $_____ billion.

H. If, instead of decreasing government purchases by $100 billion in Question 4F, the government decreased transfer payments by $100 billion, the new short-run equilibrium output would equal $_____ billion.

I. In comparing the answers to Questions 4F-H, it is apparent that a change in government purchases has a (greater/lesser/equal) _____ effect on the short-run equilibrium output than does an equal change in transfer payments or taxation.

IV. Becoming an Economic Naturalist: Case Study

The Economic Naturalist 26.3 discusses the impact of the Japanese recession on its neighboring countries of East Asia. The Japanese economy's slump during the 1990s resulted in less household and business spending on imports from these economies and, therefore, autonomous expenditures in the East Asian economies declined. The fall in autonomous expenditures subsequently led to a recessionary gap in those economies. Based on the textbook discussion of stabilization policy within the context of the basic Keynesian model, explain what the appropriate fiscal policy would have been to close the recessionary gap in the East Asian economies. Also, discuss the limitations of the use of fiscal policy to close the recessionary gap.

Answer:

V. Self-Test Solutions

Key Terms
1. m
2. f
3. b
4. l
5. k
6. d
7. i
8. g

9. j
10. c
11. h
12. a
13. e

Multiple-Choice Questions

1. B
2. D
3. C
4. A
5. B
6. E
7. E $250 billion + [.6(Y - $200 billion)] + $180 billion + $75 billion + (-$40 billion) = $345 billion + .6Y
8. C
9. D
10. A
11. B
12. C
13. A
14. C
15. A
16. D
17. D
18. E
19. A
20. C

Short Answer Problems

1.
A.

Consumption
($bil.)

Disposable Income ($ bil.)

B. $175 billion + .75(Y - $100 billion) + $50 billion + $75 billion + (-$75) billion; $150 billion + .75Y

C.

D. $150 billion (= $175 billion - $75 billion + $50 billion + 75 billion - $75 billion); vertical

E. $300 billion (= .75 x $400 billion)

2. A. B. C.

(1) Output (Y)	(2) Planned Aggregate Expenditure	(3) Y– PAE	(4) Y = PAE?
$3,000	$3,200	$-200	No
3,500	3,650	-150	No
4,000	4,100	-100	No
4,500	4,550	-50	No
5,000	5,000	0	Yes
5,500	5,450	50	No
6,000	5,900	100	No

C. $5,000

D. increase

E. decrease

3.

A. PAE = $400 billion + .8Y

B.

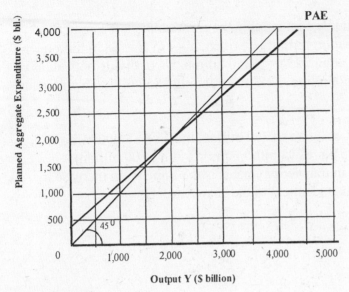

C. $2,000 billion

D. recesionary gap; $500

E. $2,800 billion (= $400 billion + .8($3,000 billion); $200 billion (Y − PAE, or $3,000 billion − $2,800 billion); decrease

F. .8 ; 5 ($= \frac{1}{1-.8} = \frac{1}{.2}$)

G. downward; decrease

H.

; $1,500 billion (The change in equilibrium output is − $100 billion x 5 = − $500 billion. Subtracting the change in equilibrium output from the initial equilibrium output, $2,000 billion - $500 billion, gives us the new equilibrium output og $1,500 billion.)

4.

A. $400 billion + .75 (Y - $200 billion) + $250 billion + $300 billion + $50 billion

B. AD = $850 billion + .75Y

C. Y = $850 billion + .75Y;

D. Y= $3,400 billion (The solution is found by first moving the .75 Y to the left side of the equation and subtracting it from Y. In equation form it is written, Y – .75 Y = $850 billion. Reducing the left-hand side yields the equation, .25Y = $850 billion. Next, divide both sides of the equation by .25. This gives us Y = $850 billion / .25, and dividing $850 billion by .25 equals $3,400 billion. Thus Y= $3,400 billion)

E. $3,400 billion

F. $3,000 billion (Y – .75Y =$750 billion, or .25Y = $750 billion, thus Y= $3,000 billion)

G. $3,100 billion (Y – .75 Y = $675, or .25Y = $775 billion, thus Y = $3,100 billion)

H. $3,100 billion (the effect of a decrease in transfer payments is the same as an increase in taxation, and thus the numerical derivation is identical to the answer to 4G).

I. greater

Chapter 27
Stabilizing the Economy:
The Role of the Fed

I. Pretest: What Do You Really Know?
Circle the letter that corresponds to the best answer. (Answers appear immediately after the final question).

1. Monetary policy is _____ flexible than fiscal policy because monetary policy changes are made by _____, while fiscal policy changes must be made by _____.
   A. more; the FOMC; legislative action
   B. more; legislative action; the FOMC
   C. more; the President; legislative action
   D. less; the FOMC; the President
   E. less; the President; legislative action

2. The benefit of holding money is _____, while the opportunity cost of holding money is _____.
   A. the nominal interest rate; the fees charged by banks
   B. the nominal interest rate; its usefulness in carrying out transactions
   C. increased income; lost purchasing power
   D. its usefulness in carrying out transactions; the nominal interest rate
   E. its usefulness in carrying out transactions; the price of wallets and billfolds

3. The following table shows Alex's estimated annual benefits of holding different amounts of money.

Average money holdings ($)	Total benefit ($)
300	30
400	39
500	46
600	51
700	54

   How much money will Alex hold if the nominal interest rate is 8 percent? (Assume she wants her money holdings to be in multiples of $100.)

A. 300
B. 400
C. 500
D. 600
E. 700

4. Lower real income ____ the demand for money and a lower price level ___ the demand for money.
   A. increases; increases
   B. increases; decreases
   C. increases; does not change
   D. decreases; decreases
   E. decreases; increases

5. Which of the following would be expected to increase the demand for money in the U.S.?
   A. Competition among brokers forces down the commission charge for selling bonds or stocks.
   B. The economy enters a recession.
   C. Political instability increases dramatically in developing nations.
   D. On-line banking allows customers to transfer funds between checking and stock mutual funds 24 hours a day.
   E. Financial investors become less concerned about the riskiness of stocks.

6. If the nominal interest rate is below the equilibrium value, then money demand is _____ than money supply, bond prices will ____, and the nominal interest rate will ____.
   A. greater; fall; increase
   B. greater; fall; decrease
   C. greater; rise; increase
   D. less; fall; increase
   E. less; rise; decrease

7. If the Fed wishes to increase nominal interest rates, it must engage in an open market ____ of bonds that ____ the money supply.
   A. sale; increases
   B. sale; decreases
   C. sale; does not change
   D. purchase; increases
   E. purchase; decreases

8. The Fed's control over real interest rates is;
   A. absolute
   B. greater than its control over nominal interest rates
   C. less than its control over nominal interest rate
   D. impossible
   E. unimportant

9. The interest rate that commercial banks charge each other for very short-term loans is called the:
   A. prime rate.
   B. federal funds rate.
   C. Federal Reserve discount rate.
   D. commercial paper rate.
   E. bank loan rate.

10. A lower real interest rate _____ investment spending and _____ consumption spending.
   A. increases; increases
   B. increases; decreases
   C. does not change; does not change
   D. decreases; increases
   E. decreases; decreases

Solutions and Feedback to Pretest

For each question you incorrectly answered, we strongly recommend taking the time to review the appropriate material before continuing. In the table below are listed for each question the pertinent Learning Objective from the following Key Point Review.

Correct Answer	Learning Objective
1. A	5
2. D	2
3. B	2
4. D	3
5. C	3
6. A	4
7. B	5
8. C	7
9. B	6
10. A	8

II. Key Point Review
The Forest

This chapter focuses on an examination of the workings of monetary policy, one of the two major types of stabilization policy. The central questions you need to be able to answer are:

- What factors affect the demand for money?
- What determines the money market equilibrium interest rate?
- How does the Fed uses its ability to control the money supply to influence nominal and real interest rates?
- How do interest rates affect planned aggregate expenditures and the short-run equilibrium output?

The Trees

Learning Objective 1: Define demand for money

As explained in an earlier chapter, the Fed uses three tools to control the money supply. This chapter shows that the Fed's control of the money supply is tantamount to controlling nominal interest rates. The nominal interest rate is the price of money and is determined by the supply and demand for money. The **demand for money** is the result of choices made by households and businesses. The demand for money is the amount of wealth an individual chooses to hold in the form of money. Households and businesses demand money to carry out transactions (i.e., use it as a medium of exchange) and as a way of holding wealth (i.e., the store of value function of money).

Hint: When economists talk about household and business demand for money they are **not** asking how much money do you want. The answer to that question is always "more." The demand for money refers to how much of your wealth you want to hold in the form of money (and, by implication, how much of your wealth will be held in non-money forms).

Learning Objective 2: Define portfolio allocation decision and explain how it relates to the demand for money

There are almost an infinite number of forms in which wealth can be held. The decision about the forms in which to hold one's wealth is called the **portfolio allocation decision**. How much money one chooses to hold is based on the costs and benefits of holding money. The opportunity cost of holding money is the interest that could have been earned if the person had chosen to hold interest-bearing assets instead of money. The higher the prevailing interest rate, the greater the opportunity cost of holding money, and hence the less money individuals and businesses will demand. The principle benefit of holding money is its usefulness in carrying out transactions. The amount of money demanded to carry out transactions is affected at the macroeconomic level by real output and the price level. An increase in aggregate real output or income raises the quantity of goods and services that people and businesses want to buy and, thus, raises the demand for money. The higher the price of goods and services, the more dollars needed to make a given set of transactions and, therefore, a higher demand for money.

Learning Objective 3: Discuss macroeconomic factors that affect the demand for money and the effects of changes on the money demand curve

Macroeconomists are primarily interested in the aggregate, or economy-wide, demand for money, represented by the money demand curve. The **money demand curve** relates the aggregate quantity of money demand, M, to the nominal interest rate, i. Because an increase in the nominal interest rate increases the opportunity cost of holding money, which reduces the quantity of money demanded, the money demand curve slopes down. An increase in real output or the price level will cause the money demand curve to increase (shift to the right), while a fall in either will cause it to decrease (shift to the left). Other factors, such as technological and financial advances, also cause the money demand curve to shift.

Learning Objective 4: Identify the money market equilibrium

The supply of money is controlled by the Fed (the central bank of the United States). Its primary tool for controlling the money supply is open-market operations. The Fed has two additional tools to control the money supply: **discount window lending** and changing **reserve requirements**. When a bank has insufficient reserves, it may choose to borrow reserves from the Fed to increase its reserves. The interest rate the Fed charges banks on borrowed reserves is called the **discount rate**. By raising the discount rate the Fed discourages banks from increasing their reserves via discount window lending; lowering the discount rate has the opposite objective. The Fed is also responsible for setting the minimum reserve requirement. Although the Fed seldom uses this tool for the purpose of affecting the money supply, it can expand the money supply by lowering the minimum reserve requirement, or reduce the money supply by raising the minimum reserve requirement. Because the Fed can control the supply of money, the money supply curve is a vertical line that intercepts the horizontal axis at the quantity of money chosen by the Fed. The equilibrium in the market for money occurs at the intersection of the supply and demand for money curves. The equilibrium amount of money in circulation is the amount of money the Fed chooses to supply. The equilibrium nominal interest rate is the interest rate at which the quantity of money demanded by the public equals the fixed supply of money made available by the Fed.

> **Note:** Money is a commodity and can be exchanged in the market. Like any other goods, it can satisfy wants and, therefore, households and businesses demand money. Unlike most other goods, the supply of money is controlled by the Fed to achieve public goals rather than to maximize profits. The money market, thus, behaves much like any other commodity market, but also has some unique features.

Learning Objective 5: Explain how monetary policy is used to control nominal interest rates

When the Fed increases the money supply by purchasing government bonds from the public, it drives up the price of bonds and, thus, lowers the equilibrium nominal interest rate. Similarly, if the banks borrow reserves via the discount window or the Fed lowers the minimum reserve requirements, the money supply increases and the equilibrium nominal interest rate decreases. When the Fed decreases the money supply through open-market sales of government bonds to the public, the price of bonds is driven down and, therefore, the equilibrium nominal interest rate must rise. Likewise, if the banks borrow fewer reserves via the discount window or the Fed raises the minimum reserve requirements, the money supply decreases and the equilibrium nominal interest rate increases.

> **Note:** Recall from our earlier discussion, there is an inverse relationship between bond prices and interest rates, i.e., when the price of bonds rise, market interest rates will go down.

Learning Objective 6: Define the federal funds rate and explain why the Fed has focused on it

Although there are thousands of different interest rates determined in the financial markets, the textbook authors use the phrase *the nominal interest rate* to refer to an average measure of these interest rates because they tend to rise and fall together. Of all the market interest rates, the one that is most closely watched by the public, politicians, and the media, however, is the federal funds rate. The **federal funds rate** is the interest rate commercial banks charge each other for very short-term (usually overnight) loans. It is closely watched because for the past 35 years, the Fed has expressed its policies in terms of a target value for the federal funds rate. Because interest rates tend to move together, an action by the Fed to change the federal funds rate generally causes other interest rates to change in the same direction. The tendency of interest rates to move together, however, is not an exact relationship. This means that the Fed's control over other interest rates is somewhat less precise than its control over the federal funds rate.

Learning Objective 7: Discuss the Fed's ability to control the real rate of interest

Similarly, the Fed's control over real interest rates is less complete than its control over nominal interest rates. The real interest rate equals the nominal interest rate minus the rate of inflation. Because inflation tends to change relatively slowly in response to changes in policy or economic conditions, actions by the Fed to change nominal interest rates allows it to control real interest rates in the short run. In the long run, however, the inflation rate and other variables will adjust, and the balance of saving and investment will determine the real interest.

> **Note:** The reason it is important that the Fed be able to influence (if not control) changes in real (not nominal) interest rates cause changes in economic behavior. Therefore, if the Fed is to be effective in formulating and implementing monetary policy it must be able to influence real interest rates.

Learning Objective 8: Explain how interest rates affect consumption and investment spending, aggregate demand, and short-run equilibrium output

Because the Fed can control the money supply and interest rates (at least, in the short run), monetary policy can be used to eliminate output gaps and stabilize the economy. Consumption and planned investment spending are inversely related to real interest rates, that is, a decrease in real interest rates will cause consumption and planned investment spending to increase. Because consumption and planned investment spending are components of planned aggregate expenditures, changes in real interest rates cause changes in planned aggregate expenditures. By adjusting real interest rates, the Fed can move planned aggregate expenditures in the desired direction. For example, an expansionary monetary policy, or monetary easing, is a reduction in interest rates by the Fed, made with the intention of reducing a recessionary gap. If the economy faces a recessionary gap, the Fed could reduce real interest rates to stimulate consumption and investment spending. This will increase planned aggregate expenditures and, as a result, output will rise and the recessionary gap will be reduce or eliminated. When the economy experiences inflationary pressures, the Fed may implement a contractionary monetary policy, or monetary tightening, by increasing interest rates with the intention of reducing an expansionary gap.

Learning Objective 9: Define and discuss the Fed's policy reaction function
Economists often try to summarize the behavior of the Fed in terms of a **policy reaction function,** describing how the action a policymaker takes depends on the state of the economy. An example of a monetary policy reaction function that will be used in the next few chapters is: $r = r^* + g(\pi - \pi^*)$, where r = the actual real interest rate set by the Fed, r^* = the Fed's long-run target for the real interest rate, π = the actual inflation rate, π^* = the Fed's long-run target for the inflation rate, and g = a positive number chosen by the Fed. The policy reaction function indicates that when actual inflation is greater than the Fed's long-run target inflation rate, the Fed will push up the real interest rate; conversely, when actual inflation is less than the Fed's long-run target inflation rate, the Fed will lower the real interest rate. The policy reaction function can be represented in a graph showing the Fed's target real interest rate on the vertical axis and the target rate of inflation on the horizontal axis. An upward sloping curve represents the policy reaction function with the slope of the curve equal to g (in the above equation). The more aggressive the Fed's monetary policy the steeper the slope of the curve while a flatter slope represents a more conservative monetary policy. It is up to the Fed to determine how aggressive or conservative its policy reaction function will be at any point in time. Doing so is a complex process, involving a combination of statistical analysis of the economy and human judgment.

III. Self-Test

Key Terms
Match the term in the right-hand column with the appropriate definition in the left-hand column by placing the letter of the term in the blank in front of its' definition. (Answers are given at the end of the chapter.)

1. ____ The choice about which forms to hold one's wealth.	a. demand for money
2. ____ The interest rate that commercial banks charge each other for very short-term (usually overnight) loans.	b. discount rate
3. ____ Shows the relationship between the aggregate quantity of money demanded and the nominal interest rate.	c. discount window lending
4. ____ Describes how the action a policymaker takes depends on the state of the economy.	d. federal funds rate
5. ____ The amount of wealth an individual chooses to hold in the form of money.	e. money demand curve
6. ____ The lending of reserves by the Federal Reserve to commercial banks.	f. policy reaction function
7. ____ The Fed's long-run target for the real interest rate.	g. portfolio allocation decision
8. ____ The interest rate that the Fed charges commercial banks to borrow reserves.	h. reserve requirements
9. ____ The Fed's long-run target for the inflation rate.	i. target inflation rate
10.____ The minimum values of the ratio of bank reserves to bank deposits that commercial banks are allowed to maintain._	j. target real interest rate

Multiple-Choice Questions

Circle the letter that corresponds to the best answer. (Answers are given at the end of the chapter.)

1. The portfolio allocation decision is related to the demand for money because
   A. money can be used to buy a portfolio.
   B. money is one of the many forms in which wealth can be held and is a part of most asset portfolios.
   C. the portfolio allocation decision determines how much of an individual's money is going to be held in the form of currency and how much in the form of balances in a checking account.
   D. money is the main form of wealth for most people.
   E. portfolio allocation explains why the amount of money people hold is directly related to interest rates.

2. E-Buy, a web-based auction firm receives an average of $25,000 in payments for its services each day that it deposits in its bank account at the end of each day. E-Commerce Management Systems, Inc. proposed a computerized cash management system to track E-Buys' inflows and outflows of payments and electronically transfer the funds to an interest-bearing bank account. The cost of the system is $500 per year and E-Buys estimates that it would reduce its cash holding by approximately $10,000 per day. E-Buy should
   A. accept the proposal.
   B. reject the proposal.
   C. accept the proposal if the average interest rate they can earn on the funds is at least 10 percent.
   D. reject the proposal if the average interest rate they can earn on the funds is less than 10 percent.
   E. accept the proposal if the average interest rate they can earn on the funds is greater than 5 percent.

3. As the number of ATM machines increases in a country
   A. the supply of money will increase.
   B. the supply of money will decrease.
   C. people will hold more of their wealth in the form of money. (i.e., the demand for money will increase).
   D. people will hold less of their wealth in the form of money (i.e., the demand for money will decrease).
   E. interest rates will increase.

4. When the Fed buys government bonds, bond prices
   A. increase and interest rates fall.
   B. decrease and interest rates fall.
   C. increase and interest rates rise.
   D. decrease and interest rates rise.
   E. and interest rates fall.

5. The Fed communicates its monetary policy to the public in terms of targets for the federal funds rate because it is
    A. the only interest rate that they can control.
    B. the interest rate that most individuals pay when they borrow money to buy a car, a household appliance, or a house.
    C. the interest rate that the Fed has the greatest control over.
    D. one of the tools of monetary policy.
    E. the most important of all the interest rates that are determined in the various financial markets.

6. The real interest rate
    A. cannot be controlled by the Fed because monetary policy only affects nominal interest rates.
    B. can be controlled by the Fed in the short run, but not in the long run.
    C. can be controlled by the Fed in the long run, but not in the short run.
    D. equals the nominal interest rate plus the inflation rate.
    E. equals the inflation rate minus the nominal interest rate.

7. If the Fed implements an open-market sale of government bonds, the
    A. money market equilibrium interest rate will rise.
    B. money market equilibrium interest rate will fall.
    C. price of bonds will rise.
    D. supply of money will increase.
    E. demand for bonds will decrease

8. If the Fed implements an open-market purchase of government bonds, this will cause a(n)
    A. decrease in consumption spending, an increase in investment spending, and an increase in planned aggregate expenditures.
    B. increase in consumption and investment spending, and an increase in planned aggregate expenditures.
    C. decrease in consumption and investment spending, and an increase in planned aggregate expenditures.
    D. decrease in consumption spending, a decrease in investment spending, and an increase in planned aggregate expenditures.
    E. increase in consumption spending, a decrease in investment spending, and a decrease in planned aggregate expenditures.

9. To close a recessionary gap the Fed should
    A. sell government bonds to increase bond prices and lower interest rates, causing consumption, investment spending, and planned aggregate expenditures to increase.
    B. sell government bonds to decrease bond prices and lower interest rates, causing consumption, investment spending, and planned aggregate expenditures to increase.
    C. buy government bonds to increase bond prices and lower interest rates, causing consumption, investment spending, and planned aggregate expenditures to increase.
    D. buy government bonds to decreases bond prices and increase interest rates, causing consumption, investment spending, and planned aggregate expenditures to decrease.

E. buy government bonds to decreases bond prices and lower interest rates, causing consumption, investment spending, and planned aggregate expenditures to increase.

10. An expansionary monetary policy will cause a(n)
    A. decrease in interest rates, an increase in planned aggregate expenditures, and is designed to reduce an expansionary gap.
    B.   increase in interest rates, a decrease in planned aggregate expenditures, and is designed to reduce an expansionary gap.
    C. decrease in interest rates, a decrease in planned aggregate expenditures, and is designed to reduce a recessionary gap.
    D. decrease in interest rates, an increase in planned aggregate expenditures, and is designed to reduce a recessionary gap.
    E. increase in interest rates, increase in planned aggregate expenditures, and is designed to reduce a recessionary gap.

11. The Fed's policy reaction function
    A. is mandated by law.
    B. is a model of the behavior of the Fed.
    C. can be determined by statistical analysis of the economy.
    D. is determined by its short-run target rate of inflation.
    E. only provides information about the central bank's inflation target.

12. The more aggressive the Fed's monetary policy
    A. the higher the value of g in the policy reaction function and the flatter the slope of the policy reaction curve.
    B. the lower the value of g in the policy reaction function and the flatter the slope of the policy reaction curve.
    C. The higher the value of g in the policy reaction function and the steeper the slope of the policy reaction curve.
    D. the lower the value of g in the policy reaction function and the steeper the slope of the policy reaction curve.
    E. the lower the real interest rate will be for a given rate of inflation.

13. The higher the price of bonds, with no change in the cost of transferring funds between bonds and checkable deposits, the
    A. more likely people are to hold their wealth in the form of bonds than money.
    B. more likely people are to hold their wealth in the form of money than bonds.
    C. the greater the differential between nominal and real interest rates.
    D. the smaller the quantity of money demanded.
    E. the greater the demand for money.

14. A decrease in aggregate real output or income will
    A. decrease the quantity of goods and services that people and businesses want to buy and sell and, thus, decrease the demand for money.
    B. decrease the quantity of goods and services that people and businesses want to buy and sell and, thus, increase the demand for money.

C. increase the quantity of goods and services that people and businesses want to buy and sell and, thus, decrease the demand for money.

D. increase the quantity of goods and services that people and businesses want to buy and sell and, thus, increase the demand for money.

E. decrease the quantity of goods and services that people and businesses want to buy and sell, but have no effect on the demand for money.

15. A contractionary monetary policy
   A. is achieved if the Fed implements an open-market purchase of government bonds.
   B. will decrease the money market equilibrium interest rate.
   C. will increase the money market equilibrium interest rate.
   D. will raise the price of bonds.
   E. will shift the money supply curve to the right.

16. The Fed can control real interest rates only in the short run because
   A. the U.S. Congress has not given it the legal authority to control interest rates in the long run.
   B. nominal interest rates only adjust slowly to changing economic conditions and policy.
   C. saving and investment are not relevant to short-run real interest rates.
   D. saving and investment are not relevant to long-run real interest rates.
   E. the inflation rate only adjusts slowly to changing economic conditions and policy.

17. If the Fed wants to lower the money market equilibrium interest rate, it should
   A. decrease the supply of money.
   B. shift the supply of money to the left.
   C. sell government bonds.
   D. purchase government bonds.
   E. decrease the price of bonds.

18. A contractionary monetary policy is designed to produce a(n)
   A. increase in planned aggregate expenditures, and reduce an expansionary gap.
   B. decrease in planned aggregate expenditures, and reduce an expansionary gap.
   C. increase in planned aggregate expenditures, and reduce a recessionary gap.
   D. decrease in planned aggregate expenditures, and reduce a recessionary gap.
   E. increase in planned aggregate expenditures, and increase an expansionary gap.

19. If the Fed purchases government bonds, this will cause a(n)
   A. increase in planned aggregate expenditures and output and reduce a recessionary gap.
   B. increase in planned aggregate expenditures and output and reduce an expansionary gap.
   C. decrease in planned aggregate expenditures and output and reduce a recessionary gap.
   D. decrease in planned aggregate expenditures and output and reduce an expansionary gap.
   E. increase in planned aggregate expenditures, decrease output, and reduce an expansionary gap.

20. If the Fed wants to increase the money market equilibrium interest rate, it should
    A. lower the reserve requirement.
    B. decrease the discount rate.
    C. increase the discount rate.
    D. buy government bonds.
    E. tell banks to increase the federal funds rate.

Short Answer Problems
(Answers and solutions are given at the end of the chapter.)

1. Cost and Benefit of Holding Money
The following table shows the estimated annual benefits to Siam of holding different amounts of money.

Average Money Holdings	Total Annual Benefit	Marginal Annual Benefit
$1,000	$60	XXXXXXXX
1,100	72	
1,200	82	
1,300	90	
1,400	96	
1,500	100	
1,600	102	
1,700	102	

A. Complete column 3 by calculating the extra benefit of each additional $100 in money holdings greater than $100.
B. How much money will Siam hold if the nominal interest rates is 10 percent? $_____; if the nominal interest rates is 8 percent? $_____; if the nominal interest rates is 6 percent? $_____; if the nominal interest rate is 4 percent $_____; if the nominal interest rate is 2 percent $_____?
C. On the graph below plot Siam's money demand curve for nominal interest rates between 2 and 12 percent.

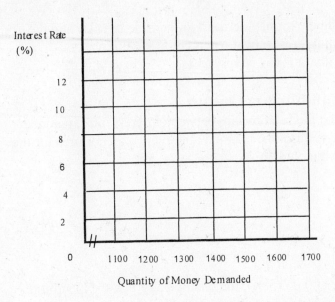

Quantity of Money Demanded

D. If Siam won a million-dollar lottery, his money demand curve shift to the (right/left) _____ representing a(n) (increase/decrease) _____ in the demand for money.

2. Money Market and Equilibrium Interest Rate

This problem focuses on the Fed's control of the money supply to achieve targeted nominal interest rates. Assume that the price level and real GDP are at levels such that the money demand is initially at MD_1.

Quantity of Money Demanded

A. If the Fed wants to set the nominal equilibrium interest rate at 4 percent, it should set the money supply at $ _____.
B. If real GDP increases so that the money demand rises to MD_2 and the Fed wants to keep the nominal equilibrium interest rate at 4 percent, it should (increase/decrease) _____ the nominal money supply to $ _____.
C. If the Fed now decides to raise the nominal equilibrium interest rate to 6 percent, it should (increase/decrease) _____ the nominal money supply to $ _____.

D. If the price level subsequently rises causing the money demand to increase to MD_3 and the Fed wants to keep the nominal equilibrium interest rate at 6 percent, it should (increase/decrease) _____ the nominal money supply to $_____.

3. Monetary Policy and Short-Run Equilibrium Output

This problem will help you to better understand the relationship between interest rates, planned aggregate expenditures, output, and monetary policy. The planned aggregate expenditures for the economy of Hinderland is given by the following equations:

$C = \$750 + 0.75(Y - T) - 300r$
$I^P = \$400 - 600r$
$G = \$500$
$T = \$400$
$NX = -\$55$

A. If the Fed sets the nominal interest rate (r) at 0.05 (5 %), the planned aggregate expenditures for the Hinderland economy would be represented by the equation $PAE = \$$_____ + .75Y.

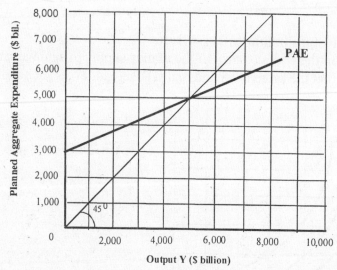

B. Given the Hinderland planned aggregate expenditures in the above graph, the short-run equilibrium output would equal $_____ .
C. If potential output (Y^*) in the Hinderland economy equals $5,050, there would be a(n) _____ gap of $_____ .
D. If the Fed wanted to close the output gap, it should implement a(n) (expansionary/ contractionary) _____ monetary policy.

Note: Questions 3E – 3F require an algebraic solution using the PAE equation from question 3A. The use of algebraic equations to determine monetary policy is discussed in Appendix A of the textbook chapter.

E. To close the gap, the Fed would need to (decrease/ increase) _____ nominal interest rates to _____ percent.

F. Following the expansionary monetary policy, assume the recessionary gap is closed at $Y =$ $5,050, and the Fed determines that the inflation rate is 1.5%. Applying the Taylor rule, this would suggest that the real interest rate in the economy would equal_____ %.

IV. Becoming an Economic Naturalist: Case Study

In the Economic Naturalist 27.4, the Fed's role in responding to the economic expansion of 2002-04 and its "pre-emptive strike against inflation" that began in June 2004 are discussed. During the latter half of 2004 and first half of 2005, the Fed has continued to raise the discount rate and the market determined federal funds rate has also risen. How would an economist characterize the monetary policy (expansionary or contractionary) during the latter half of 2004 and first half of 2005? Looking at the discount rate and federal funds rate since July 2005, has the Fed maintained the same direction in its monetary policy? Explain your answer.

Answer:

V. Self-Test Solutions

Key Terms
1. g
2. d
3. e
4. f
5. a
6. c
7. j
8. b
9. i
10. h

Multiple-Choice Questions
1. B
2. E $10,000 x 0.05 = $500. Therefore, an interest rate of greater than 5% would imply that the benefit would be greater than the cost.
3. D
4. A
5. C
6. B
7. A
8. B
9. C
10. D
11. B
12. C
13. B

14. A
15. C
16. E
17. D
18. B
19. A
20. C

Short Answer Problems

1.

A.

Average Money Holdings	Total Annual Benefit	Marginal Annual Benefit
$1,000	$60	XXXXXXXX
1,100	72	12
1,200	82	10
1,300	90	8
1,400	96	6
1,500	100	4
1,600	102	2
1,700	102	0

B. $1,200; $1,300; $1,400; $1,500; $1,600

C.

D. right; increase

2.

A. $1300
B. increase; $1,400
C. decrease; $1,300
D. increase; $1,400

3.

A. $1,250 ($750 + .75(Y − $400) − $300(.05) + $400 − $600(.05) + $500 + (−$55)

B. $5,000

C. recessionary gap; $50 (Y* − Y = output gap)

D. expansionary

E. decrease; 3.6 ($5,050 = $1,295 + .75($5,050) − 900i, or $5,050 = $1,295 + $3,787.5 − 900$i$. Combining the constant values gives us −$32.5 = − 900$i$., or 3.6 = i)

F. 1.75 [r = 0.01 − 0.5 ($\dfrac{\$5,050 - \$5,050}{\$5,050}$) + 0.5(.015)]

Chapter 28
Inflation, Aggregate Supply, and Aggregate Demand

I. Pretest: What Do You Really Know?

Circle the letter that corresponds to the best answer. (Answers appear immediately after the final question).

1. All else equal, an increase in the rate of inflation _____ aggregate demand and _____ short-run equilibrium output.
   A. increases; increases
   B. increases; decreases
   C. does not change; does not change
   D. decreases; increases
   E. decreases; decreases

2. Suppose in an economy PAE = $5,000 + .75 Y - 10,000r and the central bank acts according to the following policy reaction function:

Rate of inflation (π)	Real interest rate set by central bank (r)
0.00 (=0%)	0.03 (=3%)
0.01	0.04
0.02	0.05
0.03	0.06
0.04	0.07

   If inflation is 1%, the central bank will set a real interest rate of _____ percent and short-run equilibrium output will equal _____.
   A. 3; 18,400
   B. 4; 18,400
   C. 6; 18,400
   D. 6; 17,600
   E. 6; 15,000

3. High levels of inflation _____ the real value of money and, hence, _____ aggregate demand.
   A. reduce; increase
   B. reduce; decrease

C. have no impact on; have no impact on
D. increase; decrease
E. increase; increase

4. Which of the following will shift the aggregate demand curve to the left?
    A. Income taxes are lowered.
    B. The government increases spending on education.
    C. Consumers become optimistic about the future.
    D. A new technology is developed that will increase profits.
    E. Foreign economies fall into recession, reducing their demand for domestic exports.

5. If for any given inflation rate, the Fed raises interest rates more than normal, this is called a
    monetary _____ and the aggregate demand curve shifts to the _____.
    A. tightening; right
    B. tightening; left
    C. gap; right
    D. easing; right
    E. easing; left

6. An upward shift in the Fed's policy reaction function is a monetary _____ and the aggregate
    demand curve _____.
    A. tightening; shifts right
    B. tightening; shifts left
    C. tightening; does not shift
    D. easing; shifts right
    E. easing; shifts left

7. An increase in interest rates by the Fed based on a given policy reaction function represents a
    _____ the aggregate demand curve, but higher than normal interest rates resulting from an
    upward shift in the Fed's policy reaction function represents a _____ the aggregate demand
    curve.
    A. shift left of; movement up
    B. shift left of ; shift right of
    C. movement up; movement down
    D. movement up; shift left of
    E. movement down; shift left of

8. The tendency for inflation to change relatively slowly from year to year in industrial
    countries is called:
    A. the inflation gap
    B. inflation expectations.
    C. inflation inertia.
    D. potential inflation.
    E. autonomous inflation.

9. When actual output is less than potential output there is ____ output gap and the rate of inflation will tend to ____.
    A. an expansionary; increase
    B. an expansionary; decrease
    C. no; remain the same
    D. a recessionary; increase
    E. a recessionary; decrease

10. Within the context of the Aggregate Demand-Aggregate Supply Diagram, the long-run equilibrium occurs where the:
    A. long-run aggregate supply and short-run aggregate supply curves intersect.
    B. short-run aggregate supply and aggregate demand curves intersect.
    C. short-run aggregate supply, long-run aggregate supply and aggregate demand curves intersect.
    D. actual output is less than potential output.
    E. actual output is greater than potential output.

Solutions and Feedback to Pretest

For each question you incorrectly answered, we strongly recommend taking the time to review the appropriate material before continuing. In the table below are listed for each question the pertinent Learning Objective from the following Key Point Review.

Correct Answer	Learning Objective
1. E	2
2. B	5
3. B	1
4. E	2
5. B	2
6. B	2
7. D	2
8. C	3
9. E	6
10. C	6

II. Key Point Review
The Forest

This chapter focuses on the development of the aggregate demand/aggregate supply diagram to analyze how macroeconomic policies affect inflation and discusses the sources of inflation. The central questions you need to be able to answer are:
- What factors determine the aggregate demand in the macroeconomy?
- What factors determine the short-run and long-run aggregate supply ?
- Where do the short-run and long-run equilibria occur on the aggregate demand-aggregate supply diagram?
- How does the economy self-correct when the short-run equilibrium does not equal potential output?

- What are the sources of inflation?
- How does fiscal policy affect the aggregate supply?

The Trees

Learning Objective 1: Define aggregate demand curve and explain why it is downward sloping

To incorporate inflation into the model, a new relationship is introduced between aggregate demand (AD) and the rate of inflation (π). Graphically, this relationship is called the aggregate demand curve. Because short-run equilibrium output equals aggregate demand, the **aggregate demand curve** not only shows the relationship between AD and inflation, but also shows the relationship between short-run equilibrium output and inflation. When the Fed raises real interest rates in response to higher inflation rates, aggregate demand and the short-run equilibrium output decrease. The aggregate demand curve is, therefore, downward sloping. In addition to the effect of inflation on monetary policy, there are three other reasons why inflation reduces aggregate demand. First, higher inflation reduces the real value of money held by households and businesses causing them to restrain spending and, thus, reduces aggregate demand. Second, higher inflation affects income distribution as it redistributes resources from relatively high-spending, less-affluent households to relatively high-saving, more-affluent households, causing overall spending to decline. Third, as domestic goods become relatively more expensive to prospective foreign purchasers, export sales decline, reducing aggregate demand. To summarize, changes in the Fed's response to higher inflation, and the effects of inflation on the real value of money, income distribution, and net exports, cause a movement along the aggregate demand curve.

Learning Objective 2: Identify the factors that cause the AD curve to shift

In addition to the above factors that cause movements along the aggregate demand curve, there are also factors that cause the aggregate demand curve to shift. For a given level of inflation, any change in the economy that affects the aggregate demand and short-run equilibrium will cause the AD curve to shift. This chapter focuses on two sorts of changes in the economy that shift the aggregate demand curve: changes in spending cause by factors other than output or interest rates (refer to as exogenous changes in spending) and changes in the Fed's policy reaction function. The components of planned aggregate expenditures include consumption, investment spending, government purchases, and net exports. A change in any other these components that is caused by something other than a change in output or interest rates is called a change in exogenous spending. An increase in exogenous spending will cause the AD curve to shift to the right, while a decrease in exogenous spending will cause the AD curve to shift to the left. If the Fed's policy reaction function shifts upward, (i.e., the Fed chooses a "tighter" monetary policy by setting the real interest rate higher than normal for a given rate of inflation), the aggregate demand curve will shift to the left. An easing of monetary policy (the Fed's policy reaction function shifts downward) causes the AD curve to shift to the right.

Learning Objective 3: Explain the importance of inflation inertia in determining the short-run aggregate supply (SRAS)

The rate of inflation in low-inflation industrial economies tends to change relatively slowly from year to year (**inflation inertia**). Inflation inertia is due to (1) the public's inflation expectations for the next few years, which are highly influenced by the recent inflation experience, and (2) long-term wage and price contracts, which tend to build the effects of people's inflation expectations into current price level. Although the rate of inflation is inertial, it does change over time.

Hint: You can think of inflation inertia as a virtuous cycle, in which low inflation begets successive periods of low inflation. If inflation begins to rise, however, a vicious cycle can set in, with high inflation creating inflationary expectations that will lead to successive period of high inflation.

Learning Objective 4: Explain the relationship between output gaps and changes in inflation

One factor that can cause inflation to change is the output gap. If the output gap is zero, the rate of inflation will tend to remain the same. When an expansionary gap exists, the rate of inflation will tend to increase; and a recessionary gap tends to cause the rate of inflation to decrease. For example, if a recessionary gap exists, firms will be selling less than their capacity to produce, and they will have an incentive to reduce the *relative* price of their product in order to sell more of it. Cutting the *relative* price means that firms will raise their prices by less than the increase in their costs, as determined by the current inflation rate. As a result, the rate of inflation will tend to fall when a recessionary gap exists. On the other hand, if an expansionary gap exists, firms will be selling more than their normal production and they will ultimately increase the relative price of their product. Doing so will mean that they raise prices by an amount greater than the increase in their costs. In this manner, inflation will tend to rise when an expansionary gap exists.

Learning Objective 5: Define long-run and short-run aggregate supply lines, and short-run and long-run equilibrium

The adjustment of inflation in response to output gaps can be conveniently shown using the AD/AS diagram. The AD/AS diagram is a tool economists use to determine the level of output prevailing at any particular time. The aggregate supply component of the AD/AS diagram is represented by two curves called the long-run aggregate supply line and the short-run aggregate supply line. The **short-run aggregate supply line**, or SRAS line, is a horizontal line showing the current rate of inflation, as determined by past expectations and pricing decisions. The AD/AS diagram can be used to determine the level of output prevailing at any particular time, called the **short-run equilibrium** output. The short-run equilibrium occurs when inflation equals the value determined by past expectations and pricing decisions and output equals the level of short-run equilibrium output that is consistent with that inflation rate. Graphically, the short-run equilibrium occurs at the intersection of the AD curve and the SRAS line. The **long-run aggregate supply line**, or LRAS line, is a vertical line at the economy's potential output (Y^*). This point is referred to as the long-run equilibrium of the economy. The **long-run equilibrium** occurs where actual output equals potential output and the inflation rate is stable. Graphically, long-run equilibrium occurs when the AD curve, the SRAS line and the LRAS line all intersect

438

Chapter 28

at a single point. An expansionary gap at the short-run equilibrium output would set in motion a similar adjustment process, but in the opposite direction (e.g., inflation rate would rise, SRAS line shifts upward).

Learning Objective 6: Discuss the self-correcting tendency of the economy
The AD/AS diagram makes the important general point that the economy tends to be self-correcting. That is, given enough time, output gaps tend to disappear without changes in monetary or fiscal policy. This view contrasts with the basic Keynesian model, which does not include a self-correcting mechanism. This difference derives from the fact that the basic Keynesian model concentrates on the short-run period, during which prices do not adjust, while the extended AD/AS model focuses on the changes in prices and inflation over the long-run period. Whether monetary and fiscal policies are needed to stabilize output then depends crucially on the speed with which the self-correction process takes place. If self-correction takes place slowly, active use of monetary and fiscal policy can help to stabilize output. If it takes place rapidly, however, an active stabilization policy is not only unnecessary, but is probably harmful. The speed with which a particular economy corrects itself depends upon the prevalence of long-term contracts and the efficiency and flexibility of product and labor markets. In addition, the larger the size of the output gap, the longer the self-correction will take. The self-correcting tendency of the economy also explains why the income-expenditure multiplier is smaller in practice than the basic Keynesian model suggests.

Note: How long is the long-run period? The long run is not defined in concrete measures, such as months or years. It is conceptually defined as a period sufficiently long to allow the economy to fully adjust prices and output. In concrete terms, the long run can vary depending upon a variety of factors that impact the economy's ability to adjust. Some economies may adjust faster than others, and a given economy can adjust faster to some circumstances, but more slowly under other circumstances.

Learning Objective 7: Show the effects of excessive aggregate demand and supply shocks on inflation
The analysis of the AD/AS diagram indicates that inflation rises and falls in response to output gaps. But, what causes output gaps? An expansionary output gap may result from excessive aggregate spending that puts upward pressure on prices ("too much money chasing too few goods"). Wars and military buildups have historically been one reason for excessive aggregate spending. Inflation may also arise from an **aggregate supply shock**, either an inflation shock or a shock to potential output. An **inflation shock** is a sudden change in the normal behavior of inflation, unrelated to the nation's output gap. For example, a large increase in energy or food prices (an adverse inflation shock) shifts the SRAS line upward. An adverse inflation shock creates stagflation, a combination of recession and higher inflation, creating a difficult dilemma for policymakers. If they take no action, eventually inflation will subside and output will recover, but in the interim the economy may suffer a protracted period of recession. Monetary or fiscal policy, on the other hand, can be used to shorten the recession, but will lock in higher inflation. A **shock to potential output** is a sharp change in potential output, shifting the LRAS line. Like an inflation shock, an adverse shock to potential output results in stagflation. The adverse shock

to potential output, however, implies that productive capacity has fallen and, therefore, output does not recover as it does following an inflation shock.

Learning Objective 8: Explain how fiscal policy may have supply-side impacts.
Fiscal policy, government spending and taxation such as public capital expenditures (for roads, airports, or schools), not only affects aggregate expenditures but also may increase potential output if it changes firms' costs of production. Government tax and transfer programs affect incentives, and, thus, the economic behavior of households and businesses. Households and business may respond to changes in their marginal tax rates by working more or less, investing more or less, and taking more or less risk. These changes may cause the aggregate supply curves to shift.

III. Self-Test

<u>Key Terms</u>
Match the term in the right-hand column with the appropriate definition in the left-hand column by placing the letter of the term in the blank in front of its' definition. (Answers are given at the end of the chapter.)

1. _____ Either an inflation shock or a shock to potential output.

2. _____ A horizontal line showing the current rate of inflation, as determined by past expectations and pricing decisions.

3. _____ Shows the relationship between short-run equilibrium output and inflation.

4. _____ A situation in which actual output equals potential output and the inflation rate is stable.

5. _____ A substantial reduction in the rate of inflation.

6. _____ A sudden change in the normal behavior of inflation, unrelated to the nation's output gap

7. _____ A vertical line showing the economy's potential output (Y*).

8. _____ A situation in which inflation equals the value determined by past expectations and pricing decisions, and output equals the level of short-run equilibrium output that is consistent with that inflation.

9. _____ A policy that affects potential output.

10. _____ The amount by which taxes rise when before-tax income rises by one dollar.

11. _____ Total taxes divided by total before-taxes income.

a. aggregate demand (AD) curve

b. aggregate supply shock

c. average tax rate

d. disinflation

e. inflation shock

f. long-run aggregate supply (LRAS) line

g. long-run equilibrium

h. marginal tax rate

i. short-run aggregate supply (SRAS) line

j. short-run equilibrium

k. supply-side policy

Multiple-Choice Questions
Circle the letter that corresponds to the best answer. (Answers are given at the end of the chapter.)

1. When the Fed responds to higher inflation by raising real interest rates
   A. consumption and investment spending rise and, thus, total spending increases.
   B. consumption and investment spending fall and, thus, total spending increases.
   C. consumption and investment spending rise and, thus, total spending decreases.
   D. consumption and investment spending fall and, thus, total spending decreases.
   E. the Fed changes its policy reaction function.

2. A decrease in taxes will cause a
   A. movement downward along the AD curve.
   B. movement upward along the AD curve.
   C. rightward shift in the AD curve.
   D. leftward shift in the AD curve.
   E. decrease in AD.

3. Inflation inertia is attributable to
   A. inflation shocks and shocks to potential output.
   B. output gaps and inflation shock.
   C. disinflation and inflation shock.
   D. output gaps and disinflation.
   E. inflation expectations and long-term wage and price contracts.

4. When an expansionary gap exists, the rate of inflation will
   A. tend to rise.
   B. tend to fall.
   C. remain unchanged.
   D. become disinflation.
   E. shift the SRAS line downward.

5. If, at the short-run equilibrium output, a recessionary gap exists, the
   A. SRAS line will move upward until actual output equals potential output.
   B. SRAS line will move downward until actual output equals potential output.
   C. LRAS line will move upward until actual output equals potential output.
   D. LRAS line will move downward until actual output equals potential output.
   E. LRAS line and SRAS line will move upward until actual output equals potential output.

6. The tendency for the economy to be self-correcting
   A. is highlighted by the AD/AS diagram.
   B. is highlighted by the basic Keynesian model.
   C. is an underlying assumption of all macroeconomic models.
   D. implies that fiscal and monetary policies are not needed to stabilize output.
   E. has been called into question by the analysis of the AD/AS diagram.

7. Excessive aggregate demand can result in
   A. a recessionary gap and a rising inflation rate.
   B. too many goods chasing too little spending.
   C. an expansionary gap and an increasing inflation rate.
   D. an expansionary gap and an increasing unemployment rate.
   E. a recessionary gap and a rising unemployment rate.

8. If the inflation rate has risen to a level inconsistent with economic efficiency and long-term growth, and the Fed tightens monetary policy, the
   A. the monetary policy reaction function shifts upward and the SRAS curve will shift downward.
   B. the monetary policy reaction function shifts downward and the AD curve will shift to the left.
   C. the monetary policy reaction function shifts upward and the AD curve will shift to the right.
   D. the monetary policy reaction function shifts upward AD curve shifts to the left.
   E. the monetary policy reaction function shifts downward and the AD curve shifts to the right.

9. The distributional effects of inflation contribute to a downward-sloping AD curve because inflation redistributes income from
   A. less affluent, lower-spending families to more affluent families who spend more, causing overall spending to decline.
   B. relatively higher-spending, less-affluent families to relatively higher-saving, more-affluent families, causing overall spending to decline.
   C. relatively lower-spending, more-affluent families to relatively higher spending, less-affluent families, causing overall spending to decline.
   D. relatively lower-spending, less-affluent families to relatively higher spending, more-affluent families, causing overall spending to decline.
   E. relatively higher-spending, more-affluent families to relatively lower saving, less-affluent families, causing overall spending to decline.

10. If the Fed were to shift its policy reaction function downward (i.e., an easing of monetary policy), the
    A. SRAS line would shift upward.
    B. LRAS line would shift upward.
    C. SRAS line would shift downward.
    D. AD curve would shift to the left.
    E. AD curve would shift to the right.

11. A current high rate of inflation will tend to promote a
    A. virtuous circle of high expected inflation and a high rate of actual inflation.
    B. virtuous circle of low expected inflation and a low rate of actual inflation.
    C. vicious circle of high expected inflation and a high rate of actual inflation.
    D. vicious circle of low expected inflation and a low rate of actual inflation.
    E. built-in expectation of low inflation in the future.

12. A short-run equilibrium with an output gap of zero implies
    A. zero inflation in the near future.
    B. the rate of inflation will remain the same.
    C. the rate of inflation will rise.
    D. the rate of inflation will fall.
    E. firms have no incentive to raise the prices of their goods and services.

13. If an expansionary gap exists at the short-run equilibrium output, the
    A. SRAS line will move upward until actual output equals potential output.
    B. SRAS line will move downward until actual output equals potential output.
    C. LRAS line will move upward until actual output equals potential output.
    D. LRAS line will move downward until actual output equals potential output.
    E. LRAS line and SRAS line will move downward until actual output equals potential output.

14. If the self-correction process of the economy takes place very slowly, so that actual output differs from potential output for protracted periods of time, then active
    A. stabilization policies are probably not justified.
    B. stabilization policies may end up doing more harm than good.
    C. use of monetary and fiscal policy can cause actual output to overshoot potential output.
    D. use of monetary and fiscal policy can help to stabilize output.
    E. stabilization policy can cause the output gap to become larger.

15. Inflation escalated to the double-digit level in the United States during the 1970s because of
    A. excessive aggregate demand due to the military buildup under President Reagan.
    B. an adverse inflation shock caused by the military buildup under President Reagan.
    C. adverse inflation shocks caused by two oil crises that significantly raised world oil prices.
    D. a positive inflation shock that resulted in high inflation and a recessionary gap.
    E. a positive inflation shock that resulted in two periods of stagflation.

16. At high rates of inflation, the purchasing power of money
    A. declines and households restrain their spending, causing aggregate demand to decline.
    B. rises and household increase their spending, causing aggregate demand to rise.
    C. rises and households restrain their spending, causing aggregate demand to decline.
    D. declines and households restrain their spending, causing aggregate demand to increase.
    E. declines and households increase their spending, causing aggregate demand to decline.

17. The development of new cost-saving technology would
    A. increase exogenous spending and, thus, cause a movement down along the AD curve.
    B. increase exogenous spending and, thus, cause a movement up along the AD curve to the left.
    C. increase exogenous spending and, thus, shift the AD curve to the right.
    D. increase exogenous spending and, thus, shift the AD curve to the left.
    E. decrease exogenous spending and, thus, shifts the AD curve to the right.

18. A short-run equilibrium with an recessionary gap implies that
    A. firms will raise the prices of their goods and services more than needed to fully cover their increases in costs.
    B. firms will raise the prices of their goods and services as much as needed to fully cover their increases in costs.
    C. negative inflation.
    D. firms have incentives to lower the relative prices of their goods and services..
    E. firms have incentives to raise the relative prices of their goods and services.

19. Unlike an adverse inflation shock, a shock to potential output causes
    A. lower output and higher inflation.
    B. higher output and lower inflation.
    C. no output losses.
    D. only temporary output losses.
    E. permanent output losses.

20. A cut in marginal tax rates will
    A. increase aggregate demand and decrease aggregate supply.
    B. decrease aggregate demand and decrease aggregate supply.
    C. increase aggregate demand and increase aggregate supply.
    D. decrease aggregate demand and decrease aggregate supply.
    E. decrease aggregate demand and increase aggregate supply.

Short Answer Problems
(Answers and solutions are given at the end of the chapter.)

1. Aggregate Demand Curve
This problem is designed to help you better understand why the AD curve is downward sloping and the factors that can cause the AD curve to shift. Assume the planned aggregate expenditures is given by the equation, $PAE = \$950 + .75Y - 900r$

A. The inflation rates and interest rates in the table below show the Fed's policy reaction function. Complete the table by calculating the level of aggregate demand for each combination of inflation rate and interest rate.

Inflation rate, π	Interest rate, r	aggregate demand, AD
0.00	0.03	
0.01	0.04	
0.02	0.05	
0.03	0.06	
0.04	0.07	
0.05	0.08	
0.06	0.09	

B. On the graph below, draw the AD curve that is shown in the above table, label it AD.

Output ($)

C. Assume that the Fed shifts its policy reaction function downward by reducing the nominal interest rates 1% at each rate of inflation. Complete column 2 of the following table, by indicating the new interest rates for rates of inflation from 0 to 6 percent.

Inflation Rate, π	Interest Rate, r	Aggregate Demand, AD
0.00		
0.01		
0.02		
0.03		
0.04		
0.05		
0.06		

D. Complete column 3 of the above table, by calculating the new levels of aggregate demand for rates of inflation from 0 to 6 percent.

E. On the graph above, draw the new AD curve shown in the above table and label it AD_1.

F. If new technological innovations caused the autonomous investment spending to increase by $20, in the table below calculate the new levels of aggregate demand for rates of inflation from 0 to 6 percent.

Inflation Rate, π	Interest Rate, r	Aggregate Demand, AD
0.00	0.02	
0.01	0.03	
0.02	0.04	

0.03	0.05	
0.04	0.06	
0.05	0.07	
0.06	0.08	

G. On the graph above, plot the new AD curve shown in the last table and label it AD$_2$.

2. AD/AS Diagram

This problem will give you practice drawing the SRAS and LRAS lines, determining the short-run and long-run equilibria, analyzing output gaps, and analyzing the economic adjustments to output gaps.

A. Assuming the current inflation rate in the economy is 3 percent, draw the short-run aggregate supply (SRAS) line on the graph below.

3500   3550   3600   3650   3700   3750

Output ($)

B. Given the AD curve and SRAS line on the graph above, the short-run equilibrium output is $_____ .

C. Assuming the potential output in the economy is $3,650 billion, insert the long-run aggregate supply (LRAS) line on the graph above.

D. Given the short-run equilibrium output and the potential output, the graph indicates that a(n) _____ gap exists.

E. The output gap will cause the inflation rate to (increase/decrease/ remain unchanged) _____ .

F. As the inflation rate adjusts to the output gap, the (SRAS / LRAS) _____ line will shift (upward/downward) _____ until the actual output equals the potential output.

G. When the actual output equals potential output, the economy will settle into its
_____ equilibrium at $_____ .

3. Sources of Inflation

This problem focuses on the effects of excessive aggregate demand on the economy in the short run and long run. Assume the economy is initially in long-run equilibrium at the point where the AD curve, and the SRAS and LRAS lines intersect on the graph below.

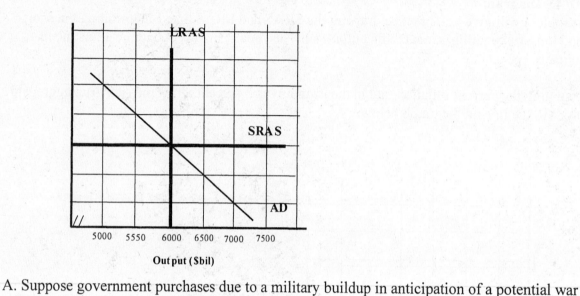

Output ($bil)

A. Suppose government purchases due to a military buildup in anticipation of a potential war cause the AD to increase by $500 billion. As a result, the (AD curve / SRAS line / LRAS line) _____ will shift _____. Draw the new curve on the graph above.

B. The new short-run equilibrium output will equal $_____ billion.

C. In the short run, the military buildup has caused the actual output to become (greater than / less than / equal to) _____ the potential output, creating a(n) _____ gap.

D. The output gap eventually will cause the inflation rate to (rise / fall) _____ and the (AD curve / SRAS line / LRAS line) _____ will shift _____.

E. Draw the new curve on the above graph showing its location after the self-correcting process is complete.

F. The economy will achieve its long-run equilibrium output at $_____ billion and the inflation rate will equal _____ percent.

G. The long-run equilibrium output after the military buildup is (greater than / less than / equal to) _____ the initial long-run equilibrium output, and the inflation rate is (greater than / less than / equal to) _____ the initial long-run equilibrium inflation rate.

H. If the policymakers decided that the inflation rate had risen to a level incompatible with long run economic growth, the Fed might implement a(n) (tight / easy) _____ monetary policy that would shift the (AD curve / SRAS line / LRAS line) _____ to the _____ .

I. In comparison to a "do nothing policy," in the short run such a monetary policy would cause a(n) _____, with output (increasing/decreasing / remaining unchanged) _____, and the rate of inflation (increased/decreased/ unchanged) _____ .

J. In the long run, such a monetary policy would leave output (greater than / less than / equal to) _____ a "do nothing policy," and the rate of inflation would be (greater than / less than / equal to) _____ a "do nothing policy."

4. Aggregate Supply Shocks

This problem focuses on the effects of aggregate supply shocks on the economy in the short run and long run. Assume the economy is initially in long-run equilibrium at the point where the AD curve and that the SRAS and LRAS lines intersect on the graph below.

Output ($bil)

A. Because of a disruption in the worldwide supply of crude oil, the price of energy rises and drives the inflation rate to 4%. As a result, the (AD curve / SRAS line / LRAS line) _____ will shift _____ . Draw the new curve on the graph above.

B. The new short-run equilibrium output will equal $ _____ billion.

C. The adverse supply shock has created a(n) _____, combined with a (higher / lower) _____ rate of inflation. This combination is referred to as _____ .

D. The output gap eventually will cause the inflation rate to (rise / fall) _____ and the (AD curve / SRAS line / LRAS line) _____ will shift _____ .

E. When the self-correcting process is complete, the economy will achieve its long-run equilibrium output at $ _____ billion, and the inflation rate will equal _____ percent.

F. The long-run equilibrium output after the adverse supply shock is (greater than / less than / equal to) _____ the initial long-run equilibrium, and the inflation rate is (greater / less / equal) _____ the initial long-run equilibrium.

G. If the policy makers chose to eliminate the output gap more quickly than the self-correcting process, the Fed might implement a(n) (tight / easy) _____ monetary policy that would shift the (AD curve / SRAS line / LRAS line) _____ to the

_____.

H. If the policymakers chose to eliminate the output gap more quickly, the long-run equilibrium output would be (greater than / less than / equal to) _____ a "do nothing policy," and the inflation rate would be (greater than / less than / equal to) _____ a "do nothing policy".

IV. Becoming an Economic Naturalist: Case Study

The Economic Naturalist 28.2 discusses the affects of the OPEC oil embargo and the Iranian Revolution on the oil prices and the U.S. economy. Both constituted an adverse inflation shock that resulted in higher inflation and recession in the U.S. during much of the 1970s. Explain the economic consequences for the U. S. economy if significantly greater production of energy supplies (either through new discoveries of oil, or new technologies such as hydrogen produced energy) were to be achieved during the second decade of the 21st century.
Answer:

V. Self-Test Solutions

Key Terms
1. b
2. i
3. a
4. g
5. d
6. e
7. f
8. j
9. k
10. h
11. c

Multiple-Choice Questions

1. D
2. C Taxes are a component of autonomous aggregate demand and a decrease in taxation, therefore, cause the AD curve to shift to the right.
3. E
4. A
5. B
6. A
7. C
8. D
9. B
10. E
11. C
12. B
13. A
14. D
15. C
16. A
17. C
18. D
19. E
20. C

Short Answer Problems

1.

A.

Inflation Rate, π	Interest Rate, r	Aggregate Demand, AD
0.00	0.03	$3,692
0.01	0.04	3,656
0.02	0.05	3,620
0.03	0.06	3,584
0.04	0.07	3,548
0.05	0.08	3,512
0.06	0.09	3,476

B.

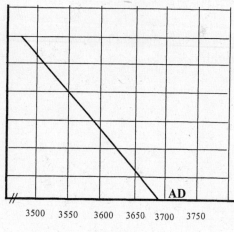

Output ($)

C. , D.

Inflation Rate, π	Interest Rate, r	Aggregate Demand, AD
0.00	0.02	$3,728
0.01	0.03	3,692
0.02	0.04	3,656
0.03	0.05	3,620
0.04	0.06	3,584
0.05	0.07	3,548
0.06	0.08	3,512

E.

Output ($)

F.

Inflation Rate, π	Interest Rate, r	Aggregate Demand, AD
0.00	0.02	$3,808
0.01	0.03	3,772
0.02	0.04	3,736
0.03	0.05	3,700
0.04	0.06	3,664
0.05	0.07	3,628
0.06	0.08	3,592

G.

2.

A.

B. $3,600

C.

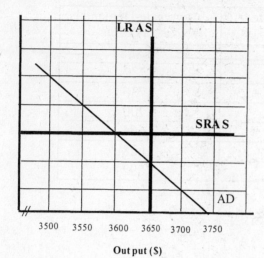

D. recessionary
E. decrease
F. SRAS; downward
G. long-run; $3,650

3.
A. AD curve; rightward;

B. $6,500 billion
C. greater than; expansionary gap
D. rise; SRAS line; upward

E.

Output ($bil)

F. $6,000 billion; 4 percent
G. equal; greater
H. tight; AD curve; left
I. recessionary gap; decreasing; unchanged;
J. equal; less

4.
A. SRAS line; upward;

Output ($bil)

B. $5,500 billion
C. recessionary gap; higher; stagflation
D. fall; SRAS line; downward
E. $6,000 billion; 3
F. equal; equal
G. easy; AD curve; right
H. equal; greater

Chapter 29
The Practice and Pitfalls of Macroeconomic Policy

I. PreTest: What Do You Really Know?

Circle the letter that corresponds to the best answer. (Answers appear immediately after the final question).

1. The monetary policy reaction function indicates a
   A. positive relationship between nominal interest rates and the inflation rate.
   B. negative relationship between nominal interest rates and the inflation rate.
   C. positive relationship between real interest rates and the inflation rate.
   D. negative relationship between real interest rates and the inflation rate.
   E. positive relationship between nominal interest rates and the real interest rates.

2. The effect of the Fed implementing a tighter monetary policy by reducing the target inflation rate is to
   A. shift the monetary policy reaction function up (to the left).
   B. shift the monetary policy reaction function down (to the right).
   C. move down the monetary policy reaction function.
   D. move up the monetary policy reaction function.
   E. move up or down the monetary policy reaction function depending upon whether people have anchored expectations.

3. If the Fed determines that the current inflation target is impeding long-run economic growth and lowers the target inflation rate
   A. the SRAS curve will shift down causing the AD curve to shift to the left and reduce the short-run equilibrium output.
   B. the SRAS curve will shift up causing the AD curve to shift to the right and increase the short-run equilibrium output.
   C. the AD curve to shift to the left causing the short-run equilibrium output to increase and ultimately the SRAS curve will shift down.
   D. the AD curve to shift to the right causing the short-run equilibrium output to increase and ultimately the SRAS curve will shift up.
   E. the AD curve to shift to the left causing the short-run equilibrium output to decline and

ultimately the SRAS curve will shift down.

4. At the long-run equilibrium with a stable monetary policy,
   A. the target inflation rate equals the target interest rate equals actual interest rate and potential output.
   B. the target inflation rate equals the target interest rate equals actual interest rate, and equilibrium output equals potential output.
   C. the target inflation rate equals the target interest rate equals actual interest rate, and equilibrium output equals natural rate of unemployment.
   D. the target inflation rate equals the actual inflation, target interest rate equals actual interest rate, and output equals potential output.
   E. the target inflation rate equals the target interest rate equals actual interest rate and the natural rate of unemployment.

5. The double-digit inflation of the late 1970s was conquered
   A. through tighter monetary policy, but at the expense of lower output and higher unemployment during the early 1980s.
   B. through tighter monetary policy, but at the expense of lower output and higher unemployment throughout 1980s.
   C. through tighter monetary policy without suffering lower output and higher unemployment during the 1980s.
   D. through tighter fiscal policy, but at the expense of lower output and higher unemployment during the early 1980s.
   E. through easier monetary policy, but at the expense of lower output and higher unemployment during the early 1980s.

6. When responding to shocks in aggregate spending, the Fed
   A. must choose between inflation and output stability, but does not face this dilemma when responding to shocks in aggregate supply.
   B. does not face the dilemma of choosing between inflation and output stability as it does when responding to shocks in aggregate supply.
   C. must choose between inflation and output stability, just as it does when responding to shocks in aggregate supply.
   D. must choose between adjusting its inflation targets or adjusting its interest rate targets, but does not face this dilemma when responding to shocks in aggregate supply.
   E. does not face the dilemma of choosing between adjusting its inflation targets or adjusting its interest rate targets as it does when responding to shocks in aggregate supply.

7. When people have anchored inflationary expectations
   A. the SRAS curve will shift down more slowly when an adverse inflation shock creates a recession.
   B. the SRAS curve will shift up more slowly when an adverse inflation shock creates a recession.
   C. the SRAS curve will shift down faster when an adverse inflation shock creates a recession.
   D. the SRAS curve will shift up more slowly when an adverse inflation shock creates a

recession.
   E. the Fed is more likely to accommodate higher inflation rates.

8. The core rate of inflation includes rate of increase in
   A. all prices in the economy.
   B. the price of energy and food.
   C. all prices except energy, food and transportation.
   D. all prices except energy and food.
   E. all prices except basic commodities.

9. The credibility of monetary policy
   A. is determined by people's anchored inflationary expectations.
   B. is the degree to which the public believe the central bank's promises to keep inflation low without imposing short-run economic costs.
   C. is less important in advanced economies like the U.S. and Europe and then it is in developing economies such as Mexico and Thailand.
   D. is enhanced if central bankers are insulated from short-term political considerations, announce numerical inflation targets and are inflation doves.
   E. determines whether inflationary expectation are anchored and is largely determined by the characteristics of the central bank.

10. Macroeconomic policymaking is
   A. an exact science.
   B. as much art as science.
   C. the equivalent of operating a car with the policymaker as driver.
   D. all art and no science.
   E. all science and no art.

Solutions and Feedback to PreTest
For each question you incorrectly answered, we strongly recommend taking the time to review the appropriate material before continuing. In the table below are listed for each question the pertinent Learning Objective from the following Key Point Review.

Correct Answer	Learning Objective
1. C	1
2. A	1
3. E	1
4. D	1
5. A	2
6. B	2
7. C	3
8. D	3
9. E	4
10. B	5

II. Key Point Review
<u>The Forest</u>

This chapter focuses on the use of monetary policy to reduce inflation and to maintain low inflation when the economy is hit by shocks to aggregate demand and aggregate supply. The central questions you need to be able to answer are
- What are the short-run and long-run economic effects of an anti-inflationary monetary policy?
- What policy options are available to the Fed in response to a shock in aggregate demand?
- What policy options are available to the Fed in response to a shock in aggregate supply?
- What institutional characteristics determine the credibility of monetary policy?
- Why is macroeconomic policymaking an inexact science?

<u>The Trees</u>

Learning Objective 1: Explain the short-run and long-run effects of an anti-inflationary monetary policy.
When the Fed adopts a tighter monetary policy, i.e., reducing its target inflation rate, the monetary policy reaction function shifts to the left (or upwards).The Fed actions will cause market interest rates to increase and, thus, consumption and investment spending will decline causing aggregate demand to decrease at every inflation rate (AD curve shifts to the left). The leftward shift in the AD curve will now intersect the short-run aggregate supply (SRAS) curve at a lower output level, indicating a decrease in the short-run equilibrium output. The new equilibrium output will also be less than the potential output, indicating that the Fed's action has allowed a recessionary gap to develop, with the unemployment rate greater than the natural rate of unemployment. Because of inflation inertia there will be no immediate impact on inflation, but eventually the recessionary gap will cause inflation to fall and the SRAS curve will gradually decline. As the inflation rate falls the Fed can begin to lower interest rates, spurring new investment spending. The new investment spending will help the economy to recover from the recession and output will move back toward the level of potential output. The long-run equilibrium will be achieved when the output returns to the level of potential output, but it will now be combined with a lower level of inflation (than when the tighter monetary policy was initiated).

Learning Objective 2: Discuss the Fed's policy options when faced with a rising inflation rate due to increased aggregate demand.
When the economy has reached a long-run equilibrium (at the level of potential output), an increase in aggregate demand will initially cause output to rise (without any impact on inflation in the short run) creating an expansionary gap. The expansionary gap will eventually put upward pressure on prices and the inflation rate will increase. At this point, the Fed has a choice. If the Fed acts to implement an **accommodating policy** that allows inflation to rise about its target inflation rate, the inflation rate will rise. The higher inflation rate will eventually cause the SRAS curve to shift upward and the output will move back to the potential output level at a permanently higher inflation rate (with both inflation and real interest rates above the Fed's targets). The alternative is for the Fed to prevent inflation from rising by raising its target for the real interest rate. An increase in the Fed's target real interest rate will shift the Fed's monetary

policy reaction function up (to the left), raising real interest rates in the economy. The higher real interest rates will shift the AD curve to the back to the left and output will remain at the level of potential output, but unlike the results of the accommodating policy, inflation will remain at the initial level.

Learning Objective 3: Discuss the Fed's policy options when faced with a rising inflation rate due to adverse shocks in aggregate supply.

When faced with rising inflation due to shocks in aggregate demand the Fed can potentially choose inflation and output stability, but shocks to aggregate supply create a dilemma of stabilizing inflation **or** output, but not both simultaneously. When faced with an aggregate supply shock, if the Fed wants to maintain its initial target inflation rate, the economy may face a protracted recessionary or expansionary gap. For example, if an adverse aggregate supply shock shifts the SRAS curve upward, the economy would experience higher inflation and a recessionary gap in the short run. At this point the Fed faces a dilemma. If the Fed maintains its target inflation rate (i.e., no change in the monetary policy reaction function), the recessionary gap will eventually induce firms to lower prices and the SRAS will gradually shift back down as the inflation rate returns to the initial level. In the long run, thus, inflation returns to the initial rate and output returns to its potential level, but in the interim the economy experiences a recession. Alternatively, the Fed may choose to avoid the recession by adjusting its target inflation rate upward (i.e., shifting the monetary policy reaction function down – to the right) causing the AD curve to shift to the right. This will quickly alleviate the recession as output returns to the potential, but the inflation rate will be permanently higher. In making such a choice the Fed might like to know how long it would take the economy to return to its long-run equilibrium if it did not change monetary policy. In part, this depends on whether or not people have **anchored inflationary expectations**. That is, if people's expectations of future inflation do not change when inflation temporarily rises, the economy will more quickly return to it long-run equilibrium. In general, inflationary expectations tend to be less anchored when the Fed has more frequently implemented accommodating policies. Thus, the Fed has a stake in convincing the public that it will maintain its original inflation target. Many economists believe that a bulge in inflation is not inevitable when there is an adverse supply shock if the Fed can prevent a change in inflationary expectations. To allow a temporary increase in inflation but keep long-term inflationary expectations from rising, the Fed can focus on the **core rate of inflation**. The core rate of inflation is the rate of increase of all prices except energy and food, the two items most frequently responsible for aggregate supply shocks. A focus on the core rate of inflation means that the Fed would only adopt a tighter monetary policy if the core rate of inflation exceeds its target inflation rate.

Learning Objective 4: Identify the institutional characteristics that determine whether inflationary expectations are anchored.

Most economists believe that the credibility of monetary policy determines whether inflationary expectations are anchored. The credibility of monetary policy, in turn, is determined by a number of institutional characteristics, including central bank independence, announcement of a numerical inflation target, the central banks reputation as an inflation fighter. The credibility of monetary policy may be enhanced if the central bank is insulated from short-term political considerations. Independence can allow the central bank to take a long-term view of the economy and, for example, pursue anti-inflationary policy even if it leads to a temporary recession. Four of the many factors that can contribute to a central bank's independence are: the length of appointments to the central bank; whether the central bank's actions are subject to frequent interference, review or veto by the legislative branch; whether the central bank has an obligation to finance the national deficit by buying newly issued government bonds; and the degree to which the central bank's budget is controlled by the legislative or executive branches of government. A second institutional characteristic that affects the credibility of monetary policy is whether the central bank announces its target inflation rate to the public. By announcing the target, the central bank provides more information, reduces uncertainty in the financial markets and allows people to plan more effectively. Not all economists believe a public announcement of a specific inflation target is necessary. Some argue that such a system is too rigid and may reduce the central bank's flexibility to deal with unexpected circumstances. Ultimately, monetary credibility is won and maintained by the central bank's performance. A central bank's performance will depend partly on its reputation as being an **inflation hawk** (someone committed to achieving and maintaining low inflation even at the cost of reduced output and employment in the short run) or an **inflation dove** (someone not strongly committed to achieving and maintaining low inflation).

Learning Objective 5: Explain why is macroeconomic policymaking an inexact science.
Monetary policy is an inexact science because we lack perfect information about the current state of the economy, the future path of the economy, the precise value of potential output, and how the economy will respond to changes in fiscal and monetary policy. A lack of information about the current state of the economy may prevent policy makers from acting in a timely manner, while imperfect information about the future path of the economy may cause policymakers to take unnecessary and unwise actions. The inability to precisely measure potential output means that we can't determine the existence of an output gap, or how large it may be, at any point in time. This obviously hinders our ability to formulate macroeconomic policy. Even if we were able to formulate appropriate macroeconomic policies, the timing of its implementation and impact will affect the outcome. Because policymakers often take a long time to implement appropriate policy there is an **inside lag**, the delay between the date the policy change is needed and the date it is implemented, that hinders the effectiveness of macroeconomic policy. In addition, the **outside lag** of macroeconomic policy, the delay between the date a policy change is implemented and the date by which most of its effects on the economy have occurred, further hinders the timeliness and effectiveness of macroeconomic policy. In sum, macroeconomic policy is both an art as well as a science.

> **Note:** The inside lag is substantially shorter for monetary policy than for fiscal policy, because the Federal Open Market Committee meets eight times per year to formulate monetary policy. Fiscal policy, on the other hand, is the responsibility of both houses of Congress and the President. Even after Congress has approved a policy change and the President has signed the bill into law, it may take a long time to implement tax changes or make additional expenditures.

III. Self-Test

Key Terms
Match the term in the right-hand column with the appropriate definitions in the left-hand column by placing the letter of the term in the blank in front of its' definition. (Answers are given at the end of the chapter.)

1. ____ A substantial reduction in the rate of inflation.

2. ____ A policy that allows the effects of a shock to occur.

3. ____ The delay between the date a policy change is implemented and the date by which most of its effects on the economy have occurred.

4. ____ The rate of increase of all prices except energy and food.

5. ____ Someone who is committed to achieving and maintaining low inflation, even at some short-run cost in reduced output and employment.

6. ____ When central bankers are insulated from short-term political considerations and are allowed to take a long-term view of the economy.

7. ____ The degree to which the public believes the central bank's promises to keep inflation low, even if doing so may impose short-run economic costs.

8. ____ Someone who is not strongly committed to achieving and maintaining low inflation.

9. ____ The delay between the date a policy change is needed and the date it is implemented.

10. ___ When people's expectations of future inflation do not change even if inflation rises temporarily.

a. accommodating policy

b. anchored expectations

c. central bank independence

d. core rate of inflation

e. credibility of monetary policy

f. disinflation

g. inflation dove

h. inflation hawk

i. inside lag

j. outside lag

Multiple-Choice Questions
Circle the letter that corresponds to the best answer. (Answers are given at the end of the chapter.)

1. With the economy initially in a long-run equilibrium, if the Fed reduces its target inflation rate, the
   A. monetary policy reaction function shifts left (upward) causing the aggregate demand curve to shift to the left.
   B. monetary policy reaction function shifts right (downward) causing the aggregate demand curve to shift to the left.
   C. monetary policy reaction function shifts left (upward) causing the aggregate demand curve to shift to the right.
   D. monetary policy reaction function shifts right (upward) causing the aggregate demand curve to shift to the right.
   E. monetary policy reaction function shifts left (upward) causing the SRAS curve to shift to the left.

2. With the economy initially in a long-run equilibrium, if the Fed reduces its target inflation rate, in the short-run the
   A. actual inflation rate will decrease and the target interest rate will decline.
   B. actual inflation rate will increase and the target interest rate will rise.
   C. economy will experience a recessionary gap as higher interest rates decrease aggregate expenditures.
   D. economy will experience a expansionary gap as lower interest rates increase aggregate expenditures.
   E. SRAS curve will shift downward and the equilibrium output will equal the potential output.

3. With the economy initially in a long-run equilibrium, if the Fed reduces its target inflation rate, in the long-run the
   A. inflation rate and interest rates will rise and the economy will experience a recessionary gap.
   B. inflation rate and interest rates will fall and the economy will experience a recessionary gap.
   C. inflation rate and interest rates will rise and the economy will experience a expansionary gap.
   D. inflation rate and interest rates will rise, SRAS curve will shift downward and the equilibrium output will equal the potential output.
   E. inflation rate and interest rates will fall, SRAS curve will shift downward and the equilibrium output will equal the potential output.

4. In the late 1970s, under the direction of Chairman Paul Volcker, the Fed implemented an anti-inflationary monetary policy. The U.S. macroeconomic data for the late 1970s to the mid-1980s
   A. does not support the theoretical analysis because the economy experienced recession during 1979-82 and disinflation and eventually a return to potential output by the mid-1980s.
   B. does not support the theoretical analysis as the economy experienced recession during 1979-82 and rising inflation and unemployment by the mid-1980s.
   C. supports the theoretical analysis as the economy experienced recession during 1979-82 and rising inflation and unemployment by the mid-1980s.
   D. supports the theoretical analysis as the economy experienced recession during 1979-82 and disinflation and eventually a return to potential output by the mid-1980s.
   E. partially supports the theoretical analysis as the economy experienced recession during 1979-82 and disinflation and eventually a return to potential output by the mid-1980s, but the higher interest rates throughout the period were not predicted by the theory.

5. When the economy is experiencing an expansionary gap caused by excessive growth in aggregate demand, if the Fed implements an accommodating policy,
   A. inflation will rise and output will gradually move back to the potential output level in the long run.
   B. inflation will fall and output will gradually move back to the potential output level in the long run.

C. a recessionary gap will develop and gradually inflation will fall as the economy moves back to the potential output level in the long run.

D. a recessionary gap will develop and gradually inflation will rise as the economy moves back to the potential output level in the long run.

E. the SRAS curve will shift downward and gradually inflation will fall as the economy moves back to the potential output level in the long run.

6. When the economy is experiencing an expansionary gap caused by excessive growth in aggregate demand, if the Fed does NOT implement an accommodating policy,
   A. it must lower its target real interest rate which shifts its monetary policy reaction function up (to the left) and causes the AD curve to shift to the left.
   B. it must raise its target real interest rate which shifts its monetary policy reaction function up (to the left) and causes the AD curve to shift to the left.
   C. it must lower its target real interest rate which shifts its monetary policy reaction function down (to the right) and causes the AD curve to shift to the left.
   D. it must raise its target real interest rate which shifts its monetary policy reaction function up (to the left) and causes the AD curve to shift to the right.
   E. a recessionary gap will develop and gradually inflation will rise as the economy moves back to the potential output level in the long run.

7. If the economy is in a long-run equilibrium with $Y=Y^*$, $\pi=\pi^*$, and $r=r^*$, an adverse shock to aggregate supply will
   A. create a dilemma in which the Fed must choose between avoiding a higher interest rates and avoiding higher inflation.
   B. create a dilemma in which the Fed must choose between avoiding a recession and avoiding an expansionary gap.
   C. create a dilemma in which the Fed must choose between avoiding a recession and avoiding higher inflation.
   D. result in the AD curve shifting to the left if the Fed does not implement an accommodating policy.
   E. result in the AD curve shifting to the left if the Fed implements an accommodating policy.

8. If the economy is in a long-run equilibrium with $Y=Y^*$, $\pi=\pi^*$, and $r=r^*$, and the Fed responds to an adverse shock to aggregate supply by maintaining its target inflation rate
   A. the monetary policy reaction function will shift down (to the right), real interest rates will fall and inflation will be permanently higher.
   B. the monetary policy reaction function will shift up (to the left), real interest rates will rise and a recession will follow.
   C. the monetary policy reaction function will NOT shift, but real interest rates will fall and inflation will be permanently higher.
   D. real interest rates will rise and a recessionary gap will exist until the SRAS curve shifts downward to a long-run equilibrium at the initial inflation rate.
   E. real interest rates will remain unchanged, the AD curve will shift to the right, and output will quickly return to the potential level, but inflation will be permanently higher.

9. If the economy is in a long-run equilibrium with Y=Y*, $\pi=\pi^*$, and r=r*, and the Fed responds to an adverse shock to aggregate supply by implementing an accommodating policy
    A. real interest rates will rise and a recessionary gap will exist until the SRAS curve shifts downward to a long-run equilibrium at the initial inflation rate.
    B. the inflation rate will rise and a recessionary gap will exist until the SRAS curve shifts downward to a long-run equilibrium at the initial inflation rate.
    C. the MPRF curve will shift down, the AD curve will shift to the right, and a recessionary gap will exist until the SRAS curve shifts downward to a long-run equilibrium at the initial inflation rate.
    D. the MPRF curve will shift up, the AD curve will shift to the right, and output will quickly return to the potential level, but inflation will be permanently higher.
    E. the MPRF curve will shift down, the AD curve will shift to the right, and output will quickly return to the potential level, but inflation will be permanently higher.

10. Assume the economy is in a long-run equilibrium with Y=Y*, $\pi=\pi^*$, and r=r*, and the Fed responds to an adverse shock to aggregate supply by maintaining its target inflation rate. The SRAS curve will shift downward more quickly if
    A. workers ask for inflationary wage increases and firms rise prices.
    B. the Fed has a history of frequently accommodating higher inflation rates.
    C. people have anchored inflationary expectations.
    D. central bank's actions are frequently reviewed by the legislature.
    E. If the central bank has an obligation to finance the national debt by buying newly issued government bonds.

11. Since the mid-1980s, real GDP growth and inflation rates in the U.S. have become much less volatile (variability in real GDP declines by half and inflation by two-thirds) than previously. Monetary policy is one factor that has contributed to this trend because since the 1980s the Fed has
    A. more consistently implemented accommodating policies.
    B. more consistently maintained its target inflation rate.
    C. adopted new technologies that have improved the ability of the economy to absorb shocks.
    D. increased openness of the U.S. economy to trade and international capital flows.
    E. deregulated the U.S. economy.

12. Unlike the oil price increases of the 1970s, the run up in oil prices during 2002-05 has not led to a recession nor to substantial increases in inflation in the U.S. Which of the following factors has contributed to the different response during the more recent oil price increases?
    A. The real price of oil was higher in 2005, exceeding $60 per barrel, than it was in 1981 ($35 per barrel).
    B. Even though the U.S. continues to be a manufacturing-oriented economy, increased energy efficiency since the 1970s has reduced the impact of higher oil prices on the economy.
    C. Inflationary expectations are less anchored than they were during the 1970s.
    D. Inflationary expectations are more anchored than they were during the 1970s.
    E. The Fed has acquired a reputation for implementing accommodating policy since the

1980s.

13. In order to allow a temporary bulge in inflation from a supply shock, but keep long-term inflationary expectations from rising, the Fed should
   A. focus on controlling the core rate of inflation.
   B. focus on controlling the price of energy and food.
   C. implement accommodating monetary policy.
   D. raise its target inflation rate.
   E. lower the real interest rate.

14. A central bank's independence and the credibility of monetary policy are enhanced when
   A. appointments to the central bank are shortened.
   B. its actions are subject to frequent reviews or veto by the legislative branch of government.
   C. The central bank is obliged to finance the national debt by buying newly issued government bonds.
   D. the central bank is allowed to set and control its own budget.
   E. the central bank's budget is set and control by the legislature.

15. Advocates of central banks announcing explicit numerical targets for inflation believe
   A. the inflation target should be zero.
   B. the experience of the U.S. since the 1980s confirms the benefits of such announcements.
   C. that inflation targets must be adhered to strictly in order to be effective.
   D. that the targets work well in industrialized economies such as the U.S. and Europe, but are less effective in developing countries like Brazil, Chile and Mexico.
   E. the targets reduce uncertainty in financial markets and allow people to plan more effectively.

16. In late 2002, the Fed had reduced the federal funds rate to 1.75% and with the inflation rate of 1.5% at the time, the
   A. real interest rate on federal funds was negative.
   B. Fed was concerned that the inflation rate in the U.S. was too low.
   C. Fed was concerned that the inflation rate in the U.S. was too high.
   D. Fed subsequently raised the federal funds rate to ensure that the real interest rate was positive.
   E. Fed subsequently raised the inflation rate to ensure that the real interest rate was positive.

17. Central banks that have acquired reputations as inflation hawks
   A. find it easier to anchor inflationary expectations.
   B. find it more difficult to anchor inflationary expectations.
   C. are more likely to implement accommodating monetary policy.
   D. are less likely to achieve credibility of their monetary policy.
   E. more often allow inflation to rise skyward.

18. A central bank can acquire a reputation as an inflation hawk by
   A. announcing numerical inflation targets

B. appointing people to the central bank who have a professional or academic background.
C. maintaining target inflation rates regardless of the short-term economic consequences.
D. maintaining target real interest rates regardless of the short-term economic consequences.
E. refusing to associate with inflation doves.

19. Macroeconomic policymaking is made more difficult by
   A. accurate knowledge of the current state of the economy.
   B. certainty about the future path of the economy.
   C. our inability to precisely measure potential output.
   D. anchored inflationary expectations
   E. our inability to precisely measure the unemployment rate.

20. When policy changes are needed, it can take a long time for policymakers to implement the appropriate policy changes. The policy making lags include
   A. the inside lag, or the delay between the date a policy change is implemented and the date by which most of its effects on the economy have occurred.
   B. the outside lag, or the delay between the date a policy change is needed and the date it is implemented.
   C. the middle lag, or the delay between the date a policy change is recommended and the date is it adopted.
   D. the inside lag, or the delay between the date a policy change is needed and the date it is implemented.
   E. the outside lag, or the delay between the date a policy change is recommended and the date is it adopted.

Short Answer Problems
(Answers and solutions are given at the end of the chapter.)

1. Accommodating Monetary Policy
This problem will aid you in reviewing the short-run and long-run effects of accommodating monetary policy. Assume that the economy is initially in long-run equilibrium with actual inflation equal to the Fed's target rate of inflation of 6 percent.

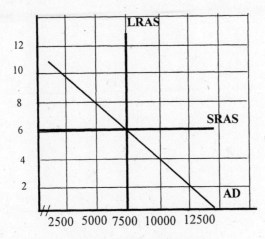

Aggregate Demand ($ bil.)

A. An increase in AD results in a new short-run equilibrium of $10,000 billion. Draw the new curve (parallel to the initial AD curve) and label the new equilibrium point A.

B. The increased in AD will result in a(n) _____ (recessionary/ expansionary) gap.

C. The output gap will cause inflation to _____ (rise/fall) and the SRAS curve will shift _____ (up/down). Draw the new SRAS curve and label it SRAS₁.

D. Assume the Fed implements an accommodating monetary policy. Indicate on the above graph the new long-run equilibrium by labeling the point B.

E. As a result of the accommodating monetary policy, point B indicates that the new equilibrium output is $_____, which is _____ (greater than / less than / equal to) the potential output.

F. Also, as a result of the accommodating monetary policy, point B indicates that the inflation rate is permanently _____ (equal to / higher / lower) than the Fed's initial target inflation rate.

2. Anti-inflationary Monetary Policy

This problem will aid you in reviewing the short-run and long-run effects of anti-inflationary monetary policy. Assume that the economy is initially in long-run equilibrium with actual inflation equal to the Fed's target rate of inflation of 6 percent.

Aggregate Demand ($ bil.)

A. An increase in AD results in a new short-run equilibrium of $12,500 billion. Draw the new curve (parallel to the initial AD curve) and label the new equilibrium point A.

B. The increased in AD will result in a(n) _____ (recessionary/ expansionary) gap.

C. The output gap will cause inflationary pressures to _____ (rise/fall).

D. Assume the Fed does not want inflation to rise above its target. This implies that the Fed would need to _____ (raise / lower) its target real interest rate to _____%.

E. Maintaining its target inflation in response to the increase AD, further implies that the monetary policy reaction function (MRPF) curve will shift _____ (up / down), and the AD curve will shift to the _____ (left / right).

F. As a result of maintaining its target inflation, indicate on the above graph the new long-run equilibrium by labeling the point C.

G. Point C indicates that the new equilibrium output is $_____, which is _____ (greater than / less than / equal to) the potential output.

F. Also, as a result of the accommodating monetary policy, point B indicates that the inflation rate is permanently _____ (equal to / higher / lower) than the Fed's initial target inflation rate.

3. Adverse Inflation Shock
This problem will aid you in reviewing the short-run and long-run effects of an adverse inflation shock. Assume that the economy is initially in long-run equilibrium with actual inflation equal to the Fed's target rate of inflation of 6 percent.

A. Assume there is an increase in the price of energy such that the current inflation rate rises to 8 percent. This would be reflected on the AS/AD graph by a(n) _____ (upward / downward) shift of the _____ (SRAS / LRAS / AD). Draw the new curve in the appropriate position and identify it with a subscript 1.

B. As a result of the adverse inflation shock, the economy moves to a short-run equilibrium at $_____ and a(n) _____ (expansionary / recessionary) gap is created. Label the short-run equilibrium point A.

C. If the Fed accommodates the inflation shock by raising its target inflation to 8%, the MRPF curve will shift _____ (up / down). Draw the new MRPF curve and label if $MRPF_1$.

D. In addition, the accommodating policy will result in a shift of the AD curve to the _____ (right / left). Draw the new AD curve and label AD_1.

E. On the graph above, indicate the new long-run equilibrium point, label it B.

F. At the new long-run equilibrium the output is _____(greater than / less than / equal to) the potential output, and the inflation rate is permanently _____ (equal to / higher / lower) than the Fed's initial target inflation rate.

G. If, on the other hand, the Fed does NOT change its target inflation rate, the AD and MPRF curves _____ (will / will not) shift. The short-run equilibrium the would be represented by point _____ and the economy would experience a(n) _____ (expansionary / recessionary) gap.

H. The output gap will gradually shift the _____ (SRAS / LRAS / AD) curve _____ (down /up) until a new long-run equilibrium was achieved (label this point C).

I. By maintaining its target inflation rate in response to an adverse inflation shock, the long-run equilibrium the output is _____(greater than / less than / equal to) the potential output, and the inflation rate is permanently _____ (equal to / higher / lower) than the Fed's initial target inflation rate.

IV. Becoming an Economic Naturalist: Case Study

In the textbook, Table 29.2 provides data on the CPI inflation and the core inflation rates for the U.S. during 2003-04. The data show that during 2003-04, despite substantial increases in the price of crude oil and the general inflation rate, the core inflation rate increased only slightly. This would suggest that the Fed was maintaining its target inflation rate in the face of an adverse inflation shock during that period. Has the Fed continued this monetary policy since 2004? Visit the web site of the Bureau of Labor Statistics at http://www.bls.gov/cpi/home.htm#data to examine the CPI and core inflation data and explain why you believe the Fed has or has not continued the policy of maintaining its target inflation rate since 2004.
Answer:

V. Self-Test Solutions

Key Terms
1. f
2. a
3. j
4. d
5. h
6. c
7. e
8. g
9. i
10. b

Multiple-Choice Questions
1. A
2. C
3. E
4. D
5. A
6. B
7. C
8. D
9. E
10. C
11. B
12. D
13. A
14. D
15. E
16. B
17. A
18. C
19. C
20. D

Short Answer Problems
1. A.

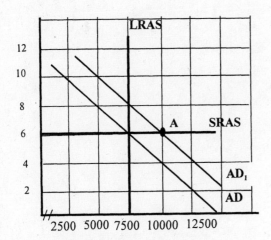

Aggregate Demand ($ bil.)

B. expansionary

C. rise; up

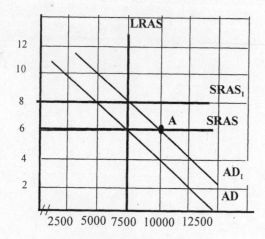

Aggregate Demand ($ bil.)

D.

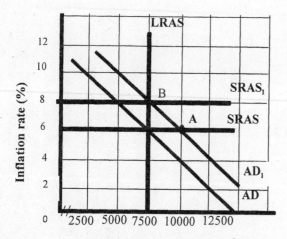

Aggregate Demand ($ bil.)

E. $7.500; equal to

F. higher

2. A.

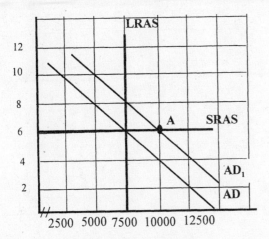

Aggregate Demand ($ bil.)

B. expansionary
C. rise
D. raise; 8%
E. up; left
F.

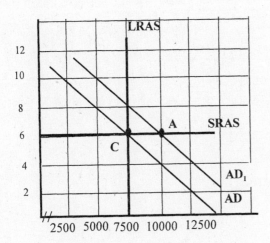

Aggregate Demand ($ bil.)

G. $7,500; equal to
F. equal to

3. A. upward; SRAS

B. $5,000; recessionary

C. down

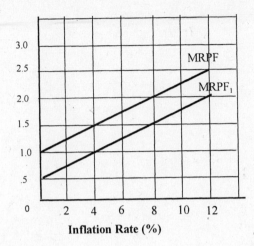

Inflation Rate (%)

D. right;

Aggregate Demand ($ bil.)

E.

Aggregate Demand ($ bil.)

F. equal to; higher
G. will not; A; recessionary
H. SRAS; down
I. equal to; equal to

Chapter 30
Exchange Rates and the Open Economy

I. Pretest: What Do You Really Know?
Circle the letter that corresponds to the best answer. (Answers appear immediately after the final question).

1. The nominal exchange rate is the
   A. market on which currencies of various nations are traded for one another.
   B. price of the average domestic good or service relative to the price of the average foreign good or service, when prices are expressed in terms of a common currency
   C. quantity of foreign currency assets held by a government for the purpose of purchasing the domestic currency in the foreign exchange market.
   D. rate at which two currencies can be traded for each other.
   E. rate at which a good in one country can be traded for the same good in another country.

2. The following table provides the nominal exchange rates for the U.S. dollar.

Country	Foreign currency/dollar	Dollar/foreign currency
Saudi Arabia (riyal)	6.167	.162
Brazil (real)	1.850	.541

   Based on these data, the nominal exchange rate equals _____ Brazilian reals per Saudi riyal or equivalently _____ Saudi riyals per Brazilian real.
   A. 1.053; .95
   B. .95; 1.053
   C. .30; 3.33
   D. 3.33; .30
   E. 6.490; .154

3. An exchange rate that varies according to the supply and demand for the currency in the foreign exchange market is called a(n) _____ exchange rate.
   A. overvalued
   B. undervalued
   C. fixed
   D. flexible
   E. real

4. The real exchange rate is the
   A. market on which currencies of various nations are traded for one another.
   B. price of the average domestic good or service relative to the price of the average foreign good or service, when prices are expressed in terms of a common currency
   C. quantity of foreign currency assets held by a government for the purpose of purchasing the domestic currency in the foreign exchange market.
   D. rate at which two currencies can be traded for each other.
   E. rate at which a good in one country can be traded for the same good in another country.

5. Net exports will tend to be high when the real exchange rate _____.
   A. is high
   B. is low
   C. equals the nominal exchange rate
   D. appreciates
   E. is strong

6. If a certain automotive part can be purchased in Mexico for 45 pesos or in the United States for $6.25 and if the nominal exchange rate is 9 pesos per U.S. dollar, then the real exchange rate for automotive part equals
   A. 1.25
   B. 51.20
   C. .125
   D. 0.8
   E. 8

7. The theory that nominal exchange rates are determined as necessary for the law of one price to hold is called
   A. the fixed-exchange-rate rule.
   B. the equilibrium principle.
   C. the law of supply and demand.
   D. purchasing power parity.
   E. international equality.

8. The price of gold is $300 per ounce in New York and 2,850 pesos per ounce in Mexico City. If the law of one price holds for gold, the nominal exchange rate is _____ pesos per U.S. dollar.
   A. .105
   B. 1.053
   C. 9.5
   D. 95.5
   E. 25

9. The purchasing power parity theory is not a good explanation of nominal exchange rate determination in the short run because
   A. there is no evidence that low inflation is association with less rapid nominal exchange rate depreciation.
   B. there is no evidence that high inflation is associated with more rapid nominal exchange rate depreciation.
   C. most goods and services are traded internationally and are standardized.
   D. many goods and services are nontraded and not all traded goods are standardized.
   E. most nominal exchange rates are fixed and foreign exchange markets do not bring the supply and demand for currencies into equilibrium.

10. The U.S. dollar exchange rate, e, where e is the nominal exchange rate expressed as Japanese yen per U.S. dollar, will appreciate when:
   A. real GDP in the U.S. increases.
   B. real GDP in Japan decreases.
   C. the U.S. Federal Reserve tightens monetary policy.
   D. U.S. consumers increase their preference for Japanese cars.
   E. the Bank of Japan tightens monetary policy.

Solutions and Feedback to Pretest
For each question you incorrectly answered, we strongly recommend taking the time to review the appropriate material before continuing. In the table below are listed for each question the pertinent Learning Objective from the following Key Point Review.

Correct Answer	Learning Objective
1. D	1
2. C	1
3. D	1
4. B	2
5. B	2
6. A	2
7. D	3
8. C	1
9. D	3
10. C	4

II. Key Point Review
The Forest

This chapter focuses on the role of exchange rates in open economies. The central questions you need to be able to answer are:
   • What distinguishes the nominal exchange rate from the real exchange rate?
   • How are flexible and fixed exchange rates exchange rates are determined?
   • What are the relative merits of fixed and flexible exchange rates?

The Trees

Learning Objective 1: Define nominal exchange rate, appreciation, and depreciation
The economic benefits of trade between nations in goods, services, and assets are similar to the benefits of trade within a nation. There is, however, a difference between the two cases. Trade within a nation normally involves only a single currency, while trade between nations involves different currencies. Because international transactions generally require that one currency be traded for another currency, the relative values of different currencies are an important factor in international economic relations. The rate at which two currencies can be traded for each other is called the **nominal exchange rate**, or simply the exchange rate. Exchange rates can be of two broad types flexible or fixed exchange rates. A **flexible exchange rate** is not officially fixed, but varies according to the supply and demand for the currency in the **foreign exchange market** – the market in which currencies of various nations are traded for one another. Flexible exchange rates change over time. An increase in the value of one currency relative to other currencies is called **appreciation,** and a decrease in the value of that currency relative to other currencies is called **depreciation.** A **fixed exchange rate** is an exchange rate whose value is set by official government policy.

Note: Exchange rates can be expressed as the amount of foreign currency needed to purchase one unit of domestic currency, or as the number of units of the domestic currency needed to purchase one unit of the foreign currency. These two ways of expressing the exchange rate are equivalent; each being the reciprocal of the other. Although the exchange rate can be expressed either way, to simply the discussion, the textbook authors have chosen to define the nominal exchange rate (e) as the number of units of foreign currency that domestic currency will buy.

Learning Objective 2: Define real exchange rates, and explain the economic importance of the real exchange rate
It is important to distinguish the nominal exchange rate from the real exchange rate. As indicated above, the nominal exchange rate tells us the price of the domestic currency in terms of a foreign currency. The **real exchange rate** tells us the price of the average domestic good or service in terms of the average foreign good or service, when prices are expressed in terms of a common currency. The real exchange rate is equal to the nominal exchange rate times the price of the average domestic good divided by the price of the average foreign good. Consequently, the nominal and real exchange rates tend to move in the same direction. The real exchange rate has important implications for a nation's trade. A high real exchange rate implies that domestic producers will have a hard time exporting to other countries, while foreign goods will sell well in the home country. Thus, when the real exchange rate is high, net exports will tend to be low. Conversely, if the real exchange rate is low, domestic producers will find it easier to export and foreign producers will have difficulty selling in the domestic market. Net exports, therefore, will be high when the real exchange rate is low. This cause-and-effect relationship suggests that a strong currency does not necessarily reflect a strong economy.

Learning Objective 3: Define the law of one price and purchasing power parity (PPP), and explain the PPP theory of exchange rate determination, its implications and shortcomings
What determines the value of flexible exchanges rates? The most basic theory of how nominal exchange rates are determined is called **purchasing power parity**, or PPP. To understand the PPP theory, one first has to understand the law of one price. The **law of one price** states that if transportation costs are relatively small, the price of an internationally traded commodity must be the same in all locations. If the law of one price were to hold for all goods and services, then the value of the exchange rate between two currencies would be determined by dividing the price of the average good in one country by the price of the average good in the other country. An implication of the PPP theory is that, in the long run, the currencies of countries that experience significant inflation will tend to depreciate. The rationale is sound because inflation implies that a nation's currency is losing purchasing power in the domestic market, while exchange-rate depreciation implies that the nation's currency is losing purchasing power in international markets.

Empirical studies have found that the PPP theory is useful for predicting changes in nominal exchange rates over the long run. The theory is less successful, however, in predicting short-run movements in exchange rates. One reason that the PPP works less well in the short run is that the law of one price works best for standardized commodities that are widely traded. Not all goods, however, are standardized commodities and not all goods are traded internationally. In general, the greater the share of traded and standardized goods and services in a nation's output, the more precisely the PPP theory will apply to the country's exchange rate.

Hint: Recall also that the PPP theory rest on the assumption that transportation costs are relatively small. Depending upon the composition of an economy's output, transportation costs of its goods may be substantial and, thus, PPP theory may not be a good predictor of the country's exchange rate.

Learning Objective 4: Use supply-and-demand analysis to determine the short-run movements in flexible exchange rates
Supply and demand analysis is more useful for understanding the short-run movements of exchange rates. Anyone who holds a currency is a potential supplier of that currency, but, in practice, the principal suppliers of a currency to the foreign exchange market are that nation's households and firms. The demanders of a currency are, in practice, households and firms that want to purchase foreign assets or goods and services. The supply curve of a currency is upward sloping and the demand curve is downward sloping. The equilibrium value of a currency, also called the **fundamental value of the exchange rate**, is the exchange rate at which the quantity supplied equals the quantity demanded. Factors that cause shifts in the supply and demand for a currency will cause the equilibrium value of the currency to change. Some factors that cause an increase in the supply of the domestic currency are an increased preference for foreign goods, an increase in the domestic real GDP, and an increase in the real interest rate on foreign assets.

Factors that cause an increased demand for the domestic currency include an increased preference for domestic goods, an increase in real GDP abroad, and an increase in the real interest rate on domestic assets. Of the many factors affecting a country's exchange rate, among the most important is the monetary policy of a country's central bank. A tightening of a country's monetary policy increases domestic real interest rates, raising the demand for its currency and causing the currency to appreciate. Easing of monetary policy has the opposite effects. In an open economy with a flexible exchange rate, the exchange rate serves as another channel for monetary policy that reinforces the effects of real interest rates. Higher interest rates, for example, reduce domestic consumption and investment. They also cause appreciation of the currency and, as a result, imports rise and exports fall, reducing net exports. The decline in net exports, thus, reinforces the domestic effects of the tightened monetary policy. Monetary policy, therefore, is more effective in an open economy with flexible exchange rates.

Learning Objective 5: Define fixed exchange rates, devaluation and revaluation

Fixed exchange rates are a historically important alternative to flexible exchange rates. Fixed exchange rates also are still used in many countries, especially small and developing nations. A **fixed exchange rate** is an exchange rate whose value is set by official government policy (in practice, usually the by the finance ministry or treasury department, in cooperation with the country's central bank). Fixed exchange rates today are usually set in terms of a major currency (e.g., the dollar or yen), or relative to a "basket" of currencies, typically those of the country's trading partners. Historically, currency values were fixed in terms of gold or other precious metals. Once an exchange rate has been fixed, the government usually attempts to keep it unchanged for some time. Economic circumstances, however, can force the government to change the value of the exchange rate. A reduction in the official value of a currency is called **devaluation**; and increase in the official value is called a **revaluation**.

Learning Objective 6: Explain the fundamental value of the exchange rate and the implications of an overvalued or undervalued currency

Fixed exchange rates are not always consistent with the fundamental value of a currency (as determined by supply and demand). When the officially fixed value of an exchange rate is greater than its fundamental value, the exchange rate is **overvalued**, and when it is less that its fundamental value, it is **undervalued**. When the officially set value of an exchange rate is overvalued, the government has several alternatives for dealing with the inconsistency. It could devalue its currency, restrict international transactions, or become a demander of its currency. The most common approach is for the government to become a demander of its currency. To be able to purchase its own currency and maintain an overvalued exchange rate, a government (usually the central bank) must hold foreign-currency assets called **international reserves**, or simply reserves. Because a government must use part of its reserves to maintain an overvalued currency, over time its reserves will decline. The net decline in a country's stock of international reserves over a year is called its **balance-of-payments deficit**. Conversely, if a country experiences a net increase in its international reserves over a year, it has a **balance-of-payments surplus**. Although a government can maintain an overvalued exchange rate for some time by purchasing its own currency, there is a limit to this strategy because no government's reserves are unlimited. Eventually a government will run out of reserves, and the fixed exchange rate will collapse. A **speculative attack**, involving massive selling of domestic-currency assets by financial investors, can quickly end a government's attempt to maintain an overvalued currency. Such an attack is most likely to occur when financial investors fear that an overvalued currency will be devalued. A speculative attack, therefore, can be self-fulfilling.

> **Hint:** Because the fundamental value of a currency is not readily known, whether a currency is overvalued is a matter of conjecture. Thus, a speculative attack may take place if currency traders *believe* a currency is overvalued. If enough traders *believe*, it can be a self-fulfilling prophecy. Thus, in part, governments must guard against any suggestion that its currency is overvalued to avoid the possibility of its becoming an accepted "fact" that can then be self-fulfilling.

As an alternative to trying to maintain an overvalued currency, a government can take actions to try to increase the fundamental value of its currency and eliminate the overvaluation problem. The most effective way to increase the fundamental value of a currency is through monetary policy. A tightening of monetary policy that raises real interest rates will increase the demand for a currency and, in turn, will raise its fundamental value. Although monetary policy can be used in this manner, it has some drawbacks. In particular, if monetary policy is used to set the fundamental value of the exchange rate equal to the official value, it is no longer available for stabilizing the domestic economy. The conflict between using monetary policy to set the fundamental value of a currency or using it to stabilize the domestic economy is most severe when the exchange rate is under a speculative attack.

Learning Objective 6: Compare fixed and flexible exchange rate systems

There are two important issues in comparing flexible and fixed exchange rates – the effects on monetary policy and the effects on trade and economic integration. A flexible exchange rate strengthens the impact of monetary policy on aggregate demand, when a fixed exchange rate prevents policymakers from using monetary policy to stabilize the domestic economy. Large economies should almost always employ flexible exchange rates because it seldom makes sense for them to give up the power to stabilize the domestic economy via monetary policy. For small economies, however, giving up this power may make sense when their history suggests an inability to use monetary policy to control domestic inflation. On the issue of trade and economic integration, supporters of fixed exchange rates have argued that an officially fixed exchange rate reduces or eliminates uncertainty about future exchange rates and, thus, provides incentives for firms to expand export business. The problem with this argument is that a fixed exchange rate is not guaranteed to remain fixed forever, especially if the currency comes under a speculative attack. Some countries, such as some of the European nations, have tried to solve the problem of uncertain exchange rates by adopting a common currency.

III. Self-Test

Key Terms
Match the term in the right-hand column with the appropriate definition in the left-hand column by placing the letter of the term in the blank in front of its' definition. (Answers are given at the end of the chapter.)

1. ____The exchange rate that equates the quantities of the currency supplied and demanded in the foreign exchange market.

a. appreciation

2. ____ An exchange rate that has an officially fixed value greater than its fundamental value.

b. balance-of-payments deficit

3. ____ The price of the average domestic good or service relative to the price of the average foreign good or service, when prices are expressed in terms of a common currency.

c. balance-of-payments surplus

4. ____ A massive selling of domestic currency assets by financial investors.

d. depreciation

5. ____A reduction in the official value of a currency (in a fixed-exchange-rate system).

e. devaluation

6. ____ If transportation costs are relatively small, the price of an internationally traded commodity must be the same in all locations.

f. fixed exchange rate

7. ____ An exchange rate whose value is not officially fixed but varies according to the supply and demand for the currency in the foreign exchange market.

g. flexible exchange rate

8. ____ The rate at which two currencies can be traded for each other.

h. foreign-exchange market

9. ____ Foreign currency assets held by a government for the purpose of purchasing the domestic currency in the foreign exchange market.

i. fundamental value of the exchange rate

10.____ An exchange rate whose value is set by official government policy.

j. international reserves

11.____ The net increase in a country's stock of international reserves over a year.

k. law of one price

12.____ An exchange rate that has an officially fixed value less than its fundamental value.

l. nominal exchange rate

13.____ An increase in the value of a currency relative to other currencies.

m.   overvalued exchange rate

14.____ The market on which currencies from various nations are traded for one another.

n. purchasing power parity (PPP)

15.____ An increase in the official value of a currency (in a fixed-exchange-rate system).

o. real exchange rate

16.____ The theory that nominal exchange rates are determined as necessary for the law of one price to hold.

p. revaluation

17.____ The net decline in a country's stock of international reserves over a year.

q. speculative attack

18.____ A decrease in the value of a currency relative to other currencies.

r. undervalued exchange rate

Multiple-Choice Questions
Circle the letter that corresponds to the best answer. (Answers are given at the end of the chapter.)

1. During summer 2005, the nominal exchange rate was one U.S. dollar to 10.6 Mexican pesos. The dollar per peso equivalent exchange rate equaled
   A. 10.6 dollars per peso.
   B. .106 dollars per peso.
   C. 9.4 dollars per peso.
   D. .094 dollars per peso.
   E. 106 dollars per peso.

2. A disposable camera cost $8 in the United States and 110 peso in Mexico during the summer of 2005. The exchange rate at that time was 10.6 pesos per dollar. The real exchange rate of the dollar (for disposable cameras) equaled
   A. 10.6.
   B. .77.
   C. 83.0.
   D. 84.8.
   E. .106.

3. During the 1980s, the United States had a balance-of-payments deficit with South Korea and Taiwan. The U.S. government complained that the governments of those two nations were manipulating their exchange rates to promote exports to the United States. Apparently, the White House believed that the
   A. currencies of South Korea and Taiwan were overvalued relative to the dollar.
   B. currencies of South Korea and Taiwan were undervalued relative to the dollar.
   C. South Korean currency was overvalued relative to the currency of Taiwan.
   D. South Korean currency was undervalued relative to the currency of Taiwan.
   E. dollar should be allowed to appreciate against the currencies of South Korea and Taiwan.

4. Between 1973 and 1999, annual inflation in developing nations that export mainly manufactured goods averaged 23 percent, while inflation averaged 59 percent in countries that mainly export raw materials. Other things equal, the PPP theory would predict that, in the long run, the currencies of the raw materials exporting countries should have
   A. been approximately stable relative to the currencies of countries exporting manufactured goods.
   B. appreciated relative to the currencies of countries exporting manufactured goods.
   C. depreciated relative to the currencies of countries exporting manufactured goods.
   D. had no predictable relationship to the currencies of countries exporting manufactured goods.
   E. been perfectly stable relative to the currencies of countries exporting manufactured goods because they maintained fixed exchange rates.

5. The PPP theory works better in the long run than it does in the short run because
   A. the law of one price only pertains to the long run.
   B. not all goods and services are traded internationally, and not all goods are heterogeneous commodities.
   C. all goods and services are traded internationally, and not all goods are heterogeneous commodities.
   D. not all goods and services are traded internationally, and not all goods are standardized commodities.
   E. all goods and services are traded internationally, and all goods are standardized commodities.

6. In the early 1980s, high interest rates in the United States attracted enormous amounts of capital into the United States to buy stocks, bonds, real estate, and other assets. All other things equal, supply-and-demand analysis of exchange rates would predict that the U.S. dollar would experience _____ relative to other currencies.
   A. depreciation
   B. appreciation
   C. devaluation
   D. revaluation
   E. purchasing price parity

7. During 2004 and 2005, the U.S. Federal Reserve Bank tightened its monetary policy and interest rates in the United States increased in order to reduce domestic consumption and investment spending. In the short-run, one would predicate a(n)
   A. depreciation of the dollar and an increase in net exports.
   B. depreciation of the dollar and a decrease in net exports.
   C. devaluation of the dollar and a decrease in net exports.
   D. appreciation of the dollar and an increase in net exports.
   E. appreciation of the dollar and a decrease in net exports.

8. The value of a fixed exchange rate in contemporary economies is
   A. determined by the supply and demand for a currency in the foreign exchange market.
   B. set by the government, usually in terms of gold or some other precious metal.
   C. set by the government, usually in terms of the currency (or basket of currencies) of the country's major trading partner(s).
   D. set by agreement of the central banks of the major trading countries of the world.
   E. determined by economic forces.

9. During the 1990s, the government of Malaysia fixed the exchange rate of the Baht to the dollar. During the spring of 1998, investors perceived that the Baht was overvalued and a speculative attack ensued. What alternatives did the Malaysian government have to deal with this problem?
   A. It could have revalued the Baht, limited international transactions, purchased Baht on the foreign exchange market, or tightened domestic monetary policy.
   B. It could have devalued the Baht, limited international transactions, purchased Baht on the foreign exchange market, or tightened domestic monetary policy.

C. It could have devalued the Baht, limited international transactions, sold Baht on the foreign exchange market, or tightened domestic monetary policy.

D. It could have revalued the Baht, limited international transactions, sold Baht on the foreign exchange market, or eased domestic monetary policy.

E. It could have revalued the Baht, limited international transactions, sold Baht on the foreign exchange market, or tightened domestic monetary policy.

10. During the 1930s, the United States was on the gold standard, creating a system of fixed exchange rates between the dollar and other currencies whose values were also set in terms of gold. As a result, monetary policy

A. could not be used to stabilize the U.S. economy during the Great Depression.

B. could be used to stabilize the U.S. economy during the Great Depression.

C. was immune to a speculative attack because devaluation was not possible.

D. was eased to counteract the banking panic and the bank failures during the Great Depression.

E. was used to decrease interest rates to counteract the economic decline brought on by the bank failures during the Great Depression.

11. When the real exchange rate of a country's currency is low, the home country will;

A. find it easier to import, while domestic producers will have difficulty exporting.

B. find it easier to export, while domestic residents will buy more imports.

C. find it harder to export, while domestic residents will buy fewer imports.

D. find it easier to export, while domestic residents will buy fewer imports.

E. find it harder to export, while domestic residents will buy more imports.

12. Between 1990 and 1999, inflation in the United States averaged 2-3% per year, while Mexico experienced double-digit average annual inflation rates. Since the Mexican government did not try to maintain a fixed exchange rate, the PPP theory would suggest that, in the long run, the Mexican peso would

A. appreciate against the dollar and Mexico's net exports to the United States decreased.

B. appreciate against the dollar and Mexico's net exports to the United States increased.

C. depreciate against the dollar and Mexico's net exports to the United States increased.

D. depreciate against the dollar and Mexico's net exports to the United States decreased.

E. remain stable relative to the dollar, with no change in Mexico's net exports to the United States.

13. The PPP theory would be most useful in predicting

A. short-run changes in the exchange rate for a country that mainly produces heavily traded, standardized goods.

B. long-run changes in the exchange rate for a country that mainly produces heavily traded, standardized goods.

C. short-run changes in the exchange rate for a country that mainly produces lightly traded, standardized goods.

D. long-run changes in the exchange rate for a country that mainly produces lightly traded, non-standardized goods.

E. short-run changes in the exchange rate for a country that mainly produces lightly traded, standardized goods.

14. The fundamental value of a country's exchange rate is
A. constant over a prolonged period of time.
B. determined by the supply of the country's currency in the foreign exchange market.
C. determined by the demand for the country's currency in the foreign exchange market.
D. determined by the supply of and demand for the country's currency in the domestic financial market.
E. determined by the supply of and demand for the country's currency in the foreign exchange market.

15. During the latter half of the 1990s, real GDP in the United States grew faster than in most other industrial countries. All other things equal, supply-and-demand analysis of exchange rates would predict that, in the short run, the U.S. dollar would _____ relative to the currencies of the other industrialized countries.
A. appreciate
B. depreciate
C. devaluate
D. revaluate
E. remain constant

16. If the central bank of England were to respond to a slowdown in the domestic economy by easing monetary policy, all other things equal, one would predict in the short run a(n)
A. increase in the real interest rate, an increase in demand for the pound, and an appreciation in the pound.
B. decrease in the real interest rate, an increase in demand for the pound, and an appreciation in the pound.
C. decrease in the real interest rate, a decrease in demand for the pound, and a depreciation in the pound.
D. increase in the real interest rate, a decrease in demand for the pound, and a depreciation in the pound.
E. increase in the real interest rate, an increase in demand for the pound, and a depeciation in the pound.

17. If a country fixes the exchange rate for its currency relative to other currencies, and if the official exchange rate is overvalued relative to its fundamental value, then
A. the most likely ultimate outcome is a depreciation of its currency.
B. the most likely ultimate outcome is a devaluation of its currency.
C. the most likely ultimate outcome is a revaluation of its currency.
D. it will likely be able to indefinitely support its value by using its international reserves to buy its currency on the foreign exchange market.
E. it can ease its monetary policy to increase the fundamental value of its currency and eliminate the overvalued status.

18. If exchange rates are flexible, a surplus in a nation's balance of payments would imply that the
    A. government will have to devalue the nation's currency.
    B. government will have to revalue the nation's currency.
    C. nation's exchange rate will remain unchanged.
    D. nation's exchange rate will appreciate.
    E. nation's exchange rate will depreciate.

19. Other things being equal, a recession in the United States combined with rapid economic growth in Japan would be expected to cause
    A. the dollar to appreciate against the yen.
    B. the dollar to depreciate against the yen.
    C. the yen to appreciate against the dollar.
    D. no predictable change in the dollar-yen exchange rate.
    E. Japan's demand curve for dollars to shift to the left.

20. In comparison to a fixed exchange rate system, a flexible exchange rate system
    A. weakens the impact of monetary policy on aggregate demand.
    B. strengthens the impact of monetary policy on aggregate demand.
    C. increases uncertainty about the future exchange rate.
    D. decreases uncertainty about the future exchange rate.
    E. is more likely to suffer from speculative attacks.

Short Answer Problems
(Answers and solutions are given at the end of the chapter.)

1. Nominal Exchange Rates

In this problem you can practice calculating the nominal exchange rates of currencies in terms of the amount of foreign currency needed to purchase one dollar and the number of dollars needed to purchase one unit of the foreign currency.

Nominal Exchange Rate for the U.S. Dollar (August 18, 2005)

Country	Foreign currency / dollar	Dollar / foreign currency
Britain (Pound)		1.08599
Canada (Dollar		0.824062
China (Yuan)		6.67466
Europe (Euro)	0.8148	
Japan (Yen)	109.84	
Mexico (Peso)	10.6345	

Source: *http://www.refcofx.com/currency-trading.html*

A. Based on the number of dollars needed to purchase one unit of the foreign currency, calculate the amount of foreign currency needed to purchase one dollar for the British pound, Canadian dollar, and the Chinese yuan in Column 2 of the above table.

B. Based on the amount of foreign currency needed to purchase one dollar, calculate the number of dollars needed to purchase one unit of the foreign currency for the European euro, Japanese yen, and Mexican peso in Column 3 of the above table.

C. During August 2005, in the Monterrey, Mexico, newspaper, *El Norte*, a popular American/ German make of automobile was advertised at the price of 152,100 pesos. During the same time, it was advertised in the *Austin American Statesman* newspaper for 18,995 dollars. Based on the above peso–dollar exchange rate and the advertised prices for the automobile, the real exchange rate (for the automobile) equaled _____ (round your answer to the nearest hundredth).

D. The real exchange rate for the automobile implies that the price of the U.S. automobile is (more/ less) _____ expensive than the Mexican automobile, putting the (U.S. / Mexican) _____ product at a disadvantage.

2. Supply and Demand Analysis of the Exchange Rate

Supply and demand analysis is applied to the determination of the exchange rate in this problem. You will determine the equilibrium exchange rate and analyze the effects of changes in various factors on the supply of or demand for dollars to determine the impact on the equilibrium exchange rate. Answer the questions below based on the following graph illustrating the supply and demand for dollars in the euro-dollar market.

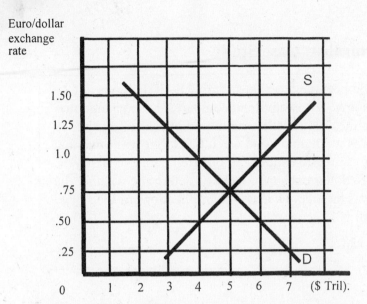

Euro/dollar
exchange
rate

A. The equilibrium exchange rate of the dollar equals _____ euro(s) per dollar.
B. If European consumers' and businesses' preferences for American goods increases, the
    (supply/demand) _____ for dollars in the foreign exchange market will (increase/
    decrease) _____ and the euro/dollar exchange will (increase/decrease)

    _____ .
C. If the U.S. GDP increases, the (supply/demand) _____ for dollars in the foreign
    exchange market will (increase/decrease) _____ and the euro/dollar exchange will
    (increase/decrease) _____ .
D. An increase in the real interest rate on European assets will (increase/decrease)
    _____ the (supply/demand) _____ of (for) dollars in the foreign
    exchange market and the euro/dollar exchange will (increase/decrease) _____ .
E. If the Fed tightens U.S. monetary policy, the (supply/demand) _____ for dollars
    in the foreign exchange market will (increase/decrease) _____ and the euro/dollar
    exchange will (increase/decrease) _____ .

3. Fundamental Value of a Currency and the Balance of Payments Deficit

The demand and supply for Surican pesos in the foreign exchange market are given by the
following equations (*e* is the Surican exchange rate measured in dollars per Surican peso).
Demand = 55,000 − 88,000 *e*
Supply = 25,000 + 32,000 *e*

A. The fundamental value of the Surican peso (*e*) equals _____ .
B. If the Surican government set the official exchange rate at .333 dollars per peso, the demand
    for Surican pesos would equal _____, and the supply of Surican pesos would be

    _____ .
C. The quantity supplied of Surican pesos would be (greater than/less than/equal to)
    _____ the quantity demanded for Surican pesos.
D. To maintain the fixed exchange rate, the Surican government would have to purchase
    _____ Surican pesos. Since the Surican peso is purchased at the official rate of 3
    pesos to the dollar, the balance of payments deficit in dollars would equal $_____ .

IV. Becoming an Economic Naturalist: Case Study

In Economic Naturalist 30.1, the authors explain why a strong U.S. dollar does not necessarily imply a strong U.S. economy. For example, it compares the exchange rate of the U.S. dollar during 1973, when the dollar was worth more in terms of other major currencies and the economy was weak, and 2000 when the dollar was lower but the economy was stronger. Go to http://research.stlouisfed.org/fred/data/exchange.html to find the latest data on the U.S. dollar exchange rate and determine whether the dollar is stronger or weaker than it was in 2000. Discuss the implications of the change in the exchange on the current U.S. economy.

Answer:

V. Self-Test Solutions

Key Terms
1. i
2. m
3. o
4. q
5. e
6. k
7. g
8. l
9. j
10. f
11. c
12. r
13. a
14. h
15. p
16. n
17. b
18. d

Multiple-Choice Questions
1. D (=1/10.6)
2. B (=[10.6*8] / 110)
3. A
4. C
5. D
6. B
7. E
8. C
9. B

10. A
11. D
12. C
13. B
14. E
15. B
16. C
17. B
18. D
19. A
20. B

Short Answer Problems

1. A and B

Nominal Exchange Rate for the U.S. Dollar (August 18, 2005)

Country	Foreign currency / dollar	Dollar / foreign currency
Britain (Pound)	0.9208 (1/1.08599)	1.08599
Canada (Dollar	1.2135	0.824062
China (Yuan)	0.1498	6.67466
Europe (Euro)	0.8148	1.22729 (1/0.8148)
Japan (Yen)	109.84	0.009104
Mexico (Peso)	10.6345	0.094033

Source: *http://www.refcofx.com/currency-trading.html*

C. 1.33 (= [9.91 x 18,995]/ 152,100)

D. more; U.S.

2.

A. .75

B. demand; increase; increase

C. supply; increase; decrease

D. increase; supply; decrease

E. demand; increase; increase

3.

A. .25 (55,000 – 88,000e = 25,000 + 32,000e or 30,000 = 120,000e)

B. 25,696 (=55,000 – 88,000 x .333); 35,656 (=25,000 + 32,000 x .333)

C. greater than

D. 9,960 (=35,656 – 25,696)

E. $3,320 (=9,960 / 3)